SPSS Advanc
Models™ 9.0

For more information about SPSS® software products, please visit our WWW site at *http://www.spss.com* or contact

Marketing Department
SPSS Inc.
233 South Wacker Drive, 11th Floor
Chicago, IL 60606-6307
Tel: (312) 651-3000
Fax: (312) 651-3668

Preface

SPSS® 9.0 is a powerful software package for microcomputer data management and analysis. The Advanced Models option is an add-on enhancement that provides additional statistical analysis techniques. The procedures in Advanced Models must be used with the SPSS 9.0 Base and are completely integrated into that system.

The Advanced Models option includes procedures for:

- GLM—General linear models, which can accommodate analysis of variance (ANOVA), regression, and analysis of covariance (ANCOVA), in both univariate and multivariate models. Repeated measures and doubly repeated measures models are also available.
- Variance components.
- Model selection loglinear analysis (hierarchical).
- General loglinear analysis.
- Logit loglinear analysis.
- Survival analysis, including life tables, Kaplan-Meier survival analysis, and Cox regression.

Installation

To install Advanced Models, follow the instructions for adding and removing features in the installation instructions supplied with the SPSS Base. (To start, double-click on the SPSS Setup icon.)

Compatibility

The SPSS system is designed to operate on many computer systems. See the materials that came with your system for specific information on minimum and recommended requirements.

Serial Numbers

Your serial number is your identification number with SPSS Inc. You will need this serial number when you call SPSS Inc. for information regarding support, payment, or an upgraded system. The serial number was provided with your Base system. Before using the system, please copy this number to the registration card.

Registration Card

Don't put it off: *fill out and send us your registration card.* Until we receive your registration card, you have an unregistered system. Even if you have previously sent a card to us, please fill out and return the card enclosed in your Advanced Models package. Registering your system entitles you to:

- Technical support services
- New product announcements and upgrade announcements

Customer Service

If you have any questions concerning your shipment or account, contact your local office, listed on page vi. Please have your serial number ready for identification when calling.

Training Seminars

SPSS Inc. provides both public and onsite training seminars for SPSS. All seminars feature hands-on workshops. SPSS seminars will be offered in major U.S. and European cities on a regular basis. For more information on these seminars, call your local office, listed on page vi.

Technical Support

The services of SPSS Technical Support are available to registered customers. Customers may call Technical Support for assistance in using SPSS products or for installation help for one of the supported hardware environments. To reach Technical Support, see the SPSS home page on the World Wide Web at *http://www.spss.com*, or call your local office, listed on page vi. Be prepared to identify yourself, your organization, and the serial number of your system.

Additional Publications

Additional copies of SPSS product manuals may be purchased from Prentice Hall, the exclusive distributor of SPSS publications. To order, fill out and mail the Publications order form included with your system or call toll-free. If you represent a bookstore or have an account with Prentice Hall, call 1-800-223-1360. If you are not an account customer, call 1-800-374-1200. In Canada, call 1-800-567-3800. Outside of North America, contact your local Prentice Hall office.

Except for academic course adoptions, manuals can also be purchased from SPSS Inc. Contact your local SPSS office, listed on page vi.

Tell Us Your Thoughts

Your comments are important. Please send us a letter and let us know about your experiences with SPSS products. We especially like to hear about new and interesting applications using the SPSS system. Write to SPSS Inc. Marketing Department, Attn: Director of Product Planning, 233 South Wacker Drive, 11th Floor, Chicago, IL 60606-6307.

About This Manual

This manual is divided into two sections. The first section documents the graphical user interface. Illustrations of dialog boxes are taken from SPSS for Windows. Dialog boxes in other operating systems are similar. In addition, this section provides examples of statistical procedures and advice on interpreting the output. The second part of the manual is a Syntax Reference section that provides complete command syntax for all of the commands included in the Advanced Models option. The Advanced Models command syntax is also available online with the CD-ROM version of SPSS.

This manual contains two indexes: a subject index and a syntax index. The subject index covers both sections of the manual. The syntax index applies only to the Syntax Reference section.

Contacting SPSS

If you would like to be on our mailing list, contact one of our offices, listed on page vi, or visit our WWW site at *http://www.spss.com*. We will send you a copy of our newsletter and let you know about SPSS Inc. activities in your area.

SPSS Inc.
Chicago, Illinois, U.S.A.
Tel: 1.312.651.3000
www.spss.com/corpinfo
Customer Service:
1.800.521.1337
Sales:
1.800.543.2185
sales@spss.com
Training:
1.800.543.6607
Technical Support:
1.312.651.3410
support@spss.com

SPSS Federal Systems
Tel: 1.703.527.6777
www.spss.com

SPSS Argentina srl
Tel: +541.814.5030
www.spss.com

SPSS Asia Pacific Pte. Ltd.
Tel: +65.245.9110
www.spss.com

SPSS Australasia Pty. Ltd.
Tel: +61.2.9954.5660
www.spss.com

SPSS Belgium
Tel: +32.162.389.82
www.spss.com

SPSS Benelux BV
Tel: +31.183.636711
www.spss.nl

SPSS Central and Eastern Europe
Tel: +44.(0)1483.719200
www.spss.com

SPSS Czech Republic
Tel: +420.2.24813839
www.spss.cz

SPSS East Mediterranea and Africa
Tel: +972.9.9526701
www.spss.com

SPSS Finland Oy
Tel: +358.9.524.801
www.spss.com

SPSS France SARL
Tel: +33.1.5535.2700
www.spss.com

SPSS Germany
Tel: +49.89.4890740
www.spss.com

SPSS Hellas SA
Tel: +30.1.7251925/7251950
www.spss.com

SPSS Hispanoportuguesa S.L.
Tel: +34.91.447.37.00
www.spss.com

SPSS Ireland
Tel: +353.1.496.9007
www.spss.com

SPSS Israel Ltd.
Tel: +972.9.9526700
www.spss.com

SPSS Italia srl
Tel: +39.51.252573
www.spss.it

SPSS Japan Inc.
Tel: +81.3.5466.5511
www.spss.co.jp

SPSS Kenya Limited
Tel: +254.2.577.262
www.spss.com

SPSS Korea
Tel: +82.2.3446.7651
www.spss.com

SPSS Latin America
Tel: 1.312.494.3226
www.spss.com

SPSS Malaysia Sdn Bhd
Tel: +60.3.704.5877
www.spss.com

SPSS Mexico SA de CV
Tel: +52.5.682.87.68
www.spss.com

SPSS Middle East and South Asia
Tel: +91.80.227.7436/221.8962
www.spss.com

SPSS Polska
Tel: +48.12.6369680
www.companion.krakow.pl

SPSS Russia
Tel: +7.095.125.0069
www.spss.com

SPSS Scandinavia AB
Tel: +46.8.506.105.50
www.spss.com

SPSS Schweiz AG
Tel: +41.1.266.90.30
www.spss.com

SPSS Singapore Pte. Ltd.
Tel: +65.533.3190
www.spss.com

SPSS South Africa
Tel: +27.11.706.7015
www.spss.com

SPSS Taiwan Corp.
Taipei, Republic of China
Tel: +886.2.25771100
www.spss.com

SPSS UK Ltd.
Tel: +44.1483.719200
www.spss.com

Contents

3 Variance Components Analysis   *33*

4 Model Selection Loglinear Analysis   *41*

5 General Loglinear Analysis   *47*

6 Logit Loglinear Analysis 55

7 Life Tables 63

8 Kaplan-Meier Survival Analysis 69

15 General Loglinear Analysis Examples   157

16 Multinomial Logit Models Examples   197

17 Life Tables Examples 233

18 Kaplan-Meier
Survival Analysis Examples 243

19 Cox Regression Examples

Syntax Reference

Appendix
Categorical Variable Coding Schemes   *459*

Bibliography   *467*

Subject Index   *471*

Syntax Index   *487*

GLM Multivariate Analysis

The GLM Multivariate procedure provides regression analysis and analysis of variance for multiple dependent variables by one or more factor variables or covariates. The factor variables divide the population into groups. Using this general linear model procedure, you can test null hypotheses about the effects of factor variables on the means of various groupings of a joint distribution of dependent variables. You can investigate interactions between factors as well as the effects of individual factors. In addition, the effects of covariates and covariate interactions with factors can be included. For regression analysis, the independent (predictor) variables are specified as covariates.

Both balanced and unbalanced models can be tested. A design is balanced if each cell in the model contains the same number of cases. In a multivariate model, the sums of squares due to the effects in the model and error sums of squares are in matrix form rather than the scalar form found in univariate analysis. These matrices are called SSCP (sums-of-squares and cross-products) matrices. If more than one dependent variable is specified, the multivariate analysis of variance using Pillai's trace, Wilks' lambda, Hotelling's trace, and Roy's largest root criterion with approximate F statistic are provided as well as the univariate analysis of variance for each dependent variable. In addition to testing hypotheses, GLM Multivariate produces estimates of parameters.

Commonly used *a priori* contrasts are available to perform hypothesis testing. Additionally, after an overall F test has shown significance, you can use post hoc tests to evaluate differences among specific means. Estimated marginal means give estimates of predicted mean values for the cells in the model, and profile plots (interaction plots) of these means allow you to visualize some of the relationships easily. The post hoc multiple comparison tests are performed for each dependent variable separately.

Residuals, predicted values, Cook's distance, and leverage values can be saved as new variables in your data file for checking assumptions. Also available are a residual SSCP matrix, which is a square matrix of sums of squares and cross-products of residuals, a residual covariance matrix, which is the residual SSCP matrix divided by the degrees of freedom of the residuals, and the residual correlation matrix, which is the standardized form of the residual covariance matrix.

WLS Weight allows you to specify a variable used to give observations different weights for a weighted least-squares (WLS) analysis, perhaps to compensate for different precision of measurement.

Example. A manufacturer of plastics measures three properties of plastic film: tear resistance, gloss, and opacity. Two rates of extrusion and two different amounts of additive are tried, and the three properties are measured under each combination of extrusion rate and additive amount. The manufacturer finds that the extrusion rate and the amount of additive individually produce significant results but that the interaction of the two factors is not significant.

Methods. Type I, Type II, Type III, and Type IV sums of squares can be used to evaluate different hypotheses. Type III is the default.

Statistics. Post hoc range tests and multiple comparisons: least significant difference, Bonferroni, Sidak, Scheffé, Ryan-Einot-Gabriel-Welsch multiple F, Ryan-Einot-Gabriel-Welsch multiple range, Student-Newman-Keuls, Tukey's honestly significant difference, Tukey's-b, Duncan, Hochberg's GT2, Gabriel, Waller Duncan t test, Dunnett (one-sided and two-sided), Tamhane's T2, Dunnett's T3, Games-Howell, and Dunnett's C. Descriptive statistics: observed means, standard deviations, and counts for all of the dependent variables in all cells; the Levene test for homogeneity of variance; Box's M test of the homogeneity of the covariance matrices of the dependent variables; and Bartlett's test of sphericity.

Plots. Spread-versus-level, residual, and profile (interaction).

Data. The dependent variables should be quantitative. Factors are categorical and can have numeric values or string values of up to eight characters. Covariates are quantitative variables that are related to the dependent variable.

Assumptions. For dependent variables, the data are a random sample of vectors from a multivariate normal population; in the population, the variance-covariance matrices for all cells are the same. Analysis of variance is robust to departures from normality, although the data should be symmetric. To check assumptions, you can use homogeneity of variances tests (including Box's *M*) and spread-versus-level plots. You can also examine residuals and residual plots.

Related procedures. Use the Explore procedure to examine the data before doing an analysis of variance. For a single dependent variable, use GLM Univariate. If you measured the same dependent variables on several occasions for each subject, use GLM Repeated Measures.

To Obtain a GLM Multivariate Analysis of Variance

▶ From the menus choose:

Analyze
General Linear Model
Multivariate...

Figure 1-1
Multivariate dialog box

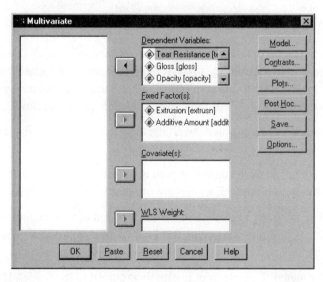

▶ Select at least two dependent variables.

Optionally, you can specify Fixed Factor(s), Covariate(s), and WLS Weight.

GLM Multivariate Model

Figure 1-2
Multivariate Model dialog box

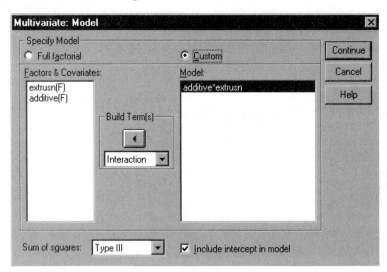

Specify Model. A full factorial model contains all factor main effects, all covariate main effects, and all factor-by-factor interactions. It does not contain covariate interactions. Select Custom to specify only a subset of interactions or to specify factor-by-covariate interactions. You must indicate all of the terms to be included in the model.

Factors and Covariates. The factors and covariates are listed with (F) for fixed factor and (C) for covariate.

Model. The model depends on the nature of your data. After selecting Custom, you can select the main effects and interactions that are of interest in your analysis.

Sum of squares. The method of calculating the sums of squares. For balanced or unbalanced models with no missing cells, the Type III sum-of-squares method is the most commonly used type.

Include intercept in model. The intercept is usually included in the model. If you can assume that the data pass through the origin, you can exclude the intercept.

Build Terms

For the selected factors and covariates:

Interaction. Creates the highest-level interaction term of all selected variables. This is the default.

Main effects. Creates a main-effects term for each variable selected.

All 2-way. Creates all possible two-way interactions of the selected variables.

All 3-way. Creates all possible three-way interactions of the selected variables.

All 4-way. Creates all possible four-way interactions of the selected variables.

All 5-way. Creates all possible five-way interactions of the selected variables.

Sums of Squares

For the model, you can choose a type of sum of squares. Type III is the most commonly used and is the default.

Type I. This method is also known as the hierarchical decomposition of the sum-of-squares method. Each term is adjusted only for the term that precedes it in the model. The Type I sum-of-squares method is commonly used for:

- A balanced ANOVA model in which any main effects are specified before any first-order interaction effects, any first-order interaction effects are specified before any second-order interaction effects, and so on.

- A polynomial regression model in which any lower-order terms are specified before any higher-order terms.

- A purely nested model in which the first-specified effect is nested within the second-specified effect, the second-specified effect is nested within the third, and so on. (This form of nesting can be specified only by using syntax.)

Type II. This method calculates the sums of squares of an effect in the model adjusted for all other "appropriate" effects. An appropriate effect is one that corresponds to all effects that do not contain the effect being examined. The Type II sum-of-squares method is commonly used for:

- A balanced ANOVA model.

- Any model that has main factor effects only.

■ Any regression model.

■ A purely nested design. (This form of nesting can be specified by using syntax.)

Type III. This method, the default, calculates the sums of squares of an effect in the design as the sums of squares adjusted for any other effects that do not contain it and orthogonal to any effects (if any) that contain it. The Type III sums of squares have one major advantage in that they are invariant with respect to the cell frequencies as long as the general form of estimability remains constant. Therefore, this type is often considered useful for an unbalanced model with no missing cells. In a factorial design with no missing cells, this method is equivalent to the Yates' weighted-squares-of-means technique. The Type III sum-of-squares method is commonly used for:

■ Any models listed in Type I and Type II.

■ Any balanced or unbalanced model with no empty cells.

Type IV. This method is designed for a situation in which there are missing cells. For any effect F in the design, if F is not contained in any other effect, then Type IV = Type III = Type II. When F is contained in other effects, Type IV distributes the contrasts being made among the parameters in F to all higher-level effects equitably. The Type IV sum-of-squares method is commonly used for:

■ Any models listed in Type I and Type II.

■ Any balanced model or unbalanced model with empty cells.

GLM Multivariate Contrasts

Figure 1-3
Multivariate Contrasts dialog box

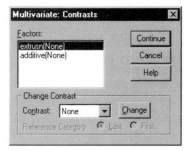

Contrasts are used to test whether the levels of an effect are significantly different from one another. You can specify a contrast for each factor in the model. Contrasts represent linear combinations of the parameters.

Hypothesis testing is based on the null hypothesis **LBM = 0**, where **L** is the contrast coefficients matrix, **M** is the identity matrix, which has dimension equal to the number of dependent variables, and **B** is the parameter vector. When a contrast is specified, SPSS creates an **L** matrix such that the columns corresponding to the factor match the contrast. The remaining columns are adjusted so that the **L** matrix is estimable.

In addition to the univariate test using F statistics and the Bonferroni-type simultaneous confidence intervals based on Student's t distribution for the contrast differences across all dependent variables, the multivariate tests using Pillai's trace, Wilks' lambda, Hotelling's trace, and Roy's largest root criteria are provided.

Available contrasts are deviation, simple, difference, Helmert, repeated, and polynomial. For deviation contrasts and simple contrasts, you can choose whether the reference category is the last or first category.

Contrast Types

Deviation. Compares the mean of each level (except a reference category) to the mean of all of the levels (grand mean). The levels of the factor can be in any order.

Simple. Compares the mean of each level to the mean of a specified level. This type of contrast is useful when there is a control group. You can choose the first or last category as the reference.

Difference. Compares the mean of each level (except the first) to the mean of previous levels. (Sometimes called reverse Helmert contrasts.)

Helmert. Compares the mean of each level of the factor (except the last) to the mean of subsequent levels.

Repeated. Compares the mean of each level (except the last) to the mean of the subsequent level.

Polynomial. Compares the linear effect, quadratic effect, cubic effect, and so on. The first degree of freedom contains the linear effect across all categories; the second degree of freedom, the quadratic effect; and so on. These contrasts are often used to estimate polynomial trends.

GLM Multivariate Profile Plots

Figure 1-4
Multivariate Profile Plots dialog box

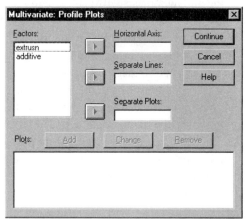

Profile plots (interaction plots) are useful for comparing marginal means in your model. Profile plots are created for each dependent variable. A profile plot is a line plot in which each point indicates the estimated marginal mean of a dependent variable (adjusted for covariates) at one level of a factor. The levels of a second factor can be used to make separate lines. Each level in a third factor can be used to create a separate plot. All fixed factors are available for plots.

A profile plot of one factor shows whether the estimated marginal means are increasing or decreasing across levels. For two or more factors, parallel lines indicate that there is no interaction between factors, which means that you can investigate the levels of only one factor. Lines that cross each other indicate an interaction.

Figure 1-5
Nonparallel plot (left) and parallel plot (right)

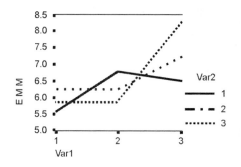
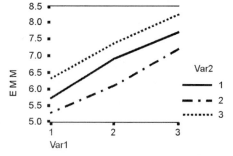

After a plot is specified by selecting factors for the horizontal axis, and optionally, factors for separate lines and separate plots, the plot must be listed in the Plots list.

GLM Multivariate Post Hoc Multiple Comparisons for Observed Means

Figure 1-6
Post Hoc Multiple Comparisons for Observed Means dialog box

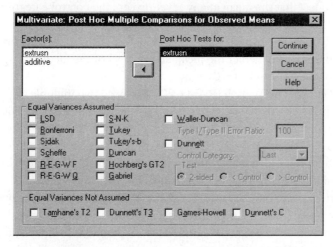

Post hoc multiple comparison tests. Once you have determined that differences exist among the means, post hoc range tests and pairwise multiple comparisons can determine which means differ. Comparisons are made on unadjusted values. These tests are used for between-subjects factors only. The post hoc multiple comparison tests are performed for each dependent variable separately.

The Bonferroni and Tukey's honestly significant difference tests are commonly used multiple comparison tests. The **Bonferroni test**, based on Student's *t* statistic, adjusts the observed significance level for the fact that multiple comparisons are made. **Sidak's *t* test** also adjusts the significance level and provides tighter bounds than the Bonferroni test. **Tukey's honestly significant difference test** uses the Studentized range statistic to make all pairwise comparisons between groups and sets the experimentwise error rate to the error rate for the collection for all pairwise comparisons. When testing a large number of pairs of means, Tukey's honestly significant difference test is more powerful than the Bonferroni test. For a small number of pairs, Bonferroni is more powerful.

Hochberg's GT2 is similar to Tukey's honestly significant difference test, but the Studentized maximum modulus is used. Usually, Tukey's test is more powerful. **Gabriel's pairwise comparisons test** also uses the Studentized maximum modulus and is generally more powerful than Hochberg's GT2 when the cell sizes are unequal. Gabriel's test may become liberal when the cell sizes vary greatly.

Dunnett's pairwise multiple comparison *t* test compares a set of treatments against a single control mean. The last category is the default control category. Alternatively, you can choose the first category. You can also choose a two-sided or one-sided test. To test that the mean at any level (except the control category) of the factor is not equal to that of the control category, use a two-sided test. To test whether the mean at any level of the factor is smaller than that of the control category, select < Control. Likewise, to test whether the mean at any level of the factor is larger than that of the control category, select > Control.

Ryan, Einot, Gabriel, and Welsch (R-E-G-W) developed two multiple step-down range tests. Multiple step-down procedures first test whether all means are equal. If all means are not equal, subsets of means are tested for equality. **R-E-G-W *F*** is based on an *F* test and **R-E-G-W *Q*** is based on the Studentized range. These tests are more powerful than Duncan's multiple range test and Student-Newman-Keuls (which are also multiple step-down procedures), but they are not recommended for unequal cell sizes.

When the variances are unequal, use **Tamhane's T2** (conservative pairwise comparisons test based on a *t* test), **Dunnett's T3** (pairwise comparison test based on the Studentized maximum modulus), **Games-Howell pairwise comparison test** (sometimes liberal), or **Dunnett's *C*** (pairwise comparison test based on the Studentized range).

Duncan's multiple range test, Student-Newman-Keuls (**S-N-K**), and **Tukey's-*b*** are range tests that rank group means and compute a range value. These tests are not used as frequently as the tests previously discussed.

The **Waller-Duncan *t* test** uses a Bayesian approach. This range test uses the harmonic mean of the sample size when the sample sizes are unequal.

The significance level of the **Scheffé test** is designed to allow all possible linear combinations of group means to be tested, not just pairwise comparisons available in this feature. The result is that the Scheffé test is often more conservative than other tests, which means that a larger difference between means is required for significance.

The least significant difference (**LSD**) pairwise multiple comparison test is equivalent to multiple individual *t* tests between all pairs of groups. The disadvantage of this test is that no attempt is made to adjust the observed significance level for multiple comparisons.

Tests displayed. Pairwise comparisons are provided for LSD, Sidak, Bonferroni, Games and Howell, Tamhane's T2 and T3, Dunnett's *C*, and Dunnett's T3. Homogeneous subsets for range tests are provided for S-N-K, Tukey's-*b*, Duncan, R-E-G-W *F*, R-E-G-W *Q*, and Waller. Tukey's honestly significant difference test, Hochberg's GT2, Gabriel's test, and Scheffé's test are both multiple comparison tests and range tests.

GLM Multivariate Save

Figure 1-7
Multivariate Save dialog box

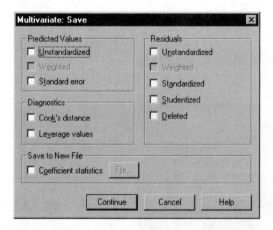

You can save values predicted by the model, residuals, and related measures as new variables in the Data Editor. Many of these variables can be used for examining assumptions about the data. To save the values for use in another SPSS session, you must save the current data file.

Predicted Values. The values that the model predicts for each case. Unstandardized predicted values and the standard errors of the predicted values are available. If a WLS variable was chosen, weighted unstandardized predicted values are available.

Diagnostics. Measures to identify cases with unusual combinations of values for the independent variables and cases that may have a large impact on the model. Available are Cook's distance and uncentered leverage values.

Residuals. An unstandardized residual is the actual value of the dependent variable minus the value predicted by the model. Standardized, Studentized, and deleted residuals are also available. If a WLS variable was chosen, weighted unstandardized residuals are available.

Save to New File. Writes an SPSS data file containing a variance-covariance matrix of the parameter estimates in the model. Also, for each dependent variable, there will be a row of parameter estimates, a row of significance values for the *t* statistics corresponding to the parameter estimates, and a row of residual degrees of freedom. For a multivariate model, there are similar rows for each dependent variable. You can use this data in other SPSS procedures.

GLM Multivariate Options

Figure 1-8
Multivariate Options dialog box

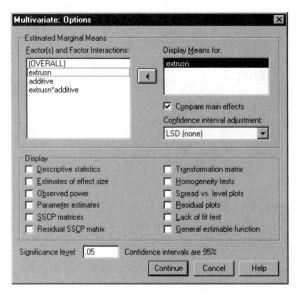

Optional statistics are available from this dialog box. Statistics are calculated using a fixed-effects model.

Estimated Marginal Means. Select the factors and interactions for which you want estimates of the population marginal means in the cells. These means are adjusted for the covariates, if any. Interactions are available only if you have specified a custom model.

■ **Compare main effects.** Provides uncorrected pairwise comparisons among estimated marginal means for any main effect in the model, for both between- and within-subjects factors. This item is available only if main effects are selected under the Display Means For list.

■ **Confidence interval adjustment.** Select least significant difference (LSD), Bonferroni, or Sidak adjustment to the confidence intervals and significance. This item is available only if Compare main effects is selected.

Display. Select Descriptive statistics to produce observed means, standard deviations, and counts for all of the dependent variables in all cells. Estimates of effect size gives a partial eta-squared value for each effect and each parameter estimate. The eta-squared statistic describes the proportion of total variability attributable to a factor. Select Observed power to obtain the power of the test when the alternative hypothesis is set based on the observed value. Select Parameter estimates to produce the parameter estimates, standard errors, t tests, confidence intervals, and the observed power for each test. You can display the hypothesis and error SSCP matrices and the Residual SSCP matrix plus Bartlett's test of sphericity of the residual covariance matrix.

Homogeneity tests produces the Levene test of the homogeneity of variance for each dependent variable across all level combinations of the between-subjects factors, for between-subjects factors only. Also, homogeneity tests include Box's M test of the homogeneity of the covariance matrices of the dependent variables across all level combinations of the between-subjects factors. The spread-versus-level and residual plots options are useful for checking assumptions about the data. This item is disabled if there are no factors. Select Residual plots to produce an observed-by-predicted-by-standardized residuals plot for each dependent variable. These plots are useful for investigating the assumption of equal variance. Select Lack of fit test to check if the relationship between the dependent variable and the independent variables can be adequately described by the model. General estimable function allows you to construct custom hypothesis tests based on the general estimable function. Rows in any contrast coefficient matrix are linear combinations of the general estimable function.

Significance level. You might want to adjust the significance level used in post hoc tests and the confidence level used for constructing confidence intervals. The specified value is also used to calculate the observed power for the test. When you specify a significance level, the associated level of the confidence intervals is displayed in the dialog box.

GLM Command Additional Features

These features may apply to univariate, multivariate, or repeated measures analysis. The SPSS command language also allows you to:

■ Specify nested effects in the design (using the DESIGN subcommand).

■ Specify tests of effects versus a linear combination of effects or a value (using the TEST subcommand).

■ Specify multiple contrasts (using the CONTRAST subcommand).

■ Include user-missing values (using the MISSING subcommand).

■ Specify EPS criteria (using the CRITERIA subcommand).

■ Construct a custom **L** matrix, **M** matrix, or **K** matrix (using the LMATRIX, MMATRIX, or KMATRIX subcommands).

■ For deviation or simple contrasts, specify an intermediate reference category (using the CONTRAST subcommand).

■ Specify metrics for polynomial contrasts (using the CONTRAST subcommand).

■ Specify error terms for post hoc comparisons (using the POSTHOC subcommand).

■ Compute estimated marginal means for any factor or factor interaction among the factors in the factor list (using the EMMEANS subcommand).

■ Specify names for temporary variables (using the SAVE subcommand).

■ Construct a correlation matrix data file (using the OUTFILE subcommand).

■ Construct a matrix data file that contains statistics from the between-subjects ANOVA table (using the OUTFILE subcommand).

■ Save the design matrix to a new data file (using the OUTFILE subcommand).

See the Syntax Reference section of this manual for complete syntax information.

GLM Repeated Measures

The GLM Repeated Measures procedure provides analysis of variance when the same measurement is made several times on each subject or case. If between-subjects factors are specified, they divide the population into groups. Using this general linear model procedure, you can test null hypotheses about the effects of both the between-subjects factors and the within-subjects factors. You can investigate interactions between factors as well as the effects of individual factors. In addition, the effects of constant covariates and covariate interactions with the between-subjects factors can be included.

In a doubly multivariate repeated measures design, the dependent variables represent measurements of more than one variable for the different levels of the within-subjects factors. For example, you could have measured both pulse and respiration at three different times on each subject.

The GLM Repeated Measures procedure provides both univariate and multivariate analyses for the repeated measures data. Both balanced and unbalanced models can be tested. A design is balanced if each cell in the model contains the same number of cases. In a multivariate model, the sums of squares due to the effects in the model and error sums of squares are in matrix form rather than the scalar form found in univariate analysis. These matrices are called SSCP (sums-of-squares and cross-products) matrices. In addition to testing hypotheses, GLM Repeated Measures produces estimates of parameters.

Commonly used *a priori* contrasts are available to perform hypothesis testing on between-subjects factors. Additionally, after an overall *F* test has shown significance, you can use post hoc tests to evaluate differences among specific means. Estimated marginal means give estimates of predicted mean values for the cells in the model, and profile plots (interaction plots) of these means allow you to visualize some of the relationships easily.

Residuals, predicted values, Cook's distance, and leverage values can be saved as new variables in your data file for checking assumptions. Also available are a residual SSCP matrix, which is a square matrix of sums of squares and cross-products of residuals, a residual covariance matrix, which is the residual SSCP matrix divided by the degrees of freedom of the residuals, and the residual correlation matrix, which is the standardized form of the residual covariance matrix.

WLS Weight allows you to specify a variable used to give observations different weights for a weighted least-squares (WLS) analysis, perhaps to compensate for different precision of measurement.

Example. Twelve students are assigned to a high- or low-anxiety group based on their scores on an anxiety-rating test. The anxiety rating is called a between-subjects factor because it divides the subjects into groups. The students are each given four trials on a learning task, and the number of errors for each trial is recorded. The errors for each trial are recorded in separate variables, and a within-subjects factor (trial) is defined with four levels for the four trials. The trial effect is found to be significant, while the trial-by-anxiety interaction is not significant.

Methods. Type I, Type II, Type III, and Type IV sums of squares can be used to evaluate different hypotheses. Type III is the default.

Statistics. Post hoc range tests and multiple comparisons (for between-subjects factors): least significant difference, Bonferroni, Sidak, Scheffé, Ryan-Einot-Gabriel-Welsch multiple *F*, Ryan-Einot-Gabriel-Welsch multiple range, Student-Newman-Keuls, Tukey's honestly significant difference, Tukey's-*b*, Duncan, Hochberg's GT2, Gabriel, Waller Duncan *t* test, Dunnett (one-sided and two-sided), Tamhane's T2, Dunnett's T3, Games-Howell, and Dunnett's *C*. Descriptive statistics: observed means, standard deviations, and counts for all of the dependent variables in all cells; the Levene test for homogeneity of variance; Box's *M*; and Mauchly's test of sphericity.

Plots. Spread-versus-level, residual, and profile (interaction).

Data. The dependent variables should be quantitative. Between-subjects factors divide the sample into discrete subgroups, such as male and female. These factors are categorical and can have numeric values or string values of up to eight characters. Within-subjects factors are defined in the Repeated Measures Define Factor(s) dialog box. Covariates are quantitative variables that are related to the dependent variable. For a repeated measures analysis, these should remain constant at each level of a within-subjects variable.

The data file should contain a set of variables for each group of measurements on the subjects. The set has one variable for each repetition of the measurement within the group. A within-subjects factor is defined for the group with the number of levels equal to the number of repetitions. For example, measurements of weight could be taken on different days. If measurements of the same property were taken on five days, the within-subjects factor could be specified as *day* with five levels.

For multiple within-subjects factors, the number of measurements for each subject is equal to the product of the number of levels of each factor. For example, if measurements were taken at three different times each day for four days, the total number of measurements is 12 for each subject. The within-subjects factors could be specified as *day(4)* and *time(3)*.

Assumptions. A repeated measures analysis can be approached in two ways, univariate and multivariate.

The univariate approach (also known as the split-plot or mixed-model approach) considers the dependent variables as responses to the levels of within-subjects factors. The measurements on a subject should be a sample from a multivariate normal distribution, and the variance-covariance matrices are the same across the cells formed by the between-subjects effects. Certain assumptions are made on the variance-covariance matrix of the dependent variables. The validity of the F statistic used in the univariate approach can be assured if the variance-covariance matrix is circular in form (Huynh and Mandeville, 1979).

To test this assumption, Mauchly's test of sphericity can be used, which performs a test of sphericity on the variance-covariance matrix of an orthonormalized transformed dependent variable. Mauchly's test is automatically displayed for a repeated measures analysis. For small sample sizes, this test is not very powerful. For large sample sizes, the test may be significant even when the impact of the departure on the results is small. If the significance of the test is large, the hypothesis of sphericity can be assumed. However, if the significance is small and the sphericity assumption appears to be violated, an adjustment to the numerator and denominator degrees of freedom can be made in order to validate the univariate F statistic. Three estimates of this adjustment, which is called **epsilon**, are available in the GLM Repeated Measures procedure. Both the numerator and denominator degrees of freedom must be multiplied by epsilon, and the significance of the F ratio must be evaluated with the new degrees of freedom.

 The multivariate approach considers the measurements on a subject to be a sample from a multivariate normal distribution, and the variance-covariance matrices are the same across the cells formed by the between-subjects effects. To test whether the variance-covariance matrices across the cells are the same, Box's M test can be used.

Related procedures. Use the Explore procedure to examine the data before doing an analysis of variance. If there are *not* repeated measurements on each subject, use GLM Univariate or GLM Multivariate. If there are only two measurements for each subject (for example, pre-test and post-test), and there are no between-subjects factors, you can use the Paired-Samples T Test procedure.

GLM Repeated Measures Define Factor(s)

GLM Repeated Measures analyzes groups of related dependent variables that represent different measurements of the same attribute. This dialog box lets you define one or more within-subjects factors for use in GLM Repeated Measures. Note that the order in which you specify within-subjects factors is important. Each factor constitutes a level within the previous factor.

To use Repeated Measures, you must set up your data correctly. You must define within-subjects factors in this dialog box. Notice that these factors are not existing variables in your data but rather factors that you define here.

Example. In a weight-loss study, suppose the weights of several people are measured each week for five weeks. In the data file, each person is a subject or case. The weights for the weeks are recorded in the variables *weight1*, *weight2*, and so on. The gender of each person is recorded in another variable. The weights, measured for each subject repeatedly, can be grouped by defining a within-subjects factor. The factor could be called *week*, defined to have five levels. In the main dialog box, the variables *weight1*, ..., *weight5* are used to assign the five levels of *week*. The variable in the data file that groups males and females (*gender*) can be specified as a between-subjects factor to study the differences between males and females.

Measures. If subjects were tested on more than one measure at each time, click Measure to define the measures. For example, the pulse and respiration rate could be measured on each subject every day for a week. These measures do not exist as variables in the data file but are defined here. A model with more than one measure is sometimes called a doubly multivariate repeated measures model.

To Obtain a GLM Repeated Measures Analysis

▶ From the menus choose:

Analyze
  General Linear Model
    Repeated Measures...

Figure 2-1
Repeated Measures Define Factor(s) dialog box

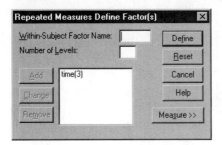

▶ Type a within-subject factor name and its number of levels.

▶ Click Add.

▶ Repeat these steps for each within-subjects factor.

To define measure factors for a doubly multivariate repeated measures design:

▶ Click Measure.

Figure 2-2

Expanded Repeated Measures Define Factor(s) dialog box

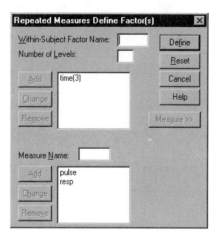

▶ Type the measure name.

▶ Click Add.

After defining all of your factors and measures:

▶ Click Define.

Figure 2-3
Repeated Measures dialog box

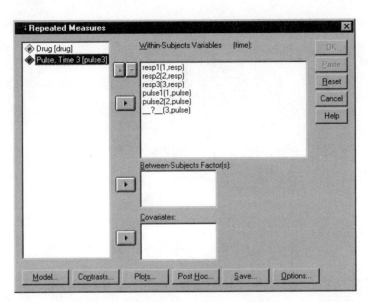

▶ Select a dependent variable that corresponds to each combination of within-subjects factors (and optionally, measures) on the list.

To change positions of the variables, use the up and down pushbuttons.

To make changes to the within-subjects factors, you can reopen the Repeated Measures Define Factor(s) dialog box without closing the main dialog box.

Optionally, you can specify between-subjects factor(s) and covariates.

GLM Repeated Measures Model

Figure 2-4
Repeated Measures Model dialog box

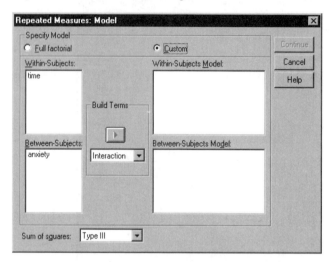

Specify Model. A full factorial model contains all factor main effects, all covariate main effects, and all factor-by-factor interactions. It does not contain covariate interactions. Select Custom to specify only a subset of interactions or to specify factor-by-covariate interactions. You must indicate all of the terms to be included in the model.

Between-Subjects. The covariates are listed with (C) for covariate.

Model. The model depends on the nature of your data. After selecting Custom, you can select the within-subjects effects and interactions and the between-subjects effects and interactions that are of interest in your analysis.

Sum of squares. The method of calculating the sums of squares for the between-subjects model. For balanced or unbalanced between-subjects models with no missing cells, the Type III sum-of-squares method is the most commonly used.

Build Terms

For the selected factors and covariates:

Interaction. Creates the highest-level interaction term of all selected variables. This is the default.

Main effects. Creates a main-effects term for each variable selected.

All 2-way. Creates all possible two-way interactions of the selected variables.

All 3-way. Creates all possible three-way interactions of the selected variables.

All 4-way. Creates all possible four-way interactions of the selected variables.

All 5-way. Creates all possible five-way interactions of the selected variables.

Sums of Squares

For the model, you can choose a type of sum of squares. Type III is the most commonly used and is the default.

Type I. This method is also known as the hierarchical decomposition of the sum-of-squares method. Each term is adjusted for only the term that precedes it in the model. The Type I sum-of-squares method is commonly used for:

- A balanced ANOVA model in which any main effects are specified before any first-order interaction effects, any first-order interaction effects are specified before any second-order interaction effects, and so on.

- A polynomial regression model in which any lower-order terms are specified before any higher-order terms.

- A purely nested model in which the first-specified effect is nested within the second-specified effect, the second-specified effect is nested within the third, and so on. (This form of nesting can be specified only by using syntax.)

Type II. This method calculates the sums of squares of an effect in the model adjusted for all other "appropriate" effects. An appropriate effect is one that corresponds to all effects that do not contain the effect being examined. The Type II sum-of-squares method is commonly used for:

- A balanced ANOVA model.

- Any model that has main factor effects only.

- Any regression model.

- A purely nested design. (This form of nesting can be specified by using syntax.)

Type III. This method, the default, calculates the sums of squares of an effect in the design as the sums of squares adjusted for any other effects that do not contain it and orthogonal to any effects (if any) that contain it. The Type III sums of squares have one major advantage in that they are invariant with respect to the cell frequencies as long as the general form of estimability remains constant. Therefore, this type is often considered useful for an unbalanced model with no missing cells. In a factorial design with no missing cells, this method is equivalent to the Yates' weighted-squares-of-means technique. The Type III sum-of-squares method is commonly used for:

- Any models listed in Type I and Type II.
- Any balanced or unbalanced model with no empty cells.

Type IV. This method is designed for a situation in which there are missing cells. For any effect F in the design, if F is not contained in any other effect, then Type IV = Type III = Type II. When F is contained in other effects, Type IV distributes the contrasts being made among the parameters in F to all higher-level effects equitably. The Type IV sum-of-squares method is commonly used for:

- Any models listed in Type I and Type II.
- Any balanced model or unbalanced model with empty cells.

GLM Repeated Measures Contrasts

Figure 2-5
Repeated Measures Contrasts dialog box

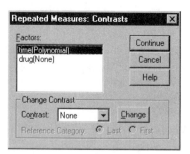

Contrasts are used to test for differences among the levels of a between-subjects factor. You can specify a contrast for each between-subjects factor in the model. Contrasts represent linear combinations of the parameters.

Hypothesis testing is based on the null hypothesis **LBM**=0, where **L** is the contrast coefficients matrix, **B** is the parameter vector, and **M** is the average matrix that corresponds to the average transformation for the dependent variable. You can display this transformation matrix by selecting Transformation matrix in the Repeated Measures Options dialog box. For example, if there are four dependent variables, a within-subjects factor of four levels, and polynomial contrasts (the default) are used for within-subjects factors, the **M** matrix will be (0.5 0.5 0.5 0.5)'. When a contrast is specified, SPSS creates an **L** matrix such that the columns corresponding to the between-subjects factor match the contrast. The remaining columns are adjusted so that the **L** matrix is estimable.

Available contrasts are deviation, simple, difference, Helmert, repeated, and polynomial. For deviation contrasts and simple contrasts, you can choose whether the reference category is the last or first category.

Contrast Types

Deviation. Compares the mean of each level (except a reference category) to the mean of all of the levels (grand mean). The levels of the factor can be in any order.

Simple. Compares the mean of each level to the mean of a specified level. This type of contrast is useful when there is a control group. You can choose the first or last category as the reference.

Difference. Compares the mean of each level (except the first) to the mean of previous levels. (Sometimes called reverse Helmert contrasts.)

Helmert. Compares the mean of each level of the factor (except the last) to the mean of subsequent levels.

Repeated. Compares the mean of each level (except the last) to the mean of the subsequent level.

Polynomial. Compares the linear effect, quadratic effect, cubic effect, and so on. The first degree of freedom contains the linear effect across all categories; the second degree of freedom, the quadratic effect; and so on. These contrasts are often used to estimate polynomial trends.

GLM Repeated Measures Profile Plots

Figure 2-6
Repeated Measures Profile Plots dialog box

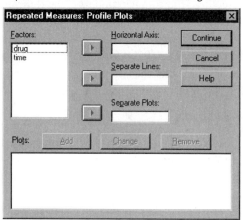

Profile plots (interaction plots) are useful for comparing marginal means in your model. A profile plot is a line plot in which each point indicates the estimated marginal mean of a dependent variable (adjusted for any covariates) at one level of a factor. The levels of a second factor can be used to make separate lines. Each level in a third factor can be used to create a separate plot. Both between-subjects factors and within-subjects factors can be used in profile plots.

A profile plot of one factor shows whether the estimated marginal means are increasing or decreasing across levels. For two or more factors, parallel lines indicate that there is no interaction between factors, which means that you can investigate the levels of only one factor. Nonparallel lines indicate an interaction.

Figure 2-7
Nonparallel plot (left) and parallel plot (right)

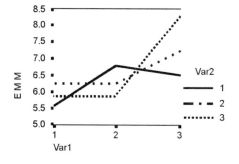 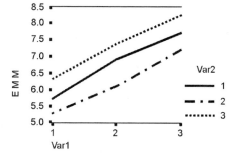

After a plot is specified by selecting factors for the horizontal axis and, optionally, factors for separate lines and separate plots, it must be added to the Plots list.

GLM Repeated Measures Post Hoc Multiple Comparisons for Observed Means

Figure 2-8
Post Hoc Multiple Comparisons for Observed Means dialog box

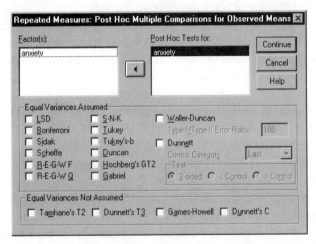

Post hoc multiple comparison tests. Once you have determined that differences exist among the means, post hoc range tests and pairwise multiple comparisons can determine which means differ. These tests are used for fixed *between-subjects* factors only. They are not available if there are no between-subjects factors. The post hoc multiple comparison tests are performed for each dependent variable separately.

The Bonferroni and Tukey's honestly significant difference tests are commonly used multiple comparison tests. The **Bonferroni test**, based on Student's *t* statistic, adjusts the observed significance level for the fact that multiple comparisons are made. **Sidak's *t* test** also adjusts the significance level and provides tighter bounds than the Bonferroni test. **Tukey's honestly significant difference test** uses the Studentized range statistic to make all pairwise comparisons between groups and sets the experimentwise error rate to the error rate for the collection for all pairwise comparisons. When testing a large number of pairs of means, Tukey's honestly significant difference test is more powerful than the Bonferroni test. For a small number of pairs, Bonferroni is more powerful.

Hochberg's GT2 is similar to Tukey's honestly significant difference test, but the Studentized maximum modulus is used. Usually, Tukey's test is more powerful. **Gabriel's pairwise comparisons test** also uses the Studentized maximum modulus and is generally more powerful than Hochberg's GT2 when the cell sizes are unequal. Gabriel's test may become liberal when the cell sizes vary greatly.

Dunnett's pairwise multiple comparison *t* test compares a set of treatments against a single control mean. The last category is the default control category. Alternatively, you can choose the first category. You can also choose a two-sided or one-sided test. To test that the mean at any level (except the control category) of the factor is not equal to that of the control category, use a two-sided test. To test whether the mean at any level of the factor is smaller than that of the control category, select < Control. Likewise, to test whether the mean at any level of the factor is larger than that of the control category, select > Control.

Ryan, Einot, Gabriel, and Welsch (R-E-G-W) developed two multiple step-down range tests. Multiple step-down procedures first test whether all means are equal. If all means are not equal, subsets of means are tested for equality. **R-E-G-W *F*** is based on an *F* test and **R-E-G-W *Q*** is based on the Studentized range. These tests are more powerful than Duncan's multiple range test and Student-Newman-Keuls (which are also multiple step-down procedures), but they are not recommended for unequal cell sizes.

When the variances are unequal, use **Tamhane's T2** (conservative pairwise comparisons test based on a *t* test), **Dunnett's T3** (pairwise comparison test based on the Studentized maximum modulus), **Games-Howell pairwise comparison test** (sometimes liberal), or **Dunnett's C** (pairwise comparison test based on the Studentized range).

Duncan's multiple range test, Student-Newman-Keuls (**S-N-K**), and **Tukey's-*b*** are range tests that rank group means and compute a range value. These tests are not used as frequently as the tests previously discussed.

The **Waller-Duncan *t* test** uses a Bayesian approach. This range test uses the harmonic mean of the sample size when the sample sizes are unequal.

The significance level of the **Scheffé test** is designed to allow all possible linear combinations of group means to be tested, not just pairwise comparisons available in this feature. The result is that the Scheffé test is often more conservative than other tests, which means that a larger difference between means is required for significance.

The least significant difference (**LSD**) pairwise multiple comparison test is equivalent to multiple individual *t* tests between all pairs of groups. The disadvantage of this test is that no attempt is made to adjust the observed significance level for multiple comparisons.

Tests displayed. Pairwise comparisons are provided for LSD, Sidak, Bonferroni, Games and Howell, Tamhane's T2 and T3, Dunnett's *C*, and Dunnett's T3. Homogeneous subsets for range tests are provided for S-N-K, Tukey's-*b*, Duncan, R-E-G-W *F*, R-E-G-W *Q*, and Waller. Tukey's honestly significant difference test, Hochberg's GT2, Gabriel's test, and Scheffé's test are both multiple comparison tests and range tests.

GLM Repeated Measures Save

Figure 2-9
Repeated Measures Save dialog box

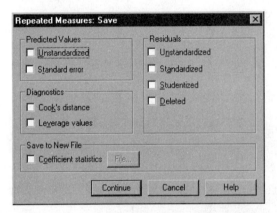

You can save values predicted by the model, residuals, and related measures as new variables in the Data Editor. Many of these variables can be used for examining assumptions about the data. To save the values for use in another SPSS session, you must save the current data file.

Predicted Values. The values that the model predicts for each case. Unstandardized predicted values and the standard errors of the predicted values are available.

Diagnostics. Measures to identify cases with unusual combinations of values for the independent variables and cases that may have a large impact on the model. Available are Cook's distance and uncentered leverage values.

Residuals. An unstandardized residual is the actual value of the dependent variable minus the value predicted by the model. Standardized, Studentized, and deleted residuals are also available.

Save to New File. Writes an SPSS data file containing a variance-covariance matrix of the parameter estimates in the model. Also, for each dependent variable, there will be a row of parameter estimates, a row of significance values for the *t* statistics corresponding to the parameter estimates, and a row of residual degrees of freedom. For a multivariate model, there are similar rows for each dependent variable. You can use this matrix file in other procedures that read an SPSS matrix file.

GLM Repeated Measures Options

Figure 2-10
Repeated Measures Options dialog box

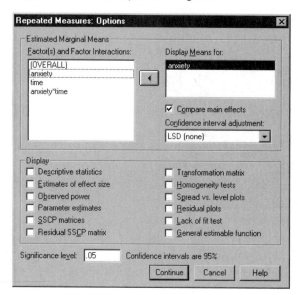

Optional statistics are available from this dialog box. Statistics are calculated using a fixed-effects model.

Estimated Marginal Means. Select the factors and interactions for which you want estimates of the population marginal means in the cells. These means are adjusted for the covariates, if any. Both within-subjects and between-subjects factors can be selected.

- **Compare main effects.** Provides uncorrected pairwise comparisons among estimated marginal means for any main effect in the model, for both between- and within-subjects factors. This item is available only if main effects are selected under the Display Means For list.

- **Confidence interval adjustment.** Select least significant difference (LSD), Bonferroni, or Sidak adjustment to the confidence intervals and significance. This item is available only if Compare main effects is selected.

Display. Select Descriptive statistics to produce observed means, standard deviations, and counts for all of the dependent variables in all cells. Estimates of effect size gives a partial eta-squared value for each effect and each parameter estimate. The eta-squared statistic describes the proportion of total variability attributable to a factor. Select Observed power to obtain the power of the test when the alternative hypothesis is set based on the observed value. Select Parameter estimates to produce the parameter estimates, standard errors, t tests, confidence intervals, and the observed power for each test. You can display the hypothesis and error SSCP matrices and the Residual SSCP matrix plus Bartlett's test of sphericity of the residual covariance matrix.

Homogeneity tests produces the Levene test of the homogeneity of variance for each dependent variable across all level combinations of the between-subjects factors, for between-subjects factors only. Also, homogeneity tests include Box's M test of the homogeneity of the covariance matrices of the dependent variables across all level combinations of the between-subjects factors. The spread-versus-level and residual plots options are useful for checking assumptions about the data. This item is disabled if there are no factors. Select Residual plots to produce an observed-by-predicted-by-standardized residuals plot for each dependent variable. These plots are useful for investigating the assumption of equal variance. Select Lack of fit test to check if the relationship between the dependent variable and the independent variables can be adequately described by the model. General estimable function allows you to construct custom hypothesis tests based on the general estimable function. Rows in any contrast coefficient matrix are linear combinations of the general estimable function.

Significance level. You might want to adjust the significance level used in post hoc tests and the confidence level used for constructing confidence intervals. The specified value is also used to calculate the observed power for the test. When you specify a significance level, the associated level of the confidence intervals is displayed in the dialog box.

GLM Command Additional Features

These features may apply to univariate, multivariate, or repeated measures analysis. The SPSS command language also allows you to:

- Specify nested effects in the design (using the DESIGN subcommand).

- Specify tests of effects versus a linear combination of effects or a value (using the TEST subcommand).

- Specify multiple contrasts (using the CONTRAST subcommand).

- Include user-missing values (using the MISSING subcommand).

- Specify EPS criteria (using the CRITERIA subcommand).

- Construct a custom **L** matrix, **M** matrix, or **K** matrix (using the LMATRIX, MMATRIX, and KMATRIX subcommands).

- For deviation or simple contrasts, specify an intermediate reference category (using the CONTRAST subcommand).

- Specify metrics for polynomial contrasts (using the CONTRAST subcommand).

- Specify error terms for post hoc comparisons (using the POSTHOC subcommand).

- Compute estimated marginal means for any factor or factor interaction among the factors in the factor list (using the EMMEANS subcommand).

- Specify names for temporary variables (using the SAVE subcommand).

- Construct a correlation matrix data file (using the OUTFILE subcommand).

- Construct a matrix data file that contains statistics from the between-subjects ANOVA table (using the OUTFILE subcommand).

- Save the design matrix to a new data file (using the OUTFILE subcommand).

See the Syntax Reference section of this manual for complete syntax information.

Variance Components Analysis

The Variance Components procedure, for mixed-effects models, estimates the contribution of each random effect to the variance of the dependent variable. This procedure is particularly interesting for analysis of mixed models such as split plot, univariate repeated measures, and random block designs. By calculating variance components, you can determine where to focus attention in order to reduce the variance.

Four different methods are available for estimating the variance components: minimum norm quadratic unbiased estimator (MINQUE), analysis of variance (ANOVA), maximum likelihood (ML), and restricted maximum likelihood (REML). Various specifications are available for the different methods.

Default output for all methods includes variance component estimates. If the ML method or the REML method is used, an asymptotic covariance matrix table is also displayed. Other available output includes an ANOVA table and expected mean squares for the ANOVA method, and an iteration history for the ML and REML methods. The Variance Components procedure is fully compatible with the GLM Univariate procedure.

WLS Weight allows you to specify a variable used to give observations different weights for a weighted analysis, perhaps to compensate for different precision of measurement.

Example. At an agriculture school, weight gains for pigs in six different litters are measured after one month. The litter variable is a random factor with six levels. (The six litters studied are a random sample from a large population of pig litters.) The investigator finds out that the variance in weight gain is attributable to the difference in litters much more than to the difference in pigs within a litter.

Data. The dependent variable is quantitative. Factors are categorical. They can have numeric values or string values of up to eight characters. At least one of the factors must be random. That is, the levels of the factor must be a random sample of possible levels. Covariates are quantitative variables that are related to the dependent variable.

Assumptions. All methods assume that model parameters of a random effect have zero means and finite constant variances and are mutually uncorrelated. Model parameters from different random effects are also uncorrelated.

The residual term also has a zero mean and finite constant variance. It is uncorrelated with model parameters of any random effect. Residual terms from different observations are assumed to be uncorrelated.

Based on these assumptions, observations from the same level of a random factor are correlated. This fact distinguishes a variance component model from a general linear model.

ANOVA and MINQUE do not require normality assumptions. They are both robust to moderate departures from the normality assumption.

ML and REML require the model parameter and the residual term to be normally distributed.

Related procedures. Use the Explore procedure to examine the data before doing variance components analysis. For hypothesis testing, use GLM Univariate, GLM Multivariate, and GLM Repeated Measures.

To Obtain a Variance Components Analysis

▶ From the menus choose:

Analyze
  General Linear Model
    Variance Components...

Figure 3-1
Variance Components dialog box

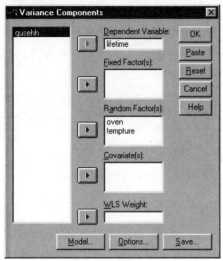

▶ Select a dependent variable.

▶ Select variables for Fixed Factor(s), Random Factor(s), and Covariate(s), as appropriate for your data. For specifying a weight variable, use WLS Weight.

Variance Components Model

Figure 3-2
Variance Components Model dialog box

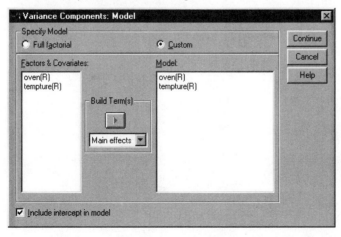

Specify Model. A full factorial model contains all factor main effects, all covariate main effects, and all factor-by-factor interactions. It does not contain covariate interactions. Select Custom to specify only a subset of interactions or to specify factor-by-covariate interactions. You must indicate all of the terms to be included in the model.

Factors and Covariates. The factors and covariates are listed with (F) for a fixed factor, (R) for a random factor, and (C) for a covariate.

Model. The model depends on the nature of your data. After selecting Custom, you can select the main effects and interactions that are of interest in your analysis. The model must contain a random factor.

Include intercept in model. Usually the intercept is included in the model. If you can assume that the data pass through the origin, you can exclude the intercept.

Build Terms

For the selected factors and covariates:

Interaction. Creates the highest-level interaction term of all selected variables. This is the default.

Main effects. Creates a main-effects term for each variable selected.

All 2-way. Creates all possible two-way interactions of the selected variables.

All 3-way. Creates all possible three-way interactions of the selected variables.

All 4-way. Creates all possible four-way interactions of the selected variables.

All 5-way. Creates all possible five-way interactions of the selected variables.

Variance Components Options

Figure 3-3
Variance Components Options dialog box

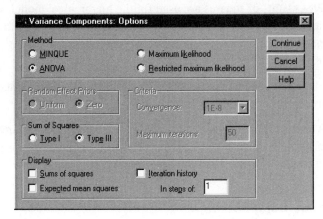

Method. You can choose one of four methods used to estimate the variance components.

■ MINQUE (minimum norm quadratic unbiased estimator) produces estimates that are invariant with respect to the fixed effects. If the data are normally distributed and the estimates are correct, this method produces the least variance among all unbiased estimators. You can choose a method for random-effect prior weights.

■ ANOVA (analysis of variance) computes unbiased estimates using either the Type I or Type III sums of squares for each effect. The ANOVA method sometimes produces negative variance estimates, which can indicate an incorrect model, an inappropriate estimation method, or a need for more data.

■ Maximum likelihood (ML) produces estimates that would be most consistent with the data actually observed, using iterations. These estimates can be biased. This method is asymptotically normal. ML and REML estimates are invariant under translation. This method does not take into account the degrees of freedom used to estimate the fixed effects.

■ Restricted maximum likelihood (REML) estimates reduce the ANOVA estimates for many (if not all) cases of balanced data. Because this method is adjusted for the fixed effects, it should have smaller standard errors than the ML method. This method takes into account the degrees of freedom used to estimate the fixed effects.

Random-Effect Priors. Uniform implies that all random effects and the residual term have an equal impact on the observations. The Zero scheme is equivalent to assuming zero random-effect variances. Available only for the MINQUE method.

Sum of Squares. Type I sums of squares are used for the hierarchical model, which is often used in variance component literature. If you choose Type III, the default in GLM, the variance estimates can be used in GLM Univariate for hypothesis testing with Type III sums of squares. Available only for the ANOVA method.

Criteria. You can specify the convergence criterion and the maximum number of iterations. Available only for the ML or REML methods.

Display. For the ANOVA method, you can choose to display sums of squares and expected mean squares. If you selected Maximum likelihood or Restricted maximum likelihood, you can display a history of the iterations.

Sums of Squares (Variance Components)

For the model, you can choose a type of sum of squares. Type III is the most commonly used and is the default.

Type I. This method is also known as the hierarchical decomposition of the sum-of-squares method. Each term is adjusted for only the term that precedes it in the model. The Type I sum-of-squares method is commonly used for:

■ A balanced ANOVA model in which any main effects are specified before any first-order interaction effects, any first-order interaction effects are specified before any second-order interaction effects, and so on.

■ A polynomial regression model in which any lower-order terms are specified before any higher-order terms.

■ A purely nested model in which the first-specified effect is nested within the second-specified effect, the second-specified effect is nested within the third, and so on. (This form of nesting can be specified only by using syntax.)

Type III. This method, the default, calculates the sums of squares of an effect in the design as the sums of squares adjusted for any other effects that do not contain it and orthogonal to any effects (if any) that contain it. The Type III sums of squares have one major advantage in that they are invariant with respect to the cell frequencies as long as the general form of estimability remains constant. Therefore, this type is often considered useful for an unbalanced model with no missing cells. In a factorial design with no missing cells, this method is equivalent to the Yates' weighted-squares-of-means technique. The Type III sum-of-squares method is commonly used for:

■ Any models listed in Type I.

■ Any balanced or unbalanced model with no empty cells.

Variance Components Save to New File

Figure 3-4
Variance Components Save to New File dialog box

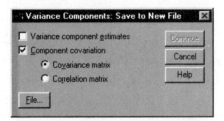

You can save some results of this procedure to a new SPSS data file.

Variance component estimates. Saves estimates of the variance components and estimate labels to a data file. These can be used in calculating more statistics or in further analysis in the GLM procedures. For example, you can use them to calculate confidence intervals or test hypotheses.

Component covariation. Saves a variance-covariance matrix or a correlation matrix to a data file. Available only if Maximum likelihood or Restricted maximum likelihood has been specified.

Save to File. Allows you to specify a filename for the file containing the variance component estimates and/or the matrix.

You can use the MATRIX command to extract the data you need from the new file and then compute confidence intervals or perform tests.

VARCOMP Command Additional Features

The SPSS command language also allows you to:

- Specify nested effects in the design (using the DESIGN subcommand).
- Include user-missing values (using the MISSING subcommand).
- Specify EPS criteria (using the CRITERIA subcommand).

See the Syntax Reference section of this manual for complete syntax information.

Model Selection Loglinear Analysis

The Model Selection Loglinear Analysis procedure analyzes multiway crosstabulations (contingency tables). It fits hierarchical loglinear models to multidimensional crosstabulations using an iterative proportional-fitting algorithm. This procedure helps you find out which categorical variables are associated. To build models, forced entry and backward elimination methods are available. For saturated models, you can request parameter estimates and tests of partial association. A saturated model adds 0.5 to all cells.

Example. In a study of user preference for one of two laundry detergents, researchers counted people in each group, combining various categories of water softness (soft, medium, or hard), previous use of one of the brands, and washing temperature (cold or hot). They found how temperature is related to water softness and also to brand preference.

Statistics. Frequencies, residuals, parameter estimates, standard errors, confidence intervals, and tests of partial association. For custom models, plots of residuals and normal probability plots.

Data. Factor variables are categorical. All variables to be analyzed must be numeric. Categorical string variables can be recoded to numeric variables before starting the model selection analysis.

Avoid specifying many variables with many levels. Such specifications can lead to a situation where many cells have small numbers of observations, and the chi-square values may not be useful.

Related procedures. The Model Selection procedure can help identify the terms needed in the model. Then you can continue to evaluate the model using General

Loglinear Analysis or Logit Loglinear Analysis. You can use Autorecode to recode string variables. If a numeric variable has empty categories, use Recode to create consecutive integer values.

To Obtain a Model Selection Loglinear Analysis

From the menus choose:

Analyze
  Loglinear
    Model Selection...

Figure 4-1
Model Selection Loglinear Analysis dialog box

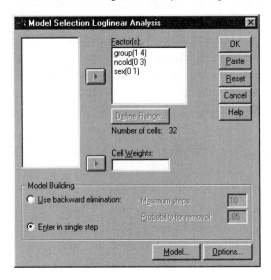

▶ Select two or more numeric categorical factors.

▶ Select one or more factor variables in the Factor(s) list, and click Define Range.

▶ Define the range of values for each factor variable.

▶ Select an option in the Model Building group.

Optionally, you can select a cell weight variable to specify structural zeros.

Loglinear Analysis Define Range

Figure 4-2
Loglinear Analysis Define Range dialog box

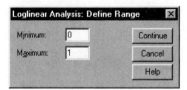

You must indicate the range of categories for each factor variable. Values for Minimum and Maximum correspond to the lowest and highest categories of the factor variable. Both values must be integers, and the minimum value must be less than the maximum value. Cases with values outside of the bounds are excluded. For example, if you specify a minimum value of 1 and a maximum value of 3, only the values 1, 2, and 3 are used. Repeat this process for each factor variable.

Loglinear Analysis Model

Figure 4-3
Loglinear Analysis Model dialog box

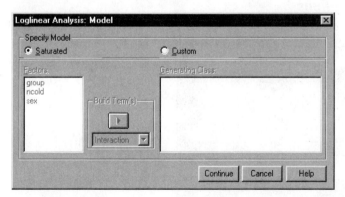

Specify Model. A saturated model contains all factor main effects and all factor-by-factor interactions. Select Custom to specify a generating class for an unsaturated model.

Generating Class. A generating class is a list of the highest-order terms in which factors appear. SPSS builds a hierarchical model containing the terms that define the generating class and all lower-order relatives. Suppose you select variables *A*, *B*, and *C* in the Factors list and then select Interaction from the Build Terms drop-down list. The resulting model will contain the specified 3-way interaction *A*B*C*, the 2-way interactions *A*B*, *A*C*, and *B*C*, and main effects for *A*, *B*, and *C*. Do not specify the lower-order relatives in the generating class.

Build Terms

For the selected factors and covariates:

Interaction. Creates the highest-level interaction term of all selected variables. This is the default.

Main effects. Creates a main-effects term for each variable selected.

All 2-way. Creates all possible two-way interactions of the selected variables.

All 3-way. Creates all possible three-way interactions of the selected variables.

All 4-way. Creates all possible four-way interactions of the selected variables.

All 5-way. Creates all possible five-way interactions of the selected variables.

Loglinear Analysis Options

Figure 4-4
Loglinear Analysis Options dialog box

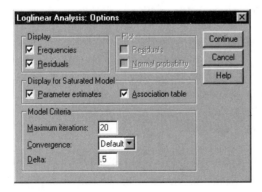

Display. You can choose Frequencies, Residuals, or both. In a saturated model, the observed and expected frequencies are equal, and the residuals are equal to 0.

Display for Saturated Model. For a saturated model, you can choose Parameter estimates. The parameter estimates may help determine which terms can be dropped from the model. An association table, which lists tests of partial association, is also available. This option is computationally expensive for tables with many factors.

Plot. For custom models, you can choose one or both types of plots, Residuals and Normal probability. These will help determine how well a model fits the data.

Model Criteria. SPSS uses an iterative proportional-fitting algorithm to obtain parameter estimates. You can override one or more of the estimation criteria by specifying Maximum iterations, Convergence, or Delta (a value added to all cell frequencies for saturated models).

HILOGLINEAR Command Additional Features

The SPSS command language also allows you to:

- Specify cell weights in matrix form (using the CWEIGHT subcommand).
- Generate analyses of several models with a single command (using the DESIGN subcommand).

See the Syntax Reference section of this manual for complete syntax information.

General Loglinear Analysis

The General Loglinear Analysis procedure analyzes the frequency counts of observations falling into each cross-classification category in a crosstabulation or a contingency table. Each cross-classification in the table constitutes a cell, and each categorical variable is called a factor. The dependent variable is the number of cases (frequency) in a cell of the crosstabulation, and the explanatory variables are factors and covariates. This procedure estimates maximum likelihood parameters of hierarchical and nonhierarchical loglinear models using the Newton-Raphson method. Either a Poisson or a multinomial distribution can be analyzed.

You can select up to 10 factors to define the cells of a table. A cell structure variable allows you to define structural zeros for incomplete tables, include an offset term in the model, fit a log-rate model, or implement the method of adjustment of marginal tables. Contrast variables allow computation of generalized log-odds ratios (GLOR).

SPSS automatically displays model information and goodness-of-fit statistics. You can also display a variety of statistics and plots or save residuals and predicted values in the working data file.

Example. Data from a report of automobile accidents in Florida are used to determine the relationship between wearing a seat belt and whether an injury was fatal or nonfatal. The odds ratio indicates significant evidence of a relationship.

Statistics. Observed and expected frequencies; raw, adjusted, and deviance residuals; design matrix; parameter estimates; odds ratio; log-odds ratio; GLOR; Wald statistic; and confidence intervals. Plots: adjusted residuals, deviance residuals, and normal probability.

Data. Factors are categorical, and cell covariates are continuous. When a covariate is in the model, SPSS applies the mean covariate value for cases in a cell to that cell.

Contrast variables are continuous. They are used to compute generalized log-odds ratios. The values of the contrast variable are the coefficients for the linear combination of the logs of the expected cell counts.

A cell structure variable assigns weights. For example, if some of the cells are structural zeros, the cell structure variable has a value of either 0 or 1. Do not use a cell structure variable to weight aggregated data. Instead, choose Weight Cases from the Data menu.

Assumptions. Two distributions are available in General Loglinear Analysis: Poisson and multinomial.

Under the Poisson distribution assumption:

■ The total sample size is not fixed before the study, or the analysis is not conditional on the total sample size.

■ The event of an observation being in a cell is statistically independent of the cell counts of other cells.

Under the multinomial distribution assumption:

■ The total sample size is fixed, or the analysis is conditional on the total sample size.

■ The cell counts are not statistically independent.

Related procedures. Use the Crosstabs procedure to examine the crosstabulations. Use the Logit Loglinear procedure when it is natural to regard one or more categorical variables as the response variables and the others as the explanatory variables.

To Obtain a General Loglinear Analysis

▶ From the menus choose:

Analyze
  Loglinear
    General...

Figure 5-1
General Loglinear Analysis dialog box

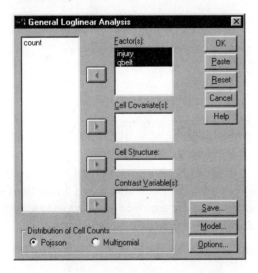

▶ In the General Loglinear Analysis dialog box, select up to 10 factor variables.

Optionally, you can:

■ Select cell covariates.

■ Select a cell structure variable to define structural zeros or include an offset term.

■ Select a contrast variable.

General Loglinear Analysis Model

Figure 5-2
General Loglinear Analysis Model dialog box

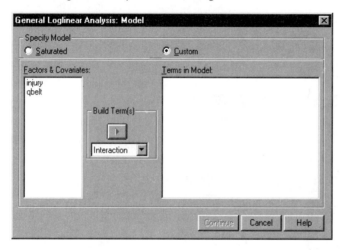

Specify Model. A saturated model contains all main effects and interactions involving factor variables. It does not contain covariate terms. Select Custom to specify only a subset of interactions or to specify factor-by-covariate interactions.

Factors and Covariates. The factors and covariates are listed, with (Cov) indicating a covariate.

Terms in Model. The model depends on the nature of your data. After selecting Custom, you can select the main effects and interactions that are of interest in your analysis. You must indicate all of the terms to be included in the model.

Build Terms

For the selected factors and covariates:

Interaction. Creates the highest-level interaction term of all selected variables. This is the default.

Main effects. Creates a main-effects term for each variable selected.

All 2-way. Creates all possible two-way interactions of the selected variables.

All 3-way. Creates all possible three-way interactions of the selected variables.

All 4-way. Creates all possible four-way interactions of the selected variables.

All 5-way. Creates all possible five-way interactions of the selected variables.

General Loglinear Analysis Options

Figure 5-3
General Loglinear Analysis Options dialog box

The General Loglinear Analysis procedure displays model information and goodness-of-fit statistics. In addition, you can choose one or more of the following:

Display. Several statistics are available for display—observed and expected cell frequencies; raw, adjusted, and deviance residuals; a design matrix of the model; and parameter estimates for the model.

Plot. Plots, available for custom models only, include two scatterplot matrices (adjusted residuals or deviance residuals against observed and expected cell counts). You can also display normal probability and detrended normal plots of adjusted residuals or deviance residuals.

Confidence Interval. The confidence interval for parameter estimates can be adjusted.

Criteria. The Newton-Raphson method is used to obtain maximum likelihood parameter estimates. You can enter new values for the maximum number of iterations, the convergence criterion, and delta (a constant added to all cells for initial approximations). Delta remains in the cells for saturated models.

To Specify Options

▶ From the menus choose:

Analyze
  Loglinear
    General...

▶ In the General Loglinear Analysis or Logit Loglinear Analysis dialog box, click Options.

General Loglinear Analysis Save

Figure 5-4
General Loglinear Analysis Save dialog box

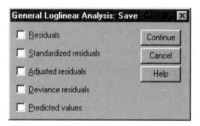

Select the values you want to save as new variables in the working data file. The suffix *n* in the new variable names increments to make a unique name for each saved variable.

The saved values refer to the aggregated data (cells in the contingency table), even if the data are recorded in individual observations in the Data Editor. If you save residuals or predicted values for unaggregated data, the saved value for a cell in the contingency table is entered in the Data Editor for each case in that cell. To make sense of the saved values, you should aggregate the data to obtain the cell counts.

Four types of residuals can be saved: raw, standardized, adjusted, and deviance. The predicted values can also be saved.

GENLOG Command Additional Features

The SPSS command language also allows you to:

- Calculate linear combinations of observed cell frequencies and expected cell frequencies, and print residuals, standardized residuals, and adjusted residuals of that combination (using the GERESID subcommand).

- Change the default threshold value for redundancy checking (using the CRITERIA subcommand).

- Display the standardized residuals (using the PRINT subcommand).

See the Syntax Reference section of this manual for complete syntax information.

Logit Loglinear Analysis

The Logit Loglinear Analysis procedure analyzes the relationship between dependent (or response) variables and independent (or explanatory) variables. The dependent variables are always categorical, while the independent variables can be categorical (factors). Other independent variables, cell covariates, can be continuous, but they are not applied on a case-by-case basis. The weighted covariate mean for a cell is applied to that cell. The logarithm of the odds of the dependent variables is expressed as a linear combination of parameters. A multinomial distribution is automatically assumed; these models are sometimes called multinomial logit models. This procedure estimates parameters of logit loglinear models using the Newton-Raphson algorithm.

You can select from 1 to 10 dependent and factor variables combined. A cell structure variable allows you to define structural zeros for incomplete tables, include an offset term in the model, fit a log-rate model, or implement the method of adjustment of marginal tables. Contrast variables allow computation of generalized log-odds ratios (GLOR). The values of the contrast variable are the coefficients for the linear combination of the logs of the expected cell counts.

SPSS automatically displays model information and goodness-of-fit statistics. You can also display a variety of statistics and plots or save residuals and predicted values in the working data file.

Example. A study in Florida included 219 alligators. How does the alligators' food type vary with their size and the four lakes in which they live? The study found that the odds of a smaller alligator preferring reptiles to fish is 0.70 times lower than for larger alligators; also, the odds of selecting primarily reptiles instead of fish were highest in lake 3.

Statistics. Observed and expected frequencies; raw, adjusted, and deviance residuals; design matrix; parameter estimates; generalized log odds ratio; Wald statistic; and confidence intervals. Plots: adjusted residuals, deviance residuals, and normal probability plots.

Data. The dependent variables are categorical. Factors are categorical. Cell covariates can be continuous, but when a covariate is in the model, SPSS applies the mean covariate value for cases in a cell to that cell. Contrast variables are continuous. They are used to compute generalized log odds ratios (GLOR). The values of the contrast variable are the coefficients for the linear combination of the logs of the expected cell counts.

A cell structure variable assigns weights. For example, if some of the cells are structural zeros, the cell structure variable has a value of either 0 or 1. Do not use a cell structure variable to weight aggregate data. Instead, use Weight Cases on the Data menu.

Assumptions. The counts within each combination of categories of explanatory variables are assumed to have a multinomial distribution. Under the multinomial distribution assumption:

- The total sample size is fixed, or the analysis is conditional on the total sample size.
- The cell counts are not statistically independent.

Related procedures. Use the Crosstabs procedure to display the contingency tables. Use the General Loglinear Analysis procedure when you want to analyze the relationship between an observed count and a set of explanatory variables.

To Obtain a Logit Loglinear Analysis

▶ From the menus choose:

Analyze
  Loglinear
    Logit...

Figure 6-1
Logit Loglinear Analysis dialog box

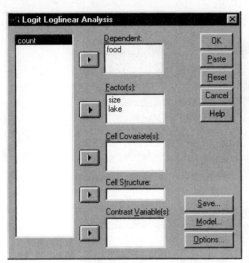

▶ In the Logit Loglinear Analysis dialog box, select one or more dependent variables.

▶ Select one or more factor variables.

The total number of dependent and factor variables must be less than or equal to 10.

Optionally, you can:

■ Select cell covariates.

■ Select a cell structure variable to define structural zeros or include an offset term.

■ Select one or more contrast variables.

Logit Loglinear Analysis Model

Figure 6-2
Logit Loglinear Analysis Model dialog box

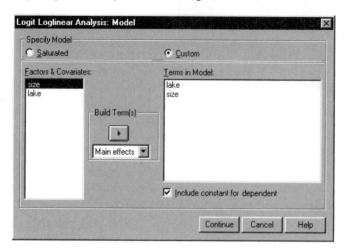

Specify Model. A saturated model contains all main effects and interactions involving factor variables. It does not contain covariate terms. Select Custom to specify only a subset of interactions or to specify factor-by-covariate interactions.

Factors and Covariates. The factors and covariates are listed, with (Cov) indicating a covariate.

Terms in Model. The model depends on the nature of your data. After selecting Custom, you can select the main effects and interactions that are of interest in your analysis. You must indicate all of the terms to be included in the model.

Terms are added to the design by taking all possible combinations of the dependent terms and matching each combination with each term in the model list. If Include constant for dependent is selected, there is also a unit term (1) added to the model list.

For example, suppose variables *D1* and *D2* are the dependent variables. A dependent terms list is created by the Logit Loglinear Analysis procedure (*D1*, *D2*, *D1*D2*). If the Terms in Model list contains *M1* and *M2* and a constant is included, the model list contains 1, *M1*, and *M2*. The resultant design includes combinations of each model term with each dependent term:

D1, D2, D1*D2
M1*D1, M1*D2, M1*D1*D2
M2*D1, M2*D2, M2*D1*D2.

Include constant for dependent. Includes a constant for the dependent variable in a custom model.

Build Terms

For the selected factors and covariates:

Interaction. Creates the highest-level interaction term of all selected variables. This is the default.

Main effects. Creates a main-effects term for each variable selected.

All 2-way. Creates all possible two-way interactions of the selected variables.

All 3-way. Creates all possible three-way interactions of the selected variables.

All 4-way. Creates all possible four-way interactions of the selected variables.

All 5-way. Creates all possible five-way interactions of the selected variables.

Logit Loglinear Analysis Options

Figure 6-3
Logit Loglinear Analysis Options dialog box

The Logit Loglinear Analysis procedure displays model information and goodness-of-fit statistics. In addition, you can choose one or more of the following options:

Display. Several statistics are available for display: observed and expected cell frequencies; raw, adjusted, and deviance residuals; a design matrix of the model; and parameter estimates for the model.

Plot. Plots available for custom models include two scatterplot matrices (adjusted residuals or deviance residuals against observed and expected cell counts). You can also display normal probability and detrended normal plots of adjusted residuals or deviance residuals.

Confidence Interval. The confidence interval for parameter estimates can be adjusted.

Criteria. The Newton-Raphson method is used to obtain maximum likelihood parameter estimates. You can enter new values for the maximum number of iterations, the convergence criterion, and delta (a constant added to all cells for initial approximations). Delta remains in the cells for saturated models.

To Specify Options

▶ From the menus choose:

Analyze
  Loglinear
    Logit...

▶ In the Logit Loglinear Analysis dialog box, click Options.

Logit Loglinear Analysis Save

Figure 6-4
Logit Loglinear Analysis Save dialog box

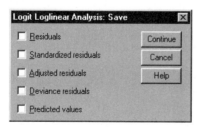

Select the values you want to save as new variables in the working data file. The suffix n in the new variable names increments to make a unique name for each saved variable.

The saved values refer to the aggregated data (to cells in the contingency table), even if the data are recorded in individual observations in the Data Editor. If you save residuals or predicted values for unaggregated data, the saved value for a cell in the contingency table is entered in the Data Editor for each case in that cell. To make sense of the saved values, you should aggregate the data to obtain the cell counts.

Four types of residuals can be saved: raw, standardized, adjusted, and deviance. The predicted values can also be saved.

GENLOG Command Additional Features

The SPSS command language also allows you to:

- Calculate linear combinations of observed cell frequencies and expected cell frequencies, and print residuals, standardized residuals, and adjusted residuals of that combination (using the GERESID subcommand).

- Change the default threshold value for redundancy checking (using the CRITERIA subcommand).

- Display the standardized residuals (using the PRINT subcommand).

See the Syntax Reference section of this manual for complete syntax information.

Life Tables

There are many situations in which you would want to examine the distribution of times between two events, such as length of employment (time between being hired and leaving the company). However, this kind of data usually includes some cases for which the second event isn't recorded (for example, people still working for the company at the end of the study). This can happen for several reasons: for some cases, the event simply doesn't occur before the end of the study; for other cases, we lose track of their status sometime before the end of the study; still other cases may be unable to continue for reasons unrelated to the study (such as an employee becoming ill and taking a leave of absence). Collectively, such cases are known as **censored cases**, and they make this kind of study inappropriate for traditional techniques such as *t* tests or linear regression.

A statistical technique useful for this type of data is called a follow-up **life table**. The basic idea of the life table is to subdivide the period of observation into smaller time intervals. For each interval, all people who have been observed at least that long are used to calculate the probability of a terminal event occurring in that interval. The probabilities estimated from each of the intervals are then used to estimate the overall probability of the event occurring at different time points.

Example. Is a new nicotine patch therapy better than traditional patch therapy in helping people to quit smoking? You could conduct a study using two groups of smokers, one of which received the traditional therapy and the other of which received the experimental therapy. Constructing life tables from the data would allow you to compare overall abstinence rates between the two groups to determine if the experimental treatment is an improvement over the traditional therapy. You can also plot the survival or hazard functions and compare them visually for more detailed information.

Statistics. Number entering, number leaving, number exposed to risk, number of terminal events, proportion terminating, proportion surviving, cumulative proportion surviving (and standard error), probability density (and standard error), and hazard rate (and standard error) for each time interval for each group; median survival time for each group; and Wilcoxon (Gehan) test for comparing survival distributions between groups. Plots: function plots for survival, log survival, density, hazard rate, and one minus survival.

Data. Your time variable should be quantitative. Your status variable should be dichotomous or categorical, coded as integers, with events being coded as a single value or a range of consecutive values. Factor variables should be categorical, coded as integers.

Assumptions. Probabilities for the event of interest should depend only on time after the initial event—they are assumed to be stable with respect to absolute time. That is, cases that enter the study at different times (for example, patients who begin treatment at different times) should behave similarly. There should also be no systematic differences between censored and uncensored cases. If, for example, many of the censored cases are patients with more serious conditions, your results may be biased.

Related procedures. The Life Tables procedure uses an actuarial approach to this kind of analysis (known generally as Survival Analysis). The Kaplan-Meier Survival Analysis procedure uses a slightly different method of calculating life tables that does not rely on partitioning the observation period into smaller time intervals. This method is recommended if you have a small number of observations, such that there would be only a small number of observations in each survival time interval. If you have variables that you suspect are related to survival time or variables that you want to control for (covariates), use the Cox Regression procedure. If your covariates can have different values at different points in time for the same case, use Cox Regression with Time-Dependent Covariates.

To Create a Life Table

▶ From the menus choose:

Analyze
  Survival
    Life Tables...

Figure 7-1
Life Tables dialog box

▶ Select one numeric survival variable.

▶ Specify the time intervals to be examined.

▶ Select a status variable to define cases for which the terminal event has occurred.

▶ Click Define Event to specify the value of the status variable that indicates that an event occurred.

Optionally, you can select a first-order factor variable. Actuarial tables for the survival variable are generated for each category of the factor variable.

You can also select a second-order *by factor* variable. Actuarial tables for the survival variable are generated for every combination of the first- and second-order factor variables.

Life Tables Define Event for Status Variable

Figure 7-2
Life Tables Define Event for Status Variable dialog box

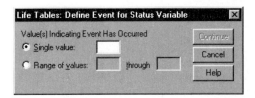

Occurrences of the selected value or values for the status variable indicate that the terminal event has occurred for those cases. All other cases are considered to be censored. Enter either a single value or a range of values that identifies the event of interest.

Life Tables Define Range

Figure 7-3
Life Tables Define Range dialog box

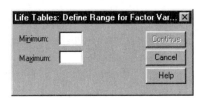

Cases with values for the factor variable in the range you specify will be included in the analysis, and separate tables (and plots, if requested) will be generated for each unique value in the range.

Life Tables Options

Figure 7-4
Life Tables Options dialog box

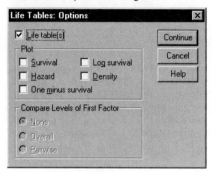

You can control various aspects of your Life Tables analysis.

Life tables. To suppress the display of life tables in the output, deselect Life tables.

Plot. Allows you to request plots of the survival functions. If you have defined factor variable(s), plots are generated for each subgroup defined by the factor variable(s). Available plots are survival, log survival, hazard, density, and one minus survival.

Compare Levels of First Factor. If you have a first-order control variable, you can select one of the alternatives in this group to perform the Wilcoxon (Gehan) test, which compares the survival of subgroups. Tests are performed on the first-order factor. If you have defined a second-order factor, tests are performed for each level of the second-order variable.

SURVIVAL Command Additional Features

The SPSS command language also allows you to:

- Specify more than one dependent variable.
- Specify unequally spaced intervals.
- Specify more than one status variable.
- Specify comparisons that do not include all the factor and all the control variables.
- Calculate approximate, rather than exact, comparisons.

See the Syntax Reference section of this manual for complete syntax information.

Kaplan-Meier Survival Analysis

There are many situations in which you would want to examine the distribution of times between two events, such as length of employment (time between being hired and leaving the company). However, this kind of data usually includes some censored cases. Censored cases are cases for which the second event isn't recorded (for example, people still working for the company at the end of the study). The Kaplan-Meier procedure is a method of estimating time-to-event models in the presence of censored cases. The Kaplan-Meier model is based on estimating conditional probabilities at each time point when an event occurs and taking the product limit of those probabilities to estimate the survival rate at each point in time.

Example. Does a new treatment for AIDS have any therapeutic benefit in extending life? You could conduct a study using two groups of AIDS patients, one receiving traditional therapy and the other receiving the experimental treatment. Constructing a Kaplan-Meier model from the data would allow you to compare overall survival rates between the two groups to determine whether the experimental treatment is an improvement over the traditional therapy. You can also plot the survival or hazard functions and compare them visually for more detailed information.

Statistics. Survival table, including time, status, cumulative survival and standard error, cumulative events, and number remaining; and mean and median survival time, with standard error and 95% confidence interval. Plots: survival, hazard, log survival, and one minus survival.

Data. The time variable should be continuous, the status variable can be categorical or continuous, and the factor and strata variables should be categorical.

Assumptions. Probabilities for the event of interest should depend only on time after the initial event—they are assumed to be stable with respect to absolute time. That is, cases that enter the study at different times (for example, patients who begin treatment at different times) should behave similarly. There should also be no systematic differences between censored and uncensored cases. If, for example, many of the censored cases are patients with more serious conditions, your results may be biased.

Related procedures. The Kaplan-Meier procedure uses a method of calculating life tables that estimates the survival or hazard function at the time of each event. The Life Tables procedure uses an actuarial approach to survival analysis that relies on partitioning the observation period into smaller time intervals and may be useful for dealing with large samples. If you have variables that you suspect are related to survival time or variables that you want to control for (covariates), use the Cox Regression procedure. If your covariates can have different values at different points in time for the same case, use Cox Regression with Time-Dependent Covariates.

To Obtain a Kaplan-Meier Survival Analysis

▶ From the menus choose:

Analyze
  Survival
    Kaplan-Meier...

Figure 8-1
Kaplan-Meier dialog box

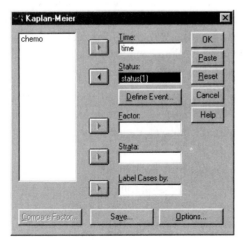

▶ Select a time variable.

▶ Select a status variable to identify cases for which the terminal event has occurred. This variable can be numeric or short string. Then click Define Event.

Optionally, you can select a factor variable to examine group differences. You can also select a strata variable, which will produce separate analyses for each level (stratum) of the variable.

Kaplan-Meier Define Event for Status Variable

Figure 8-2
Kaplan-Meier Define Event for Status Variable dialog box

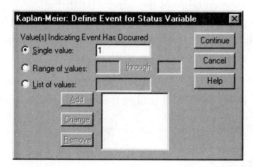

Enter the value or values indicating that the terminal event has occurred. You can enter a single value, a range of values, or a list of values. The Range of Values option is available only if your status variable is numeric.

Kaplan-Meier Compare Factor Levels

Figure 8-3
Kaplan-Meier Compare Factor Levels dialog box

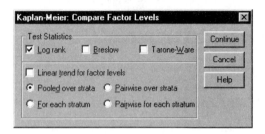

You can request statistics to test the equality of the survival distributions for the different levels of the factor. Available statistics are log rank, Breslow, and Tarone-Ware. Select one of the alternatives to specify the comparisons to be made: pooled over strata, for each stratum, pairwise over strata, or pairwise for each stratum.

Linear trend for factor levels. Allows you to test for a linear trend across levels of the factor. This option is available only for overall (rather than pairwise) comparisons of factor levels.

Kaplan-Meier Save New Variables

Figure 8-4
Kaplan-Meier Save New Variables dialog box

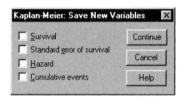

You can save information from your Kaplan-Meier table as new variables, which can then be used in subsequent analyses to test hypotheses or check assumptions. You can save survival, standard error of survival, hazard, and cumulative events as new variables.

Kaplan-Meier Options

Figure 8-5
Kaplan-Meier Options dialog box

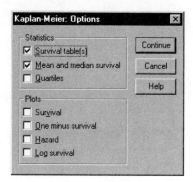

You can request various output types from Kaplan-Meier analysis.

Statistics. You can select statistics displayed for the survival functions computed, including survival table(s), mean and median survival, and quartiles. If you have included factor variables, separate statistics are generated for each group.

Plots. Plots allow you to examine the survival, hazard, log-survival, and one-minus-survival functions visually. If you have included factor variables, functions are plotted for each group.

KM Command Additional Features

The SPSS command language also allows you to:

- Obtain frequency tables that consider cases lost to follow-up as a separate category from censored cases.
- Specify unequal spacing for the test for linear trend.
- Obtain percentiles other than quartiles for the survival time variable.

See the Syntax Reference section of this manual for complete syntax information.

Cox Regression Analysis

Like Life Tables and Kaplan-Meier survival analysis, Cox Regression is a method for modeling time-to-event data in the presence of censored cases. However, Cox Regression allows you to include predictor variables (covariates) in your models. For example, you could construct a model of length of employment based on educational level and job category. Cox Regression will handle the censored cases correctly, and it will provide estimated coefficients for each of the covariates, allowing you to assess the impact of multiple covariates in the same model. You can also use Cox Regression to examine the effect of continuous covariates.

Example. Do men and women have different risks of developing lung cancer based on cigarette smoking? By constructing a Cox Regression model, with cigarette usage (cigarettes smoked per day) and gender entered as covariates, you can test hypotheses regarding the effects of gender and cigarette usage on time-to-onset for lung cancer.

Statistics. For each model: –2LL, the likelihood-ratio statistic, and the overall chi-square. For variables in the model: parameter estimates, standard errors, and Wald statistics. For variables not in the model: score statistics and residual chi-square.

Data. Your time variable should be quantitative and your status variable can be categorical or continuous. Independent variables (covariates) can be continuous or categorical; if categorical, they should be dummy or indicator coded (there is an option in the procedure to recode categorical variables automatically). Strata variables should be categorical, coded as integers or short strings.

Assumptions. Observations should be independent, and the hazard ratio should be constant across time; that is, the proportionality of hazards from one case to another should not vary over time. The latter assumption is known as the **proportional hazards assumption**.

Related procedures. If the proportional hazards assumption does not hold (see above), you may need to use the Cox with Time-Dependent Covariates procedure. If you have no covariates, or if you have only one categorical covariate, you can use the Life Tables or Kaplan-Meier procedure to examine survival or hazard functions for your sample(s). If you have no censored data in your sample (that is, every case experienced the terminal event), you can use the Linear Regression procedure to model the relationship between predictors and time-to-event.

To Obtain a Cox Regression Analysis

▶ From the menus choose:

Analyze
  Survival
    Cox Regression...

Figure 9-1
Cox Regression dialog box

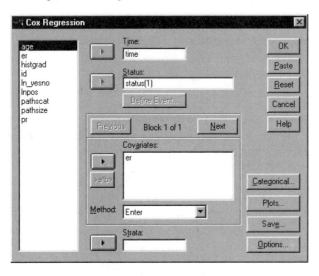

▶ Select a time variable.

▶ Select a status variable, and then click Define Event.

▶ Select variables to use as covariates.

Optionally, you can compute separate models for different groups by defining a strata variable.

Cox Regression Define Categorical Variables

Figure 9-2
Cox Regression Define Categorical Covariates dialog box

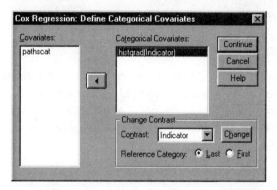

You can specify details of how the Cox Regression procedure will handle categorical variables.

Covariates. Contains a list of all of the covariates specified in the main dialog box, either by themselves or as part of an interaction, in any layer. If some of these are string variables or are categorical, you can use them only as categorical covariates.

Categorical Covariates. Lists variables identified as categorical. Each variable includes a notation in parentheses indicating the contrast coding to be used. String variables (denoted by the symbol < following their names) are already present in the Categorical Covariates list. Select any other categorical covariates from the Covariates list and move them into the Categorical Covariates list.

Change Contrast. Allows you to change the contrast method. Available contrast methods are:

- **Indicator.** Contrasts indicate the presence or absence of category membership. The reference category is represented in the contrast matrix as a row of zeros.

- **Simple.** Each category of the predictor variable except the reference category is compared to the reference category.

- **Difference.** Each category of the predictor variable except the first category is compared to the average effect of previous categories. Also known as reverse Helmert contrasts.

- **Helmert.** Each category of the predictor variable except the last category is compared to the average effect of subsequent categories.

- **Repeated.** Each category of the predictor variable except the first category is compared to the category that precedes it.

- **Polynomial.** Orthogonal polynomial contrasts. Categories are assumed to be equally spaced. Polynomial contrasts are available for numeric variables only.

- **Deviation.** Each category of the predictor variable except the reference category is compared to the overall effect.

If you select Deviation, Simple, or Indicator, select either First or Last as the reference category. Note that the method is not actually changed until you click Change.

String covariates *must* be categorical covariates. To remove a string variable from the Categorical Covariates list, you must remove all terms containing the variable from the Covariates list in the main dialog box.

Cox Regression Plots

Figure 9-3
Cox Regression Plots dialog box

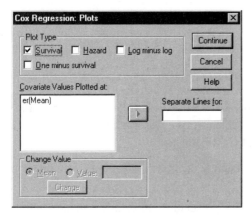

Plots can help you to evaluate your estimated model and interpret the results. You can plot the survival, hazard, log-minus-log, and one-minus-survival functions.

Because these functions depend on values of the covariates, you must use constant values for the covariates to plot the functions versus time. The default is to use the mean of each covariate as a constant value, but you can enter your own values for the plot using the Change Value control group.

You can plot a separate line for each value of a categorical covariate by moving that covariate into the Separate Lines For text box. This option is available only for categorical covariates, which are denoted by (Cat) after their names in the Covariate Values Plotted At list.

Cox Regression Save New Variables

Figure 9-4
Cox Regression Save New Variables dialog box

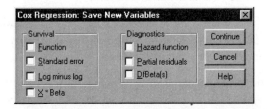

You can save various results of your analysis as new variables. These variables can then be used in subsequent analyses to test hypotheses or to check assumptions.

Survival. Allows you to save the survival function, standard error, and log-minus-log estimates as new variables.

Diagnostics. Allows you to save the hazard function, partial residuals, and DfBeta(s) for the regression as new variables.

If you are running Cox with a time-dependent covariate, DfBeta(s) are the only variables that you can save. You can also save the linear predictor variable X*Beta.

Cox Regression Options

Figure 9-5
Cox Regression Options dialog box

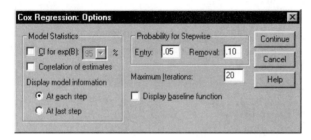

You can control various aspects of your analysis and output.

Model Statistics. You can obtain statistics for your model parameters, including confidence intervals for exp(*B*) and correlation of estimates. You can request these statistics either at each step or at the last step only.

Probability for Stepwise. If you have selected a stepwise method, you can specify the probability for either entry or removal from the model. A variable is entered if the significance level of its *F*-to-enter is less than the Entry value, and a variable is removed if the significance level is greater than the Removal value. The Entry value must be less than the Removal value.

Maximum Iterations. Allows you to specify the maximum iterations for the model, which controls how long the procedure will search for a solution.

Display baseline function. Allows you to display the baseline hazard function and cumulative survival at the mean of the covariates. This display is not available if you have specified time-dependent covariates.

Cox Regression Define Event for Status Variable

Enter the value or values indicating that the terminal event has occurred. You can enter a single value, a range of values, or a list of values. The Range of Values option is available only if your status variable is numeric.

COXREG Command Additional Features

The SPSS command language also allows you to:

- Obtain frequency tables that consider cases lost to follow-up as a separate category from censored cases.

- Select a reference category, other than first or last, for the deviation, simple, and indicator contrast methods.

- Specify unequal spacing of categories for the polynomial contrast method.

- Specify additional iteration criteria.

- Control the treatment of missing values.

- Specify the names for saved variables.

- Write output to an external SPSS system file.

- Hold data for each split-file group in an external scratch file during processing. This can help conserve memory resources when running analyses with large data sets. This is not available with time-dependent covariates.

See the Syntax Reference section of this manual for complete syntax information.

10

Computing Time-Dependent Covariates

There are certain situations in which you would want to compute a Cox Regression model but the proportional hazards assumption does not hold. That is, hazard ratios change across time; the values of one (or more) of your covariates are different at different time points. In such cases, you need to use an extended Cox Regression model, which allows you to specify **time-dependent covariates**.

In order to analyze such a model, you must first define your time-dependent covariate. (Multiple time-dependent covariates can be specified using command syntax.) To facilitate this, a system variable representing time is available. This variable is called $T\_$. You can use this variable to define time-dependent covariates in two general ways:

- If you want to test the proportional hazards assumption with respect to a particular covariate or estimate an extended Cox regression model that allows nonproportional hazards, you can do so by defining your time-dependent covariate as a function of the time variable $T\_$ and the covariate in question. A common example would be the simple product of the time variable and the covariate, but more complex functions can be specified as well. Testing the significance of the coefficient of the time-dependent covariate will tell you whether the proportional hazards assumption is reasonable.

- Some variables may have different values at different time periods but aren't systematically related to time. In such cases, you need to define a **segmented time-dependent covariate**, which can be done using **logical expressions**. Logical expressions take the value 1 if true and 0 if false. Using a series of logical expressions, you can create your time-dependent covariate from a set of measurements. For example, if you have blood pressure measured once a week for the four weeks of your study (identified as *BP1* to *BP4*), you can define your time-dependent covariate as

$$(T\_ < 1) * BP1 + (T\_ \geq 1 \ \& \ T\_ < 2) * BP2 + (T\_ \geq 2 \ \& \ T\_ < 3) * BP3$$
$$+ (T\_ \geq 3 \ \& \ T\_ < 4) * BP4$$

Notice that exactly one of the terms in parentheses will be equal to 1 for any given case and the rest will all equal 0. In other words, this function means that if time is less than one week, use *BP1*; if it is more than one week but less than two weeks, use *BP2*, and so on.

For segmented time-dependent covariates, cases that are missing any values are removed from the analysis. Therefore, you must be sure that all cases have values for all measured time points on the covariate, even for time points after the case is removed from the risk set (due to event or censoring). These values are not used in the analysis, but they must be valid SPSS values to prevent the cases from being dropped. For example, with the definition given above, a case censored at the second week must still have values for *BP3* and *BP4* (they can be 0 or any other number, since they are not used in the analysis).

In the Compute Time-Dependent Covariate dialog box, you can use the function-building controls to build the expression for the time-dependent covariate, or you can enter it directly in the Expression for T_COV_ text area. Note that string constants must be enclosed in quotation marks or apostrophes, and numeric constants must be typed in American format, with the dot as the decimal delimiter. The resulting variable is called *T_COV_* and should be included as a covariate in your Cox Regression model.

To Compute a Time-Dependent Covariate

▶ From the menus choose:

Analyze
  Survival
    Cox w/ Time-Dep Cov...

Figure 10-1
Compute Time-Dependent Covariate dialog box

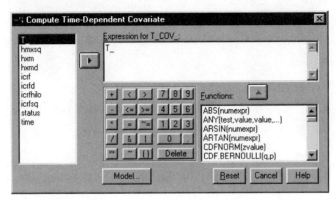

▶ Enter an expression for the time-dependent covariate.

▶ Click Model to proceed with your Cox Regression.

Note: Be sure to include the new variable *T_COV_* as a covariate in your Cox Regression model.

For more information about the model-building process, see Chapter 9.

Cox Regression with Time-Dependent Covariates
Additional Features

The SPSS command language also allows you to specify multiple time-dependent covariates.

Other command syntax features are available for Cox Regression with or without time-dependent covariates.

See the Syntax Reference section of this manual for complete syntax information.

GLM Multivariate Examples

Multivariate analysis of variance considers the effects of factors on several dependent variables at once, using a general linear model. The factors divide the cases (or subjects) into groups. The hypotheses tested are similar to those in univariate analysis, except that in multivariate analysis, a vector of means replaces the individual means.

In addition to the output in univariate analysis, multivariate *F* tests are available. You can also display the hypothesis and error sums-of-squares and cross-product (SSCP) matrices for each effect in the design, the transformation coefficient table (**M** matrix), Box's *M* test for equality of covariance matrices, and Bartlett's test of sphericity.

This chapter includes the following examples:

Example 1: Multivariate ANOVA: Multivariate two-way fixed-effects model with interaction. The effects of two measurements, the amount of an additive and the rate of extrusion of plastic film, are studied simultaneously on three properties of the manufactured plastic film. The SSCP (sums-of-squares and cross-products) matrices are displayed for the main effects and the interaction effect. These values are used by SPSS to calculate the *F* values for hypothesis testing on the three dependent variables. The conclusion is that the main effects of amount of additive and rate of extrusion are significant, but their interaction is not.

Example 2: Profile analysis: Setting up custom linear hypotheses. In a survey, 30 couples were given questions designed to rate companionate and passionate love on a five-point scale. A plot of the mean answers of husbands and wives is used to set up hypotheses that will investigate the differences between groups. The **L** and **M** matrices are used together in the model to define contrasts, where **LBM = 0**. The conclusion is that the parallelism and the coincidence of the profiles of husbands and wives is not rejected. However, the equality of means of the four answers is rejected.

Example 1
Multivariate ANOVA: Multivariate Two-Way Fixed-Effects Model with Interaction

How can the optimum conditions for extruding plastic film be evaluated by using a statistical technique called evolutionary operation? A study was conducted to examine how the amount of an additive and the rate of extrusion affected the conditions for extruding plastic film. The data are from Johnson and Wichern (1988). The amount of additive and rate of extrusion are two fixed factors that may interact so that the model is a two-way fixed-effects model with interaction. Three properties of the extruded film were measured: tear resistance, gloss, and opacity. These are the three dependent variables in this multivariate model. Evolutionary operation, the statistical method for process improvement used here, was described by Box and Draper (1969).

Figure 11-1
Effects of rate of extrusion and amount of additive on plastic film

Independent Factors		Dependent Variables		
Change in rate of extrusion	Amount of additive	Tear resistance	Gloss	Opacity
1	1	6.5	9.5	4.4
1	1	6.2	9.9	6.4
1	1	5.8	9.6	3.0
1	1	6.5	9.6	4.1
1	1	6.5	9.2	0.8
1	2	6.9	9.1	5.7
1	2	7.2	10.0	2.0
1	2	6.9	9.9	3.9
1	2	6.1	9.5	1.9
1	2	6.3	9.4	5.7
2	1	6.7	9.1	2.8
2	1	6.6	9.3	4.1
2	1	7.2	8.3	3.8
2	1	7.1	8.4	1.6
2	1	6.8	8.5	3.4
2	2	7.1	9.2	8.4
2	2	7.0	8.8	5.2
2	2	7.2	9.7	6.9
2	2	7.5	10.1	2.7
2	2	7.6	9.2	1.9

The data are recorded in the SPSS file *plastic*, in the order shown in Figure 11-1. There are two independent factors in the model: the change in rate of extrusion (*extrusn*) and the amount of additive (*additive*). The *extrusn* factor has two levels: low and high (indicated by 1 and 2, respectively, in the data). The *additive* factor has two levels: 1.0% and 1.5% (indicated by 1 and 2, respectively, in the data). In addition to these two main factors, their interaction *extrusn*additive* is included in the model. Since three dependent variables are studied at the same time, multivariate analysis of variance is used.

SSCP Matrices

In univariate fixed-effects analysis of variance, the total sum of squares of the model is partitioned into sums of squares due to the effects in the model and the error sum of squares. Each effect in the model is then evaluated by using an *F* statistic, which is the ratio of the sum of squares due to the effect and the error sum of squares. In a multivariate model, there is more than one dependent variable; hence, the sums of squares due to the effects in the model and the error sums of squares are no longer scalars. Instead, they are replaced by square matrices. For each of these square matrices, the dimension is equal to the number of dependent variables. In univariate analysis, there is only one dependent variable, and the matrix reduces to a scalar, which is the same as the sum of squares of the corresponding effect.

In a multivariate model, these square matrices are called the sums-of-squares and cross-products (**SSCP**) matrices. Analogous to the univariate test of an effect, the "ratio" of the SSCP matrix due to the effect being tested (**H**) and the SSCP matrix of the appropriate error (**E**) is used to evaluate the effect of interest. Since **H** and **E** are matrices, this "ratio" in a multivariate model is evaluated by the determinant of $\mathbf{HE}^{-1}$, where $\mathbf{E}^{-1}$ is the inverse of **E**. The **H** matrix, which is the SSCP matrix of the effect being tested, is called the hypothesis SSCP matrix, and the **E** matrix, which is the SSCP matrix of the appropriate error, is called the error SSCP matrix. In a fixed-effects multivariate analysis of variance, the hypothesis SSCP matrix for testing any effect in the model is its own SSCP matrix due to that effect, and the error SSCP matrix for all tests in the model is always the SSCP matrix due to error in the model.

Running the Tests

To produce the output shown in this example, from the menus choose:

Analyze
General Linear Model
Multivariate...

▶ Dependent variables: tear_res, gloss, opacity
▶ Fixed Factor(s): extrusn, additive

Options...
☑ Hypothesis and error SSCP matrices

 Activate the multivariate tests table and drag the Effect icon from the row tray to the layer tray. Click the arrows on the Effect icon to cycle through the layers.

The hypothesis SSCP matrices for testing the effects in the model are shown in Figure 11-2. These are the matrices that are used in calculating the *F* values.

Figure 11-2
Between-subjects SSCP matrix

			TEAR_RES	GLOSS	OPACITY
Hypothesis	Intercept	TEAR_RES	920.724	1264.05	533.979
		GLOSS	1264.045	1735.38	733.090
		OPACITY	533.979	733.090	309.684
	EXTRUSN	TEAR_RES	1.740	-1.505	.855
		GLOSS	-1.505	1.301	-.740
		OPACITY	.855	-.740	.421
	ADDITIVE	TEAR_RES	.760	.682	1.930
		GLOSS	.682	.612	1.732
		OPACITY	1.930	1.732	4.900
	EXTRUSN*ADDITIVE	TEAR_RES	.000	.016	.044
		GLOSS	.016	.544	1.468
		OPACITY	.044	1.468	3.960
Error		TEAR_RES	1.764	.020	-3.070
		GLOSS	.020	2.628	-.552
		OPACITY	-3.070	-.552	64.924

Based on Type III Sum of Squares

The results of the multivariate analysis of variance are shown in Figure 11-3. Each effect is shown as a layer.

Figure 11-3

Multivariate tests

Effect: Intercept

	Value	F	Hypothesis df	Error df	Sig.	Noncent. Parameter	Observed Power[1]
Pillai's Trace	.999	5950.906[2]	3.000	14.000	.000	17852.717	1.000
Wilks' Lambda	.001	5950.906[2]	3.000	14.000	.000	17852.717	1.000
Hotelling's Trace	1275.194	5950.906[2]	3.000	14.000	.000	17852.717	1.000
Roy's Largest Root	1275.194	5950.906[2]	3.000	14.000	.000	17852.717	1.000

1. Computed using alpha = .05
2. Exact statistic

Effect: EXTRUSN

	Value	F	Hypothesis df	Error df	Sig.	Noncent. Parameter	Observed Power[1]
Pillai's Trace	.618	7.554[2]	3.000	14.000	.003	22.663	.948
Wilks' Lambda	.382	7.554[2]	3.000	14.000	.003	22.663	.948
Hotelling's Trace	1.619	7.554[2]	3.000	14.000	.003	22.663	.948
Roy's Largest Root	1.619	7.554[2]	3.000	14.000	.003	22.663	.948

1. Computed using alpha = .05
2. Exact statistic

Effect: ADDITIVE

	Value	F	Hypothesis df	Error df	Sig.	Noncent. Parameter	Observed Power[1]
Pillai's Trace	.477	4.256[2]	3.000	14.000	.025	12.767	.744
Wilks' Lambda	.523	4.256[2]	3.000	14.000	.025	12.767	.744
Hotelling's Trace	.912	4.256[2]	3.000	14.000	.025	12.767	.744
Roy's Largest Root	.912	4.256[2]	3.000	14.000	.025	12.767	.744

1. Computed using alpha = .05
2. Exact statistic

Multivariate tests (Continued)

Effect: EXTRUSN * ADDITIVE

	Value	F	Hypothesis df	Error df	Sig.	Noncent. Parameter	Observed Power[1]
Pillai's Trace	.223	1.339^2	3.000	14.000	.302	4.016	.280
Wilks' Lambda	.777	1.339^2	3.000	14.000	.302	4.016	.280
Hotelling's Trace	.287	1.339^2	3.000	14.000	.302	4.016	.280
Roy's Largest Root	.287	1.339^2	3.000	14.000	.302	4.016	.280

[1.] Computed using alpha = .05

[2.] Exact statistic

Above the upper left corner in each of these layer tables is the effect in the model being tested, and the first column lists the names of the test statistics. Four commonly used test statistics for multivariate analysis are displayed in the output: Pillai's trace, Wilks' lambda, Hotelling's trace, and Roy's largest root. The next column displays the value of the test statistics, followed by the F statistic, which is a transformed value of the corresponding test statistic and has an approximate F distribution. The hypothesis and error degrees of freedom of the F distribution are shown. The noncentrality parameter estimate of the F distribution and observed power of detecting an effect of observed magnitude are displayed in the last two columns.

Of the four test statistics, Wilks' lambda has the virtue of being convenient and related to the likelihood-ratio criterion. However, for some practical situations (see Olsen, 1976), Pillai's trace may be the most robust and powerful criterion among the others. Choice of these multivariate statistics may depend on the situation. Their F statistics may sometimes, although not necessarily, be the same. Whenever the F statistic has an exact F distribution, a footnote is displayed as a reminder.

In the test of the interaction effect *extrusn*additive*, the four F statistics are all the same, with a value of 1.339. Since the F value is not significant at the 0.05 alpha level, we conclude that there is no interaction effect. The F statistics for testing *extrusn* and *additive* are 7.554 and 4.256, respectively. Both are significant at $\alpha = 0.05$, indicating that changes in both the rate of extrusion and the amount of additive affect the three dependent variables.

Example 2
Profile Analysis: Setting Up Custom Linear Hypotheses

Do husbands and wives share the same point of view on love and marriage? An investigation was performed to study the points of view of married couples on love and marriage. A set of four questions was answered by a sample of 30 couples. The first two questions concerned the feeling of passionate love, while the second two questions were about the feeling of companionate love. All four questions were rated on a five-point scale, ranging from "None at all" to "A tremendous amount." The data are taken from Johnson and Wichern (1988).

Figure 11-4 shows a plot of the means of the answers to the four questions. The mean rating by husbands and the mean rating by wives for each question are plotted on separate lines.

Figure 11-4
Plot of husbands' and wives' profiles

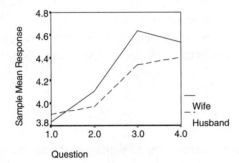

The plot suggests three queries:

- Parallelism of profiles: Are the population mean profiles of husbands and wives parallel to each other?

- Equality of husbands' and wives' profiles: Assuming parallelism, are the profiles of husbands and wives equal?

- Equality of answer means: Assuming parallelism, are the answer means equal?

In order to satisfy parallelism of profiles, the two profile plots should be parallel to each other for each line segment between adjacent questions. This query can be viewed as testing the hypothesis of no response by group interaction. Testing the equality of the two profiles is equivalent to testing whether there is any difference between the husbands' and wives' answers. Testing the equality of answer means is equivalent to testing for any differences between husbands and wives in each of the four survey questions. In the next section, we will study each of the three queries related to the plot by specifying the **L** matrix and the **M** matrix, using a multivariate linear model.[*]

Setting Up Contrast Matrices

In the SPSS data file *love*, *Q1*, *Q2*, *Q3*, and *Q4* are variables that represent the answers to the four love and marriage questions, on a five-point scale. The variable *spouse* divides the cases into two groups, husbands and wives. You can form a multivariate linear model with *Q1*, *Q2*, *Q3*, and *Q4* as the dependent variables and *spouse* as the factor.

To answer the three queries listed in the previous section, you can use the LMATRIX and the MMATRIX syntax subcommands, which correspond to the **L** matrix and **M** matrix of the general multivariate linear hypothesis **LBM = 0**. The **B** matrix is the parameter matrix in which each column corresponds to the parameter vector for the linear model on each of the dependent variables. In this example, the four dependent variables correspond to the four columns of **B**. Since there is only one factor, *spouse,* in the model, and it has only two levels, *husband* and *wife*, each column of **B** has three parameters to be estimated: the overall intercept and the two parameters for each level of *spouse*. The **L** matrix sets up contrasts for the factor in the model, and the **M** matrix sets up contrasts for the dependent variables.

Testing Parallelism

To test for parallelism, you must set up both the **L** matrix and the **M** matrix. Since the first query asks whether the line segments between adjacent answers are parallel, the **M** matrix should be set for contrasts, which can compare adjacent answers. In other words, comparisons should be made of the mean of *Q1* against *Q2*, *Q2* against *Q3*, and *Q3* against *Q4*. The **M** matrix will be a 4×3 matrix of the following form:

$$\begin{bmatrix} 1 & 0 & 0 \\ -1 & 1 & 0 \\ 0 & -1 & 1 \\ 0 & 0 & -1 \end{bmatrix}$$

[*]This problem would normally be handled by using a repeated measures effect. However, the example here is used to illustrate the use of LMATRIX and MMATRIX subcommands.

Because the **M** matrix is used to test whether the line segments of the husband group and the wife group are parallel, the **L** matrix compares the husband group with the wife group. The **L** matrix will be a 1×3 matrix of the following form:

$$\begin{bmatrix} 0 & 1 & -1 \end{bmatrix}$$

where the first value, 0, corresponds to the overall intercept parameter in the linear model, and the pair 1 and -1 compares the husband group with the wife group.

To produce the output in this section, from the menus choose:

Analyze
 General Linear Model
  Multivariate...

▶ Dependent variables: q1, q2, q3, q4
▶ Fixed Factor(s): spouse
Model...
   ⊙ Custom
   ▶ Model: spouse

Paste

To the pasted syntax, add the LMATRIX and MMATRIX subcommands as shown:

```
GLM q1 q2 q3 q4 BY spouse
 /METHOD = SSTYPE(3)
 /INTERCEPT = INCLUDE
 /CRITERIA = ALPHA(.05)
 /DESIGN spouse
 /LMATRIX = spouse 1 -1
 /MMATRIX = q1 1 q2 -1;
            q2 1 q3 -1;
            q3 1 q4 -1.
```

To run the GLM command, click the Run Current tool. The syntax indicates that there are four dependent variables, *Q1, Q2, Q3,* and *Q4*, in the model, and one factor, *spouse*. The DESIGN subcommand indicates the model. The subcommands METHOD, INTERCEPT, and CRITERIA are default specifications (with which we are not concerned here).

The **L** matrix is specified by using the LMATRIX subcommand, followed by the factor name *spouse* and the contrast for the factor. The **M** matrix is specified by the MMATRIX subcommand, followed by an equals sign, the name of one dependent variable, its coefficient, the name of the dependent variable being compared with the first, and its coefficient. Each of the three comparisons is listed in a similar manner. If a dependent variable and its coefficient are not specified, the coefficient of that dependent variable is assumed to be 0. A semicolon (;) is used to indicate the end of one column in the **M** matrix.

Parallelism Test Results

The results of the custom hypothesis test of parallelism are shown in Figure 11-5.

Figure 11-5
Multivariate test results

	Value	F	Hypothesis df	Error df	Sig.	Noncent. Parameter	Observed Power[1]
Pillai's trace	.121	2.580[2]	3.000	56.000	.063	7.740	.604
Wilks' lambda	.879	2.580[2]	3.000	56.000	.063	7.740	.604
Hotelling's trace	.138	2.580[2]	3.000	56.000	.063	7.740	.604
Roy's largest root	.138	2.580[2]	3.000	56.000	.063	7.740	.604

[1]. Computed using alpha = .05
[2]. Exact statistic

With $p = 0.063$, the test is not significant at $\alpha = 0.05$. Parallelism of the mean profiles of husbands and wives will be assumed.

Testing for Equality of Profiles

To test the equality of husbands' and wives' profiles, the means of the four answers for the husband group and the wife group are compared. In this case, the **M** matrix corresponds to the average of the four answers, and the **L** matrix corresponds to the contrast used to compare husbands and wives.

To produce the output in this section, recall the GLM Multivariate dialog box and paste, or from the menus choose:

Analyze
  General Linear Model
    Multivariate...

▶ Dependent variables: q1, q2, q3, q4
▶ Fixed Factor(s): spouse
Model...
    ⊙ Custom
    ▶ Model: spouse

Paste

To the pasted syntax, add the **LMATRIX** and **MMATRIX** subcommands as shown:

```
GLM q1 q2 q3 q4 BY spouse
 /METHOD = SSTYPE(3)
 /INTERCEPT = INCLUDE
 /CRITERIA = ALPHA(.05)
 /DESIGN spouse
 /LMATRIX = spouse 1 -1
 /MMATRIX = q1 .25 q2 .25 q3 .25 q4 .25.
```

To run the **GLM** command, click the Run Current tool. The results are shown in Figure 11-6.

Figure 11-6
Univariate test results

Source	Transformed Variable	Type III Sum of Squares	df	Mean Square	F	Sig.	Noncentrality Parameter	Observed Power
Contrast	T1	.234	1	.234	1.533	.221	1.533	.230
Error	T1	8.869	58	.153				

Since the **M** matrix has only one column, the univariate result is used. The p value for the test is 0.221, which is not significant at $\alpha = 0.05$. This means that equality of the husbands' and wives' profiles can be assumed. That is, the answers from the husbands and the wives to the four questions can be assumed to be the same.

Testing for Equality of Answer Means

To test the equality of answer means, the means of the husbands' group and wives' group for the four answers are compared with each other. In this case, the **M** matrix is the one used in testing parallelism, while the **L** matrix corresponds to taking the average of each group. It is [1 0.5 0.5]. The value 1 corresponds to the intercept, and the two values of 0.5 correspond to the husbands' group and the wives' group, respectively.

To produce the output in this section, recall the GLM Multivariate dialog box and paste, or from the menus choose:

Analyze
  General Linear Model
    Multivariate...

▶ Dependent variables: q1, q2, q3, q4
▶ Fixed Factor(s): spouse
Model...
    ⊙ Custom
    ▶ Model: spouse

Paste

To the pasted syntax, add the LMATRIX and MMATRIX subcommands as shown:

```
GLM Q1 Q2 Q3 Q4 BY spouse
 /DESIGN spouse
 /METHOD = SSTYPE(3)
 /INTERCEPT = INCLUDE
 /CRITERIA = ALPHA(.05)
 /LMATRIX = INTERCEPT 1 spouse .5 .5
 /MMATRIX = Q1 1 Q2 -1;
            Q2 1 Q3 -1;
            Q3 1 Q4 -1.
```

The contrast coefficients are specified in the **L** matrix, and the transformation coefficients are specified in the **M** matrix. The results are displayed in Figure 11-7.

Figure 11-7
Multivariate test results

	Value	F	Hypothesis df	Error df	Sig.	Noncent. Parameter	Observed Power[1]
Pillai's trace	.305	8.188[2]	3.000	56.000	.000	24.564	.988
Wilks' lambda	.695	8.188[2]	3.000	56.000	.000	24.564	.988
Hotelling's trace	.439	8.188[2]	3.000	56.000	.000	24.564	.988
Roy's largest root	.439	8.188[2]	3.000	56.000	.000	24.564	.988

[1]. Computed using alpha = .05
[2]. Exact statistic

For each test, $p < 0.0005$, which is significant. It means that the equality of answers cannot be assumed.

Figure 11-8
Univariate test results for each individual contrast on the dependent variables

Source	Transformed Variable	Type III Sum of Squares	df	Mean Square	F	Sig.	Noncentrality Parameter	Observed Power
Contrast	T1	1.667	1	1.667	2.433	.124	2.433	.335
	T2	12.150	1	12.150	13.973	.000	13.973	.957
	T3	1.667E-02	1	1.7E-02	.212	.647	.212	.074
Error	T1	39.733	58	.685				
	T2	50.433	58	.870				
	T3	4.567	58	7.9E-02				

Figure 11-8 displays the univariate results for this custom hypothesis on each difference of adjacent answers. The three columns in the **M** matrix each correspond to one contrast (or transformation) on the dependent variables. The right side of the first column in Figure 11-8 displays the name of the transformed variable. The first transformed variable, *T1*, corresponds to the first column of the **M** matrix, which compares *q1* with *q2*. The second transformed variable, *T2,* corresponds to the second column of the **M** matrix, which compares *q2* with *q3*. The last transformed variable,

T3, corresponds to the last column of the **M** matrix, which compares *q3* with *q4*. The three contrast results, taken as a set, imply that the first two population means are the same, but differ from the last two, which do not differ from each other.

GLM Repeated Measures Examples

Repeated measures analysis applies to situations where the same measurement is made multiple times on each subject or case. A within-subjects factor that encompasses each set of repeated measurements is defined. Between-subjects factors that divide the cases into groups can be specified as well as covariates.

This chapter includes the following examples:

Example 1: Repeated measures analysis of variance. Twelve students were each tested four times on a learning task. They were also rated for high anxiety or low anxiety. The data are arranged with four trial variables so that the four scores are recorded in one case for each student. A within-subjects factor, *trial,* is defined, and the *anxiety* factor is specified as a between-subjects factor because it divides the group of subjects into two groups. The *anxiety* factor is shown to be not significant, while the *trial* effect is significant. In checking assumptions, Box's *M* and Mauchly's test of sphericity are used.

Example 2: Doubly multivariate repeated measures analysis of variance. A new drug is tested against a placebo in its effects on respiration and pulse. Half of the patients receive the new drug, and half receive the placebo. The variable *drug* divides the subjects into the new-drug group and the placebo group and is used as a between-subjects factor. Both effects, respiration and pulse, are measured together at three different times, making six variables in the data file. The newly defined within-subjects variable is called *time*, with three levels for the three times.

Example 1
Repeated Measures Analysis of Variance

Does the anxiety of a person affect performance on a learning task? Twelve subjects were assigned to one of two anxiety groups on the basis of an anxiety test, and the number of errors made in four blocks of trials on a learning task was measured. In this example, we use a repeated measures analysis-of-variance technique to study the data.

In the data file *anxiety2*, there is one case for each subject (*subject*). Four trial variables (*trial1*, *trial2*, *trial3*, and *trial4*) contain the scores for all of the subjects (see Figure 12-1).

Figure 12-1
Data arrangement

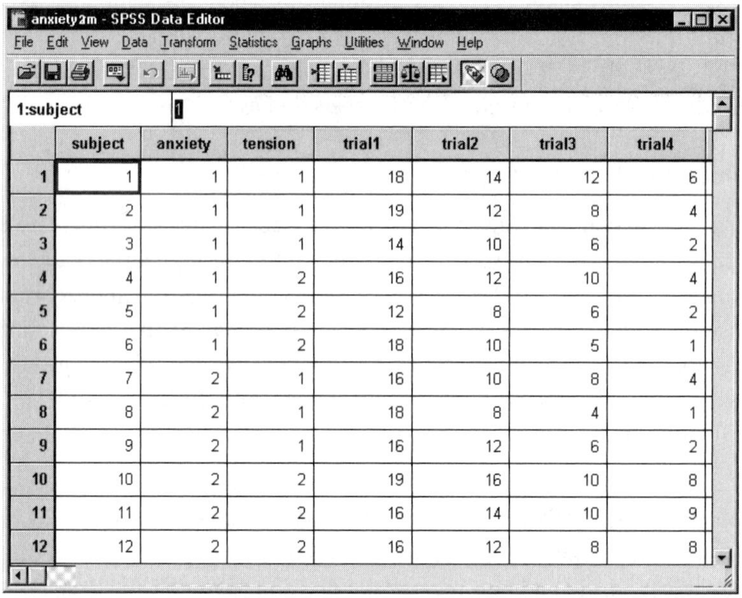

	subject	anxiety	tension	trial1	trial2	trial3	trial4
1	1	1	1	18	14	12	6
2	2	1	1	19	12	8	4
3	3	1	1	14	10	6	2
4	4	1	2	16	12	10	4
5	5	1	2	12	8	6	2
6	6	1	2	18	10	5	1
7	7	2	1	16	10	8	4
8	8	2	1	18	8	4	1
9	9	2	1	16	12	6	2
10	10	2	2	19	16	10	8
11	11	2	2	16	14	10	9
12	12	2	2	16	12	8	8

anxiety2m - SPSS Data Editor

File Edit View Data Transform Statistics Graphs Utilities Window Help

1:subject   1

To use the repeated measures analysis-of-variance technique, we distinguish two types of factors in the model: between-subjects factors and within-subjects factors. A **between-subjects factor** is any factor that divides the sample of subjects or cases into discrete subgroups. For example, the factor *anxiety* is a between-subjects factor because it divides the 12 subjects into two groups: one with high anxiety measurement scores and one with low anxiety measurement scores. A **within-subjects factor** is any factor that distinguishes measurements made on the same subject or case rather than distinguishing different subjects or cases. For example, the factor *trial* is a within-subjects factor in this analysis because it distinguishes the four measurements of error taken for each of the subjects.

A repeated measures analysis consists of the analysis of a within-subjects model, which describes the model for the within-subjects factors, plus the analysis of a between-subjects model, which describes the model for the between-subject factors. For example, in the current repeated measures analysis, the within-subjects part of the model consists of the within-subjects factor *trial* and the interaction, and the between-subjects part of the model consists of the between-subjects factor *anxiety*.

In the data file *anxiety2*, the variables *trial1*, *trial2*, *trial3*, and *trial4* contain the number of errors made at each of the four trials by each subject.

To produce the output in this example, from the menus choose:

Analyze
  General Linear Model
    Repeated Measures...

Within-Subject Factor Name: trial
Number of Levels: 4

Click Add and click Define.

▶ Within-Subjects Variables (trial): trial1, trial2, trial3, trial4
▶ Between-Subjects Factor(s): anxiety

Options...
    ☑ Homogeneity tests

 Activate the tests of within-subjects effects table and drag the Epsilon Corrections icon from the row tray to the layer tray.

In the above choices, for the within-subjects factor, a new name, *trial*, is typed, which designates the measurements made on the same subject. The number of levels is the number of measurements made on each subject (4). Each of the four within-subjects variables, *trial1*, *trial2*, *trial3*, and *trial4*, corresponds to one measurement for each subject.

Between-Subjects Tests

For repeated measures analysis, the results for testing the effects in the model from a multivariate approach and a univariate approach are both provided. For testing the between-subjects effects in the model, both approaches yield the same results. This test is constructed by summing all of the within-subjects variables in the model and dividing by the square root of the number of within-subjects variables. Then an analysis of variance is performed on the result. In this example, since there is only one between-subjects factor, *anxiety*, the test for the between-subjects effects is performed by a one-way analysis of variance using

$$\frac{trial_1 + trial_2 + trial_3 + trial_4}{\sqrt{4}}$$

as the dependent variable. The results from testing the between-subjects effect, *anxiety*, are shown in Figure 12-2. The significance $p = 0.460$ indicates that this effect is not significant at $\alpha = 0.05$.

Figure 12-2
Test of between-subjects effects

Measure: MEASURE_1

Transformed Variable: Average

Source	Type III Sum of Squares	df	Mean Square	F	Sig.	Eta Squared	Noncent. Parameter	Observed Power[1]
Intercept	4800.000	1	4800.000	280.839	.000	.966	280.839	1.000
ANXIETY	10.083	1	10.083	.590	.460	.056	.590	.107
Error	170.917	10	17.092					

[1]. Computed using alpha = .05

Multivariate Tests

The multivariate table contains tests of the within-subjects factor, *trial*, and the interaction of the within-subjects factor and the between-subjects factor, *trial*anxiety*. The results are shown in Figure 12-3.

Figure 12-3
Multivariate tests

Effect		Value	F	Hypothesis df	Error df	Sig.	Noncent. Parameter	Observed Power[1]
TRIAL	Pillai's Trace	.961	64.854[2]	3.000	8.000	.000	194.561	1.000
	Wilks' Lambda	.039	64.854[2]	3.000	8.000	.000	194.561	1.000
	Hotelling's Trace	24.320	64.854[2]	3.000	8.000	.000	194.561	1.000
	Roy's Largest Root	24.320	64.854[2]	3.000	8.000	.000	194.561	1.000
TRIAL * ANXIETY	Pillai's Trace	.479	2.451[2]	3.000	8.000	.138	7.354	.408
	Wilks' Lambda	.521	2.451[2]	3.000	8.000	.138	7.354	.408
	Hotelling's Trace	.919	2.451[2]	3.000	8.000	.138	7.354	.408
	Roy's Largest Root	.919	2.451[2]	3.000	8.000	.138	7.354	.408

1. Computed using alpha = .05
2. Exact statistic

Four test statistics—Pillai's trace, Wilks' lambda, Hotelling's trace and Roy's largest root—are provided. In this example, the *F* statistics for all four tests are the same. The *p* value for testing the *trial* effect is less than 0.001, which is significant at $\alpha = 0.05$, while the *p* value for testing the *trial*anxiety* effect is 0.138, which is not significant at $\alpha = 0.05$.

Checking Assumptions

The assumption for the multivariate approach is that the vector of the dependent variables follows a multivariate normal distribution, and the variance-covariance matrices are equal across the cells formed by the between-subject effects. Box's *M* test for this assumption is shown in Figure 12-4. The significance is 0.315, indicating that the null hypothesis (that the observed variance-covariance matrices are equal across the two levels of the *anxiety* effect) is not rejected.

Figure 12-4
Test for equality of covariance matrices

Box's Test of Equality of Covariance Matrices[a]

Box's M	21.146
F	1.161
df1	10
df2	478
Sig.	.315

Tests the null hypothesis that the observed covariance matrices of the dependent variables are equal across groups.

a. Design: Intercept+ANXIETY
Within Subjects Design: TRIAL

Testing for Sphericity

To use the univariate results for testing the within-subjects factor, *trial,* and the interaction of the within-subjects factor and the between-subjects factor, *trial*anxiety,* some assumptions about the variance-covariance matrices of the dependent variables should be checked. The validity of the *F* statistic used in the univariate approach can be assured when the variance-covariance matrix of the dependent variables is *circular* in form (Huynh and Mandeville, 1979). Mauchly (1940) derived a test that verifies this variance-covariance matrix structure by performing a test of sphericity on the orthonormalized transformed dependent variable. This test, which is automatically performed when a repeated measures analysis is used, is shown in Figure 12-5. The significance of this test is 0.053, which is slightly larger the 0.05 alpha level, indicating that the variance-covariance matrix assumption is just barely satisfied.

Figure 12-5
Mauchly's test of sphericity

Mauchly's Test of Sphericity[1]

Measure: MEASURE_1

Within Subjects Effect	Mauchly's W	Approx. Chi-Square	df	Sig.	Epsilon[2]		
					Greenhouse-Geisser	Huynh-Feldt	Lower-bound
TRIAL	.283	11.011	5	.053	.544	.701	.333

Tests the null hypothesis that the error covariance matrix of the orthonormalized transformed dependent variables is proportional to an identity matrix.

[1.] Design: Intercept+ANXIETY
Within Subjects Design: TRIAL

[2.] May be used to adjust the degrees of freedom for the averaged tests of significance. Corrected tests are displayed in the layers (by default) of the Tests of Within Subjects Effects table.

What if the significance indicated rejection? If the above sphericity test were to be rejected, sphericity could not be assumed. Then an adjustment value, called epsilon, would be needed for multiplying the numerator and denominator degrees of freedom in the *F* test. The significance of the *F* test would then be evaluated with the new degrees of freedom. The last three columns in Figure 12-5 display three possible values of epsilon, based on three different criteria: Greenhouse-Geisser, Huynh-Feldt, and lower-bound. The Greenhouse-Geisser epsilon is conservative, especially for a small sample size. The Huynh-Feldt epsilon is an alternative that is not as conservative as the Greenhouse-Geisser epsilon; however, it may be a value greater than 1. When its calculated value is greater than 1, the Huynh-Feldt epsilon is displayed as 1.000, and this value is used in calculating the new degrees of freedom and significance. The lower-bound epsilon takes the reciprocal of the degrees of freedom for the within-subjects factor. This represents the most conservative approach possible, since it indicates the most extreme possible departure from sphericity. SPSS displays results for each of the values of epsilon.

Testing Hypotheses

The univariate tests for the within-subjects factor, *trial,* and the interaction term, *trial*anxiety,* are shown in Figure 12-6, with all layers displayed.

Figure 12-6

Tests of within-subjects effects

Source	Measure		Type III Sum of Squares	df	Mean Square	F	Sig.	Eta Squared	Noncent. Parameter	Observed Power[1]
TRIAL	MEASURE_1	Sphericity Assumed	991.500	3	330.500	128.627	.000	.928	385.881	1.000
		Greenhouse-Geisser	991.500	1.632	607.468	128.627	.000	.928	209.943	1.000
		Huynh-Feldt	991.500	2.102	471.773	128.627	.000	.928	270.329	1.000
		Lower-bound	991.500	1.000	991.500	128.627	.000	.928	128.627	1.000
TRIAL * ANXIETY	MEASURE_1	Sphericity Assumed	8.417	3	2.806	1.092	.368	.098	3.276	.265
		Greenhouse-Geisser	8.417	1.632	5.157	1.092	.346	.098	1.782	.194
		Huynh-Feldt	8.417	2.102	4.005	1.092	.357	.098	2.295	.220
		Lower-bound	8.417	1.000	8.417	1.092	.321	.098	1.092	.157
Error(TRIAL)	MEASURE_1	Sphericity Assumed	77.083	30	2.569					
		Greenhouse-Geisser	77.083	16.322	4.723					
		Huynh-Feldt	77.083	21.016	3.668					
		Lower-bound	77.083	10.000	7.708					

[1]. Computed using alpha = .05

The significance for each test when sphericity is assumed, or when any of the three epsilons is used, is displayed. The third column indicates what type of epsilon is used in evaluating the significance of the test. For example, the row labeled *Sphericity Assumed* indicates that the assumption about the variance-covariance matrix is assumed and that the significance is evaluated using the original degrees of freedom. The row labeled *Greenhouse-Geisser* indicates that the Greenhouse-Geisser epsilon is used and that the significance in this row is evaluated using the Greenhouse-Geisser epsilon adjustment. In this example, because the variance-covariance matrix assumption is assumed to be satisfied (by the result of the Mauchly's test), the conclusion can be drawn based on the row labeled *Sphericity Assumed.* The *trial* effect is significant, with a *p* value of less than 0.001, and the *trial*anxiety* interaction effect is not significant, with a *p* value of 0.368. Notice that the same conclusion can be drawn using any three of the epsilons.

Contrasts

It is sometimes useful to introduce contrasts among the within-subjects variables in order to study the levels of the within-subjects factors. To specify contrasts for the within-subjects variables, recall the dialog box for Repeated Measures and choose:

Contrasts...
 Factors: trial
 Contrast: Repeated (Click Change)

This set of contrasts does not affect the results of the univariate and multivariate analyses. It is useful only for comparing the levels of the within-subjects factor. The tests of within-subjects contrasts are shown in Figure 12-7.

Figure 12-7
Within-subjects contrasts

Tests of Within Subjects Contrasts

Measure: MEASURE_1

Source	Transformed Variable	Type III Sum of Squares	df	Mean Square	F	Sig.	Noncentrality Parameter	Observed Power[1]
TRIAL	TRIAL_1	300.000	1	300.000	52.023	.000	52.023	1.000
	TRIAL_2	168.750	1	168.750	83.678	.000	83.678	1.000
	TRIAL_3	147.000	1	147.000	78.750	.000	78.750	1.000
TRIAL*ANXIETY	TRIAL_1	.333	1	.333	.058	.815	.058	.055
	TRIAL_2	4.083	1	4.083	2.025	.185	2.025	.252
	TRIAL_3	16.333	1	16.333	8.750	.014	8.750	.760
Error(TRIAL)	TRIAL_1	57.667	10	5.767				
	TRIAL_2	20.167	10	2.017				
	TRIAL_3	18.667	10	1.867				

1. Computed using alpha = .050

A repeated contrast compares one level of *trial* with the subsequent level. The first column indicates the effect being tested. For example, the label *TRIAL* tests the hypothesis that, averaged over the two anxiety groups, the mean of the specified contrast is 0.

 The transformed variable names under the repeated contrast are in the second column. The first name, *TRIAL_1,* represents the contrast that compares the first level of *trial* with the second level of *trial*. Notice that the first dependent variable, *trial1,* corresponds to the observation of the first level of *trial* and that the second dependent variable, *trial2,* corresponds to the observation of the second level of *trial*, and so on. The first contrast, *TRIAL_1,* corresponds to the transformation $trial1 - trial2$.

Similarly, the second contrast, *TRIAL_2*, represents the transformation $trial2 - trial3$, which compares the second level of *trial* with the third level. The third contrast, *TRIAL_3*, represents the transformation $trial3 - trial4$, which compares the third level with the fourth level. In the above table, all three specified contrasts—*TRIAL_1*, *TRIAL_2*, and *TRIAL_3*—are significant at $\alpha = 0.01$.

The label *TRIAL*ANXIETY* tests the hypothesis that the mean of the specified contrast is the same for the two anxiety groups. Except for the last specified contrast, *TRIAL_3*, which may be significant at $\alpha = 0.05$, all others are not significant at $\alpha = 0.01$.

Example 2
Doubly Multivariate Repeated Measures Analysis of Variance

Can a new drug improve respiratory and pulse scores? A study was performed to determine whether a new drug has any effect on the respiratory score and pulse score of a patient. Twelve randomly selected patients having similar medical conditions were randomly divided into two groups. Patients in one group were treated with the new drug, and patients in another group were treated with a placebo. The respiratory score and the pulse were measured at three different times. The data, created for this example, are shown in Figure 12-8.

Figure 12-8
Respiratory and pulse measurements

Drug	Respiratory Score			Pulse		
	Time 1	Time 2	Time 3	Time 1	Time 2	Time 3
New Drug	3.4	3.3	3.3	77	77	73.5
New Drug	3.4	3.4	3.3	77	77	77
New Drug	3.3	3.4	3.4	80.5	80.5	80.5
New Drug	3.4	3.4	3.4	80.5	80.5	80.5
New Drug	3.3	3.4	3.3	77	77	84
New Drug	3.3	3.3	3.3	70	70	84
Placebo	3.3	3.3	3.3	98	98	94.5
Placebo	3.2	3.3	3.4	91	91	94.5
Placebo	3.2	3.2	3.2	94.5	94.5	94.5
Placebo	3.2	3.2	3.2	91	91	101.5
Placebo	3.2	3.3	3.3	94.5	94.5	101.5
Placebo	3.3	3.2	3.1	91	91	98

The data are stored in the file *new drug*, with one case for each subject. The respiratory scores are stored in three variables (*resp1, resp2,* and *resp3*), one for each time. The pulses are stored in three variables (*pulse1, pulse2,* and *pulse3*), again, one for each time. The variable *drug* has two values, 1 for the group that received the new drug and 2 for the group that received the placebo.

The type of drug divides the patients into two groups; therefore, it is a between-subjects factor. The three time points distinguish measurements taken on the same patient, making *time* a within-subjects factor. Notice that two measurements, respiratory score and pulse score, are taken for all patients at each factor combination—this is a doubly multivariate repeated measures design.

To produce the output shown in this example, from the menus choose:

Analyze
  General Linear Model
    Repeated Measures...

Within-Subject Factor Name: time
Number of Levels: 3 (Click Add)

Measure>>
  Measure Name: resp pulse (Click Add for each measure)

Click Define.

▶ Within-Subjects Variables (time): resp1, resp2, resp3, pulse1, pulse2, pulse3
▶ Between-Subjects Factor(s): drug

The within-subjects factor name is a new name that you specify to designate groups of measurements made on the same subject—in this example, *time* for the three times. The number of levels indicates the number of groups for the within-subjects factor. A measure name is a new name that you specify to designate the group of like scores measured at different times. In this example, the measure names indicate the respiratory score and the pulse. Notice the order of the within-subjects variables. All three respiratory score names appear first, and then the three pulse names, matching the order on Measure Name.

The multivariate results of the analysis are shown in Figure 12-9 and Figure 12-10. In this example, the *TIME* effect and the *TIME*DRUG* effect are not significant. However, the *DRUG* effect is significant at $p < 0.0005$, indicating that the new drug has an effect on the respiratory and pulse scores.

Chapter 12

Figure 12-9

Multivariate tests

Multivariate Tests[1]

Effect			Value	F	Hypothesis df	Error df	Sig.	Noncent. Parameter	Observed Power[2]
Between Subjects	Intercept	Pillai's Trace	1.000	32480.4[3]	2.000	9.000	.000	64960.841	1.000
		Wilks' Lambda	.000	32480.4[3]	2.000	9.000	.000	64960.841	1.000
		Hotelling's Trace	7217.871	32480.4[3]	2.000	9.000	.000	64960.841	1.000
		Roy's Largest Root	7217.871	32480.4[3]	2.000	9.000	.000	64960.841	1.000
	DRUG	Pillai's Trace	.956	98.177[3]	2.000	9.000	.000	196.354	1.000
		Wilks' Lambda	.044	98.177[3]	2.000	9.000	.000	196.354	1.000
		Hotelling's Trace	21.817	98.177[3]	2.000	9.000	.000	196.354	1.000
		Roy's Largest Root	21.817	98.177[3]	2.000	9.000	.000	196.354	1.000
Within Subjects	TIME	Pillai's Trace	.612	2.761[3]	4.000	7.000	.114	11.044	.464
		Wilks' Lambda	.388	2.761[3]	4.000	7.000	.114	11.044	.464
		Hotelling's Trace	1.578	2.761[3]	4.000	7.000	.114	11.044	.464
		Roy's Largest Root	1.578	2.761[3]	4.000	7.000	.114	11.044	.464
	TIME * DRUG	Pillai's Trace	.496	1.722[3]	4.000	7.000	.249	6.887	.301
		Wilks' Lambda	.504	1.722[3]	4.000	7.000	.249	6.887	.301
		Hotelling's Trace	.984	1.722[3]	4.000	7.000	.249	6.887	.301
		Roy's Largest Root	.984	1.722[3]	4.000	7.000	.249	6.887	.301

[1]. Design: Intercept+DRUG
   Within Subjects Design: TIME

[2]. Computed using alpha = .05

[3]. Exact statistic

Figure 12-10
Between-subjects effects

Tests of Between-Subjects Effects

Transformed Variable: Average

Source	Measure	Type III Sum of Squares	df	Mean Square	F	Sig.	Noncent. Parameter	Observed Power[1]
Intercept	RESP	391.380	1	391.380	69750.941	.000	69750.941	1.000
	PULSE	224.001	1	224.001	14197.254	.000	14197.254	1.000
DRUG	RESP	.100	1	.100	17.871	.002	17.871	.967
	PULSE	2.454	1	2.454	155.563	.000	155.563	1.000
Error	RESP	5.611E-02	10	5.611E-03				
	PULSE	.158	10	1.578E-02				

1. Computed using alpha = .05

Variance Components Examples

What components contribute to variation in the absorption of calcium by turnip leaves? Can you estimate the size of the individual components? Is variance in testing of ovens due to their nonhomogeneity? These questions can be investigated by using the Variance Components procedure. In this chapter, you can find illustrations of four different methods as well as technical background information.

Factors, Effects, and Models

A key concept in the variance components model is the idea of fixed and random effects. Factors make up the effects, and then the effects are combined into a model.

Types of Factors

Since effects in the model are composed of factors, first consider the types of factors. When the levels of a factor are all of the possible values in the entire population or all of the levels of interest to the researchers, then it is a **fixed factor**. For example, imagine that researchers for a computer magazine conduct a study to compare the lifetimes of five types of laptop computer batteries: Nickel Cadmium (*NiCad*), Nickel Metal Hydride (*NiMH*), Lead Acid, and Lithium Ion (*LiIon*). The variable labeled *Type of battery* is treated as a fixed factor either when these five types are the only ones on the market or when the researchers are interested in making inferences about only these five types.

A factor is said to be **random** when the levels of the factor represent a random sample of all possible values from a population and inferences will be made on the entire population. Suppose, in the above example, that the study of battery types is conducted using batteries from five different manufacturers. It is not unreasonable to think of those manufacturers as a randomly chosen sample from a population of battery manufacturers. The lifetime of batteries from any one of these five manufacturers may have no particular interest in and of itself to the researchers. The five manufacturers are chosen with the objective of treating them as representative of the population of all laptop computer battery manufacturers, and inferences can and will be made about the whole population. Thus, *Manufacturer* is treated as a random factor.

Types of Effects

Effects are made up of factors, and in the Variance Components procedure, they also inherit the random nature of the composing factors. An effect is treated as a **fixed effect** when all of its composing factors are fixed factors; otherwise, the effect is treated as a **random effect**.

In the laptop computer battery example, the main effect *Type of Battery* is a fixed effect, and the nested effect *Manufacturer within Type of Battery* is a random effect.

Types of Models

If all effects in a model are random effects, the model is called a **random-effects model**. Similarly, a model with only fixed effects and the residual term is called a **fixed-effects model**. It is common to find models where some effects are random and some are fixed. In this case, the model is a **mixed model**. Since the intercept is generally treated as a fixed effect, a model including the intercept and one or more random factors is by default a mixed model. Using the above laptop computer battery example, an example of a mixed model is:

Intercept + Type of Battery + Manufacturer within Type of Battery + Residual

while an example of a fixed-effects model is:

Intercept + Type of Battery + Residual

Model for One-Way Classification

For a first example of variance components, classification by one factor provides a simple model. This section deals with the one-way classification model generally, using one data set to demonstrate two methods of variance component estimation. Consider the turnip leaf data that appeared in Table 13.3.1 of Snedecor and Cochran (1980). As mentioned in the authors' book, the data presented here are a small subset of the original data collected from a larger experiment on the precision of estimation of calcium concentration in percentage dry weight of turnip greens. Four determinations were made on each of the four leaves from a single plant. The data are shown in Figure 13-1.

Figure 13-1
Calcium concentration in turnip greens (% dry weight)

Leaf	% Calcium Determination			
	1	**2**	**3**	**4**
1	3.28	3.09	3.03	3.03
2	3.52	3.48	3.38	3.38
3	2.88	2.80	2.81	2.76
4	3.34	3.38	3.23	3.26

In the SPSS data file, each measurement is one case. The variables are leaf (*leaf*), percentage of calcium (*pctca*), and determination (*determ*).

Consider how the mean calcium concentration varies with *leaf*. You can use the Summarize (Case Summaries) procedure to compute the observed means and the observed standard deviations for each level of *leaf*. The results are shown in Figure 13-2.

Figure 13-2
Case summaries

Percentage of Calcium

Leaf	Mean	Std. Deviation
1	3.1075	.1184
2	3.4400	.0712
3	2.8125	.0499
4	3.3025	.0695
Total	3.1656	.2540

It is apparent that the means vary among these four leaves; thus, *leaf* is a plausible effect. Now the question is: Are you really interested in (1) the different percentages of calcium in the four specific leaves chosen, or (2) the variation in all leaves from which the four leaves may have been drawn? Since the leaf i ($i = 1, 2, 3, 4$) is just one from among randomly picked leaves, the answer should be (2), and the *leaf* effect must be treated as a random effect.

Let y_{ij} be the *j*th determination on leaf i. The mathematical model that relates the expected percentage on leaf i to the grand mean and the *leaf* effect is

$$y_{ij} = \mu + \alpha_i + \varepsilon_{ij} \qquad \text{for } j = 1, 2, 3, 4$$

where μ is the grand mean, α_i are the main effects ($i = 1, 2, 3, 4$), and ε_{ij} are residual errors. The errors are independent, and each follows a distribution with a mean of 0 and variance *Var(Error)*. For readers who are familiar with the general linear model, this equation looks exactly like the one for a one-way ANOVA model. However, some underlying assumptions are different: the main effects (α_i) are random variables whose values depend on which four leaves are picked. Thus, they follow certain probability distributions. It is usually assumed that the α_i are independent, and each has a mean of 0 and the same variance *Var(LEAF)*. Moreover, the main effects and the residuals are also assumed to be independent. It follows from these assumptions that

$$\text{Var}(y_{ij}) = \text{Var}(\text{LEAF}) + \text{Var}(\text{Error})$$

The total variance, then, of y_{ij} is the sum of the two components, *Var(LEAF)* and *Var(Error)*—hence the name **variance components**. If *leaf* has no effects on the percentage of calcium, then the component *Var(LEAF)* equals 0. You can use the GLM Univariate procedure to test this null hypothesis (discussed in the *SPSS Base User's Guide*.) However, GLM cannot estimate the variance *Var(LEAF)*, while the Variance Components procedure does estimate the variance.

Estimation Methods

Four estimation methods are available in the Variance Components procedure: ANOVA, minimum norm quadratic unbiased estimator (MINQUE), maximum likelihood (ML), and restricted maximum likelihood (REML). For illustration purposes, both the ANOVA method using Type I sums of squares and the maximum likelihood method are used in this example.

ANOVA Method

The ANOVA method does not require any knowledge of the distributions of the random effect *leaf* and the residual error other than their means and the variances. This method estimates the variance components by equating the expected mean squares of the random effects and the residual to their observed mean squares. The expected and the observed mean squares vary depending on the type of sum of squares used. The Variance Components procedure offers two types of sums of squares: Type I and Type III. If you are new to these types, see Chapter 3 for general information. For a one-way classification model (one factor), both types produce the same sums of squares. For the sake of simplicity, only Type I results are shown here.

To produce the output, from the menus choose:

Analyze
  General Linear Model
    Variance Components...

▸ Dependent variable: pctca
▸ Random factor: leaf

Options...
  Method
  ⊙ ANOVA
  Sum of Squares
  ⊙ Type I
  Display
  ☑ Sums of squares
  ☑ Expected mean squares

The expected mean squares table is shown in Figure 13-3 and the ANOVA table, in Figure 13-4.

Figure 13-3
Expected mean squares

Source	Variance Components		Quadratic Term
	Var(LEAF)	Var(Error)	
Intercept	4.000	1.000	Intercept
LEAF	4.000	1.000	
Error	.000	1.000	

Figure 13-4
ANOVA table

Source	Type I Sum of Squares	df	Mean Square
Corrected Model	.888	3	.296
Intercept	160.339	1	160.339
LEAF	.888	3	.296
Error	7.923E-02	12	6.602E-03
Total	161.306	16	
Corrected Total	.968	15	

Dependent Variable: PCTCA

Since the Variance Components procedure does not perform hypothesis testing, only the sums of squares, degrees of freedom, and mean squares are reported in the ANOVA table.

Reading from the expected mean squares table (Figure 13-3), the expected mean squares of *LEAF* and *Error* are:

$$\text{EMS(LEAF)} = 4 \times \text{Var(LEAF)} + \text{Var(Error)}$$
$$\text{EMS(Error)} = \text{Var(Error)}$$

Equating these expected mean squares with the corresponding observed mean squares in the ANOVA table produces the following two equations:

$$0.296 = 4 \times \text{Var(LEAF)} + \text{Var(Error)}$$
$$0.006602 = \text{Var(Error)}$$

Solving for the variances yields:

$$\text{Var(Error)} = 0.006602$$
$$\text{Var(LEAF)} = \left(\frac{0.296 - 0.006602}{4} \right) = 0.0723$$

These solutions are the ANOVA Type I variance estimates. SPSS calculates these variances and displays full precision values of the estimates in the variance estimates table (Figure 13-5).

Figure 13-5
Variance estimates

Component	Estimate
Var(LEAF)	7.238E-02
Var(Error)	6.602E-03

The ANOVA Type I variance estimates are $Var(LEAF) = 0.07238$ and $Var(Error) = 0.006602$, which agree with the estimates given in Table 13.3.1 in Snedecor and Cochran (1980).

Maximum Likelihood Method

The maximum likelihood method requires distributional assumptions other than those on the means and the variances of the main effects *leaf* and the residual error, which were the assumptions required for the ANOVA method. Maximum likelihood assumes that the data are normally distributed. Although this is a considerably strong assumption, it is unlikely to be seriously violated in many situations. Moreover, the likelihood principle behind the maximum likelihood method is known to give estimates with useful statistical properties and estimates superior to those computed by the ANOVA method, when the data are approximately normally distributed.

Under the normality assumption, the likelihood function is maximized with respect to a set of parameters. In practice, the natural logarithm of the likelihood function (called the log-likelihood function) is maximized. The parameters include all of the fixed effects and all of the variance components. In the turnip-leaf example, there are three parameters: the intercept term, the variance *Var(LEAF)*, and the residual variance *Var(Error)*. The set of parameter values at which the log-likelihood function attains its maximum value are called the maximum likelihood estimates. The Variance Components procedure adopts an iterative algorithm that combines the rapid convergence property of the Newton-Raphson method with the robustness property of the Fisher scoring method to find the maximum likelihood estimates (robustness against the initial estimate).

Although the complete set of parameters includes the intercept term, its estimate is not displayed. The variance estimates table in Figure 13-6 displays the maximum likelihood estimates for the two variance components.

To produce this output, recall the dialog box and choose:

Options...
   Method
    ⊙ Maximum likelihood
   Display
    ☑ Iteration history

Figure 13-6
Variance estimates

Component	Estimate
Var(LEAF)	5.387E-02
Var(Error)	6.602E-03

The maximum likelihood variance estimates are *Var(LEAF)* = 0.05387 and *Var(Error)* = 0.006602. Comparing with the ANOVA Type I estimates, we find that the two methods give different estimates for *Var(LEAF)*. This difference is expected, primarily because the maximum likelihood method assumes normality in addition to the assumptions required by the ANOVA method.

    Another reason that the maximum likelihood method is sometimes preferred to the ANOVA method is that it readily gives an asymptotic variance-covariance matrix of the variance estimates as a by-product of the iteration procedure. In contrast, the sampling variance-covariance matrix of the ANOVA method estimates is often very difficult to derive.

    The Variance Components procedure always displays the asymptotic covariance matrix table along with the variance estimates table. Using the asymptotic normality property of the maximum likelihood estimators, the asymptotic variance-covariance matrix can be used in establishing confidence intervals and testing hypotheses about the variance components.

Figure 13-7
Asymptotic covariance matrix

	Var(LEAF)	Var(Error)
Var(LEAF)	1.542E-03	-1.816E-06
Var(Error)	-1.816E-06	7.265E-06

Dependent Variable: PCTCA
Method: Maximum Likelihood Estimation

For example, variance for the estimated *Var(LEAF)*, as read from Figure 13-7, is 0.001542. Taking the positive square root of this number gives the standard error for *Var(LEAF)*, which is 0.03927. Thus, an asymptotic 95% confidence interval can be constructed. To calculate the upper 2.5% point of the standard normal distribution, from the Transform menu, choose Compute and enter

$Z = \text{IDF.NORMAL}(0.975, 0, 1)$

The z value, found in the Data Editor, is 1.9600. The confidence interval, then, is

Var(LEAF) $\pm 1.9600 \times$ standard error of Var(LEAF)

Since the estimate of *Var(LEAF)* is 0.05387 and the standard error of *Var(LEAF)* is 0.03927, the asymptotic 95% confidence interval for *Var(LEAF)* is (–0.02310, 0.1308). Often the interval is reported as (0, 0.1308) because *Var(LEAF)* is a non-negative quantity by definition. For more about negative variances, see "Negative Variance Estimates" on p. 124.

Similarly, the asymptotic 95% confidence interval for *Var(Error)* is (0.001319, 0.01188).

You can examine the estimates at various stages of the iteration by requesting the iteration history table. It helps to identify problems when the iteration fails to converge within the maximum number of iterations or is terminated because iteration cannot be continued. For this example, the iteration table (Figure 13-8) does not indicate any problems, and the iteration converged at the seventh iteration with the desired precision.

Figure 13-8
Iteration history

Iteration	Log-likelihood	Var(LEAF)	Var(Error)
0	10.071	7.403E-02	4.952E-03
1	10.319	3.893E-02	6.602E-03
2	10.414	4.785E-02	6.743E-03
3	10.428	5.253E-02	6.632E-03
4	10.429	5.380E-02	6.604E-03
5	10.429	5.387E-02	6.602E-03
6	10.429	5.387E-02	6.602E-03
7	10.429[1]	5.387E-02	6.602E-03

Dependent Variable: PCTCA
Method: Maximum Likelihood Estimation
[1] Convergence achieved.

Negative Variance Estimates

Variances by definition are non-negative quantities. Indeed, you might think that estimates for the variance components are always non-negative; but computationally, the ANOVA method and the minimum normal quadratic unbiased estimation method sometimes produce negative estimates. There is no mechanism in the ANOVA method or the minimum normal quadratic unbiased estimation method that will prevent negative variance estimates from occurring. However, such occurrences do not imply that the computational algorithms are incorrect.

When a negative variance estimate is obtained, an immediate question is: What does a negative variance estimate indicate? There seems to be no definite answer to this question. Such negative variance estimates are associated with the data or the model. Some possible explanations are:

- The variation of observations may be too large for the sample size, producing negative variance estimates even though the true variances are positive. Try to collect more data in the hope that a larger sample size will then yield positive estimates.

- Outliers or erroneously recorded observations are in the data. Identify these observations and handle them appropriately.

- The true value of the variance component may be small or 0. This is usually the case when the negative estimate has a large absolute value. Taking the variance component to be 0 is equivalent to dropping the corresponding random effects from the model.

- The method of estimation is not appropriate. For example, using the ANOVA method on a highly unbalanced data set with empty cells is more likely to produce negative variance estimates. You may want to use the maximum likelihood or the restricted maximum likelihood methods.

- The specified model is not correct. The covariance structure of data assumed under the variance components model may not be appropriate for your data. Sometimes a negative variance estimate indicates that observations in your data are negatively correlated.

The above reasons are some of the common possibilities, and they are in no way exhaustive. Users interested in the problem of negative estimates can find more information in LaMotte (1973) and Hocking (1985). Although it is hard to predict when a negative estimate will occur, one thing is sure—such occurrences lead to some embarrassment: a variance that by definition is non-negative is being estimated as a negative number.

Nested Design Model for Two-Way Classification

A more complicated model can include more than one factor, and the factors can be crossed or nested. Consider the data about test ovens described in Bowker and Lieberman (1972). A quality assurance engineer for an electronics components manufacturing firm claims that the 36 ovens used by this firm for testing the life of the various components are not homogeneous. To determine whether or not the claim can be justified, the engineer conducted an experiment using a single type of electronic component. Three randomly selected ovens were used for the experiment. The electronic component was tested at the two temperatures normally used for life testing of that component. Each component was operated in an oven until it failed. Then the lifetime, in minutes, of the component was recorded. Three components were tested per oven-temperature combination. The original data are shown in Figure 13-9.

Figure 13-9
Lifetimes of electronic components in minutes

Temperature	Oven 1	Oven 2	Oven 3
550°F	237, 254, 246	208, 178, 187	<u>192</u>, 186, 183
600°F	178, 179, <u>183</u>	146, 145, 141	142, 125, 136

Hemmerle and Hartley (1973) deliberately excluded two values (underlined in the above table) in the oven data to introduce a set of unbalanced data. This new set of data is analyzed in this section.

The factor *oven* is clearly a random factor because the three ovens used in the experiment are just a sample of the larger population of 36 ovens. Temperature is also treated as a random factor because 550° F and 600° F were just two of the many temperatures that could be used for testing. Since there is no information on whether or not the ranges of temperature for testing were the same for all of the ovens, we further assume that temperature is nested within oven. Hence, a nested design model is used.

The SPSS data file contains four variables: *oven*, *tempture*, *lifetime*, and *qusehh*, with one case for each lifetime recorded. *Lifetime* is the lifetime of a component that is the dependent variable, *oven* is the oven factor with three levels, *tempture* is the temperature factor with two levels, *tempture(oven)* is the temperature within the oven, and *qusehh* is the SPSS weight variable that is used to exclude the two cases not considered in Hemmerle and Hartley (1973) by assigning zero weights to them and unit weights to all other cases. Using these variables, the nested design model is represented as:

LIFETIME = Constant + OVEN + TEMPTURE(OVEN) + Residual

where both *OVEN* and *TEMPTURE(OVEN)* are random effects.

SPSS offers several methods to estimate the variance components *Var(OVEN)*, *Var(TEMPTURE(OVEN))* and *Var(Error)*. However, not all of them are suitable for unbalanced data; for example, the ANOVA Type I method is not suitable. The minimum norm quadratic unbiased estimation (MINQUE) method is used here because it involves no normality assumption. Without any knowledge of what prior values should be used, estimates using both prior values schemes, MINQUE(0) and MINQUE(1), are computed.

To produce the output, from the menus choose:

Data
 Weight Cases...

⊙ Weight cases by: qusehh

Analyze
 General Linear Model
  Variance Components...

▶ Dependent Variable: lifetime
▶ Random Factor(s): oven tempture

Model...
  ⊙ Custom
  ▶ Model: oven tempture

Options...
  Method:
  ⊙ MINQUE
  Random Effect Priors
  ⊙ Zero

Paste

In the syntax window, at the end of the DESIGN subcommand, type (oven) to specify the nesting effect, TEMPTURE(OVEN). The modified syntax is

```
VARCOMP LIFETIME BY OVEN TEMPTURE
 /RANDOM = OVEN TEMPTURE
 /METHOD = MINQUE(0)
 /DESIGN = OVEN TEMPTURE(OVEN)
 /INTERCEPT = INCLUDE.
```

Run the syntax by clicking the Run Current tool. For MINQUE with the other prior values scheme, change the method to

```
/METHOD = MINQUE(1)
```

and run the syntax again. The results for both methods are shown in Figure 13-10.

Figure 13-10
Variance estimates for the MINQUE(0) and MINQUE(1) methods

Component	Estimate
Var(OVEN)	85.923
Var(TEMPTURE(OVEN))	1940.664
Var(Error)	-157.119[1]

Dependent Variable: LIFETIME
Method: Minimum Norm Quadratic Unbiased Estimation (Weight = 0 for Random Effects, 1 for Residual)

1. For the ANOVA and MINQUE methods, negative variance component estimates may occur. Some possible reasons for their occurrence are: (a) the specified model is not the correct model, or (b) the true value of the variance equals zero.

Component	Estimate
Var(OVEN)	102.839
Var(TEMPTURE(OVEN))	1545.921
Var(Error)	70.067

Dependent Variable: LIFETIME
Method: Minimum Norm Quadratic Unbiased Estimation (Weight = 1 for Random Effects and Residual)

Estimates of the residual variance based on the two prior value schemes contradict each other. In order to decide which scheme gives a more reasonable answer, estimates based on another method are computed. The ANOVA Type III method is used, since Type III sums of squares are suitable for unbalanced data. Also, the ANOVA method does not require any normality assumption. The results are shown in Figure 13-11.

Figure 13-11
Variance estimates for the ANOVA Type III method

Component	Estimate
Var(OVEN)	9.750
Var(TEMPTURE(OVEN))	1475.803
Var(Error)	78.633

Dependent Variable: LIFETIME
Method: ANOVA (Type III Sum of Squares)

The first finding is that the signs of the MINQUE(1) estimates and the ANOVA Type III estimates do agree. Second, values of the corresponding variance estimates are close except that of *Var(OVEN)*. Based on these findings, it seems that the second scheme of prior values is more appropriate than the first scheme for this data.

Based on the MINQUE(1) estimates (using the uniform scheme of prior values) in Figure 13-10, the variability among the ovens is about one and a half times the size of the residual variance, and it contributes

$$102.839/(102.839 + 1545.921 + 70.067) = 5.98\%$$

to the total variance. This result supports the engineer's claim, and efforts should be spent on improving homogeneity of the ovens. Notice that the variance of the temperature-within-oven effect is substantially larger than the residual variance—22 times, to be exact. This effect alone explained

$$1545.921/(102.839 + 1545.921 + 70.067) = 89.94\%$$

of total variance. This strongly suggests that a very significant and important part of the variance of an electronic component's lifetime is attributed to the temperature used for testing.

Univariate Repeated Measures Analysis Using a Mixed Model Approach

A notable property of longitudinal studies and repeated measures experiments is that each subject is observed at several different times (not necessarily equally spaced) or under different experimental conditions. A classical technique is to apply a univariate mixed model to the data (see Winer, Brown, and Michels, 1991). This model assumes that observations from the same subject have a constant variance and a common correlation. In other words, the variance-covariance matrix of observations from each subject exhibits the **compound symmetry** structure. The common correlation is often called the **intra-class correlation**. In this example, we show how to estimate this intra-class correlation using the Variance Components procedure.

A study was designed to investigate whether boys and girls have different growth rates. Using the distance, in millimeters, from the center of the pituitary to the pteryo-maxillary fissure as a measure of growth, data were collected from each of 11 girls and 16 boys at ages 8, 10, 12 and 14 by investigators at the University of North Carolina Dental School. Occasionally, this distance decreases with age because the distance represents the relative position of two points. The data appeared in Potthoff and Roy

(1964) and were again analyzed by Jennrich and Schluchter (1986). The complete data are shown in Figure 13-12.

Figure 13-12
Data for growth study

		Girl				Boy			
		8	10	12	14	8	10	12	14
Distance (mm) from center of pituitary to pteryo-maxillary fissure	1	21.0	20.0	21.5	23.0	26.0	25.0	29.0	31.0
	2	21.0	21.5	24.0	25.5	21.5	22.5	23.0	26.5
	3	20.5	24.0	24.5	26.0	23.0	22.5	24.0	27.5
	4	23.5	24.5	25.0	26.5	25.5	27.5	26.5	27.0
	5	21.5	23.0	22.5	23.5	20.0	23.5	22.5	26.0
	6	20.0	21.0	21.0	22.5	24.5	25.5	27.0	28.5
	7	21.5	22.5	23.0	25.0	22.0	22.0	24.5	26.5
	8	23.0	23.0	23.5	24.0	24.0	21.5	24.5	25.5
	9	20.0	21.0	22.0	21.5	23.0	20.5	31.0	26.0
	10	16.5	19.0	19.0	19.5	27.5	28.0	31.0	31.5
	11	24.5	25.0	28.0	28.0	23.0	23.0	23.5	25.0
	12	.	.	.	.	21.5	23.5	24.0	28.0
	13	.	.	.	.	17.0	24.5	26.0	29.5
	14	.	.	.	.	22.5	25.5	25.5	26.0
	15	.	.	.	.	23.0	24.5	26.0	30.0
	16	.	.	.	.	22.0	21.5	23.5	25.0

You may need to rearrange data so that it is most convenient to specify a univariate mixed model using SPSS. In this example, a categorical variable named *subject* is created to give each individual a unique identification. Girls 1 to 11 in Figure 13-12 are assigned subject values 1 to 11. Boys 1 to 16 are assigned values 12 to 27. A second categorical variable called *age* is created with four levels that correspond to the four ages (8, 10, 12, and 14). A third categorical variable called *gender* uses the characters *F* for female and *M* for male. Finally, *distance* is the dependent variable. There is one case for each distance.

Using repeated measures terminology, *gender* is a between-subjects factor and *age* is a within-subjects factor because each subject is observed at these four ages. Both *gender* and *age* are fixed factors. The variable *subject,* on the other hand, is a random factor because its levels are arbitrarily chosen solely for identification purpose.

The following design uses a common technique (for example, see Winer, Brown, and Michels, 1991) to formulate a repeated measures analysis as a mixed model:

DISTANCE = Constant + GENDER + SUBJECT(GENDER) + AGE
+ AGE*GENDER + Residual

with the effect *SUBJECT(GENDER)* being random. The corresponding mathematical model is:

$$d_{ijk} = \mu + g_i + s_{k(i)} + a_j + (ag)_{ij} + e_{ijk}$$

$$k = 1, ..., n_i, j = 1, 2, 3, 4 \text{ and } i = 1, 2$$

where $n_1 = 11$, $n_2 = 16$, d_{ijk} is the distance of the kth individual observed for the ith level of *gender* and the jth level of *age*, and g_i is the fixed-effect parameter corresponding to the ith level of *gender*. Similarly, a_j and $(ag)_{ij}$ are the fixed-effect parameters that correspond respectively to the jth level of *age* and the (i,j)th level of the interaction effect *age*gender*. $s_{k(i)}$ is a random-effect parameter that corresponds to the kth individual within the ith level of *gender*, and e_{ijk} is the residual. The usual assumptions are: $s_{k(i)}$ are uncorrelated, each has zero mean and variance σ_s^2, and the residuals are also uncorrelated, while each has zero mean and variance σ_e^2. Furthermore, the random-effect parameters and the residuals are uncorrelated also.

Consider, for example, the distance observed from the first boy at age 10 (that is, d_{221}). It follows from the above distributional assumptions that the variance of this observation is $\sigma_s^2 + \sigma_e^2$. Next consider the distance observed from the same boy at age 14 (that is, d_{241}). Its variance also equals $\sigma_s^2 + \sigma_e^2$. The covariance between these two distances is σ_s^2 because the two corresponding residuals are uncorrelated. In general, all distances observed from any boy or girl have equal variances and the common value is $\sigma_s^2 + \sigma_e^2$. Also, the covariance between any two distances observed at two different ages is equal to σ_s^2. Therefore, the correlation between any two distances observed at two different ages is the same. The common correlation value is called the intra-class correlation. In this example, it is equal to $\sigma_s^2 / (\sigma_s^2 + \sigma_e^2)$. Since both the numerator and the denominator are positive, the intra-class correlation is also positive.

All estimation methods except the maximum likelihood method give the same variance component estimates. For purposes of illustration, only estimates based on the maximum likelihood method and those based on the restricted maximum likelihood method are displayed here. In order to obtain maximum precision, the tables are edited and up to eight decimal points are shown.

To produce the output, from the menus choose:

Analyze
  General Linear Model
    Variance Components...

Dependent Variable: distance
Fixed Factor(s): gender age
Random Factor(s): subject

Model...
  ⊙ Custom
  Model: gender age subject age*gender

Options...
  Method
  ⊙ Maximum likelihood
  Display
  ☑ Iteration history

Paste

After you paste the syntax, indicate nesting by adding (**gender**) after subject. The modified syntax is

```
VARCOMP distance  BY gender age  subject
 /RANDOM = subject
 /METHOD = ML
 /CRITERIA = ITERATE(50)
 /CRITERIA = CONVERGE(1.0E-8)
 /PRINT = HISTORY (1)
 /DESIGN = gender subject(gender) age age*gender
 /INTERCEPT = INCLUDE .
```

 Double-click the variance estimates table, highlight the cells containing numbers, and change the format (Cell Properties) to eight decimal places. You may need to drag the right boundary of the cells to display this larger number of decimal places.

Change the method to REML and run the command again. The variance estimates are shown in Figure 13-13 and Figure 13-14.

Figure 13-13
Variance estimates for ML

Component	Estimate
Var(SUBJECT(GENDER))	3.04202616
Var(Error)	1.82873878

Dependent Variable: DISTANCE
Method: Maximum Likelihood Estimation

Figure 13-14

Variance estimates for REML

Component	Estimate
Var(SUBJECT(GENDER))	3.28538826
Var(Error)	1.97503788

Dependent Variable: DISTANCE
Method: Restricted Maximum Likelihood Estimation

Based on the maximum likelihood estimates, the estimate for intra-class correlation is

$$\rho = \frac{3.04202616}{(3.04202616 + 1.82873878)} = 0.62454793$$

whereas the correlation estimate based on the restricted maximum likelihood estimates is

$$\rho = \frac{3.28538826}{(3.28538826 + 1.97503788)} = 0.62454793$$

Although the variance component estimates are different, the two intra-class correlation estimates are surprisingly close (up to eight decimal points). In order to compute the asymptotic standard errors for these two correlation estimates, you need the asymptotic variance-covariance matrices for the variance component estimates. They are shown in Figure 13-15 and Figure 13-16.

Figure 13-15

Asymptotic covariance matrix for ML

	Var(SUBJECT(GENDER))	Var(Error)
Var(SUBJECT(GENDER))	.91215920	-.02064374
Var(Error)	-.02064374	.08257495

Dependent Variable: DISTANCE
Method: Maximum Likelihood Estimation

Figure 13-16

Asymptotic covariance matrix for REML

	Var(SUBJECT(GENDER))	Var(Error)
Var(SUBJECT(GENDER))	1.14905789	-.02600516
Var(Error)	-.02600516	.10402066

Dependent Variable: DISTANCE
Method: Restricted Maximum Likelihood Estimation

Using the delta method (see Johnson, Kotz, and Kemp, 1992), the variance of the intra-class correlation is approximated by

$$\mathrm{var}(\rho) = \mathrm{var}(\sigma_s^2/(\sigma_s^2 + \sigma_e^2))$$

$$= (\sigma_e^4 \mathrm{var}(\sigma_s^2) + \sigma_s^4 \mathrm{var}(\sigma_e^2) - 2\sigma_s^2\sigma_e^2 \mathrm{cov}(\sigma_s^2, \sigma_e^2))/(\sigma_s^2 + \sigma_e^2)^4$$

With the maximum likelihood method,

$$\mathrm{var}(\sigma_s^2) = 0.91215920, \ \mathrm{var}(\sigma_e^2) = 0.08257495 \ \text{and}$$

$$\mathrm{cov}(\sigma_s^2, \sigma_e^2) = -0.02064374$$

The approximate variance of the intra-class correlation is

$$\mathrm{var}(\rho) \approx \frac{\left(1.82873878^2 \times 0.91215920 + 3.04202616^2 \times 0.08257495 - 2 \times 3.04202616 \times 1.82873878 \times (-0.02064374)\right)}{\left(3.04202616 + 1.82873878\right)^4}$$

$$= \ 0.00718555$$

Taking the square root of $\mathrm{var}(\rho)$ gives the standard error of the intra-class correlation. Based on the maximum likelihood estimates, the standard error equals 0.08476761.

Since the maximum likelihood variance estimates are asymptotically normally distributed, it follows that the intra-class correlation is also asymptotically normal. Thus, you can compute an asymptotic 95% confidence interval for this intra-class correlation as $\rho \pm Z_{0.025} \times \mathrm{se}(\rho)$ where Z is the upper 2.5% point of the standard normal distribution. From the Transform menu, choose Compute and enter

$$Z_{0.025} = \text{IDF.NORMAL}(0.975, 0, 1)$$

The $Z_{0.025}$ value is 1.95996400. Hence, the asymptotic 95% confidence interval is (0.45840647, 0.79068939).

Similarly, based on the restricted maximum likelihood variance estimates, the standard error of the intra-class correlation is 0.08809308. The asymptotic 95% confidence interval for the intra-class correlation is (0.45188866, 0.79720720). Although both the maximum likelihood and the restricted maximum likelihood methods give very close estimates for the intra-class correlation, the maximum likelihood method does produce a narrower confidence interval.

For an intra-class correlation estimate based on the ANOVA method, see Searle, Casella and McCulloch (1992).

Background Information

The following sections include technical background information about variance components models and the types of estimation methods. For readers who are interested in a thorough discussion of this subject, see Rao and Kleffe (1988) and Searle, Casella, and McCulloch (1992).

Model

A variance components model analyzes the contribution of each random effect to the total variation in each cross-classification category. Each cross-classification constitutes a cell and each categorical variable is called a factor. A variance components model formulates the value of the dependent variable in each cell as the sum of a linear combination of parameters and a residual error term. The parameters are identified by association with the categorical variables and the covariates in the model. The parameters are then classified into fixed-effects parameters and random-effects parameters. The classification is based on the nature (fixed or random) of the effects with which the parameters are associated. The residual error term is assumed to have a zero mean and a constant variance across all the cells. The mathematical model for the observed value of the dependent variable in a cell is given by

$$y_{ik} = \mathbf{x}_{io}\beta_o + \sum_{s=1}^{m} \mathbf{x}_{is}\beta_s + \varepsilon_{ik}, \qquad k = 1,\dots,n_i \text{ and } i = 1,\dots,r$$

where y_{ik} is the kth repetition within the ith cell, x_{io} is the portion of the ith row of the design matrix associated with the fixed effects, β_o is the vector of fixed-effects parameters, $\mathbf{x}_{is}$ is the portion of the ith row of the design matrix associated with the sth random effect, β_s is the vector of the sth random-effect parameters, ε_{ik} is the residual error associated with the value y_{ik}, n_i is the number of repetitions within the ith cell, m is the number of random effects, and r is the number of cells.

When there are no random effects (that is, $m = 0$) this equation corresponds to a general linear model with fixed effects only.

Distribution Assumptions

Various assumptions are made when you use variance components analysis.

Random Effects

Under a variance components model, the vectors $\beta_1, \ldots, \beta_m$ are random vectors. In other words, elements of these vectors are random variables. Therefore, these random vectors have their expected values and variance-covariance matrices.

For the sth random effect:

- Each element of the vector β_s has zero expected value.

- Variances of the elements of the vector β_s are the same. Denote the common variance as σ_s^2.

- Elements of the vector β_s are uncorrelated. In other words, covariance between *any* two elements is 0.

It is further assumed that the random vectors $\beta_1, \ldots, \beta_m$ are mutually uncorrelated. Thus, covariance between an element from a random vector and an element from a different random vector is always 0.

Residual Error Term

It is often assumed that:

- The residual error term has zero expectation and constant variance across all cells. Denote the constant variance as σ_ε^2.

- The residuals from different cells are uncorrelated.

- The residual error term is uncorrelated with all elements of the random-effect vectors.

Variance Decomposition

With the above assumptions, the total variance of an observation in the ith cell is

$$\text{var}(y_{ik}) = \sum_{s=1}^{m} \sigma_s^2 \|\mathbf{x}_{is}\|^2 + \sigma_\varepsilon^2, \quad k = 1, ..., n_i \text{ and } i = 1, ..., r$$

where $\|\mathbf{x}_{is}\|^2$ is the sum of squares of all elements of the row vector $\mathbf{x}_{is}$. Hence the data variance is decomposed into a weighted sum of the variances of the random effects and the residual variance. Variance of a random effect is called a **variance component**.

A logical conclusion from the above assumptions is that observations in a variance components model are correlated. This correlation clearly distinguishes between a variance components model and a general linear model. Because the observations are correlated, special estimation methods are used to estimate the variance components.

Estimation Methods

The following four estimation methods are available in the Variance Components procedure:

■ ANOVA

■ Minimum norm quadratic unbiased estimation (MINQUE)

■ Maximum likelihood (ML)

■ Restricted maximum likelihood (REML)

ANOVA Method

The ANOVA method first computes sums of squares and expected mean squares for all effects following the general linear model approach. Then a system of linear equations is established by equating the sums of squares of the random effects to their expected mean squares. The variables in the equations are the variance components and the residual variance. Any solution, if one exists, to this system of linear equations constitutes a set of estimates for the variance components.

This method is computationally less laborious and the estimates are statistically unbiased. However, negative variance estimates can happen and the variance-covariance matrix of the estimates is difficult to obtain even asymptotically.

The Variance Components procedure offers two types of sums of squares: Type I and Type III. For detailed descriptions of these two types of sums of squares, see Chapter 3. A discussion of choosing the appropriate type can be found in Speed (1979).

MINQUE Method

The MINQUE method requires a set of *a priori* values for the variance components or the ratios of the components to the residual variance. The estimators are then functions of the data and of the prior values. When the prior values are proportional to the true but unknown values of each variance component (or ratios of each component to the residual variance), the estimates achieve minimum variance in the class of all unbiased, translation invariant quadratic estimators. Since the variance components are unknown, the correct prior values are seldom found. Therefore, the estimators are unlikely to possess the above optimal properties in reality. Despite this fact, the MINQUE method is popular because of its considerable flexibility with respect to the form of models that can be fitted. For a summary of the method, see Rao (1973). For an in-depth discussion of the method, see Rao and Kleffe (1988).

The Variance Components procedure offers two schemes of prior values. The first scheme, MINQUE(0), assigns zero prior values to ratios of variance components to the residual variance. The second scheme, MINQUE(1), gives the ratios unit prior values. With either scheme, a system of linear equations is established based on the prior values and the data. The variables are the ratios of the variance components to the residual variance, and the residual variance itself. The system of linear equations is then solved to obtain the MINQUE estimates. Details of the estimation procedure can be found in Giesbrecht (1983).

Maximum Likelihood Method

The maximum likelihood method finds a set of values, called the maximum likelihood estimates, at which the log-likelihood function attains its local maximum. The estimators are the fixed-effects parameters, the variance components, and the residual variance. The maximum likelihood estimates are obtained by an iterative procedure that uses both the Newton-Raphson method and the Fisher scoring method. Although the fixed-effects parameters are part of the estimators, their values are not displayed. As a by-product of the iterative procedure, the asymptotic variance-covariance matrix of the variance component estimates are also obtained.

For technical details of computing the maximum likelihood estimates, see Hemmerle and Hartley (1973), Jennrich and Sampson (1976), and Searle, Casella and McCulloch (1992).

Restricted Maximum Likelihood Method

The restricted maximum likelihood method is basically the same as the maximum likelihood method except for one difference: the restricted maximum likelihood method takes into account the degrees of freedom used for estimating fixed effects when estimating variance components, while the maximum likelihood method does not. Instead of using the original data vector, the restricted maximum likelihood method operates on linear combinations of the observations, chosen in such a way that those combinations are invariant to the values of the fixed-effect parameters. These linear combinations turn out to be equivalent to residuals calculated after fitting by ordinary least squares (weighted least squares if a regression weight is specified) only the fixed effects part of the model. Thus, the method performs maximization over a restricted vector space.

For balanced data, the restricted maximum likelihood estimates are identical to the ANOVA estimates, although their variance-covariance matrices are different. Because of this property, the restricted maximum likelihood method is preferred to the maximum likelihood method for balanced data. Also, computational burdens are smaller for the restricted maximum likelihood method, since it maximized with respect to a smaller number of variables.

For more information about this method, see Patterson and Thompson (1971), Corbeil and Searle (1976), and Searle, Casella and McCulloch (1992).

Model Selection
Loglinear Analysis Examples

When examining the relationship between two categorical variables, the straightforward approach, familiar to most researchers, is to construct a contingency table and compute the appropriate chi-square statistic to test the hypothesis of independence. But what happens when you have more than two categorical variables? One approach would be to construct a series of two-way tables and compute corresponding chi-square statistics for each one. However, this strategy is flawed in the sense that results will be confounded by interactions between variables. Interpretation also becomes more difficult as the number of variables increases. The ideal solution would allow you to examine the relationships among all of the variables simultaneously, including interactions among groups of variables.

The Loglinear Model

By using a structured kind of model called a **loglinear model**, we can do just that. Loglinear models attempt to predict cell frequencies based on values of the categorical variables in the model. It is analogous to factorial ANOVA in that it allows you to partition variance in your cell frequencies into subsets attributable to main effects and interaction effects of the variables of interest.

Figure 14-1
Exposure and sickness

		Exposed to event?		
		No	Yes	
Got sick?	No	A	B	P
	Yes	C	D	Q
		R	S	N

For example, let's assume that we're investigating the relationship between exposure to a traumatic event and sickness. Given the contingency table shown in Figure 14-1, we can build a model of the cell frequencies (which we can call F), including a parameter θ, representing the overall sample size (this corresponds to the "grand mean" in ANOVA), a parameter λ_x, representing the effect of exposure to the event (X), a parameter λ_y for the effect of getting sick (Y), and a parameter λ_{xy} for the joint effect of being exposed to the event *and* getting sick (the interaction term):

$$\ln F = \theta + \lambda_x + \lambda_y + \lambda_{xy}$$

This gives us a linear model, which allows us to compute values for the parameters. Using this model allows us to isolate effects of each of the variables from each other and from their combined effect. (The natural log of cell frequency is used to simplify both computation and interpretation of parameter estimates.)

Notice that in this model there are four parameters (θ and the three λ parameters), and there are four cell frequencies to be estimated (A, B, C, and D). Because there are as many parameters as there are values to be estimated, this model will always reproduce the original contingency table values perfectly. Models such as this, which include all possible effects of individual variables and combinations of variables, are called **saturated models**.

It is also possible to analyze a particular contingency table with a model that omits one or more possible effects. For example, we could use the following model for Figure 14-1:

$$\ln F = \theta + \lambda_x + \lambda_y$$

Notice that this model does not include the interaction term. That is, it assumes that exposure and sickness do *not* have a joint influence on cell frequency. Notice also that the model contains only three parameters but is still used to estimate four values (the cell frequencies). Because of this, unless exposure and sickness are perfectly independent, there will be some discrepancies between the estimated values we get from the model and the observed values. We can measure these discrepancies and determine whether the model estimates are significantly different from the observed values. If we have a good model, the estimates will be close to the observed values.

There are three procedures in SPSS for handling loglinear models: General Loglinear Analysis, Model Selection Loglinear Analysis, and Logit Loglinear Analysis. Use General Loglinear Analysis if you have a specific model with specific effects in mind that you want to test. Use Model Selection Loglinear Analysis if you need to explore many possible models to determine the best model to use for your data.

Use Logit Loglinear Analysis if you have one variable in your set that you want to define as a dependent variable (outcome) to be predicted based on the other variables.

The Likelihood-Ratio Chi-Square

To test the discrepancy between an unsaturated model and the data we are modeling, we use the **likelihood-ratio chi-square** instead of the traditional Pearson chi-square. It is computed using the following formula:

$$G^2 = 2\sum_i O_i \ln\left(\frac{O_i}{E_i}\right)$$

where O_i is the observed frequency for cell i and E_i is the expected frequency for cell i. The likelihood-ratio chi-square statistic has the desirable property that it is additive, in the same sense that sums of squares in simple ANOVA are additive—the sum of the chi-square values for the individual effects in the model equals the chi-square for the total model. Therefore, if you take the difference between two likelihood-ratio chi-square statistics for related models, the result is another likelihood-ratio chi-square statistic. This property allows you to make two important inferences in your analysis: you can *compare nested models,* and you can *assess individual effects.*

Nested Models

One model is said to be nested within another model if the effects in the nested model are a subset of the effects in the more complex model. For example, the model

$$\ln F = \theta + \lambda_x + \lambda_y \qquad\qquad \text{Equation 14-1}$$

is nested within the model

$$\ln F = \theta + \lambda_x + \lambda_y + \lambda_{xy} \qquad\qquad \text{Equation 14-2}$$

Notice that all of the effects in Equation 14-1, plus the interaction term, are included in Equation 14-2. By computing likelihood-ratio chi-square statistics for each of these models and then taking the difference, we get another likelihood-ratio chi-square statistic that tests the relative advantage of the more complex model (Equation 14-2) over the simpler model (Equation 14-1) in predicting cell frequencies. If the resulting value is not statistically significant, we can conclude that the models are equivalent in their predictive ability. In such cases, we would usually choose the simpler model (that is, the more parsimonious model) that still explains the observed data.

Individual Effects

Each model is an attempt to capture the variability of cell frequencies in terms of the variables involved. The total variability of cell frequencies can be measured by the difference in likelihood-ratio chi-squares for the full model and a baseline model. This baseline model assumes that no effects are present, and cases are expected to be evenly distributed across all cells of the contingency table. The complete independence model is given by the following equation:

$$\ln F = \theta$$

where θ is simply the natural log of the average number of cases per cell.

The total variability, as measured by the likelihood-ratio chi-square, can be partitioned into effect variance in a manner similar to the partitioning of the sum of squares in ANOVA. As explained above, taking the difference between the likelihood-ratio chi-square values for two nested models allows you to test how much better the saturated model (Equation 14-2) fits the data than the simpler model (Equation 14-1). This can also be thought of as a test of the contribution of the interaction term, λ_{xy}, to the model. In fact, all of the effects in the model can be tested this way, each in turn, to give a relative index of each effect's contribution to the model. In each case, the nested model omitting the effect of interest is compared to the model including that effect (but no higher-level interactions) to compute a likelihood-ratio chi-square, called the **partial chi-square** (see Figure 14-2). This statistic can be used as an indicator of the relative importance of each effect, and it can also be used to test the hypothesis that the effect is 0.

Figure 14-2
Testing effects

To test this effect:	Compare this model...	To this model
λ_x	$\ln F = \theta + \lambda_y$	$\ln F = \theta + \lambda_x + \lambda_y$
λ_y	$\ln F = \theta + \lambda_x$	$\ln F = \theta + \lambda_x + \lambda_y$
λ_{xy}	$\ln F = \theta + \lambda_x + \lambda_y$	$\ln F = \theta + \lambda_x + \lambda_y + \lambda_{xy}$

Note that this strategy can be generalized to test effects within unsaturated models as well. For example, in the model given in Equation 14-1, there are two effects that can be tested: the effect of X is tested by comparing the model $\ln F = \theta + \lambda_y$ to the baseline (Equation 14-1), and the effect of Y is tested by comparing the model $\ln F = \theta + \lambda_x$ to the baseline.

Hierarchical Model Selection

As Einstein said, "Things should be made as simple as possible, but no simpler." If we include only the main effects and exclude any interactions among variables, we risk overlooking some important effects, and our model probably won't fit the data very well. On the other hand, if we include every possible effect and interaction, we will have a complicated model with as many parameters as there are table cells. Thus, we will not have simplified anything. Sometimes it can be difficult to find the right compromise between the two extremes. A strategy of testing a series of nested models can help you identify the appropriate amount of complexity for your model. The strategy is based on sequentially considering orders of complexity to select the simplest model that provides reasonable prediction of cell frequencies. Suppose that we have three categorical variables, X, Y, and Z. There are three orders of complexity involved: the main effects (simplest), the two-way interactions (more complex), and the three-way interaction (most complex). We can start with the most complex model, the saturated model:

$$\ln F = \theta + \lambda_x + \lambda_y + \lambda_z + \lambda_{xy} + \lambda_{xz} + \lambda_{yz} + \lambda_{xyz}$$

and then compare this third-order model with the second-order model:

$$\ln F = \theta + \lambda_x + \lambda_y + \lambda_z + \lambda_{xy} + \lambda_{xz} + \lambda_{yz}$$

which, in turn, is compared to the first-order model:

$$\ln F = \theta + \lambda_x + \lambda_y + \lambda_z$$

which is finally compared to the zero-order model:

$$\ln F = \theta$$

At each stage, we assess the change in fit, using the likelihood-ratio chi-square. If the change is not significant, then we conclude that we can simplify the model at that level without sacrificing much predictive ability, and we proceed to the next stage. We continue through the levels until the change is significant; this tells us that we have found the point of "diminishing returns"—the point at which the loss of predictive power becomes too large to ignore.

Notice that if a higher-level effect is in the model, then the corresponding lower-level effects are also in the model. That is, with three variables X, Y, and Z, if λ_{xy} is in the model, then λ_x and λ_y are also in the model (although λ_z may or may not be). Models that meet this requirement are called **hierarchical loglinear models**. For models that operate under this constraint, we can identify a model simply by specifying the effects at the highest level of complexity at which they appear. For example, if we specify that λ_{xy} is included in the model, then we know that λ_x and λ_y are also included. Thus, we can abbreviate this model using the shorthand $X*Y$. This specification is called the **generating class** of the model. Figure 14-3 shows some more examples of generating classes and the corresponding models.

Figure 14-3
Generating classes and corresponding models

Generating Class	Model
X,Y	$\ln F = \theta + \lambda_x + \lambda_y$
X*Y,Z	$\ln F = \theta + \lambda_x + \lambda_y + \lambda_z + \lambda_{xy}$
X*Y*Z	$\ln F = \theta + \lambda_x + \lambda_y + \lambda_z + \lambda_{xy} + \lambda_{xz} + \lambda_{yz} + \lambda_{xyz}$
X*Y, X*Z	$\ln F = \theta + \lambda_x + \lambda_y + \lambda_z + \lambda_{xy} + \lambda_{xz}$

The Model Selection Loglinear procedure can analyze only hierarchical models. If you need to analyze nonhierarchical models, use the General Loglinear procedure.

Strategy for Using Model Selection

In an ideal world, you would have specific expectations about relationships among your variables, based on theory or prior research. However, in many situations, you may not have such bases for developing specific hypotheses about your data. In such cases, you must take an exploratory approach to finding an appropriate model for your data. Model Selection Loglinear Analysis is designed to help you explore a range of models in an organized fashion in order to find a model that maximizes predictive ability while minimizing model complexity. Here is a useful approach to exploring relationships in your categorical data:

- Select your variables carefully. Don't just include everything—include only the variables that will be most interesting or useful.

- Identify a specific model using Model Selection Loglinear Analysis. Use this procedure to find the appropriate level of complexity for your model and to identify which effects should be included and which should be excluded.

- Test the resulting model using the General Loglinear Model procedure. This procedure lets you test a specific model more thoroughly (for example, by printing parameter estimates for unsaturated models) and allows you to save residuals and predicted values as new variables for further analysis.

Example 1: Examining a saturated model. This is a model of the relationships among exposure to a traumatic event, health, and gender. The saturated model is used to examine the relationships and interactions among these variables.

Example 2: Using backward elimination to select a suitable model. A method using automatic elimination of extraneous effects is demonstrated here. We examine the same set of variables, with the goal of reducing the complexity of the model without sacrificing predictive validity.

Example 1
Examining a Saturated Model

Is it true that exposure to a traumatic event can cause adverse effects on health? Are there differences in this effect between males and females? In this first example, we will look at a saturated model of the relationships among these variables.

The variables involved were measured as follows (all variables are based on responses to questionnaire items):

Exposure to traumatic event. The event studied was a crowd accident at a college football stadium. Students trying to rush onto the field after a football game were crushed against a metal gate by the mass of the crowd, causing difficulty in breathing and injury in some students. Each student was assigned to one of four categories:

- Control (coded as 1): The student was not at the football game and was not exposed to the event at all.

- Witness (coded as 2): The student was at the football game and witnessed the event but was not directly involved.

- Non-injured (coded as 3): The student was involved in the crush (was part of the crowd moving toward the gate) but was not injured.

- Injured (coded as 4): The student was in the crowd and was injured as a result of the crush.

Gender. Student gender was recorded as *Male* (coded as 0) or *Female* (coded as 1).

Health effect. This was assessed by asking students to indicate the number of colds they had experienced in the two months following the stadium incident. The assumption is that an adverse impact on health will be reflected in an increased number of colds reported. The variable is coded as zero colds in the last two months, one cold, two colds, or three or more colds (coded as 0, 1, 2, or 3, respectively).

Notice that the variables are coded numerically. All variables used in the Model Selection Loglinear Analysis procedure must be coded numerically. If you have string variables that you want to use in this procedure, you will need to recode them using Recode or Automatic Recode (on the Transform menu) before you begin your model selection loglinear analysis.

To produce this output, from the menus choose:

Analyze
  Loglinear
    Model Selection...

Click Reset to restore dialog box defaults, and then select:

▶ Factor(s): group, ncold, sex
    Define Range for each variable

⊙ Enter in single step

Model...
    ⊙ Saturated

Options...
    Display for Saturated Model
    ☑ Parameter estimates
    ☑ Association table
    Model Criteria
    Delta: 0

The first table presented in the output (Figure 14-4) is the table of observed and expected frequencies for all cells. Because this is a saturated model, the observed and expected values are equal, and residuals are all equal to 0.

Figure 14-4
Observed and expected frequencies and residuals

Factor	Code	OBS count	EXP count	Residual	Std Resid
GROUP	CONTROL				
NCOLD	0				
SEX	MALE	18.0	18.0	.00	.00
SEX	FEMALE	29.0	29.0	.00	.00
NCOLD	1				
SEX	MALE	43.0	43.0	.00	.00
SEX	FEMALE	70.0	70.0	.00	.00
NCOLD	2				
SEX	MALE	19.0	19.0	.00	.00
SEX	FEMALE	37.0	37.0	.00	.00
NCOLD	3				
SEX	MALE	12.0	12.0	.00	.00
SEX	FEMALE	32.0	32.0	.00	.00
GROUP	WITNESS				
NCOLD	0				
SEX	MALE	14.0	14.0	.00	.00
SEX	FEMALE	15.0	15.0	.00	.00
NCOLD	1				
SEX	MALE	20.0	20.0	.00	.00
SEX	FEMALE	34.0	34.0	.00	.00
NCOLD	2				
SEX	MALE	15.0	15.0	.00	.00
SEX	FEMALE	16.0	16.0	.00	.00
NCOLD	3				
SEX	MALE	7.0	7.0	.00	.00
SEX	FEMALE	13.0	13.0	.00	.00
GROUP	NON-INJU				
NCOLD	0				
SEX	MALE	17.0	17.0	.00	.00
SEX	FEMALE	2.0	2.0	.00	.00
NCOLD	1				
SEX	MALE	33.0	33.0	.00	.00
SEX	FEMALE	19.0	19.0	.00	.00
NCOLD	2				
SEX	MALE	22.0	22.0	.00	.00
SEX	FEMALE	19.0	19.0	.00	.00
NCOLD	3				
SEX	MALE	7.0	7.0	.00	.00
SEX	FEMALE	6.0	6.0	.00	.00
GROUP	INJURED				
NCOLD	0				
SEX	MALE	1.0	1.0	.00	.00
SEX	FEMALE	7.0	7.0	.00	.00
NCOLD	1				
SEX	MALE	4.0	4.0	.00	.00
SEX	FEMALE	8.0	8.0	.00	.00
NCOLD	2				
SEX	MALE	5.0	5.0	.00	.00
SEX	FEMALE	8.0	8.0	.00	.00
NCOLD	3				
SEX	MALE	3.0	3.0	.00	.00
SEX	FEMALE	2.0	2.0	.00	.00

Following the observed and expected frequencies and residuals are the goodness-of-fit statistics. Again, because this is a saturated model, the chi-square fit statistics equal 0, indicating perfect fit.

Figure 14-5
Goodness-of-fit test statistics

```
Likelihood ratio chi square =     .00000   DF = 0  P = 1.000
            Pearson chi square =     .00000   DF = 0  P = 1.000
```

The next table helps us assess the level of complexity required in our model. It tests the hypothesis that the k-way and higher-order effects are 0. We can see that the third-order effect ($X*Y*Z$) is not significantly different from 0 at the 5% level ($G^2 = 12.999$, $p = 0.1626$) and thus could be omitted from the model without unduly reducing model fit. The second-order effects ($X*Y$, $X*Z$, and $Y*Z$) and first-order effects (X, Y, and Z), however, appear to be significantly different from 0, so we must keep these levels in order to maintain model fit.

Figure 14-6
Tests that k-way and higher-order effects are 0

K	DF	L.R. Chisq	Prob	Pearson Chisq	Prob	Iteration
3	9	12.999	.1626	12.121	.2066	3
2	24	55.247	.0003	51.335	.0010	2
1	31	343.028	.0000	384.788	.0000	0

The next table reports the contribution of each order of effect by itself, as opposed to the previous table, which tests the contribution of all levels at or above the level being tested. For our example, the statistics reported for the second-order effects in Figure 14-6 test whether the model is still accurate, omitting both second- and third-order effects. In Figure 14-7, the statistics given for second-order effects consider the second-order effects by themselves. This can be seen clearly by noting that the sum of G^2 values for the second-order and third-order effects equals the G^2 for the second-order effects from the previous table (within rounding error): 42.247 + 12.999 = 55.246.

Figure 14-7
Tests that k-way effects are 0

K	DF	L.R. Chisq	Prob	Pearson Chisq	Prob	Iteration
1	7	287.781	.0000	333.453	.0000	0
2	15	42.247	.0002	39.214	.0006	0
3	9	12.999	.1626	12.121	.2066	0

Partial associations allow you to test the significance of each individual effect in the model. There is a term for each effect in the model, giving the degrees of freedom, the partial chi-square, the probability associated with the chi-square, and the number of iterations required to solve for the partial association. In general, terms with partial associations that do not differ from 0 (that is, that have a nonsignificant partial chi-square) can be omitted from the model without sacrificing too much predictive accuracy. In this case, it seems that the *GROUP*NCOLDS* interaction and the *SEX*NCOLDS* interaction could safely be omitted from the model.

Figure 14-8
Tests of partial associations

Tests of PARTIAL associations.

Effect Name	DF	Partial Chisq	Prob	Iter
GROUP*NCOLD	9	10.806	.2893	2
GROUP*SEX	3	28.033	.0000	2
NCOLD*SEX	3	3.147	.3696	2
GROUP	3	188.705	.0000	2
NCOLD	3	88.398	.0000	2
SEX	1	10.679	.0011	2

The last section of output reports the parameter estimates for the saturated model. (An excerpt is shown in Figure 14-9.) Each coefficient is reported, along with its standard error, z value, and confidence interval. The parameters are reported as follows:

- For main effects, there will be $k - 1$ parameters, where k is the number of categories for the main effect in question. In our example, the *GROUP* effect has three parameters $(4 - 1)$. They are numbered starting with the first category and ending with the next to the last category. The last category is redundant because of the constraint that the sum of the parameter estimates for a particular effect must equal 1.

- For interaction effects, there will be $(k_1 - 1) \times (k_2 - 1) \times \ldots \times (k_n - 1)$ parameters, where $k_1 \ldots k_n$ are the number of categories for variables $1 \ldots n$. In this example, for the *GROUP*NCOLD*SEX* interaction, there are

$(4 - 1) \times (4 - 1) \times (2 - 1) = 9$ parameters. As with main effects, the last category of each variable is redundant and is omitted from the parameters table. Parameters are labeled based on the order of categories in each variable involved in the interaction, with categories in the last variable cycling the fastest and those for the first variable cycling slowest. See Figure 14-10 for an example from the current data set for the three-way interaction *GROUP*NCOLD*SEX*. (Don't be confused by the fact that the last variable, *SEX*, has the value *Male* for all parameters; this is because the variable has only two values, so one of them is redundant and only the first category is used.)

Figure 14-9
Estimates for parameters

GROUP*NCOLD*SEX

```
Parameter      Coeff.     Std. Err.      Z-Value Lower 95 CI Upper 95 CI

       1    .0192792161       .16651       .11579    -.30707      .34563
       2    .1149988198       .11772       .97690    -.11573      .34573
       3    .0123338705       .13014       .09478    -.24273      .26740
       4    .0572037498       .18066       .31663    -.29689      .41130
       5   -.0727088092       .13559      -.53623    -.33847      .19305
       6    .1472630100       .14812       .99418    -.14306      .43759
       7    .6272222983       .25041      2.50474     .13641     1.11803
       8   -.0658713615       .14959      -.44033    -.35908      .22733
       9   -.2816769613       .15418     -1.82695    -.58387      .02051
```

Figure 14-10
*Parameters for GROUP*NCOLD*SEX*

Parameter	**Represents cases with these values**		
	GROUP	**NCOLD**	**SEX**
1	1 (Control)	0	0 (Male)
2	1 (Control)	1	0 (Male)
3	1 (Control)	2	0 (Male)
4	2 (Witness)	0	0 (Male)
5	2 (Witness)	1	0 (Male)
6	2 (Witness)	2	0 (Male)
7	3 (Non-injured)	0	0 (Male)
8	3 (Non-injured)	1	0 (Male)
9	3 (Non-injured)	2	0 (Male)

Example 2
Using Backward Elimination to Select a Suitable Model

In this example, we use the same data set and examine the same relationships. This time, however, we let the computer make decisions about which effects to include or exclude, and we can evaluate the fit of our final model.

Backward elimination uses a stepwise procedure to find a parsimonious model of cell frequencies. The procedure starts with a saturated model and examines the highest order of effects (interactions) to see if any can be removed without significantly weakening predictive power. If an effect can be removed, a nested model without the effect is evaluated, and the remaining effects are examined to see whether any can be removed. The process repeats until no more effects can be removed without sacrificing predictive power.

To produce this output, from the menus choose:

Analyze
  Loglinear
    Model Selection...

Click Reset to restore dialog box defaults, and then select:

▶ Factor(s): group, ncold, sex
  Define Range for each variable

⊙ Use backward elimination

Model...
⊙ Saturated

Options...
  Model Criteria
  Delta: 0

The first portion of the output, regarding the saturated model, is identical to the output given above and will not be repeated in this discussion. After the table shown in Figure 14-7, you will see the first step of the backward elimination, shown in Figure 14-11.

Figure 14-11
Backward elimination

```
Backward Elimination (p = .050) for DESIGN 1 with generating class

   GROUP*NCOLD*SEX

 Likelihood ratio chi square =       .00000   DF = 0  P = 1.000

 - - - - - - - - - - - - - - - - - - - - - - - - - - - - - - - - - - - -


 If Deleted Simple Effect is            DF   L.R. Chisq Change    Prob  Iter

   GROUP*NCOLD*SEX                        9              12.999   .1626    3
```

All of the effects in the saturated model are nested within the third-order interaction, so only that term can be considered for elimination at this point. Since the chi-square change for that term is not significantly different from 0, the computer deletes this term and generates the next model. After omitting the third-order interaction, the second-order effects are no longer nested under another effect, so they can be considered for removal.

Figure 14-12
Step 1

```
   The best model has generating class

        GROUP*NCOLD
        GROUP*SEX
        NCOLD*SEX

 Likelihood ratio chi square =    12.99921   DF = 9  P =  .163

 - - - - - - - - - - - - - - - - - - - - - - - - - - - - - - - - - - - -


 If Deleted Simple Effect is            DF   L.R. Chisq Change    Prob  Iter

   GROUP*NCOLD                           9              10.806   .2893    2
   GROUP*SEX                             3              28.033   .0000    2
   NCOLD*SEX                             3               3.147   .3696    2
```

The *NCOLD*SEX* interaction has the least predictive value in this model (as measured by the probability value of the chi-square change statistic), so it is removed.

Figure 14-13
Step 2

```
The best model has generating class

     GROUP*NCOLD
     GROUP*SEX

Likelihood ratio chi square =      16.14579    DF = 12  P =  .185

- - - - - - - - - - - - - - - - - - - - - - - - - - - - - - - - - - - - - - -


If Deleted Simple Effect is              DF   L.R. Chisq Change    Prob  Iter

  GROUP*NCOLD                             9              10.937   .2801    2
  GROUP*SEX                               3              28.164   .0000    2
```

The next model, with the *NCOLD*SEX* interaction excluded, is evaluated. As we can see from the chi-square change statistic, the *GROUP*NCOLD* interaction term does not improve the model significantly, so it is removed.

Figure 14-14
Step 3

```
The best model has generating class

     GROUP*SEX
     NCOLD

Likelihood ratio chi square =      27.08264    DF = 21  P =  .168

- - - - - - - - - - - - - - - - - - - - - - - - - - - - - - - - - - - - - - -


If Deleted Simple Effect is              DF   L.R. Chisq Change    Prob  Iter

  GROUP*SEX                               3              28.164   .0000    2
  NCOLD                                   3              88.398   .0000    2
```

At this point, none of the remaining effects can be excluded without weakening the predictive power of the model. The process stops, and the final model is reported. The output includes observed and expected frequencies, residuals and standardized residuals for each cell, and goodness-of-fit statistics.

Figure 14-15
Observed and expected frequencies and residuals

Observed, Expected Frequencies and Residuals.

Factor	Code	OBS count	EXP count	Residual	Std Resid
GROUP	CONTROL				
NCOLD	0				
SEX	MALE	18.0	17.0	.99	.24
SEX	FEMALE	29.0	31.1	-2.07	-.37
NCOLD	1				
SEX	MALE	43.0	38.2	4.85	.78
SEX	FEMALE	70.0	69.7	.33	.04
NCOLD	2				
SEX	MALE	19.0	23.3	-4.29	-.89
SEX	FEMALE	37.0	42.5	-5.53	-.85
NCOLD	3				
SEX	MALE	12.0	13.5	-1.54	-.42
SEX	FEMALE	32.0	24.7	7.27	1.46
GROUP	WITNESS				
NCOLD	0				
SEX	MALE	14.0	10.4	3.64	1.13
SEX	FEMALE	15.0	14.4	.58	.15
NCOLD	1				
SEX	MALE	20.0	23.2	-3.22	-.67
SEX	FEMALE	34.0	32.3	1.65	.29
NCOLD	2				
SEX	MALE	15.0	14.2	.82	.22
SEX	FEMALE	16.0	19.7	-3.75	-.84
NCOLD	3				
SEX	MALE	7.0	8.2	-1.24	-.43
SEX	FEMALE	13.0	11.5	1.52	.45
GROUP	NON-INJU				
NCOLD	0				
SEX	MALE	17.0	14.6	2.39	.63
SEX	FEMALE	2.0	8.5	-6.51	-2.23
NCOLD	1				
SEX	MALE	33.0	32.8	.24	.04
SEX	FEMALE	19.0	19.1	-.08	-.02
NCOLD	2				
SEX	MALE	22.0	20.0	2.00	.45
SEX	FEMALE	19.0	11.6	7.36	2.16
NCOLD	3				
SEX	MALE	7.0	11.6	-4.63	-1.36
SEX	FEMALE	6.0	6.8	-.77	-.30
GROUP	INJURED				
NCOLD	0				
SEX	MALE	1.0	2.4	-1.40	-.91
SEX	FEMALE	7.0	4.6	2.38	1.11
NCOLD	1				
SEX	MALE	4.0	5.4	-1.39	-.60
SEX	FEMALE	8.0	10.4	-2.37	-.74
NCOLD	2				
SEX	MALE	5.0	3.3	1.71	.94
SEX	FEMALE	8.0	6.3	1.67	.66
NCOLD	3				
SEX	MALE	3.0	1.9	1.09	.79
SEX	FEMALE	2.0	3.7	-1.68	-.88

Figure 14-16
Goodness-of-fit test statistics

```
Likelihood ratio chi square =    27.08264    DF = 21   P =  .168
            Pearson chi square =    25.41861    DF = 21   P =  .229
```

The likelihood-ratio chi-square for this reduced model is not significant, indicating that the model provides a reasonably good fit for the data. Notice also that the three effects that were eliminated from the saturated model (*GROUP*NCOLD*SEX*, *NCOLD*SEX*, and *GROUP*NCOLD*) were the same effects that we would have dropped, based on the partial chi-square statistics reported for the saturated model in "Examining a Saturated Model" on p. 145.

From here, you might examine this final model using the General Loglinear Analysis procedure. That procedure will report parameter estimates for the unsaturated model, as well as allow you to save residuals and predicted values. You can use these saved variables to evaluate your solution in more detail and to look for potential problems, such as outliers or bias in your estimates. You might also consider using the Logit Loglinear Analysis procedure to design a model where one variable is cast as a dependent variable to be predicted by the other variables. In the case of this example, you might want to see if you can predict number of colds (*NCOLD*), based on exposure to the incident (*GROUP*) and sex (*SEX*).

General Loglinear Analysis Examples

The General Loglinear Analysis (Genlog) procedure uses the Generalized Linear Model (GLM) approach to fit loglinear and logit models. Loglinear models are used to study association patterns among categorical variables, sometimes with auxiliary information provided by covariates. For example, you might study the toxicity of various concentrations of a medicine, taking into account the dosage.

Categorical data and loglinear analysis are used extensively in marketing research and the social sciences as well as in medicine and the biological sciences. Table 15-1 illustrates typical data that can be analyzed with loglinear techniques.

Table 15-1
Melanoma occurrence by age group and region

Age group	Melanoma cases, n_{ij}		Estimated population at risk, N_{ij}	
	Northern	Southern	Northern	Southern
less than 35	61	64	2880262	1074246
35–44	76	75	564535	220407
45–54	98	68	592983	198119
55–64	104	63	450740	134084
65–74	63	45	270908	70708
75 +	80	27	161850	34233

In this example, the variables are categorical and the data represent counts. One way to analyze these data would be to use the Crosstabs procedure to display a contingency table and calculate measures of association; this method deals with two variables at a time and does not estimate parameters. Loglinear analysis goes further by allowing models that take into account several variables at once and multiple categories in each variable. Loglinear analysis, in addition to testing hypotheses, also produces estimates of parameters.

In linear regression analysis, the variable to be predicted is continuous. The regression model equation has the form

$$y \;=\; B_0 + B_1 x_1 + B_2 x_2 + \dots \qquad \text{Equation 15-1}$$

The dependent variable y is expressed as a linear combination of independent factors and covariates.

In loglinear analysis, the variable to be predicted is a count (which appears on the left, as in the regression model), and the original equation is exponential, as in

$$m \;=\; e^{\,B_0 + B_1 x_1 + B_2 x_2 + \dots} \qquad \text{Equation 15-2}$$

When the natural logarithm of both sides of the equation is taken, a linear equation results:

$$\ln(m) \;=\; B_0 + B_1 x_1 + B_2 x_2 + \dots \qquad \text{Equation 15-3}$$

The log of the counts is expressed as a linear combination of factors and covariates. However, it is easy to convert the log values back to counts by calculating the exponentials. This type of conversion is demonstrated in the examples.

Several examples are analyzed in this chapter, and many more are available in the sources cited. Logit loglinear examples are in Chapter 16. The current chapter begins with two examples of parameter estimation and then provides theoretical background information, followed by more examples. The sections appear in the following order:

Parameter Estimation Examples

Example 1: Complete table. Data from a report of automobile accidents in Florida are used to determine the relationship between wearing a seat belt and the type of injury sustained. The odds ratio indicates significant evidence of a relationship.

Example 2: Incomplete table. The severity level of disabilities suffered by stroke patients was recorded at admission and at discharge. Some cells in the table are necessarily empty because of hospital rules on discharge, and these cells are treated as structural zeros. The study indicates that the final state is independent of the initial state.

Background Information

- Distribution assumptions
- Cell structure variable
- Steps in a general loglinear analysis

Model Diagnosis

- Goodness-of-fit statistics
- Residuals

Additional Examples

Example 3: Survival parametric model. The General Loglinear Analysis procedure is used to fit a special case of the proportional hazard (PH) model where survival times have an exponential distribution. The structure variable is used to include an offset term in a study of remission times for leukemia patients.

Example 4: Table standardization. The method of adjustment of marginal tables is applied to estimate population counts whose marginal distributions match those of a previous census.

Example 5: Poisson loglinear regression. The data show new melanoma cases and the population at risk for a two-year period, tabulated by areas and age groups. The generalized log-odds ratio (GLOR) values are calculated and used to compare age groups and areas.

Parameter Estimation

Analyses of a complete table and an incomplete table are illustrated in the next two sections. A complete table has observed counts for every cell, whereas an incomplete table has some empty cells, designated as **structural zeros**. In the example of an incomplete table (Table 15-3 on p. 165), the structural zeros are denoted by hyphens in the cells. For more information on structural zeros, see "Structural Zero Indicator" on p. 173.

In these examples, we are interested in estimating values of the parameters in the loglinear equations. The Genlog procedure first constructs a design matrix of all possible effects in the model equations and then applies a redundancy check to determine which columns in the design matrix are redundant in producing a unique solution to the equations (see "Design Matrix" on p. 174). The Genlog procedure adopts the easy-to-interpret convention of setting the redundant (aliased) parameters to 0.

Odds and the Log-Odds Ratio

The **odds** of an event occurring are defined as the ratio of the probability that the event will occur to the probability that it will not. For example, the odds that an ace will be drawn from a deck of 52 cards are

$$\frac{4/52}{48/52} = \frac{1}{12}$$

whereas the probability of drawing an ace is

$$\frac{4}{52} = \frac{1}{13}$$

The ratio of two odds is called the **odds ratio**. When dealing with equations involving exponentials, it is often useful to take the natural log (ln) of the exponential expression to evaluate the parameters. The log of the odds ratio is called the **log-odds ratio**. Once the natural log of an exponential expression is calculated, you can evaluate the expression by finding the value of e raised to the power you calculated for the log, where $e = 2.718$, approximately. Thus, if the log-odds ratio is 1.98, the odds ratio is

$$e^{1.98} = 7.21$$

Example 1
Complete Table

Consider Table 15-2, which is a two-way classification table showing the type of injury sustained in an automobile accident and whether seat belts were worn. The data are based on the 1988 automobile accident report of the Florida State Department of Highway Safety and Motor Vehicles cited by Agresti (1990). The Genlog procedure can be used to determine the relationship between wearing a seat belt and the type of injury sustained.

Table 15-2
1988 Florida automobile accident data

Wearing a seat belt?	Injury type	
	Fatal	Nonfatal
No	1601	162527
Yes	510	412368

Figure 15-1 shows the same data as they appear in the Data Editor.

Figure 15-1
Data structure for accident data

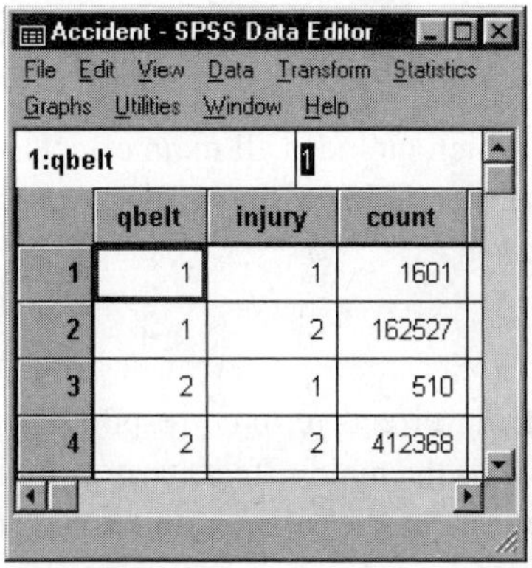

The variables to be analyzed are *qbelt* (whether a seat belt is worn) and *injury* (injury type). The variable *count* gives the number of cases for each combination of *qbelt* and *injury*. The file is weighted by *count*, simulating a data set in which there are 1601 cases with *qbelt* = 1 and *injury* = 1, 162,527 cases with *qbelt* = 1 and *injury* = 2, and so on. This way of entering categorical data using a weight variable is very common and often convenient. The analysis is the same whether the data are entered this way or whether the file actually contains all of the individual cases. To begin the analysis, from the menus choose:

Data
  Weight Cases...
  ▶ Weight cases by: count

Analyze
  Loglinear
    General...

  ▶ Factor(s): qbelt injury

Options...
  Display
      ☑ Frequencies
      ☑ Residuals
      ☑ Estimates
    Plots: deselect all plots
    Criteria
        Delta: 0

The default model is a **saturated design**, which includes all main effects and interactions involving factor variables. The natural logarithm of the expected number of fatal injuries without seat belts is expressed as

$$\ln(m_{11}) = \mu + \alpha_1 + \beta_1 + \gamma_{11}$$
Equation 15-4

where μ is the overall intercept, α_1 is the main-effects term corresponding to the first category of *qbelt* (not wearing a seat belt), β_1 is the main-effects term corresponding to the first category of *injury* (fatal injury), and γ_{11} is the interaction term corresponding to the first category of *qbelt* and the first category of *injury*. Similarly, the natural logarithms of the other expected numbers are expressed as

$$\ln(m_{12}) = \mu + \alpha_1 + \beta_2 + \gamma_{12}$$
$$\ln(m_{21}) = \mu + \alpha_2 + \beta_1 + \gamma_{21}$$
$$\ln(m_{22}) = \mu + \alpha_2 + \beta_2 + \gamma_{22}$$
Equation 15-5

The first design matrix constructed by the Genlog procedure has all of the parameters represented. In the current model, there are nine parameters but only four cells. To get a unique solution to the equations, some constraints must be applied. Before estimating parameters, the Genlog procedure uses a SWEEP process to identify aliased columns. The parameters for these aliased columns are set to 0 (see "Incorporating Cell Structure

Information" on p. 176). In this example, the Genlog procedure identifies the following five parameters as aliased and sets their values to 0:

$$\alpha_2 = 0; \quad \beta_2 = 0; \quad \gamma_{12} = 0; \quad \gamma_{21} = 0; \quad \gamma_{22} = 0 \qquad \text{Equation 15-6}$$

In Figure 15-2, the aliased parameters are indicated by an x in the column labeled *Aliased*.

Figure 15-2
Correspondence between parameters and terms of the design

```
Correspondence Between Parameters and Terms of the Design

Parameter    Aliased   Term

    1                   Constant
    2                   [QBELT = 1]
    3          x        [QBELT = 2]
    4                   [INJURY = 1]
    5          x        [INJURY = 2]
    6                   [QBELT = 1]*[INJURY = 1]
    7          x        [QBELT = 1]*[INJURY = 2]
    8          x        [QBELT = 2]*[INJURY = 1]
    9          x        [QBELT = 2]*[INJURY = 2]

Note: 'x' indicates an aliased (or a redundant) parameter.
      These parameters are set to zero.
```

If 0 is substituted for aliased parameters in Equation 15-5, the model equations become

$$\ln(m_{11}) = \mu + \alpha_1 + \beta_1 + \gamma_{11}$$
$$\ln(m_{12}) = \mu + \alpha_1$$
$$\ln(m_{21}) = \mu + \beta_1 \qquad \text{Equation 15-7}$$
$$\ln(m_{22}) = \mu$$

From Equation 15-7,

$$\mu = \ln(m_{22})$$
$$\alpha_1 = \ln(m_{12}) - \ln(m_{22}) = \ln(m_{12}/m_{22})$$
$$\beta_1 = \ln(m_{21}) - \ln(m_{22}) = \ln(m_{21}/m_{22}) \qquad \text{Equation 15-8}$$
$$\gamma_{11} = \ln(m_{11}) - \ln(m_{12}) - (\ln(m_{21}) - \ln(m_{22})) = \ln\left(\frac{m_{11}m_{22}}{m_{12}m_{21}}\right)$$

By definition of the log-odds, α_1 is the expected log-odds between the first and second categories of *qbelt* within the second category of *injury*, β_1 is the expected log-odds between the first and second categories of *injury* within the second category of *qbelt*, and γ_{11} is the expected log-odds ratio of the table. If *qbelt* and *injury* are independent, the odds ratio is 1, which corresponds to a log-odds ratio equal to 0. Hence, γ_{11} is a measure of the strength of association between *qbelt* and *injury*. Since the design is saturated, the expected counts equal the observed counts. Therefore, the parameter estimates are

$$\hat{\mu} = \ln(412368) = 12.9297$$

$$\hat{\alpha}_1 = \ln\left(\frac{162527}{412368}\right) = -0.9311$$

$$\hat{\beta}_1 = \ln\left(\frac{510}{412368}\right) = -6.6953$$

Equation 15-9

$$\hat{\gamma}_{11} = \ln\left(\frac{1601 \times 412368}{162527 \times 510}\right) = 2.0750$$

By referring to the parameter designations in Figure 15-2, you can compare these calculations with the parameter estimates of the Genlog procedure shown in Figure 15-3.

Figure 15-3
Parameter estimates for the saturated model

```
Parameter Estimates

                                            Asymptotic 95% CI
Parameter    Estimate      SE     Z-value   Lower      Upper
        1     12.9297    .0016    8302.90   12.93      12.93
        2      -.9311    .0029    -317.90    -.94       -.93
        3       .0000       .         .        .          .
        4     -6.6953    .0443    -151.11   -6.78      -6.61
        5       .0000       .         .        .          .
        6      2.0750    .0509      40.74    1.98       2.17
        7       .0000       .         .        .          .
        8       .0000       .         .        .          .
        9       .0000       .         .        .          .
```

Parameter 1 corresponds to the constant μ, parameter 2 corresponds to α_1, and so on. Parameter 6 is γ_{11}, the interaction term between not wearing a seat belt (*qbelt* 1) and fatal injury (*injury* 1).

The asymptotic 95% confidence limits for the sample log-odds ratio, as shown for parameter 6 in Figure 15-3, are 1.98 and 2.17, corresponding to an odds ratio between 7.21 and 8.80, since

$$e^{1.98} = 7.21 \qquad \text{and} \qquad e^{2.17} = 8.80$$

Equation 15-10

This means that at the 95% confidence level, the odds of fatal injury to nonfatal injury for passengers without seat belts is between 7.21 and 8.80 times the corresponding odds when seat belts are worn. From these data, therefore, there is significant evidence that wearing seat belts does help to avoid fatal injury.

Example 2
Incomplete Table

Bishop and Fienberg (1969) present data collected at Massachusetts General Hospital on the severity of disability suffered by 121 stroke patients. These data are shown in Table 15-3. On admission and again on discharge, each patient was assigned a severity level according to his or her physical disability following a stroke. There are five distinct severity levels, labeled from A through E, with A being the least severe and E, the most severe. Since no patient was discharged who did not show any sign of improvement, cells representing patients whose final states were more severe than their initial states are necessarily 0. These are **structural zeros**, which are different from zero values that just happen to occur in the data. The Genlog procedure can be used to investigate the relationship between the initial state and the final state for stroke patients who are released from the hospital.

Table 15-3
Initial and final severity levels of stroke patients

Initial state	Final state					Totals
	A	**B**	**C**	**D**	**E**	
A	5	-	-	-	-	5
B	4	5	-	-	-	9
C	6	4	4	-	-	14
D	9	10	4	1	-	24
E	11	23	12	15	8	69
Totals	35	42	20	16	8	121

Bishop et al. (1975) fit a quasi-independence model to these data. Under a quasi-independence assumption, the initial state and final state are independent, conditional on the nonstructural zero cells.

The data structure is shown in Figure 15-4. Variables *initial* and *final* are coded with numbers that represent the states *A*, *B*, *C*, *D*, and *E*. Variable *qtake* indicates whether the cell is a structural zero (0) or not (1).

Figure 15-4
Data structure for stroke data

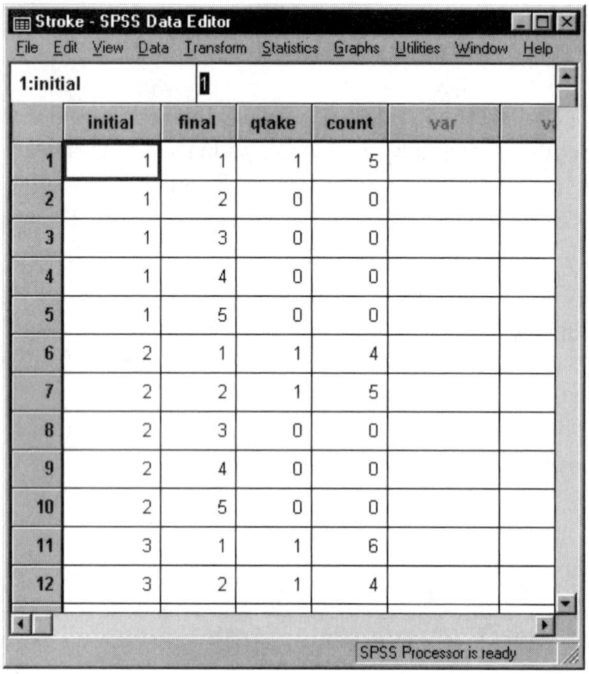

	initial	final	qtake	count	var
1	1	1	1	5	
2	1	2	0	0	
3	1	3	0	0	
4	1	4	0	0	
5	1	5	0	0	
6	2	1	1	4	
7	2	2	1	5	
8	2	3	0	0	
9	2	4	0	0	
10	2	5	0	0	
11	3	1	1	6	
12	3	2	1	4	

The data are weighted by *count*. Denoting the expected cell count for the *i*th initial state and the *j*th final state as m_{ij}, the model equations under the quasi-independence model are

$$\ln(m_{ij}) = \mu + \alpha_i + \beta_j; \quad i = 1,2,3,4,5; \text{ and } j = 1,\ldots, i \qquad \text{Equation 15-11}$$

where μ is the intercept term, α_i is the main-effects term corresponding to the *i*th category of *initial*, and β_j is the main-effects term corresponding to the *j*th category of *final*. Due to intrinsic aliasing among the model equations, the Genlog procedure identifies the following two parameters as aliased and sets their values to 0:

$$\alpha_5 = 0 \quad \text{and} \quad \beta_5 = 0 \qquad \text{Equation 15-12}$$

The equations represented in Equation 15-11, reexpressed in terms of the nonaliased parameters, can be written as follows:

$$\ln(m_{11}) = \mu + \alpha_1 + \beta_1$$
$$\ln(m_{21}) = \mu + \alpha_2 + \beta_1$$
$$\ln(m_{22}) = \mu + \alpha_2 + \beta_2$$
$$\ln(m_{31}) = \mu + \alpha_3 + \beta_1$$
$$\ln(m_{32}) = \mu + \alpha_3 + \beta_2$$
$$\ln(m_{33}) = \mu + \alpha_3 + \beta_3$$
$$\ln(m_{41}) = \mu + \alpha_4 + \beta_1$$
$$\ln(m_{42}) = \mu + \alpha_4 + \beta_2 \qquad \text{Equation 15-13}$$
$$\ln(m_{43}) = \mu + \alpha_4 + \beta_3$$
$$\ln(m_{44}) = \mu + \alpha_4 + \beta_4$$
$$\ln(m_{51}) = \mu + \beta_1$$
$$\ln(m_{52}) = \mu + \beta_2$$
$$\ln(m_{53}) = \mu + \beta_3$$
$$\ln(m_{54}) = \mu + \beta_4$$
$$\ln(m_{55}) = \mu$$

Under the quasi-independence assumption, the ratio of counts between any two final states, unless prohibited, is the same for all initial states, and vice versa. From Equation 15-13, you can derive the following:

$$\frac{m_{41}}{m_{51}} = \frac{m_{42}}{m_{52}} = \frac{m_{43}}{m_{53}} = \frac{m_{44}}{m_{54}} = e^{\alpha_4} \qquad \text{Equation 15-14}$$

and

$$\frac{m_{21}}{m_{22}} = \frac{m_{31}}{m_{32}} = \frac{m_{41}}{m_{42}} = \frac{m_{51}}{m_{52}} = e^{\beta_1 - \beta_2} \qquad \text{Equation 15-15}$$

Equation 15-14 implies that the ratios of the number of patients with initial state D (*initial* = 4) to initial state E (*initial* = 5) are the same across all possible final states. Similarly, Equation 15-15 signifies that the ratios of the number of patients with final state A (*final* = 1) to final state B (*final* = 2) are the same for all initial states.

To fit this quasi-independence model, from the menus choose:

Data
  Weight Cases...
  ▶ Weight cases by: count

Next, choose:

Analyze
  Loglinear
    General...

▶ Factor(s): initial final

Cell Structure: qtake

Model...
    ⊙ Custom
    ▶ Terms in Model (Main effects): final initial

Options...
    Display
        ☑ Frequencies
        ☑ Estimates
    Plots: deselect all plots

The fitted values are shown in Figure 15-5.

Figure 15-5
Table information for stroke data

```
Table Information
                   Observed                 Expected
Factor    Value    Count        %           Count        %
INITIAL     A
  FINAL     A        5.00 (    4.13)          5.00 (    4.13)
  FINAL     B         .00 (     .00)           .00 (     .00)
  FINAL     C         .00 (     .00)           .00 (     .00)
  FINAL     D         .00 (     .00)           .00 (     .00)
  FINAL     E         .00 (     .00)           .00 (     .00)
INITIAL     B
  FINAL     A        4.00 (    3.31)          3.75 (    3.10)
  FINAL     B        5.00 (    4.13)          5.25 (    4.34)
  FINAL     C         .00 (     .00)           .00 (     .00)
  FINAL     D         .00 (     .00)           .00 (     .00)
  FINAL     E         .00 (     .00)           .00 (     .00)
INITIAL     C
  FINAL     A        6.00 (    4.96)          4.43 (    3.66)
  FINAL     B        4.00 (    3.31)          6.20 (    5.12)
  FINAL     C        4.00 (    3.31)          3.37 (    2.79)
  FINAL     D         .00 (     .00)           .00 (     .00)
  FINAL     E         .00 (     .00)           .00 (     .00)
INITIAL     D
  FINAL     A        9.00 (    7.44)          6.16 (    5.09)
  FINAL     B       10.00 (    8.26)          8.63 (    7.13)
  FINAL     C        4.00 (    3.31)          4.69 (    3.88)
  FINAL     D        1.00 (     .83)          4.52 (    3.73)
  FINAL     E         .00 (     .00)           .00 (     .00)
INITIAL     E
  FINAL     A       11.00 (    9.09)         15.66 (   12.94)
  FINAL     B       23.00 (   19.01)         21.92 (   18.12)
  FINAL     C       12.00 (    9.92)         11.93 (    9.86)
  FINAL     D       15.00 (   12.40)         11.48 (    9.49)
  FINAL     E        8.00 (    6.61)          8.00 (    6.61)
```

To test the goodness of fit of the model, the Genlog procedure calculates chi-square statistics, as shown in Figure 15-6. The chi-square statistics are derived from comparing the fitted cell counts with the observed cell counts. Since the significance is above 0.05, the quasi-independence model fits the data fairly well.

Figure 15-6
Goodness-of-fit statistics for stroke data

```
Goodness-of-fit Statistics

                    Chi-Square      DF       Sig.

Likelihood Ratio      9.5958        6       .1427
         Pearson      8.3691        6       .2123
```

Therefore, a patient's final state at discharge is independent of his or her initial state, given the fact that a patient is discharged only if the current state is better than the initial state.

Figure 15-7 shows the parameter reference table, and Figure 15-8 shows the parameter estimates.

Figure 15-7

Parameter reference table for stroke data

```
Correspondence Between Parameters and Terms of the Design
Parameter    Aliased   Term
     1                 Constant
     2                 [FINAL = 1]
     3                 [FINAL = 2]
     4                 [FINAL = 3]
     5                 [FINAL = 4]
     6          x      [FINAL = 5]
     7                 [INITIAL = 1]
     8                 [INITIAL = 2]
     9                 [INITIAL = 3]
    10                 [INITIAL = 4]
    11          x      [INITIAL = 5]
Note: 'x' indicates an aliased (or a redundant) parameter.
      These parameters are set to zero.
```

Figure 15-8

Parameter estimates for stroke data under a quasi-independence model

```
Parameter Estimates
```

				Asymptotic 95% CI	
Parameter	Estimate	SE	Z-value	Lower	Upper
1	2.0794	.3536	5.88	1.39	2.77
2	.6717	.4091	1.64	-.13	1.47
3	1.0082	.3973	2.54	.23	1.79
4	.3998	.4267	.94	-.44	1.24
5	.3614	.4383	.82	-.50	1.22
6	.0000	.	.	.	.
7	-1.1417	.4923	-2.32	-2.11	-.18
8	-1.4294	.3661	-3.90	-2.15	-.71
9	-1.2633	.3009	-4.20	-1.85	-.67
10	-.9328	.2410	-3.87	-1.41	-.46
11	.0000	.	.	.	.

From Figure 15-7, α_4 is parameter 10. Its value is -0.9328. Thus, under the quasi-independence assumption, the number of patients with initial state D is

$$e^{-0.9328} = 0.39 \qquad \qquad \text{Equation 15-16}$$

times the number of patients with initial state E.

Again from Figure 15-7, β_1 is parameter 2 and β_2 is parameter 3. Using the values in Figure 15-8,

$$e^{\beta_1 - \beta_2} = e^{0.6717 - 1.0082} = 0.71 \qquad \qquad \text{Equation 15-17}$$

This calculation indicates that the number of patients with final state A is 0.71 times the number of patients with final state B, given that the initial state is B or lower.

Background Information

The following sections (p. 171 through p. 176) include technical background information about loglinear analysis and the types of data distributions. You may be able to follow the examples in this chapter without reading this material.

Distribution Assumptions

The Genlog procedure can be used to fit a model under either of two distribution assumptions—the **Poisson loglinear model** or the **multinomial loglinear model**. The multinomial loglinear model is a special case of the **product multinomial loglinear model** (logit model), which has its own dialog box in SPSS. For a detailed explanation of these distribution assumptions, see Agresti (1990).

A general loglinear analysis analyzes the frequency counts of observations falling into each cross-classification category. Each cross-classification constitutes a **cell**, and each categorical variable is called a **factor**. Thus, the dependent variable is the number of cases (frequency) in a cell of the crosstabulation, and the explanatory variables are factors and covariates. A general loglinear model formulates each cell count as the product of a cell-specific constant and the exponential of a linear combination of parameters. The parameters are identified by association with the categorical variables and the covariates in a design matrix (see "Design Matrix" on p. 174). The mathematical model for the expected count in a cell is given by

$$m_i = z_i e^{x_i \beta}; \qquad i = 1 \ldots, r \qquad \text{Equation 15-18}$$

where m_i is the expected cell count for the ith cell, z_i is the cell-specific constant, x_i is the ith row of the design matrix, β is the vector of parameters, and r is the number of cells.

Poisson Distribution

Under the Poisson distribution assumption:

- The total sample size is not fixed before the study, or the analysis is not conditional on the total sample size.

- The event of an observation being in a cell is statistically independent of the cell counts of other cells.

The joint probability density function of the cell counts (n_i) under the Poisson assumption is given by

$$\prod_{i=1}^{r} e^{-m_i} \frac{m_i^{n_i}}{n_i!}$$

Equation 15-19

Multinomial Distribution

Under the multinomial distribution assumption:

- The total sample size is fixed, or the analysis is conditional on the total sample size.
- The cell counts are not statistically independent.

For a multinomial distribution, the joint probability density function is given by

$$\frac{N!}{\prod_{i=1}^{r} n_i!} \prod_{i=1}^{r} \pi_i^{n_i}$$

Equation 15-20

where $\pi_i = m_i/N$.

Product Multinomial Distribution (Logit Model)

A special case of the **logit model** is the multinomial model. This model is appropriate when it is natural to regard one or more categorical variables as the response variables and the others as the explanatory variables. At each setting or combination of the categories of the explanatory variables, the subtotal sample size is fixed and the cell counts of the response variables follow a multinomial distribution. Furthermore, it is assumed that the collection of cell counts at different settings are statistically independent; thus, the joint distribution for the entire sample is the product of these independent multinomial distributions. Therefore, logit models are also called product multinomial loglinear models in this context.

The joint probability function for the product multinomial loglinear (logit) model is given by

$$\prod_{j=1}^{c} \prod_{i=1}^{r} \frac{N_j}{\prod_{i=1}^{r} n_{ij}!} \, \pi_{ij}^{n_{ij}}$$

Equation 15-21

where $\pi_{ij} = \frac{m_{ij}}{N_j}$, $N_j = \sum_{i=1}^{r} m_{ij}$, n_{ij} is the cell count, and c is the number of settings.

Cell Structure Variable

The cell structure variable is used to assign weights to the cells. It can be used for the following purposes:

- To suppress cells that you don't want to estimate by specifying structural zeros in the table (see "Incomplete Table" on p. 165).

- To include an offset term that appears in models for survival data, as illustrated in McCullagh and Nelder, 1989 (see "Survival Parametric Model" on p. 179).

- To adapt the General Loglinear Analysis procedure to fit the log-rate model described in Agresti, 1990 (see "Poisson Loglinear Regression" on p. 188).

- To implement the method of adjustment of marginal tables, as discussed in Haberman, 1979 (see "Table Standardization" on p. 184).

Details on fitting these models using the General Loglinear Analysis procedure are described in the sections cited.

Structural Zero Indicator

If the value of the cell structure variable is not positive for a cell, that particular cell is treated as a **structural zero** (called a "necessarily empty cell" by McCullagh and Nelder, 1989). Both the observed and expected counts for a structural zero are fixed as zeros. Although the cell still constitutes part of the contingency table, it is not used during the estimation.

If the cell count is 0 due to chance variation but its expected count is positive, the cell is treated as a **sampling zero** (called an "accidentally empty cell" by McCullagh and Nelder, 1989). A sampling zero is used in the estimation, and its expected cell count is estimated from the model. All cells whose cell structure values are positive are used in the estimation.

Structural zeros can occur when some combination of levels of the factors is *a priori* impossible. The subset of vegetarians who eat meat represent an example of this. In other situations, structural zeros are imposed to keep certain cells from entering into the analysis. An example is the fitting of a quasi-independence model to a square contingency table. A typical method of applying structural zeros is to declare the diagonal cells to be structural zeros and to use a cell structure variable to fit an independence model using only the off-diagonal cells.

Steps in a General Loglinear Analysis

A general loglinear analysis in SPSS performs the following steps:

■ Constructs a design matrix from the user's specifications. It creates an over-parameterized design matrix, incorporates cell structure information, and identifies and removes the aliased columns.

■ Estimates parameters.

■ Checks the model.

Design Matrix

The Genlog procedure displays the design matrix if you specify Design Matrix in the General Loglinear Analysis Options dialog box (not shown). Each column of the matrix is indexed by a unique parameter number that corresponds to a term of the design. The mapping of the parameter numbers to the terms of the design is shown in the correspondence table in Figure 15-9.

Figure 15-9
Correspondence between parameters and terms of the design

```
Correspondence Between Parameters and Terms of the Design

  Parameter   Aliased  Term

         1             Constant
         2             [QBELT = 1]
         3        x    [QBELT = 2]
         4             [INJURY = 1]
         5        x    [INJURY = 2]
         6             [QBELT = 1]*[INJURY = 1]
         7        x    [QBELT = 1]*[INJURY = 2]
         8        x    [QBELT = 2]*[INJURY = 1]
         9        x    [QBELT = 2]*[INJURY = 2]

  Note: 'x' indicates an aliased (or a redundant) parameter.
        These parameters are set to zero.
```

Each **aliased** (or redundant) term is indicated by an x in the table. The rows of the matrix are indexed by the factor combinations that define the contingency table.

Over-parameterized design matrix. The General Loglinear Analysis procedure uses a regression approach to represent the model in terms of parameters. In this approach, a dummy coding scheme is used.

First, the Genlog procedure forms an identity matrix for each factor variable, with dimension equal to the number of categories of the factor. Then, a constant vector is formed for each factor variable. Each element of the constant vector is equal to 1, and the length of the constant vector is equal to the number of categories of the factor. These identity matrices and constant vectors form the basis for the construction of the final design matrix.

For each effect, the Genlog procedure constructs the columns of the design matrix as the **Kronecker products** of the identity matrices and constant vectors. Effects involving a covariate are treated as regressor variables in the usual sense. If the effect involves a single covariate, the column of the design matrix is the covariate vector, and the associated parameter is the usual regression coefficient. Similarly, if the effect involves a factor-by-covariate interaction, multiple regression coefficients are computed—one for each combination of the categories of the factors involved (see the *SPSS Base Syntax Reference Guide* for a comparison of the GENLOG and LOGLINEAR commands). The columns are constructed using the algorithm that applies to multiple slopes in the usual regression procedure.

The Genlog procedure does not allow an interaction term between covariates. To specify an interaction effect involving more than one covariate, the products of the covariates must be calculated by a data transformation before using the Genlog procedure. You can choose Compute from the Transform menu to specify the product as a new variable, which can then be specified as a single covariate (see "Two Response Variables with Two Categories Each" on p. 205 in Chapter 16).

Logit model. For the logit model, there is one constant term for every value of the explanatory (factor) variable. The algorithm works in the same way as in the general loglinear model except for some modifications in generating the constant terms. The logit model is discussed in Chapter 16.

Incorporating Cell Structure Information

In some cases, the presence of structural zeros is the cause of aliasing in the design matrix. These aliased columns must be identified.

For each combination of values of the factors, the value of the cell structure variable is checked. If it is not positive, all elements in the corresponding row of the over-parameterized design matrix are assigned a value of 0. Otherwise, the row remains unchanged.

Identifying the aliased columns. To identify the aliased columns in the design matrix, the **cross-product matrix** (the matrix product of the transpose of the matrix multiplied by itself) is calculated. The SWEEP operations are then applied to all rows and columns sequentially. After each SWEEP operation, the diagonal elements are inspected. If the ratio of a diagonal element after the SWEEP to its original value (before the first SWEEP operation) is less than a predetermined threshold value, the corresponding column in the over-parameterized design matrix is declared to be aliased. Aliased columns are then removed from the over-parameterized design matrix. The remaining columns form a **full rank design matrix** that is subsequently used in the estimation stage.

To keep the sum of the expected cell counts equal to the sum of the observed cell counts, the constant term in a general loglinear model and the intercept-like terms in a logit model are not subjected to the redundancy test after the SWEEP operations. Therefore, these terms always stay in the model equation.

Model Diagnosis

Before conclusions or inferences are made based on the results of a selected model, it is important to check whether the model assumptions are satisfied. We usually look for two kinds of indications that the model does not fit:

- The data as a whole show systematic departures from the predicted values. This implies that the model alone is not adequate to explain the behavior of the data.

- Some isolated discrepancies are due to several particular data values, while the rest of the data agree with the predicted values. This implies that there is something unusual about these data values. They may be in areas where the model does not apply, or perhaps they are outliers or the result of typographic errors.

Goodness-of-Fit Statistics

The first step in model diagnosis is the examination of goodness of fit. Two goodness-of-fit statistics are reported in the General Loglinear and Logit Loglinear procedures—the Pearson chi-square statistic and the likelihood-ratio chi-square statistic. Using O to denote the observed value and E to denote the fitted value, the Pearson chi-square statistic is

$$\chi^2 = \sum \frac{(O-E)^2}{E}$$

Equation 15-22

For the Poisson model, the likelihood-ratio chi-square statistic is

$$G^2 = \sum (O\ln(O/E) - (O-E))$$

Equation 15-23

and for the multinomial model, it is

$$G^2 = 2\sum O\ln(O/E)$$

Equation 15-24

where the sum is over all cells that are not structural zeros and do not have zero-fitted values. It should be noted that the G^2 from Equation 15-23 and G^2 from Equation 15-24 are identical because the sum of residuals $(O-E)$ is 0 when an intercept term is included for the Poisson model (the General Loglinear Analysis procedure does include an intercept). Both χ^2 and G^2 have asymptotic chi-square distributions. The degrees of freedom depend on the number of cells excluding structural zeros, the number of non-aliased parameters, and the number of fitted values that are equal to 0. Sometimes, χ^2 is preferred to G^2, and vice versa. χ^2 provides more direct interpretation, while G^2 is useful for comparing nested models. In most cases, both χ^2 and G^2 will lead to the same conclusion.

The likelihood-ratio statistic compares how well the selected model fits the data to the fit of a corresponding saturated model. A saturated model always produces a perfect fit using the greatest number of parameters leaving zero degrees of freedom. However, by the principle of parsimony, we want to use a model with the least number of parameters that can describe the data almost as well as the saturated model. Therefore, the likelihood-ratio statistic and its p value tell us whether the selected model is statistically different from a saturated model. A small p value (labeled *Sig.* in the output) indicates that the selected model cannot adequately describe the data as the saturated model does and should include more parameters in the model.

Also, the likelihood-ratio statistic has a definite advantage because it is additive for nested models, whereas the Pearson statistic in general is not. When one model is nested within another model, the difference in G^2 statistics indicates whether the two models are different from a statistical point of view. It is known that difference has an asymptotic chi-square distribution with degrees of freedom equal to the difference of models' degrees of freedom.

If the selected model is correct, then O has mean E for both Poisson and multinomial models. In a correct model, O also has variance E under the Poisson model and variance $E(1 - E/N)$ under the multinomial model, where N is the total sample size. When N is large, the ratio E/N becomes negligible. Thus, the expression

$$\frac{O - E}{\sqrt{E}}$$

Equation 15-25

has a mean equal to 0 and a variance equal to 1 when the sample size is large. Thus, the order of magnitude of the Pearson statistic χ^2 should be at most that of the degrees of freedom. If the value of χ^2 is too large relative to the degrees of freedom, the model does not fit.

Residuals

Another step in model diagnosis is the examination of residuals. This step helps to evaluate the fit for each observation, to identify possible outliers, and sometimes to provide hints to improve the model. The General Loglinear Analysis procedure provides four types of residuals—raw, standardized, adjusted, and deviance.

Plots are selected in the General Loglinear Analysis Options dialog box. A matrix scatterplot of adjusted residuals versus observed values and adjusted residuals versus fitted values can be generated. A similar matrix scatterplot is available for deviance residuals. Furthermore, all of these residuals, along with the fitted values, can be saved in the working data file for further analyses, as selected in the General Loglinear Analysis Save dialog box. The SPSS system-missing value will be assigned if the corresponding cell contains a structural zero or an otherwise prohibited value.

A **raw residual** (or **residual**) is the difference obtained by subtracting the fitted value from the observed value. Therefore, the sum of all raw residuals is 0 because the sum of all fitted values must be equal to the sum of observed values, as one of the assumptions of the General Loglinear Analysis procedure. Raw residuals do not play an important role in model diagnosis because their magnitudes can be misleading without considering the sizes of the fitted and observed values.

A **standardized residual**, on the other hand, does take into account the size of the fitted values. For the Poisson model, the standardized residual is the raw residual divided by $\sqrt{E}$. For the multinomial model, the denominator is $\sqrt{E(1 - E/N)}$. For the Poisson model, the sum of squares of the standardized residuals is the Pearson chi-square statistic; thus, they are also known as Pearson residuals. Therefore, standardized residuals can be used to check the individual contributions to the Pearson chi-square statistic. The standardized residuals are asymptotically normal with the means equal to 0 and the variances less than 1 if the selected model is correct.

The **adjusted residual** is the standardized residual divided by its estimated standard error (Haberman, 1973). Its asymptotic distribution is standard normal with the mean equal to 0 and the variance equal to 1 under the correct model. Because of this property, the adjusted residual is preferred over the standardized residual for checking normality.

The **deviance residual** is the individual contribution to the likelihood-ratio chi-square statistic. Its sign is the same as that of the raw residual. For both the Poisson and multinomial models, the sum of squares of the deviance residuals equals the likelihood-ratio chi-square statistic. Like adjusted residuals, deviance residuals also have an asymptotic standard normal distribution.

For an example of model diagnosis, see "Model Diagnosis: Coal Miner Data Revisited" on p. 218 in Chapter 16.

Additional Examples

This section contains three examples illustrating various applications of general loglinear analysis. For applications of logit loglinear analysis, see Chapter 16.

Example 3
Survival Parametric Model

McCullagh and Nelder (1989) and Agresti (1990) discuss how to use loglinear models to analyze survival data for various parametric survival models. Detailed descriptions of the equivalence between parametric survival models and loglinear models can be found in their books. This example illustrates how to use the General Loglinear Analysis procedure to fit a special case of the proportional hazard (PH) model where survival times have an exponential distribution.

For survival data, the response is the length of time until the occurrence of some event. With an exponential assumption for survival time, the hazard rate is a constant at all time points. Using λ as the constant hazard rate, the hazard function for a PH model is expressed as

$$h(x) = \lambda e^{\beta'x} \qquad\qquad\qquad \text{Equation 15-26}$$

where x denotes a set of explanatory variables and β' is the transposed matrix. For subject i, the product of time at risk (t_i) and the hazard function gives the expected number of events:

$$m_i = t_i \lambda e^{\beta'x_i} \qquad\qquad\qquad \text{Equation 15-27}$$

Taking natural logarithms on both sides of Equation 15-27 gives

$$\ln(m_i) - \ln(t_i) = \ln(\lambda) + \beta'x_i \qquad\qquad\qquad \text{Equation 15-28}$$

The term $\ln(t_i)$ is referred to as an **offset** in most loglinear analysis literature. In this example, the structure variable is used to include the offset term.

An example of a proportional hazard model is found in data from Freireich et al. (1963), which measured the remission time of leukemia patients. The patients were divided into two groups. The treatment group received an experimental drug and the control group received a placebo. The remission time was measured in weeks. Since the observations can be assumed to be independent, the Poisson distribution is appropriate. The data structure is shown in Figure 15-10.

Figure 15-10

Data structure for leukemia data

	case	time	group	qcensor
1	1	6	1	0
2	2	6	1	1
3	3	6	1	1
4	4	6	1	1
5	5	7	1	1
6	6	9	1	0
7	7	10	1	0
8	8	10	1	1
9	9	11	1	0
10	10	13	1	1
11	11	16	1	1
12	12	17	1	0
13	13	19	1	0
14	14	20	1	0
15	15	22	1	1

	case	time	group	qcensor
20	20	34	1	0
21	21	35	1	0
22	1	1	2	1
23	2	1	2	1
24	3	2	2	1
25	4	2	2	1
26	5	3	2	1
27	6	4	2	1
28	7	4	2	1
29	8	5	2	1
30	9	5	2	1
31	10	8	2	1
32	11	8	2	1
33	12	8	2	1
34	13	8	2	1

The data are recorded in individual cases. Each case number has two entries, one for each group. The variable *group* indicates treatment (1) or control (2). Figure 15-10 shows two views of the data. Note that the entries for the controls (group 2) start with case 1 again. Thus, each case has two entries, one for each group. In the contingency table of *case* by *group*, each cell has one case. The status of each case (censored or not) is in *qcensor*. Weighting the data by *qcensor* (by using the Data menu prior to analysis) causes the cell counts to be 1 for uncensored cases and 0 for censored cases. To identify each case as an individual cell, the ID variable *case* is specified as a factor in the loglinear analysis.

By comparing Equation 15-27 with Equation 15-18, you can see that with an exponential assumption for survival time, *time* is the cell structure variable (cell-specific constant) in the General Loglinear Analysis procedure. Since the group effect is the main interest, *group* is the only explanatory variable in this model. A model with *group* as the only explanatory factor in the custom model is fitted.

From the menus choose:

Data
  Weight Cases...
▶ Weight cases by: qcensor

Analyze
  Loglinear
    General...

▶ Factor(s): case group

Cell Structure: time

Model...
  ⊙ Custom
  ▶ Terms in Model (Main effects): group

Options...
  Display
    ☑ Frequencies
    ☑ Estimates
  Plots: deselect all plots

Since *qcensor* is a status variable, the estimated cell counts and the goodness of fit are meaningless in this example. The parameter correspondence table is shown in Figure 15-11.

Figure 15-11
Parameter correspondence table

```
Correspondence Between Parameters and Terms of the Design

Parameter    Aliased   Term

       1                Constant
       2                [GROUP = 1.00000]
       3         x      [GROUP = 2.00000]
```
Note: 'x' indicates an aliased (or a redundant) parameter.
      These parameters are set to zero.

The parameter estimates, shown in Figure 15-12, are the items of interest. The parameter estimate for group 1 (parameter 2) is −1.5266 with a standard error of 0.3984. Since the parameter for group 2 (parameter 3) is identified as aliased in the parameter correspondence table, its value is 0.

Figure 15-12
Parameter estimates for leukemia data

```
Parameter Estimates

                                              Asymptotic 95% CI
Parameter   Estimate       SE    Z-value     Lower      Upper
    1        -2.1595     .2182     -9.90     -2.59      -1.73
    2        -1.5266     .3984     -3.83     -2.31       -.75
    3         .0000        .          .         .          .
```

Thus, the estimated hazard ratio for the treatment group as compared to the control group is

$$e^{-1.5266} = 0.2172 \hspace{4cm} \text{Equation 15-29}$$

The 95% confidence limits for the log-hazard difference are $(-2.31, -0.75)$, corresponding to hazard ratio limits of $(0.10, 0.47)$.

You can also use the Cox Regression procedure to analyze the same data (see Chapter 19). To use the Cox Regression procedure, from the menus choose:

Data
  Weight Cases...
  ⊙ Do not weight cases

Analyze
  Survival
    Cox Regression...

▸ Time: time

Status: qcensor(1)

Covariates: group(Cat)I

Categorical...
    Categorical Covariates: group
    Contrast: Indicator   (Click Change)

In the Cox Regression procedure output (not shown), the parameter estimate for group 1 is -1.5092 with a standard error of 0.4096. These numbers are close to, but not the same as, those of the General Loglinear Analysis procedure because the Cox Regression procedure fits Cox's proportional hazard model, which does not assume any underlying distribution for the survival time.

Example 4
Table Standardization

Occasionally, researchers want to calculate a set of fitted values that have specified marginal totals or the required marginal distributions. Haberman (1979) discussed the method of adjustment of marginal tables. The method is applied to estimate the population counts whose marginal distributions matched those of a previous census. A similar process, called table standardization (or *raking* the table), is presented in Agresti (1990). In this process, the estimated counts are standardized so that the marginal totals are all equal to 100. In both cases, the purpose is to make the pattern of association more visible and to facilitate comparisons.

Both the adjustment of marginal tables and the table standardization can be done by using the iteratively proportional fitting (IPF) technique (available in the Model Selection Loglinear Analysis procedure). However, the same results can be obtained by specifying a suitable cell structure variable in the General Loglinear Analysis procedure.

The following example is taken from Haberman (1979). Both tables show the classification of number of years of husband's education versus that of wife's education. The first data set is a sample gathered from the 1972 General Social Survey, and the second data set is from the 1970 United States census data. In this example, the 1970 marginal totals will be used to estimate the 1972 census counts using the 1972 sample under a saturated design. The variables are *yrhusb* (years of education of husband), *yrwife* (years of education of wife), *gsscnt* (GSS count), *marhusb* (census marginal count for *yrhusb*), and *marwife* (census marginal count for *yrwife*). The data are shown in Figure 15-13.

Figure 15-13
Data structure for education data

	yrhusb	yrwife	gsscnt	marhusb	marwife
1	1.00	1.00	283.00	19933782	18052065
2	1.00	2.00	141.00	19933782	17859905
3	1.00	3.00	25.00	19933782	5101589
4	1.00	4.00	4.00	19933782	3584015
5	2.00	1.00	82.00	13275913	18052065
6	2.00	2.00	180.00	13275913	17859905
7	2.00	3.00	43.00	13275913	5101589
8	2.00	4.00	14.00	13275913	3584015
9	3.00	1.00	20.00	5186966	18052065
10	3.00	2.00	104.00	5186966	17859905
11	3.00	3.00	43.00	5186966	5101589
12	3.00	4.00	20.00	5186966	3584015
13	4.00	1.00	4.00	6200883	18052065
14	4.00	2.00	52.00	6200883	17859905
15	4.00	3.00	41.00	6200883	5101589
16	4.00	4.00	69.00	6200883	3584015

Variables *yrhusb* and *yrwife* have four values, each one corresponding to a level of education ranging from grade school through high school, college, and graduate school. An initial estimate of the joint distribution is needed (like the initial estimate in the iteratively proportional fitting algorithm). Since only the marginal totals are available, the model closest to the saturated model is the independence model. Thus, the estimated values from the independence model are used as the initial values. Haberman (1979) contains examples of choosing the initial values under various scenarios.

In the independence model, the estimated cell count is the product of the corresponding marginal totals divided by the total sample size, which is 44,597,744 in this example. (The total sample size is the sum of the four unique values of *marhusb*.)

$$wgt = \frac{marhusb \times marwife}{44597774}$$ Equation 15-30

The *wgt* variable is added to the data by using the Compute Variable dialog box, accessed from the Transform menu. Then, the estimated cell counts are specified as weights by weighting cases by *wgt* (using the Data menu). The 1972 observations are specified as cell structure values. Finally, an independence model is fitted. To carry out the analysis, from the menus choose:

Transform
  Compute...
    wgt=marhusb*marwife/44597774

Data
  Weight Cases...
▶ Weight cases by: wgt

Analyze
  Loglinear
    General...

▶ Factor(s):yrhusb yrwife

Cell Structure: gsscnt

Model...
  ⊙ Custom
  ▶ Terms in Model (Main effects): yrhusb yrwife

Options...
  Display
    ☑ Frequencies
    ☑ Estimates
  Plots: deselect all plots

The fitted values are the estimated 1972 population census counts. The General Loglinear Analysis procedure displays both the observed and the fitted values by default. The output is shown in Figure 15-14.

Figure 15-14
Table information for education data

```
Table Information

                       Observed                    Expected
Factor    Value          Count        %             Count        %

YRHUSB    0-11
  YRWIFE    0-11     8068697.07  ( 18.09)        13284910.3  ( 29.79)
  YRWIFE      12     7982807.68  ( 17.90)        5598667.30  ( 12.55)
  YRWIFE   13-15     2280247.51  (  5.11)         909085.84  (  2.04)
  YRWIFE      16+    1601940.35  (  3.59)         141029.18  (   .32)

YRHUSB      12
  YRWIFE    0-11     5373757.99  ( 12.05)        3914816.89  (  8.78)
  YRWIFE      12     5316555.60  ( 11.92)        7268812.44  ( 16.30)
  YRWIFE   13-15     1518646.46  (  3.41)        1590225.64  (  3.57)
  YRWIFE      16+    1066893.41  (  2.39)         501998.52  (  1.13)

YRHUSB   13-15
  YRWIFE    0-11     2099554.28  (  4.71)         663722.05  (  1.49)
  YRWIFE      12     2077205.02  (  4.66)        2919328.37  (  6.55)
  YRWIFE   13-15      593342.81  (  1.33)        1105394.76  (  2.48)
  YRWIFE      16+     416840.62  (   .93)         498497.57  (  1.12)

YRHUSB      16+
  YRWIFE    0-11     2509962.56  (  5.63)         188522.67  (   .42)
  YRWIFE      12     2483244.60  (  5.57)        2073004.77  (  4.65)
  YRWIFE   13-15      709325.91  (  1.59)        1496856.45  (  3.36)
  YRWIFE      16+     498322.13  (  1.12)        2442471.42  (  5.48)
```

To check whether the 1972 fitted marginal totals have the same distribution (not the same values) as the 1970 census counts, you can compute generalized residuals by using the GRESID subcommand in a syntax window.

From the menus choose:

Transform
  Compute...

In the Compute Variable dialog box, set up eight new variables:

husb1=0
husb1 = 1 if yrhusb = 1
husb2=0
husb2 = 1 if yrhusb = 2
husb3=0
husb3 = 1 if yrhusb = 3
...
wife1=0
wife1 = 1 if yrwife = 1
...

and so on, for all of the values of *yrhusb* and *yrwife*. (You could also use Transform/Recode to set up the eight variables.) These are the coefficients for the generalized residuals. Then paste the syntax from the previous General Loglinear Analysis dialog box and type the following line before the period at the end of the command:

```
/GRESID = HUSB1, HUSB2, HUSB3, HUSB4, WIFE1, WIFE2, WIFE3, WIFE4
```

You can run the command by clicking the Run Current syntax tool on the toolbar. The generalized residuals are shown in Figure 15-15.

Figure 15-15
Generalized residuals

```
Generalized Residual
                Observed      Expected                            Std.        Adj.
                   Value         Value      Resid.              Resid.      Resid.
   HUSB1      19933692.61   19933692.61   1.18092E-06   2.64500E-10        .
   HUSB2      13275853.46   13275853.46   8.66130E-07   2.37712E-10        .
   HUSB3       5186942.74    5186942.74   2.11410E-07   9.28261E-11        .
   HUSB4       6200855.19    6200855.19   3.33413E-07   1.33893E-10        .
   WIFE1      18051971.90   18051971.90   1.26660E-06   2.98110E-10        .
   WIFE2      17859812.89   17859812.89   8.30740E-07   1.96574E-10        .
   WIFE3       5101562.69    5101562.69   2.68221E-07   1.18752E-10        .
   WIFE4       3583996.52    3583996.52   2.27243E-07   1.20035E-10        .
```

The 1972 fitted marginal totals have the same distribution as the 1970 census counts. For example, the ratio of the 1972 marginal totals between the first two categories of *yrhusb* is

$$\frac{19,933,692.61}{13,275,853.48} = 1.5015 \qquad \text{Equation 15-31}$$

which is the same as that for the 1970 census counts:

$$\frac{19,933,782}{13,275,913} = 1.5015 \qquad \text{Equation 15-32}$$

The results are not surprising because this is a property of the method of adjustment.

Example 5
Poisson Loglinear Regression

Poisson regression encompasses statistical methods for the analysis of the relationship between an observed count with a Poisson distribution and a set of explanatory variables. The loglinear model is the best known type of Poisson regression. The expected count for observed count n_i is m_i. Its specification is

$$m_i = N_i e^{\beta' x_i} \qquad \text{Equation 15-33}$$

for counts n_i with independent Poisson distributions, where n_i denotes the number of events for the ith sample and N_i denotes the corresponding exposure.

The following example illustrates how to use the General Loglinear Analysis procedure to fit Poisson loglinear models. The data are taken from Koch et al. (1986) and show the *age*-by-*region* cross-classification of new melanoma cases among white males during 1969–1971 and estimated populations at risk (see Table 15-4).

Table 15-4
Age-by-region cross-classification

Age group	Melanoma cases, n_{ij}		Estimated population at risk, N_{ij}	
	Northern	Southern	Northern	Southern
less than 35	61	64	2880262	1074246
35–44	76	75	564535	220407
45–54	98	68	592983	198119
55–64	104	63	450740	134084
65–74	63	45	270908	70708
75 +	80	27	161850	34233

The data contain the counts, denoted as n_{ij}, which are the numbers of new melanoma cases reported for the ith age group and jth area where $i = 1, 2, 3, 4, 5, 6$ and $j = 1, 2$. The exposures, denoted as N_{ij}, are corresponding estimated populations at risk. It is of interest to investigate whether the ratios n_{ij}/N_{ij} across areas tend to be homogeneous across age groups or whether the ratios across age groups tend to be homogeneous across areas. Such a structure can be expressed in the loglinear form

$$m_{ij} = N_{ij} e^{\mu + \alpha_i + \beta_j} \qquad \text{Equation 15-34}$$

where α_i represents the effect for ith age group and β_j represents jth area effect. The model can be fitted in the General Loglinear Analysis procedure. The data structure is shown in Figure 15-16.

Figure 15-16
Data structure for melanoma data

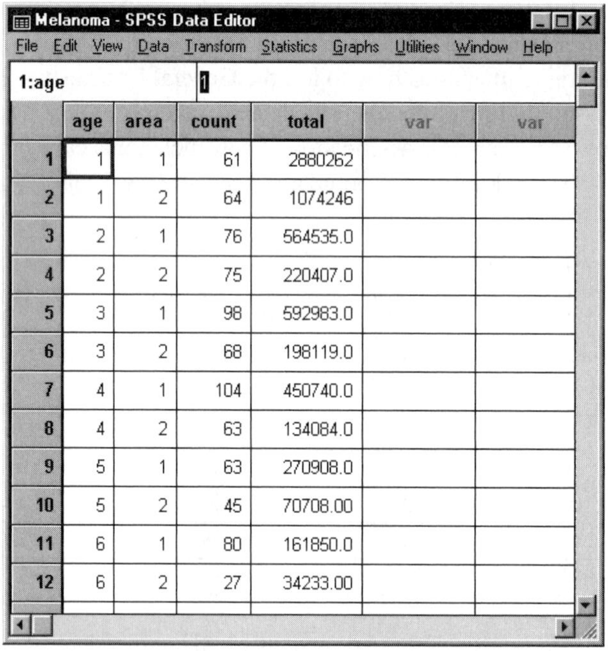

	age	area	count	total	var	var
1	1	1	61	2880262		
2	1	2	64	1074246		
3	2	1	76	564535.0		
4	2	2	75	220407.0		
5	3	1	98	592983.0		
6	3	2	68	198119.0		
7	4	1	104	450740.0		
8	4	2	63	134084.0		
9	5	1	63	270908.0		
10	5	2	45	70708.00		
11	6	1	80	161850.0		
12	6	2	27	34233.00		

The variables are *age* (age group), *area* (region), *count* (new melanoma cases), and *total* (population at risk). The data are weighted by *count* because the individual cases are already aggregated.

Data
  Weight Cases...
▶ Weight cases by: count

Analyze
  Loglinear
    General...

▶ Factor(s):age area

Cell Structure: total

Model...
  ⊙ Custom
    ▶ Terms in Model (Main effects): age area

Options...
  Display
    ☑ Frequencies
    ☑ Estimates
  Plots: deselect all plots

The goodness-of-fit statistics in Figure 15-17 show that the Poisson loglinear model fits the data fairly well (the significance values are greater than 0.05).

Figure 15-17
Goodness-of-fit statistics

```
Goodness-of-fit Statistics

                     Chi-Square        DF        Sig.
Likelihood Ratio        6.2149          5       .2859
         Pearson        6.1151          5       .2952
```

The output shows that there are nine parameters in the model, including the constant. As shown in Figure 15-18, α_6 and β_2 (parameters 7 and 9) have been identified as redundant and their parameter estimates are set to 0.

Figure 15-18
Correspondence between parameters and terms of the design

```
Parameter    Aliased   Term

      1                Constant
      2                [AGE = 1]
      3                [AGE = 2]
      4                [AGE = 3]
      5                [AGE = 4]
      6                [AGE = 5]
      7         x      [AGE = 6]
      8                [AREA = 1]
      9         x      [AREA = 2]

Note: 'x' indicates an aliased (or a redundant) parameter.
```

The estimates of the remaining six parameters are shown in Figure 15-19. The estimates for parameters 2 through 6 show that different age groups all contribute significant effects to the model and that their effects are not the same. The area effect, parameter 8, is significantly different from 0, as shown by its 95% confidence interval.

Figure 15-19
Parameter estimates

```
                                                   Asymptotic 95% CI
             Parameter   Estimate     SE    Z-value    Lower     Upper
age groups      1        -6.8941    .1079   -63.88     -7.11     -6.68
             ┌─ 2        -2.9447    .1320   -22.30     -3.20     -2.69
             │  3        -1.1473    .1268    -9.05     -1.40      -.90
             │  4        -1.0316    .1242    -8.31     -1.28      -.79
   area      │  5         -.7029    .1239    -5.67      -.95      -.46
             └─ 6         -.5790    .1364    -4.24      -.85      -.31
                7         .0000       .         .         .         .
                8        -.8195    .0710   -11.54      -.96      -.68
```

To study the difference between different age groups across areas, you can create comparison variables and specify them as contrast variables to obtain the contrast estimate and its confidence interval estimate.

For example, you can compare the second age group with the first age group—that is, $(\alpha_2 - \alpha_1)$—across areas. One way to do this is to create a contrast variable, *G1*. It has the value -1 for the first age group cells, (1,1) and (1,2), and the value 1 for the second age group cells, (2,1) and (2, 2)—the same as the coefficients of α_2 and α_1. The value is 0 for the other cells because they are not included in the comparison currently being considered.

The data with three new contrast variables, *G1*, *G2*, and *G3*, are shown in Figure 15-20. Variable *G2* is for comparing the third age group with the first age group, and *G3* is for comparing the two areas across age groups.

Figure 15-20
Data with contrast variables

Melanoma - SPSS Data Editor

File Edit View Data Transform Statistics Graphs Utilities Window Help

1:g1 -1

	age	area	count	total	g1	g2	g3
1	1	1	61	2880262	-1	-1	-1
2	1	2	64	1074246	-1	-1	1
3	2	1	76	564535.0	1	0	-1
4	2	2	75	220407.0	1	0	1
5	3	1	98	592983.0	0	1	-1
6	3	2	68	198119.0	0	1	1
7	4	1	104	450740.0	0	0	-1
8	4	2	63	134084.0	0	0	1
9	5	1	63	270908.0	0	0	-1
10	5	2	45	70708.00	0	0	1
11	6	1	80	161850.0	0	0	-1
12	6	2	27	34233.00	0	0	1

To implement the contrast variables, recall the General Loglinear Analysis dialog box and move the three new variables to the Contrast Variable(s) list. The other selections remain the same. The contrast variables *G1*, *G2*, and *G3* are shown in the output in the generalized log-odds ratio (GLOR) coefficients table (see Figure 15-21).

Figure 15-21

Generalized residual and generalized log-odds ratio coefficients

```
Factor      Value                      G1        G2        G3

AGE less than 35
   AREA     northern               -1.000    -1.000    -1.000
   AREA     southern               -1.000    -1.000     1.000

AGE         35-44
   AREA     northern                1.000      .000    -1.000
   AREA     southern                1.000      .000     1.000

AGE         45-54
   AREA     northern                 .000     1.000    -1.000
   AREA     southern                 .000     1.000     1.000

AGE         55-64
   AREA     northern                 .000      .000    -1.000
   AREA     southern                 .000      .000     1.000

AGE         65-74
   AREA     northern                 .000      .000    -1.000
   AREA     southern                 .000      .000     1.000

AGE         75 +
   AREA     northern                 .000      .000    -1.000
```

Applying *G1* to Equation 15-34 yields

$$\ln(m_{21}) - \ln(m_{11}) + \ln(m_{22}) - \ln(m_{12})$$
$$= \ln(N_{21}) - \ln(N_{11}) + \ln(N_{22}) - \ln(N_{12}) + 2(\alpha_2 - \alpha_1)$$

Equation 15-35

This equation can be solved for $(\alpha_2 - \alpha_1)$ and evaluated. The estimate for the left side of Equation 15-35 is the GLOR estimate for *G1*, which is calculated by the General Loglinear Analysis procedure. The estimate, shown in the output table in Figure 15-22, is 0.38, with a standard error of 0.24.

Figure 15-22

Generalized log-odds ratio

Generalized Log-Odds Ratio

| | | | | | 95% Confidence Interval | | | |
| | | | | | Log-Odds Ratio | | Odds Ratio | |
Variable	GLOR	SE	Wald	Sig.	Lower	Upper	Lower	Upper
G1	.38	.24	2.48	.1150	-.09	.86	.91	2.35
G2	.56	.24	5.49	.0191	.09	1.02	1.10	2.77
G3	-2.22	.43	27.02	.0000	-3.05	-1.38	.05	.25

From the data, you can calculate the first part of the right side of Equation 15-35:

$$\ln(N_{21}) - \ln(N_{11}) + \ln(N_{22}) - \ln(N_{12}) = -3.22$$

Equation 15-36

Next, subtract the result from the GLOR estimate and divide by 2:

$$\frac{0.38 - (-3.22)}{2} = 1.8$$ Equation 15-37

This is the estimate for $(\alpha_2 - \alpha_1)$. The standard error is $0.24/2 = 0.12$. Applying the same operations and using the 95% confidence interval for *G1* $(-0.09, 0.86)$ yields $(1.56, 2.04)$ as the 95% confidence interval for $(\alpha_2 - \alpha_1)$. The figures suggest that the ratio of the rate of new melanoma cases for the second age group (35–44) to the rate for first age group (less than 35) is 6, since

$$e^{1.8} = 6.0$$ Equation 15-38

Two more contrasts, *G2* and *G3*, were created; *G2* compares the third age group with the first age group, and *G3* compares the two areas (see Figure 15-21). Applying both *G2* and *G3* to the natural logarithm of *total* gives -3.27 and -7.11, respectively. Following calculations similar to those for *G1* yields

$$\frac{0.56 - (-3.27)}{2} = 1.915$$ Equation 15-39

as the estimate for $(\alpha_3 - \alpha_1)$. The corresponding 95% confidence interval is $(1.68, 2.15)$.

Similarly, using *G3*, the estimate for $(\beta_2 - \beta_1)$ is

$$\frac{-2.22 - (-7.11)}{6} = 0.815$$ Equation 15-40

It is divided by 6 because we pool the area differences across six age groups. The corresponding 95% confidence interval is $(0.68, 0.96)$, which is the same as that for parameter 8 but has the opposite sign. We can conclude that the rate in the southern area is 2.3 times higher than that of the northern area, since

$$e^{0.815} = 2.3$$ Equation 15-41

Multinomial Logit Models Examples

Multinomial logit models are a special class of loglinear models. In a multinomial logit model, variables are classified as response (or dependent) variables and explanatory (or independent) variables. As their names suggest, the behaviors of the response variables are thought to be explained by the explanatory variables. In these models, response variables are always categorical, while explanatory variables can be either categorical or continuous.

The *logarithm* of the odds of the response variables (instead of the cell count in the loglinear model) is expressed as a linear combination of parameters. Moreover, the counts within each combination of categories of explanatory variables are assumed to have a multinomial distribution. The Logit Loglinear Analysis procedure automatically specifies a multinomial distribution.

There are many kinds of logit models, especially for response variables with more than two categories. Two popular logit models are illustrated later in this chapter—baseline category logit (see "Polytomous Response Variable" on p. 211) and continuation ratio logit (see "Continuation Ratio Logit Model" on p. 225). Two other popular models are cumulative logit and adjacent category logit.

For baseline category logit and adjacent category logit models, there is an equivalent loglinear model for each. In fact, SPSS fits a logit model by fitting its equivalent loglinear model, if it exists. Also, the Logit Loglinear Analysis procedure can handle several response variables that might have more than two categories. The examples in the following sections illustrate how to specify logit models using the Logit Loglinear Analysis procedure and how to interpret the output.

Example 1: One response variable with two categories. Data from a Florida report on accidents relating types of injuries and whether the injured persons were wearing seat belts are analyzed using a Logit Loglinear model. Parameter estimates and the analysis-of-dispersion table are discussed.

Example 2: Two response variables with two categories each. The data are from a study that measured the effects of two respiratory ailments on coal miners in various age groups. The example includes an interaction between covariates.

Example 3: Polytomous response variable. This study investigates how alligators' primary food type varies with their size and the four lakes in which they live. The five categories of food make the response variable polytomous (more than two categories).

Example 4: Model diagnosis, coal miner data revisited. The data from Example 2 are used to generate another model and techniques of model diagnosis are discussed. The second model is shown to be statistically different from the first.

Example 5: Continuation ratio logit model. This model can be used when the response variable is ordinal (has ordered categories). The study investigates how various doses of a chemical affect developing fetuses in mice. Odds of deleterious effects are calculated based on the dosage.

Example 1
One Response Variable with Two Categories

This example shows how to analyze the accident data using the Logit Loglinear Analysis procedure instead of the General Loglinear Analysis procedure ("Complete Table" on p. 160 in Chapter 15). Consider the 1988 Florida automobile accident data again (see Table 16-1).

Table 16-1
1988 Florida automobile accident data

Wearing a seat belt?	Injury type	
	Fatal	Nonfatal
No	1601	162527
Yes	510	412368

The response variable is *injury* (injury type) and the explanatory variable is *qbelt* (whether a seat belt is worn). Each variable has two categories. The data structure is shown in Figure 16-1. The data are weighted by *count*.

Figure 16-1
Data structure for accident data

Consider how the odds of having a fatal injury vary with the value of *qbelt*. The observed odds are

$$\frac{n_{11}}{n_{12}} = \frac{1601}{162527} = 0.009851$$

Equation 16-1

without seat belts and

$$\frac{n_{21}}{n_{22}} = \frac{510}{412368} = 0.001237$$

Equation 16-2

with seat belts. The odds ratio is

$$\frac{n_{11}n_{22}}{n_{12}n_{21}} = 7.964905$$

Equation 16-3

These figures suggest that the odds are related to whether or not seat belts are worn. If m_{11} is the expected number of fatal injuries without seat belts, m_{12} is the expected number of nonfatal injuries without seat belts, and so on, the logit model is

$$\ln\left(\frac{m_{i1}}{m_{i2}}\right) = \lambda + \delta_i \qquad i = 1, 2 \qquad\qquad \text{Equation 16-4}$$

where λ is the baseline term and δ_i is the term due to *qbelt*. As discussed below, this logit model is equivalent to the loglinear model

$$\ln(m_{ij}) = \alpha_i + \beta_j + \gamma_{ij} \qquad i = 1, 2 \text{ and } j = 1, 2 \qquad\qquad \text{Equation 16-5}$$

where α_i is the main-effects term of *qbelt*, β_j is the main-effects term of *injury*, and γ_{ij} is the interaction term between *qbelt* and *injury*. This loglinear model is slightly different from others because the overall intercept term μ is not included in Equation 16-5. The following paragraphs explain why.

Recalling that the logarithm of a ratio is the logarithm of the numerator minus the logarithm of the denominator and using Equation 16-5, we have

$$\ln\left(\frac{m_{i1}}{m_{i2}}\right) = \ln(m_{i1}) - \ln(m_{i2})$$

Equation 16-6

$$= (\alpha_i + \beta_1 + \gamma_{i1}) - (\alpha_i + \beta_2 + \gamma_{i2}) \qquad i = 1, 2$$

Since the α_i terms cancel, Equation 16-6 can be simplified as

$$\ln\left(\frac{m_{i1}}{m_{i2}}\right) = \ln(m_{i1}) - \ln(m_{i2}) = (\beta_1 - \beta_2) + (\gamma_{i1} - \gamma_{i2}) \qquad i = 1, 2$$

Equation 16-7

Comparing Equation 16-4 and Equation 16-7 yields

$$\lambda = \beta_1 - \beta_2 \qquad \text{and} \qquad \delta_i = \gamma_{i1} - \gamma_{i2} \qquad\qquad \text{Equation 16-8}$$

Thus, the logit model in Equation 16-4 is equivalent to the loglinear model in Equation 16-5. Furthermore, terms that do not relate to the category of *injury* (that is, the index *j* terms) cancel in Equation 16-6, so it is unnecessary to include the overall intercept term μ in Equation 16-5.

Although it could be further argued that the terms α_i are also unnecessary or that they can have any values (because including them in Equation 16-5 does not affect Equation 16-4), we do need these α_i terms to equate the sum of fitted values to the sum of observed counts for each combination of levels of explanatory variables. Therefore, the Logit Loglinear procedure labels them as constants in the parameter correspondence table and displays their estimates without standard errors in the parameter estimates table.

For the accident data, to weight the data by *count*, from the menus choose:

Data
  Weight Cases...
▶ Weight cases by: count

To fit the logit model in Equation 16-4, choose:

Analyze
  Loglinear
    Logit...

▶ Dependent: injury
▶ Factor(s): qbelt

Options...
    Display
        ☑ Frequencies
        ☑ Estimates
    Plots: deselect all plots
    Criteria
        Delta: 0

The default saturated model is used.

Since the Logit Loglinear Analysis procedure fits the equivalent loglinear model in Equation 16-5, it displays estimates for parameters β_1, β_2, γ_{i1}, and γ_{i2}. Figure 16-2 shows the parameter correspondence table.

Figure 16-2
Parameter correspondence table

```
Correspondence Between Parameters and Terms of the Design

Parameter   Aliased   Term

        1             Constant for [QBELT = 1]
        2             Constant for [QBELT = 2]
        3             [INJURY = 1]
        4       x     [INJURY = 2]
        5             [INJURY = 1]*[QBELT = 1]
        6       x     [INJURY = 1]*[QBELT = 2]
        7       x     [INJURY = 2]*[QBELT = 1]
        8       x     [INJURY = 2]*[QBELT = 2]

Note: 'x' indicates an aliased (or a redundant) parameter.
      These parameters are set to zero.
```

The α_1 and α_2 terms are shown in the table as parameter 1 and parameter 2, respectively, although they are not considered as real parameters in a logit model. Parameters 4, 6, 7, and 8 (β_2, γ_{12}, γ_{21}, and γ_{22}) are identified as aliased and their values are set to 0. Figure 16-3 shows the parameter estimates table.

Figure 16-3
Parameter estimates table

```
Parameter Estimates

 Constant    Estimate

     1        11.9986
     2        12.9297

Note: Constants are not parameters under multinomial assumption.
      Therefore, standard errors are not calculated.

                                               Asymptotic 95% CI
 Parameter   Estimate       SE    Z-value      Lower      Upper
     3        -6.6953     .0443   -151.11      -6.78      -6.61
     4         .0000        .         .          .          .
     5        2.0750      .0509     40.74       1.98       2.17
     6         .0000        .         .          .          .
     7         .0000        .         .          .          .
     8         .0000        .         .          .          .
```

The parameter estimates are

$$\beta_1 = -6.6953 \qquad\qquad \text{Equation 16-9}$$

and

$$\gamma_{11} = 2.0750 \qquad\qquad \text{Equation 16-10}$$

Substituting these values into Equation 16-8 yields

$$\lambda = (-6.6953) - 0 = -6.6953$$
$$\delta_1 = 2.0750 - 0 = 2.0750 \qquad\qquad \text{Equation 16-11}$$
$$\delta_2 = 0$$

From Equation 16-4,

$$\ln\left[\frac{m_{i1}}{m_{i2}}\right] = -6.6953 + 2.0750\,I \qquad i = 1, 2 \qquad\qquad \text{Equation 16-12}$$

where $I = 1$ if $i = 1$ and $I = 0$ if $i = 2$. Hence, the log-odds of having a fatal injury without a seat beat are 2.0750 times that with a seat belt. It is equivalent to saying that the odds of having an injury without a seat belt are

$$e^{2.0750} = 7.9649$$

Equation 16-13

times higher than the odds with a seat belt.

In addition to parameter estimates, the Logit Loglinear Analysis procedure calculates other statistics useful for investigating the association between response variables and explanatory variables. Two methods for measuring association—entropy and concentration—are used in the logit loglinear model. The Logit Loglinear Analysis procedure produces an analysis-of-dispersion table containing measure-of-association statistics for both entropy and concentration. The analysis-of-dispersion table is analogous to the analysis-of-variance table in regression. The measure of association plays a role similar to R^2 in regression. Following the methods discussed in Haberman (1982), you can use these statistics, shown in Figure 16-4, to compare how the current model differs from the independence model. If the test statistics are not significant, the current model is not substantially different from the independence model.

Figure 16-4
Analysis-of-dispersion table

```
Analysis of Dispersion

Source of Dispersion      Entropy   Concentration        DF

Due to Model            1020.5789        17.0477           1
Due to Residual        12930.7232      4189.5059      577004
Total                  13951.3022      4206.5536      577005

Measures of Association

      Entropy =.0732
Concentration =  .0041
```

Consider entropy first. Denoting the entropy due to the model as $S_H(M)$, the chi-square statistic

$$\psi_H = 2\ S_H(M) \tag{Equation 16-14}$$

has an asymptotic chi-square distribution. The number of degrees of freedom is given in the column labeled *DF*. In this example,

$$\psi_H = 2 \times 1020.5789 = 2041.1578 \tag{Equation 16-15}$$

which has an asymptotic chi-square distribution with 1 degree of freedom. To calculate the *p* value, choose Compute from the Transform menu and create a variable *p*:

$$p = 1 - \text{CDF.CHISQ}(2044.1578, 1) \tag{Equation 16-16}$$

The *p* value is practically 0.

The concentration due to the model is denoted as $S_C(M)$ and the concentration due to the residual is denoted as $S_C(R)$. Then the *F* statistic

$$F_C = \frac{S_C(M)/DF(M)}{S_C(R)/DF(R)} \tag{Equation 16-17}$$

has an *F* distribution with degrees of freedom *DF(M)* and *DF(R)*. The terms *DF(M)* and *DF(R)* are the degrees of freedom due to the model and due to the residual, respectively.

Using concentration as the measurement,

$$F_C = \frac{17.0477/1}{4189.5059/577003} = 2347.9079 \tag{Equation 16-18}$$

with (1, 577003) degrees of freedom. Using the CDF.F function in the Compute Variable dialog box (accessed from the Transform menu), the *p* value is again essentially 0: $p = 1 - \text{CDF.F}(2347.8829)$. Thus, there is strong evidence that *qbelt* and *injury* are not independent.

Note that ψ_H is the same as the likelihood-ratio statistic with the same number of degrees of freedom when an independence model is fitted to these data. Also,

$$\psi_C = \frac{(DF(T)+1)S_C(M)}{S_C(T)} = 2338.4048$$

Equation 16-19

is the same as the Pearson statistic for the independence model, where $DF(T)$ represents the total of degrees of freedom. This is expected, as mentioned in Haberman (1982), because the response variable has two categories.

The association coefficients are $R_H = 0.0732$ and $R_C = 0.0041$. As mentioned in Goodman and Kruskal (1954), it is best not to interpret R_H and R_C in the same manner as we would interpret an R^2 of the same magnitude in a usual regression analysis. The observed R_H and R_C do indicate a fairly strong relation.

Since the data are in a two-way table and the model is saturated, we can calculate R_H and R_C using the Crosstabs procedure. R_H is the uncertainty coefficient with *injury* as the response. R_C is the square of Kendall's tau-*b*.

Example 2
Two Response Variables with Two Categories Each

In some studies, it is common to treat two categorical variables as response variables. We could fit a separate logit model to each response variable using the same set of explanatory variables, or we could study how the associations between response variables are affected by the explanatory variables. Consider an example illustrating the second case.

Figure 16-5 shows data from Ashford and Sowden (1970), where coal miners are classified by breathlessness, wheeze, and age. The data are from a study that measured the effects of two respiratory ailments on 18,282 coal miners in the United Kingdom. The coal miners were smokers without radiological evidence of pneumoconiosis, between 20 and 64 years of age at the time of examination. The aim of this analysis is to study how the association between breathlessness and wheeze changes across levels of age. The variables are *age*, *qbreath*, *qwheeze*, and *count*. The variable *age* is coded into nine groups. The data structure is shown in Figure 16-5.

Figure 16-5
Data structure for coal miner data

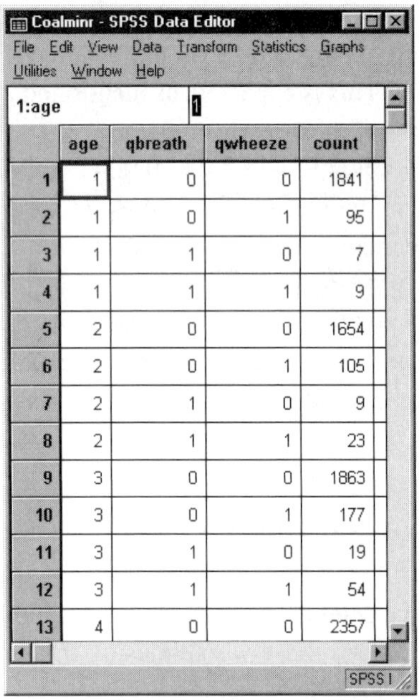

	age	qbreath	qwheeze	count
1	1	0	0	1841
2	1	0	1	95
3	1	1	0	7
4	1	1	1	9
5	2	0	0	1654
6	2	0	1	105
7	2	1	0	9
8	2	1	1	23
9	3	0	0	1863
10	3	0	1	177
11	3	1	0	19
12	3	1	1	54
13	4	0	0	2357

The data are weighted by *count*.

Agresti (1990) fitted the model

$$\ln\left(\frac{m_{11k}m_{22k}}{m_{12k}m_{21k}}\right) = \lambda + k\delta \qquad \text{Equation 16-20}$$

where m_{ijk} is the count for the *i*th category of breathlessness, the *j*th category of wheeze, and the *k*th level of age. Equation 16-20 implies that the association of breathlessness and wheeze, as measured by the log-odds ratio, varies linearly across age. The equivalent loglinear model is

$$\ln(m_{ijk}) = \alpha_k + \beta_i + \omega_j + (\alpha\beta)_{ik} + (\alpha\omega)_{jk} + (\beta\omega)_{ij} + kI\delta \qquad \text{Equation 16-21}$$

where $I = 1$ if $i = j = 1$, and $I = 0$ if *i* or *j* is not 1. The main-effects terms corresponding to *age*, *qbreath*, and *qwheeze* are α_k, β_i, and ω_j. The interaction-effects terms are then denoted by $(\alpha\beta)_{ik}$, $(\alpha\omega)_{jk}$, and $(\beta\omega)_{ij}$. Furthermore, it can be derived from Equation 16-20 and Equation 16-21 that

$$\lambda = (\beta\omega)_{11} - (\beta\omega)_{12} - (\beta\omega)_{21} + (\beta\omega)_{22} \qquad \text{Equation 16-22}$$

To begin the analysis, create a variable *delta*. From the menus choose:

Transform
  Compute...

Target Variable: delta (type the name for the new variable)

Numeric Expression: age*(qbreath=1)*(qwheeze=1)

This sets *delta* equal to the value of the age group when $i = j = 1$; otherwise, *delta* is equal to 0. This is, in fact, an example of an interaction between covariates.

To fit the model in Equation 16-21, from the menus choose:

Analyze
  Loglinear
    Logit...

▶ Dependent: qbreath qwheeze
▶ Factor(s): age
▶ Cell Covariate(s): delta

Model...
  ⊙ Custom
    ▶ Terms in Model (Main effects): age delta

Options...
  Display
      ☑ Frequencies
      ☑ Estimates
  Plot: deselect all plots

Paste

Running the Logit Loglinear Analysis procedure in the dialog box generates all possible interactions between the dependent variable list in the Logit Loglinear Analysis dialog box and the terms in the Logit Loglinear Analysis Model dialog box. To get only the relevant interactions, click Paste and then modify the syntax by removing the extra interactions. The pasted syntax is shown in Figure 16-6. Remove the interactions that are shaded (*delta* remains in the design) and click the Run Current tool.

Figure 16-6
Pasted syntax for coal miner data

```
GENLOG QBREATH QWHEEZE BY AGE WITH DELTA
  /MODEL MULTINOMIAL
  /PRINT = FREQ ESTIM
  /PLOT = NONE
  /CRITERIA =CIN(95) ITERATION(20) CONVERGE(.001) DELTA(.5)
  /DESIGN = QBREATH, QWHEEZE, QBREATH BY QWHEEZE,
          QBREATH BY AGE, QWHEEZE BY AGE,
          QBREATH BY QWHEEZE BY AGE, QBREATH BY DELTA,
          QWHEEZE BY DELTA, QBREATH BY QWHEEZE BY
          DELTA.
```

This model fits the data well, as seen from the goodness-of-fit statistics shown in Figure 16-7. The significance is well above 0.05.

Figure 16-7
Goodness-of-fit statistics

```
Goodness-of-fit Statistics

                    Chi-Square      DF      Sig.

Likelihood Ratio      6.8017        7      .4498
         Pearson      6.8083        7      .4491
```

Figure 16-8 shows the parameter correspondence table and Figure 16-9 shows the parameter estimates table.

Figure 16-8
Correspondence between parameters and terms of the design

```
Parameter    Aliased   Term
        1              Constant for [AGE = 1]
        2              Constant for [AGE = 2]
        3              Constant for [AGE = 3]
        4              Constant for [AGE = 4]
        5              Constant for [AGE = 5]
        6              Constant for [AGE = 6]
        7              Constant for [AGE = 7]
        8              Constant for [AGE = 8]
        9              Constant for [AGE = 9]
       10              [QBREATH = 0]
       11        x     [QBREATH = 1]
       12              [QWHEEZE = 0]
       13        x     [QWHEEZE = 1]
       14              [QBREATH = 0]*[AGE = 1]
       15              [QBREATH = 0]*[AGE = 2]
       16              [QBREATH = 0]*[AGE = 3]
       17              [QBREATH = 0]*[AGE = 4]
       18              [QBREATH = 0]*[AGE = 5]
       19              [QBREATH = 0]*[AGE = 6]
       20              [QBREATH = 0]*[AGE = 7]
       21              [QBREATH = 0]*[AGE = 8]
       22        x     [QBREATH = 0]*[AGE = 9]
       23        x     [QBREATH = 1]*[AGE = 1]
       24        x     [QBREATH = 1]*[AGE = 2]
       25        x     [QBREATH = 1]*[AGE = 3]
       26        x     [QBREATH = 1]*[AGE = 4]
       27        x     [QBREATH = 1]*[AGE = 5]
       28        x     [QBREATH = 1]*[AGE = 6]
       29        x     [QBREATH = 1]*[AGE = 7]
       30        x     [QBREATH = 1]*[AGE = 8]
       31        x     [QBREATH = 1]*[AGE = 9]
       32              [QWHEEZE = 0]*[AGE = 1]
       33              [QWHEEZE = 0]*[AGE = 2]
       34              [QWHEEZE = 0]*[AGE = 3]
       35              [QWHEEZE = 0]*[AGE = 4]
       36              [QWHEEZE = 0]*[AGE = 5]
       37              [QWHEEZE = 0]*[AGE = 6]
       38              [QWHEEZE = 0]*[AGE = 7]
       39              [QWHEEZE = 0]*[AGE = 8]
       40        x     [QWHEEZE = 0]*[AGE = 9]
       41        x     [QWHEEZE = 1]*[AGE = 1]
       42        x     [QWHEEZE = 1]*[AGE = 2]
       43        x     [QWHEEZE = 1]*[AGE = 3]
       44        x     [QWHEEZE = 1]*[AGE = 4]
       45        x     [QWHEEZE = 1]*[AGE = 5]
       46        x     [QWHEEZE = 1]*[AGE = 6]
       47        x     [QWHEEZE = 1]*[AGE = 7]
       48        x     [QWHEEZE = 1]*[AGE = 8]
       49        x     [QWHEEZE = 1]*[AGE = 9]
       50              [QBREATH = 0]*[QWHEEZE = 0]
       51        x     [QBREATH = 0]*[QWHEEZE = 1]
       52        x     [QBREATH = 1]*[QWHEEZE = 0]
       53        x     [QBREATH = 1]*[QWHEEZE = 1]
       54              DELTA
Note: 'x' indicates an aliased (or a redundant) parameter.
      These parameters are set to zero.
```

Figure 16-9
Parameter estimates

```
Parameter Estimates
   Constant   Estimate
          1    2.4542
          2    3.3158
          3    4.3525
          4    5.3215
          5    5.7848
          6    6.3997
          7    6.8891
          8    7.0824
          9    7.0770
```

Note: Constants are not parameters under multinomial assumption.
Therefore, standard errors are not calculated.

Parameter	Estimate	SE	Z-value	Asymptotic 95% CI Lower	Upper
10	-2.1462	.2427	-8.84	-2.62	-1.67
11	.0000	.	.	.	.
12	-2.3541	.2375	-9.91	-2.82	-1.89
13	.0000	.	.	.	.
14	4.2330	.3017	14.03	3.64	4.82
15	3.5013	.2347	14.92	3.04	3.96
16	2.9783	.1822	16.35	2.62	3.34
17	2.3722	.1424	16.66	2.09	2.65
18	1.9698	.1275	15.45	1.72	2.22
19	1.5092	.1094	13.79	1.29	1.72
20	.8009	.0989	8.10	.61	.99
21	.4213	.0959	4.39	.23	.61
22	.0000	.	.	.	.
23	.0000	.	.	.	.
24	.0000	.	.	.	.
25	.0000	.	.	.	.
26	.0000	.	.	.	.
27	.0000	.	.	.	.
28	.0000	.	.	.	.
29	.0000	.	.	.	.
30	.0000	.	.	.	.
31	.0000	.	.	.	.
32	1.6556	.1337	12.38	1.39	1.92
33	1.4169	.1287	11.01	1.16	1.67
34	1.0224	.1132	9.03	.80	1.24
35	.8957	.1046	8.56	.69	1.10
36	.5529	.1025	5.39	.35	.75
37	.3639	.0978	3.72	.17	.56
38	.3144	.0958	3.28	.13	.50
39	.2077	.0947	2.19	.02	.39
40	.0000	.	.	.	.
41	.0000	.	.	.	.
42	.0000	.	.	.	.
43	.0000	.	.	.	.
44	.0000	.	.	.	.
45	.0000	.	.	.	.
46	.0000	.	.	.	.
47	.0000	.	.	.	.
48	.0000	.	.	.	.
49	.0000	.	.	.	.
50	3.6762	.1999	18.39	3.28	4.07
51	.0000	.	.	.	.
52	.0000	.	.	.	.
53	.0000	.	.	.	.
54	-.1306	.0295	-4.43	-.19	-.07

In Figure 16-8, $(\beta\omega)_{11}$, $(\beta\omega)_{12}$, $(\beta\omega)_{21}$, and $(\beta\omega)_{22}$ are the 50th, 51st, 52nd, and 53rd parameters, respectively. Then, using Figure 16-9, λ is estimated as $3.6762 - 0 - 0 + 0 = 3.6762$, with a standard error of 0.1999.

Since δ is the 54th parameter, its estimate is -0.1306, with a standard error of 0.0295. The z value is

$$-\frac{0.1306}{0.0295} = -4.4298 \qquad\qquad \text{Equation 16-23}$$

This implies that δ is significantly far from 0, considering the large sample size. Finally, the estimated log-odds ratio at level k of age is

$$\ln\left(\frac{m_{11k}m_{22k}}{m_{12k}m_{21k}}\right) = +3.6762 - 0.1306\ k \qquad\qquad \text{Equation 16-24}$$

It is evident from Equation 16-24 that the odds ratio between breathlessness and wheeze decreases at a rate of

$$e^{-0.1306} = 0.88 \qquad\qquad \text{Equation 16-25}$$

for every level of increase in age.

Example 3
Polytomous Response Variable

A **polytomous response variable** has more than two categories. Data from Delany and Moore (1987) illustrate how to fit a logit model to a polytomous response variable. The data include 219 alligators captured in four Florida lakes in September 1985. The investigators studied how the alligators' primary food type varied with their size and the lakes in which they lived. The response variable *food* categorizes the primary food type. It has five categories—fish, invertebrate, reptile, bird, and other. The explanatory variables are *size* and *lake*. The variable *size* indicates the length of the alligators, in one of two categories. The variable *lake* identifies the area where the alligators were captured.

The data structure is shown in Figure 16-10. The lakes are designated by numbers: Lake Hancock (1), Lake Oklawaha (2), Lake Trafford (3), and Lake George (4). The data are weighted by *count*.

Figure 16-10
Data structure for alligator data

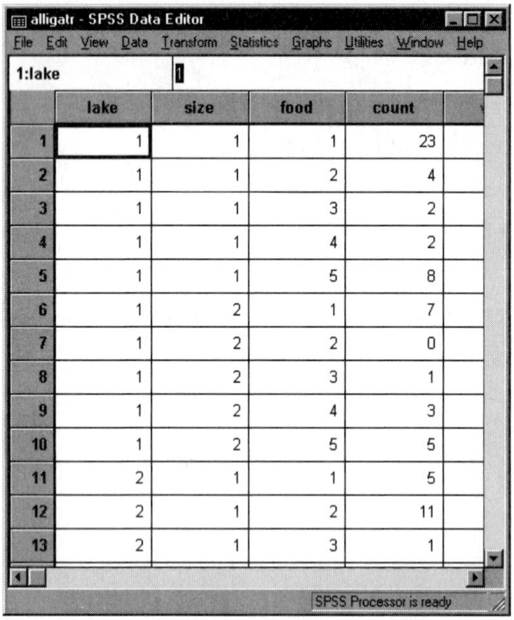

	lake	size	food	count
1	1	1	1	23
2	1	1	2	4
3	1	1	3	2
4	1	1	4	2
5	1	1	5	8
6	1	2	1	7
7	1	2	2	0
8	1	2	3	1
9	1	2	4	3
10	1	2	5	5
11	2	1	1	5
12	2	1	2	11
13	2	1	3	1

Agresti (1990) analyzes these data and fits the logit model

$$\ln\left(\frac{m_{ijk}}{m_{1jk}}\right) = \lambda_i + \omega_{ij} + \upsilon_{ik}, \qquad i = 2, 3, 4, 5 \qquad \text{Equation 16-26}$$

where i is the index for *food*, j is for *size*, and k is for *lake*. This logit model is used to study the preference for fish (*food* 1) versus any other food type. The equivalent loglinear model is

$$\ln(m_{ijk}) = (SL)_{jk} + F_i + (FS)_{ij} + (FL)_{ik} \qquad \text{Equation 16-27}$$

where $(SL)_{jk}$ is the normalizing constant for the *j*th category of *size* and *k*th category of *lake*. F_i is the main-effects term for *food*, $(FS)_{ij}$ and $(FL)_{ik}$ are the terms corresponding to *food* by *size* and *food* by *lake*. From Equation 16-26 and Equation 16-27,

$$\lambda_i = F_i - F_1$$
$$\omega_{ij} = (FS)_{ij} - (FS)_{1j} \qquad \text{Equation 16-28}$$
$$\upsilon_{ik} = (FL)_{ik} - (FL)_{1k}$$

For this logit model, from the menus choose:

Data
  Weight Cases...
▶ Weight cases by: count

Analyze
  Loglinear
    Logit...

▶ Dependent: food
▶ Factor(s): size lake

Model...
  ⊙ Custom
  ▶ Terms in Model (Main effects): lake size

Options...
  Display
      ☑ Frequencies
      ☑ Estimates
  Plot: deselect all plots

This model fits the data well, as shown in the goodness-of-fit statistics in Figure 16-11. The significance is well above 0.05.

Figure 16-11
Goodness-of-fit statistics

	Chi-Square	DF	Sig.
Likelihood Ratio	17.0798	12	.1466
Pearson	15.0435	12	.2391

The measures of association shown in Figure 16-12 are $R_H = 0.1064$ for entropy and $R_C = 0.0921$ for concentration, which suggests that *food* is associated with *lake* and *size*.

Figure 16-12
Analysis of dispersion and measures of association

```
Analysis of Dispersion

Source of Dispersion      Entropy   Concentration       DF

Due to Model              32.1413        14.2409         16
Due to Residual          270.0401       140.3253        856
Total                    302.1815       154.5662        872

Measures of Association

      Entropy =   .1064
Concentration =   .0921
```

Next, look at the parameter estimates. Figure 16-13 shows the parameter correspondence table, and Figure 16-14 shows the parameter estimates.

Figure 16-13
Correspondence between parameters and terms of the design

```
Parameter   Aliased   Term
        1             Constant for [LAKE = 1]*[SIZE = 1]
        2             Constant for [LAKE = 1]*[SIZE = 2]
        3             Constant for [LAKE = 2]*[SIZE = 1]
        4             Constant for [LAKE = 2]*[SIZE = 2]
        5             Constant for [LAKE = 3]*[SIZE = 1]
        6             Constant for [LAKE = 3]*[SIZE = 2]
        7             Constant for [LAKE = 4]*[SIZE = 1]
        8             Constant for [LAKE = 4]*[SIZE = 2]
        9             [FOOD = 1]
       10             [FOOD = 2]
       11             [FOOD = 3]
       12             [FOOD = 4]
       13      x      [FOOD = 5]
       14             [FOOD = 1]*[SIZE = 1]
       15      x      [FOOD = 1]*[SIZE = 2]
       16             [FOOD = 2]*[SIZE = 1]
       17      x      [FOOD = 2]*[SIZE = 2]
       18             [FOOD = 3]*[SIZE = 1]
       19      x      [FOOD = 3]*[SIZE = 2]
       20             [FOOD = 4]*[SIZE = 1]
       21      x      [FOOD = 4]*[SIZE = 2]
       22      x      [FOOD = 5]*[SIZE = 1]
       23      x      [FOOD = 5]*[SIZE = 2]
       24             [FOOD = 1]*[LAKE = 1]
       25             [FOOD = 1]*[LAKE = 2]
       26             [FOOD = 1]*[LAKE = 3]
       27      x      [FOOD = 1]*[LAKE = 4]
       28             [FOOD = 2]*[LAKE = 1]
       29             [FOOD = 2]*[LAKE = 2]
       30             [FOOD = 2]*[LAKE = 3]
       31      x      [FOOD = 2]*[LAKE = 4]
       32             [FOOD = 3]*[LAKE = 1]
       33             [FOOD = 3]*[LAKE = 2]
       34             [FOOD = 3]*[LAKE = 3]
       35      x      [FOOD = 3]*[LAKE = 4]
       36             [FOOD = 4]*[LAKE = 1]
       37             [FOOD = 4]*[LAKE = 2]
       38             [FOOD = 4]*[LAKE = 3]
       39      x      [FOOD = 4]*[LAKE = 4]
       40      x      [FOOD = 5]*[LAKE = 1]
       41      x      [FOOD = 5]*[LAKE = 2]
       42      x      [FOOD = 5]*[LAKE = 3]
       43      x      [FOOD = 5]*[LAKE = 4]
```

Note: 'x' indicates an aliased (or a redundant) parameter.
      These parameters are set to zero.

Figure 16-14
Parameter estimates for alligator data

```
Constant    Estimate

    1        2.2921
    2        1.1327
    3         .0746
    4         .6537
    5        1.4305
    6        1.7612
    7        1.3470
    8         .7674
```

Note: Constants are not parameters under the multinomial assumption.
Therefore, standard errors are not calculated.

Parameter	Estimate	SE	Z-value	Asymptotic 95% CI Lower	Upper
9	1.9043	.5258	3.62	.87	2.93
10	.3553	.5958	.60	−.81	1.52
11	−1.4103	1.1357	−1.24	−3.64	.82
12	−.1888	.7903	−.24	−1.74	1.36
13	.0000	.	.	.	.
14	−.0316	.4483	−.74	−1.21	.55
15	.0000	.	.	.	.
16	1.1267	.5049	2.23	.14	2.12
17	.0000	.	.	.	.
18	−.6828	.6514	−1.05	−1.96	.59
19	.0000	.	.	.	.
20	−.9622	.7127	−1.35	−2.36	.43
21	.0000	.	.	.	.
22	.0000	.	.	.	.
23	.0000	.	.	.	.
24	−.8262	.5575	−1.48	−1.92	.27
25	−.0057	.7766	−7.279E-03	−1.53	1.52
26	−1.5164	.6214	−2.44	−2.73	−.30
27	.0000	.	.	.	.
28	−2.4846	.7432	−3.34	−3.94	−1.03
29	.9316	.7968	1.17	−.63	2.49
30	−.3944	.6263	−.63	−1.62	.83
31	.0000	.	.	.	.
32	.4166	1.2605	.33	−2.05	2.89
33	2.4532	1.2938	1.90	−.08	4.99
34	1.4189	1.1892	1.19	−.91	3.75
35	.0000	.	.	.	.
36	−.1311	.8920	−.15	−1.88	1.62
37	−.6589	1.3686	−.48	−3.34	2.02
38	−.4286	.9383	−.46	−2.27	1.41
39	.0000	.	.	.	.
40	.0000	.	.	.	.
41	.0000	.	.	.	.
42	.0000	.	.	.	.
43	.0000	.	.	.	.

Consider how the size of an alligator affects the odds of its selecting primarily reptiles instead of fish. For $i = 3$, the parameter $\omega_{31} = (FS)_{31} - (FS)_{11}$. Since $(FS)_{31}$ and $(FS)_{11}$ are the 18th and the 14th parameters,

$$\omega_{31} = -0.6828 - (-0.3316) = -0.3512$$

Equation 16-29

Similarly,

$$\omega_{32} = (FS)_{32} - (FS)_{12} = 0 \qquad\qquad \text{Equation 16-30}$$

Thus, for a given lake, the estimated odds of preferring primarily reptiles to fish is

$$e^{-0.3512} = 0.70 \qquad\qquad \text{Equation 16-31}$$

times lower for the smaller alligators than for the larger ones.

Next, consider how these odds differ between lakes. One way to do this is to compute the parameter estimates υ_{31}, υ_{32}, υ_{33}, and υ_{34}. By referring to Figure 16-13 and Figure 16-14, we have

$$\upsilon_{31} = (FL)_{31} - (FL)_{11} = 0.4166 - (-0.8262) = 1.2428$$
$$\upsilon_{32} = (FL)_{32} - (FL)_{12} = 2.4532 - (-0.0057) = 2.4589$$
$$\upsilon_{33} = (FL)_{33} - (FL)_{13} = 1.4189 - (-1.5164) = 2.9353$$
$$\upsilon_{34} = (FL)_{34} - (FL)_{14} = 0 - 0 = 0$$

Equation 16-32

Therefore, the lake effects indicate that the estimated odds of selecting primarily reptiles instead of fish are relatively highest in lake 3, next in lake 2, next in lake 1, and relatively lowest in lake 4. To complete the analysis, the food effect is

$$\lambda_3 = F_3 - F_1 = -1.4103 - 1.9043 = -3.3146 \qquad\qquad \text{Equation 16-33}$$

and the estimated odds are

$$\frac{m_{311}}{m_{111}} = e^{\lambda_1 + \omega_{31} + \upsilon_{31}} = e^{-2.4230} = 0.0887$$

$$\frac{m_{312}}{m_{112}} = e^{\lambda_1 + \omega_{31} + \upsilon_{32}} = e^{-1.2069} = 0.2991$$

Equation 16-34

$$\frac{m_{313}}{m_{113}} = e^{\lambda_1 + \omega_{31} + \upsilon_{33}} = e^{-0.7305} = 0.4817$$

$$\frac{m_{314}}{m_{114}} = e^{\lambda_1 + \omega_{31} + \upsilon_{34}} = e^{-3.6658} = 0.0256$$

and

$$\frac{m_{321}}{m_{121}} = e^{\lambda_1 + \omega_{32} + \upsilon_{31}} = e^{-2.0718} = 0.1260$$

$$\frac{m_{322}}{m_{122}} = e^{\lambda_1 + \omega_{32} + \upsilon_{32}} = e^{-0.8557} = 0.4250$$

Equation 16-35

$$\frac{m_{323}}{m_{123}} = e^{\lambda_1 + \omega_{32} + \upsilon_{33}} = e^{-0.3793} = 0.6843$$

$$\frac{m_{324}}{m_{124}} = e^{\lambda_1 + \omega_{32} + \upsilon_{34}} = e^{-3.3146} = 0.0363$$

If you want standard errors or confidence intervals for these odds, you can use a contrast variable to calculate the generalized log-odds ratio (GLOR). You would construct a comparison variable (similar to the variables *G1*, *G2*, and *G3* in "Poisson Loglinear Regression" on p. 188 in Chapter 15) and specify it in the Contrast Variable(s) list in the Logit Loglinear Analysis dialog box.

Example 4
Model Diagnosis: Coal Miner Data Revisited

Consider the coal miner data again, which is discussed in "Two Response Variables with Two Categories Each" on p. 205. The model used is somewhat unusual, although it fits the data well. As in Agresti (1990), this model was developed through model diagnosis on another model. The other model is a logit model that assumes a constant odds ratio across age. The following discussion illustrates how to apply the techniques for model diagnosis to the coal miner data.

For this discussion, the previously fitted model will be called model 1 and another model, to be described below, will be called model 2. Model 2 is given by

$$\ln\left(\frac{m_{11k}m_{22k}}{m_{12k}m_{21k}}\right) = \lambda$$

Equation 16-36

where m_{ijk} is the count for the *i*th category of breathlessness, the *j*th category of wheeze, and the *k*th level of age. The equivalent loglinear model is the one with no three-way interaction. Recall that the variables are *qbreath*, *qwheeze*, and *age*. The setup for running the procedure is similar to "Two Response Variables with Two Categories Each" on p. 205. This time, do not use a covariate.

From the menus choose:

Data
  Weight Cases...
▶ Weight cases by: count

Analyze
  Loglinear
    Logit...

▶ Dependent: qbreath qwheeze
▶ Factor(s): age

Model...
    ⊙ Custom
    ▶ Terms in Model (Main effects): age

Save...
    ☑ Adjusted residuals

Options...
    Display
      ☑ Residuals
    Plot
      ☑ Deviance residuals
      ☑ Normal probability for deviance

Paste

After editing, the final syntax should be:

```
GENLOG QBREATH QWHEEZE BY AGE
 /MODEL=MULTINOMIAL
 /PRINT=RESID ADJRESID DEV
 /PLOT=RESID(DEV) NORMPROB(DEV)
 /DESIGN=QBREATH, QWHEEZE, QBREATH*QWHEEZE, QBREATH*AGE,
 QWHEEZE*AGE
 /SAVE ADJRESID DEV.
```

Figure 16-15 shows the goodness-of-fit information for model 2.

Figure 16-15
Goodness-of-fit statistics

	Chi-Square	DF	Sig.
Likelihood Ratio	26.6904	8	.0008
Pearson	26.6348	8	.0008

Since the sample size $N = 18282$ is large, the two goodness-of-fit statistics follow the chi-square distribution. Since the p values (*Sig.*) are both 0.008, which is considerably smaller than 0.05, this model is unlikely to be the right one.

Next, look at the residuals. When Residuals is selected, the Logit Loglinear Analysis procedure displays three residuals, as shown in Figure 16-16. Notice that the raw residuals and the adjusted residuals all add up to 0 within each level of *age*. This behavior is expected as a property of the multinomial logit model.

Figure 16-16
Residuals for model 2

Factor	Value	Resid.	Adj. Resid.	Dev. Resid.
AGE	20 to 24			
QBREATH No Breathlessness				
QWHEEZE	No Wheeze	1.45	.75	.03
QWHEEZE	Have Wheeze	-1.45	-.75	-.15
QBREATH Have Breathlessness				
QWHEEZE	No Wheeze	-1.45	-.75	-.52
QWHEEZE	Have Wheeze	1.45	.75	.51
AGE	25 to 29			
QBREATH No Breathlessness				
QWHEEZE	No Wheeze	5.91	2.20	.15
QWHEEZE	Have Wheeze	-5.91	-2.20	-.57
QBREATH Have Breathlessness				
QWHEEZE	No Wheeze	-5.91	-2.20	-1.65
QWHEEZE	Have Wheeze	5.91	2.20	1.36
AGE	30 to 34			
QBREATH No Breathlessness				
QWHEEZE	No Wheeze	8.05	2.10	.19
QWHEEZE	Have Wheeze	-8.05	-2.10	-.60
QBREATH Have Breathlessness				
QWHEEZE	No Wheeze	-8.05	-2.10	-1.64
QWHEEZE	Have Wheeze	8.05	2.10	1.16
AGE	35 to 39			
QBREATH No Breathlessness				
QWHEEZE	No Wheeze	9.60	1.77	.20
QWHEEZE	Have Wheeze	-9.60	-1.77	-.59
QBREATH Have Breathlessness				
QWHEEZE	No Wheeze	-9.60	-1.77	-1.30
QWHEEZE	Have Wheeze	9.60	1.77	.90
AGE	40 to 44			
QBREATH No Breathlessness				
QWHEEZE	No Wheeze	6.49	1.13	.15
QWHEEZE	Have Wheeze	-6.49	-1.13	-.39
QBREATH Have Breathlessness				
QWHEEZE	No Wheeze	-6.49	-1.13	-.85
QWHEEZE	Have Wheeze	6.49	1.13	.51
AGE	45 to 49			
QBREATH No Breathlessness				
QWHEEZE	No Wheeze	-2.79	-.42	-.07
QWHEEZE	Have Wheeze	2.79	.42	.16
QBREATH Have Breathlessness				
QWHEEZE	No Wheeze	2.79	.42	.30
QWHEEZE	Have Wheeze	-2.79	-.42	-.17
AGE	50 to 54			
QBREATH No Breathlessness				
QWHEEZE	No Wheeze	5.86	.81	.16
QWHEEZE	Have Wheeze	-5.86	-.81	-.37
QBREATH Have Breathlessness				
QWHEEZE	No Wheeze	-5.86	-.81	-.53
QWHEEZE	Have Wheeze	5.86	.81	.29
AGE	55 to 59			
QBREATH No Breathlessness				
QWHEEZE	No Wheeze	-25.71	-3.65	-.82
QWHEEZE	Have Wheeze	25.71	3.65	1.78
QBREATH Have Breathlessness				
QWHEEZE	No Wheeze	25.71	3.65	2.22
QWHEEZE	Have Wheeze	-25.71	-3.65	-1.25
AGE	60 to 64			
QBREATH No Breathlessness				
QWHEEZE	No Wheeze	-8.86	-1.44	-.38
QWHEEZE	Have Wheeze	8.86	1.44	.79
QBREATH Have Breathlessness				
QWHEEZE	No Wheeze	8.86	1.44	.89
QWHEEZE	Have Wheeze	-8.86	-1.44	-.46

Agresti (1990) observed that the adjusted residuals show a decreasing trend as age increases. Since the adjusted residuals have the same magnitudes within each age group, it would be confusing to look at adjusted residual diagnostic plots provided by the Logit Loglinear Analysis procedure. Instead, consider the diagnostic plots for the deviance residuals. Recall that Deviance residuals and Normal probability for deviance were selected. The plots are shown in Figure 16-17 and Figure 16-18.

Figure 16-17
Matrix plot of observed count versus expected count versus deviance residuals

Loglinear Model

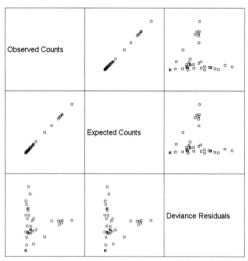

Figure 16-18
Normal Q-Q plot of deviance residuals

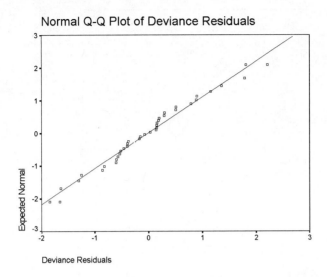

In Figure 16-17, the deviance residuals exhibit a decreasing trend as either the observed or expected count increases. The normal Q-Q plot in Figure 16-18 further suggests that the distribution is not normal.

To verify Agresti's observation, the adjusted residuals are saved into variable *Adj_1* and a scatterplot is created with the Graphs menu. *Adj_1* is plotted versus *age* for cases where *qbreath* is 1 and *qwheeze* is 1. These are the cells for *Have Breathlessness–Have Wheeze*. The scatterplot is shown in Figure 16-19.

Figure 16-19
Scatterplot of adjusted residuals versus age group

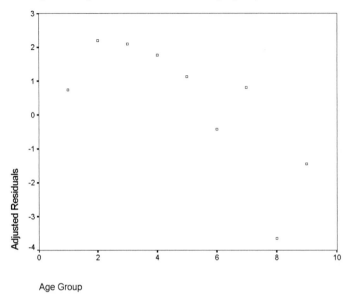

Age Group

The trend is apparent in Figure 16-19. This suggests that a covariate related to the age group number may be included in the model. Such a variable, *delta*, was created and selected as a covariate in "Two Response Variables with Two Categories Each" on p. 205. Since model 2 is nested within model 1, to test whether the two models are statistically different, you can compare their likelihood-ratio chi-square statistics. Recall that the likelihood-ratio statistic of model 1 is 6.8017 (see Figure 16-7) with 7 degrees of freedom. The difference from the model 2 statistic (see Figure 16-15) is
$26.6904 - 6.8017 = 19.8887$ with $8 - 7 = 1$ degrees of freedom.

This corresponds to a *p* value of 0.0000082. You can calculate the *p* value by choosing Compute from the Transform menu and creating a new variable $p = 1 - \text{CDF.CHISQ}(19.8887, 1)$. The small *p* value is strong evidence that model 2 is different from model 1. This is expected because model 1 fits the data well but model 2 does not.

Example 5
Continuation Ratio Logit Model

A categorical variable is called an ordinal variable when there is an unambiguous ordering of its categories. When a response variable is an ordinal variable, we can collect extra information about its association with the explanatory variables. Also, there is a larger class of models for ordinal variables. One of these models is the continuation ratio logit model. Suppose an ordinal variable has categories labeled from 1 to I. Then the jth continuation ratio logit model is defined as

$$L_j = \ln\left(\frac{\pi_j}{\pi_{j+1} + \ldots + \pi_I}\right), \qquad j = 1, \ldots, I-1 \qquad \text{Equation 16-37}$$

where π_j is the probability that an observation is from the jth category (Agresti, 1990). When I equals 2, this logit model is the same as the standard logit model.

Advantages

There are some advantages in working with continuation ratio logit models. Suppose that $\{n_i\}$ are the observed counts from a multinomial distribution with sample size N and cell probabilities $\{\pi_i\}$. We can decompose the multinomial probability density function as the product of $I-1$ dependent binomial probability density functions. The jth binomial distribution has probability $\pi_j/(\pi_{j+1} + \ldots + \pi_I)$ and sample size $n_j + \ldots + n_I$. This implies that the continuation ratio logit model can be fitted by using the algorithms or software designed for a standard logit model.

Procedure

The procedure is quite straightforward when you choose Loglinear and then Logit from the Analyze menu. Suppose that the response variable is *resp* and the design is *resp* plus a covariate.

First, choose Recode from the Transform menu to create a dichotomous variable, *resp1*. The first category of *resp1* is the same as that of *resp*. The second category of *resp1* includes the second through the last categories of *resp* combined. Then fit a logit model with the following variables:

■ Response variable *resp1*

■ Design variables *resp1* and the covariate (Logit Loglinear Analysis Model dialog box)

Save the predicted values, creating a variable, *pred1*. Then create a second dichotomous variable, *resp2*. The first category of *resp2* is the second category of *resp*. The second category of *resp2* includes the third through the last categories of *resp* combined. Next, choose Compute Variable from the Transform menu and set the values of *pred1* to 0 for the first category of *resp*. Then fit a logit model with the following variables:

■ Response variable *resp2*

■ Cell structure variable *pred1*

■ Design variables *resp2* and the covariate (Logit Loglinear Analysis Model dialog box)

Save the predicted values, creating variable *pred2*. Repeat these steps until the last category of *resp* is reached.

The overall likelihood-ratio chi-square statistic can be obtained by adding individual chi-square statistics. Furthermore, the observed proportions $n_j / (n_j + \dots + n_I)$ are each asymptotically independent. Thus, you can assess the fits of the $I - 1$ logit models independently. More details can be found in Fienberg (1980) and Agresti (1990). Although the method sounds complicated, it is in fact practical to use. The following example illustrates how to fit a continuation ratio logit model using SPSS and this method.

Toxicity Study

The data are taken from a developmental toxicity study by Price et al. (1987). The sample consists of 1435 pregnant mice. The purpose of the study was to investigate how various doses of the chemical ethylene glycol dimethyl ether (diEGdiME) affect developing fetuses. The researchers administered diEGdiME in distilled water to pregnant mice for 10 days early in the pregnancy. The mice were divided into five groups according to the concentration of diEGdiME, measured in mg/kg per day. The first group was a control group. The uterine contents of the mice were collected two days later for examination. The results show the status of the fetus. There are three possible outcomes listed in reverse order of desirability—dead, malformed, and normal. These outcomes are recorded in the variable *status* as 1, 2, and 3. The data are shown in Figure 16-20.

Figure 16-20
Data for toxicity study

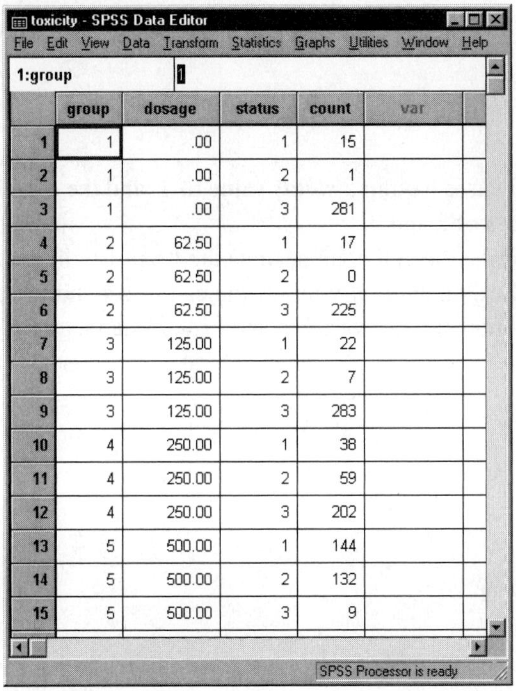
toxicity - SPSS Data Editor

File Edit View Data Transform Statistics Graphs Utilities Window Help

1:group 1

	group	dosage	status	count	var
1	1	.00	1	15	
2	1	.00	2	1	
3	1	.00	3	281	
4	2	62.50	1	17	
5	2	62.50	2	0	
6	2	62.50	3	225	
7	3	125.00	1	22	
8	3	125.00	2	7	
9	3	125.00	3	283	
10	4	250.00	1	38	
11	4	250.00	2	59	
12	4	250.00	3	202	
13	5	500.00	1	144	
14	5	500.00	2	132	
15	5	500.00	3	9	

SPSS Processor is ready

The variables are *group*, *dosage*, *status*, and *count*. The data are weighted by *count* (using the Data menu).

Since I is equal to 3, there are $I - 1 = 2$ individual logit models. The first logit model compares the number of dead fetuses to that of live fetuses (that is, malformed and normal). The second logit model compares the number of malformed fetuses to that of normal fetuses (provided they are alive). Agresti (1990) suggests the design

$$L_j = \alpha_j + \beta_j x_i \qquad j = 1, 2$$ Equation 16-38

where j is the index for *status* and x_i is the *dosage* at the ith group.

To fit the first logit model, the first dichotomous variable, *qalive*, is created.

To create *qalive*, from the menus choose:

Transform
  Recode...

status-->qalive

  Old and New Values...
    1 -->1
    2 thru 3 --> 2

The first group contains all cases having a *status* value of 1, and the second contains all cases having *status* values of 2 and 3.

You do not need to combine the cell counts, since the Logit Loglinear Analysis procedure will aggregate the data internally. Now you can fit a standard logit model with *qalive* as the response (dependent) variable and *group* as a factor.

From the menus choose:

Data
  Weight Cases...
▶ Weight cases by: count

Analyze
  Loglinear
    Logit...

▶ Dependent: qalive
▶ Factor(s): group
▶ Cell Covariate(s): dosage

Model...
  ⊙ Custom
  ▶ Terms in Model (Main effects): dosage

Save...
  ☑ Predicted values

The predicted values will be saved into variable *pre_1* for use in the next logit model.

In the second logit model, the second category of *status* is compared to the third and last category of *status*, making *status* the response variable. The first category of *status* is suppressed by declaring it missing. In the Data Editor, double-click on *status* and specify:

Missing Values...
  Discrete missing values: 1

Next, recall the Logit Loglinear dialog box and choose:

▶ Dependent: status
▶ Factor(s): group
▶ Cell Covariate(s): dosage
▶ Cell Structure: pre_1

Model...
   ⊙ Custom
   ▶ Terms in Model (Main effects): dosage

Save...
   ☐ Predicted values (deselect)

This second custom model uses *status* and the interaction *dosage* by *status* (if you paste the syntax, you can see these variables on the DESIGN subcommand). Since the second logit model is the last logit model in this example, it is not necessary to save the predicted values unless otherwise needed. The goodness-of-fit statistics from the two logit models are shown in Figure 16-21 and Figure 16-22. Both models fit fairly well at the 0.05 level because the significance values are greater than 0.05.

Figure 16-21
Goodness-of-fit statistics for first logit model

	Chi-Square	DF	Sig.
Likelihood Ratio	5.7775	3	.1230
Pearson	5.8257	3	.1204

Figure 16-22
Goodness-of-fit statistics for second logit model

	Chi-Square	DF	Sig.
Likelihood Ratio	6.0609	3	.1087
Pearson	3.9331	3	.2688

The *overall* likelihood-ratio chi-square statistic is the sum of two likelihood-ratio chi-square statistics:

$$5.7775 + 6.0609 = 11.8384 \qquad\qquad \text{Equation 16-39}$$

and there are $3 + 3 = 6$ degrees of freedom. To calculate the corresponding p value, from the Transform menu choose Compute and enter

$$p = 1 - \text{CDF.CHISQ}(11.8384,6) \qquad \text{Equation 16-40}$$

The p value is 0.0657, which is marginally acceptable. The parameter estimates are shown in Figure 16-23 and Figure 16-24.

Figure 16-23
Parameter estimates for first logit model

```
Parameter Estimates
  Constant    Estimate
      1         5.6556
      2         5.4326
      3         5.6602
      4         5.5249
      5         4.9857
Note: Constants are not parameters under multinomial assumption.
      Therefore, standard errors are not calculated.
                                              Asymptotic 95% CI
Parameter     Estimate       SE     Z-value     Lower      Upper
      6        -3.2479     .1576     -20.60      -3.56      -2.94
      7          .0000        .          .          .          .
      8          .0064     .0004      14.70   5.537E-03  7.241E-03
      9          .0000        .          .          .          .
```

In the first logit model, parameter 8 indicates that

$$\beta_1 = 0.0064 \qquad \text{Equation 16-41}$$

with a standard error of 0.0004 and a z value of 14.70.

Figure 16-24
Parameter estimates for second logit model

```
Parameter Estimates
  Constant    Estimate
      1         -.0170
      2         -.0264
      3         -.0192
      4         -.1892
      5        -3.0716
Note: Constants are not parameters under multinomial assumption.
      Therefore, standard errors are not calculated.
                                              Asymptotic 95% CI
Parameter     Estimate       SE     Z-value     Lower      Upper
      6          .0000        .          .          .          .
      7        -5.7019     .3322     -17.16      -6.35      -5.05
      8          .0000        .          .          .          .
      9          .0000        .          .          .          .
     10          .0174     .0012      14.16        .01        .02
     11          .0000        .          .          .          .
```

In the second logit model, parameter 10 indicates that

$$\beta_2 = 0.0174 \qquad \text{Equation 16-42}$$

with a standard error of 0.0012 and a z value of 14.16.

Thus, the likelihood of the less desirable fetus status (dead in the first logit model and malformed in second logit model) increases as the concentration of diEGdiME increases. From Equation 16-41, the estimated odds that a fetus is dead increase multiplicatively by a factor of

$$e^{0.0064 \times 100} = 1.9 \qquad\qquad \text{Equation 16-43}$$

for every 100 mg/kg per day increase in the concentration of diEGdiME.

Life Tables Examples

Contributed by Milton Steinberg, Marymount College.

An insurance company wants to calculate the expected number of years of life remaining for 65-year-old males with angina pectoris. A researcher wants to assess tumor-free time after rats have been injected with a putative carcinogen. The owner of a shopping mall wishes to calculate the probability that a business leasing space in the mall will continue to rent for three years. In each of these instances, the investigator is interested in **survival time**, the time to occurrence of an event, such as death, tumor growth, or rental termination.

The calculations in these situations are complicated by the fact that not all subjects or entities will experience the terminal event during the time of observation. Some of the angina pectoris patients will not die during five years of study. Some of the rats will not develop tumors during 200 days of study. Some of the businesses will not leave during the eight years that the mall has existed.

This chapter discusses techniques for assessing situations in which some of the subjects do not experience the terminal event that is the event of interest. In **life tables** and other methods of **survival analysis**, data from those subjects who do not experience the terminal event can also contribute to the calculation for the probabilities at any interval under study. The terms *survival analysis* and *life tables* refer to the fact that these techniques are often used to assess life expectancies

When to Use Life Tables

If observations can be classified into meaningful equal time intervals such as seconds, days, months, or years, the life table can be used to calculate the probability of a terminal event during any interval under study. If observations cannot be aggregated into equal time intervals, as is the case in many clinical and experimental studies, use the Kaplan-Meier technique, described in Chapter 18. To investigate the relation between survival time and a predictor variable, such as age or tumor type, use the Cox Regression procedures, described in Chapter 19.

Constructing a Life Table

The owner of a small mall with 30 shops wants to determine the probability that a business will continue its lease for three years. During the eight years that the mall has existed, a total of 100 businesses have rented space. Of these 100 businesses, 71 have terminated their leases and moved to other locations. At present, 29 of the 30 shops are occupied.

Figure 17-1 shows the first 15 records of the data as they might be presented for computer processing. There are 100 records total.

Figure 17-1
Computer-ready survival data (first 15 records)

Interval	Status
0	1
0	1
1	1
1	1
1	1
1	1
1	1
1	1
2	1
2	0
2	1
2	1
2	0
2	1
2	1

There are only two columns in this table. In the first column, time intervals are coded by their start times in years. For convenience, the cases have been sorted by interval. The first interval, coded 0, is the interval from the very beginning of a lease up to, but not including, one year. The second interval is from one year up to, but not including, two years, and so on. Each interval indicates the number of years that a business has been under lease, not the year in which the business began to lease. A business with an interval coded 2 could have begun leasing in the sixth year of the mall's eight-year lifetime.

Censored Observations

The second column in Figure 17-1, *Status*, indicates whether the terminal event, lease termination, has occurred. The first nine businesses have terminated their leases (1). The tenth business has not terminated (0). The tenth business is one of the 29 that are still leasing space at the mall even though it has been in business for only two years (two years up to, but not including, three years). This observation on the tenth business is called a **censored** observation because its outcome is hidden from view. The terminal event has not yet occurred.

Calculating Probabilities

In order to determine the probability that a business continues to lease for one year, two years, or more, it is convenient to reorganize Figure 17-1 into intervals of years, as shown in Figure 17-2. The reorganized columns plus additional computed columns constitute a more traditional life table. Notice that the *Status* column from Figure 17-1 has been reorganized into two columns, *Number Withdrawn During Interval*, showing the number of censored observations, and *Number of Terminal Events*.

Figure 17-2
Reorganization of Figure 17-1 with additional, computed columns

Interval Start Time	Number Entering this Interval	Number Withdrawn During Interval	Number of Terminal Events	Number Exposed to Risk	Proportion Terminating	Proportion Surviving	Cumulative Proportion Surviving at End
0	100	0	2	100	.0200	.9800	.9800
1	98	0	6	98	.0612	.9388	.9200
2	92	3	8	90.5	.0884	.9116	.8387
3	81	3	11	79.5	.1384	.8616	.7226
4	67	6	9	64	.1406	.8594	.6210
5	52	8	19	48	.3958	.6042	.3752
6	25	6	9	22	.4091	.5909	.2217
7	10	3	7	8.5	.8235	.1765	.0391
Total		29	71				

This table presents the following information:

- *Interval Start Time* is the start of each interval in years.

- *Number Entering this Interval* is the number of cases surviving at the beginning of the interval. All 100 businesses started leasing at 0 years.

- *Number Withdrawn During Interval* is the number of censored cases. Here, it is the number of businesses that leased less than one year ago and have continued to lease. There were no such cases for the first (0) interval, as can be seen in Figure 17-1.

- *Number of Terminal Events* is the number of cases that experienced the terminal event. Two businesses terminated their leases after less than one year, as shown in Figure 17-1.

- *Number Exposed to Risk* is the number of cases entering the interval minus half the number withdrawn during the interval. It is used to account for the contribution of censored data and will be more fully described below. This column is used as the denominator to calculate the proportion terminating and the proportion surviving.

- *Proportion Terminating* is the proportion of cases that experienced the terminal event during the interval. This is an estimate of the probability that a case will experience termination during an interval. Two businesses out of 100 left the mall during the first year. The probability of a terminal event in the first year (interval 0) is $2/100 = 0.02$.

- *Proportion Surviving* is the proportion of cases that have survived to the end of the interval. Since two businesses terminated their leases, 98 out of 100 were still leasing: $98/100 = 0.98$. This is 1 minus the proportion terminating.

- *Cumulative Proportion Surviving at End* is an estimate of the probability of surviving to the end of any specified interval. The probability for the 0 interval is 0.98. This is also the cumulative probability for the first interval.

For the interval starting at one year, the number entering the interval is 98, since 2 out of 100 were terminated in the previous interval. None of these 98 were censored (withdrawn) during the interval. Six experienced the terminal event. The proportion terminating is thus $6/98 = 0.0612$. The proportion surviving is $1 - 0.0612 = 0.9388$. The probability that a business will survive to the end of the second interval is the probability of survival in the first interval times the probability of survival in the second interval. The cumulative proportion of survival is thus $0.9800 \times 0.9388 = 0.9200$.

Effects of Censoring

The special advantage of survival analysis procedures such as life tables is the ability to use information from censored cases. Ninety-two businesses entered the third interval in the business example. Eight of these became terminal; but, in addition, three businesses are censored. They leased three years ago and are still leasing. Their outcome is unknown, but it is known that they have leased for at least three years. In order to make use of the censored cases, we assume that each of these three businesses were observed for half of the interval. Each is counted as a half-case. Instead of 92 cases, we have $92 - (3 \times 0.5) = 90.5$. This is the number that appears in the *Number Exposed to Risk* column. The number exposed to risk shows the number of cases entering the interval adjusted for censored cases. The proportion terminating becomes the number of terminal events divided by the number exposed to risk $(8/90.5 = 0.0884)$ rather than the number of terminal events divided by the number entering the interval $(8/92 = 0.0870)$. Our knowledge that the censored cases survived the interval may thus be put to use to increase the estimated probability.

The probability of a business leasing for three years is estimated to be 0.8387 (the cumulative proportion surviving the interval beginning at 2).

Before constructing a life table, you should consider carefully the cases that are to be censored. Use of life tables assumes that the reason for censoring is not related to the cause of termination. In the business example, it must be assumed that those who continued to lease into interval 7 did not do so because they were given more favorable terms than those who terminated their leases. If a cancer patient in remission dies in a workplace accident before experiencing a recurrence of the disease, the case may be considered censored and thus excluded from analysis. The researcher should look carefully at the reasons that the cases under consideration are no longer in the study and decide which cases to censor or drop. For more information on censoring, see Cox and Oakes (1984).

Censored cases, for whom the terminal event has not yet occurred but who have been followed for the duration of the study, are fundamentally different from cases that have been **lost to follow-up**. Cases lost to follow-up are those with whom the investigator has lost contact during the course of the study. They may have experienced the terminal event without the investigator's knowledge during a time period within the purview of the study. Cancer patients lost to follow-up may or may not experience death from cancer during the lifetime of the study; the investigator will not know. Furthermore, those lost to follow-up may be systematically different from those not lost to follow-up. Careful consideration should be given to assigning censored status to these cases or excluding them from the study.

SPSS Life Tables Output

Figure 17-3 shows the result of submitting the data organized as in Figure 17-1 to the SPSS Life Tables procedure.

To produce this table, from the menus choose:

Analyze
  Survival
    Life Tables...

▶ Time: interval
  Display Time Intervals 0 through 8 by 1

▶ Status: status

Define Event...
  Single value: 1

Figure 17-3
Life table

```
Life Table
   Survival Variable  INTERVAL  Interval Start Time
            Number  Number  Number                           Cumul
            Entrng  Wdrawn  Exposd  Number                    Propn   Proba-
  Intrvl    this    During  to      of      Propn   Propn     Surv    bility   Hazard
  Start     Intrvl  Intrvl  Risk    Termnl  Termi-  Sur-      at End  Densty   Rate
  Time                              Events  nating  viving
  ------    ------  ------  ------  ------  ------  ------    ------  ------   ------

     .0     100.0      .0   100.0     2.0   .0200   .9800     .9800   .0200    .0202
    1.0      98.0      .0    98.0     6.0   .0612   .9388     .9200   .0600    .0632
    2.0      92.0     3.0    90.5     8.0   .0884   .9116     .8387   .0813    .0925
    3.0      81.0     3.0    79.5    11.0   .1384   .8616     .7226   .1160    .1486
    4.0      67.0     6.0    64.0     9.0   .1406   .8594     .6210   .1016    .1513
    5.0      52.0     8.0    48.0    19.0   .3958   .6042     .3752   .2458    .4935
    6.0      25.0     6.0    22.0     9.0   .4091   .5909     .2217   .1535    .5143
    7.0      10.0     3.0     8.5     7.0   .8235   .1765     .0391   .1826   1.4000
```

The median survival time for these data is 5.49

```
          SE of   SE of
  Intrvl  Cumul   Proba-  SE of
  Start   Sur-    bility  Hazard
  Time    viving  Densty  Rate
  ------  ------  ------  ------
     .0   .0140   .0140   .0143
    1.0   .0271   .0237   .0258
    2.0   .0369   .0276   .0327
    3.0   .0455   .0329   .0447
    4.0   .0501   .0320   .0503
    5.0   .0533   .0481   .1097
    6.0   .0504   .0450   .1657
    7.0   .0303   .0506   .3779
```

This table presents the following information:

- *Interval Start Time* is the start of each interval. It extends up to, but not including, the start time of the next interval.

- *Number Entering this Interval* is the number of cases surviving at the beginning of the interval.

- *Number Withdrawn During Interval* is the number of censored cases. They have not experienced the terminal event.

- *Number Exposed to Risk* is the number of cases entering the interval minus half the number withdrawn during the interval. It is used to account for the contribution of censored data.

- *Number of Terminal Events* is the number of cases that experienced the terminal event. Two businesses terminated their leases after less than one year, as shown in Figure 17-1.

- *Proportion Terminating* is the proportion of cases that experienced the terminal event during the interval. This is an estimate of the probability that a case will experience termination during an interval. Two businesses out of 100 left the mall during the first year. The probability of a terminal event in the first year (interval 0) is $2/100 = 0.02$.

- *Proportion Surviving* is the proportion of cases that have survived to the end of the interval. Since two businesses terminated their leases, 98 out of 100 were still leasing: $98/100 = 0.98$. This is 1 minus the proportion terminating.

- *Cumulative Proportion Surviving at End* is an estimate of the probability of surviving to the end of any specified interval. The probability for the 0 interval is 0.98. This is also the cumulative probability for the first interval.

- *Probability Density* is an estimate of the probability of failure during a particular time interval.

- *Hazard Rate* is the proportion of those who have survived up to a particular interval who are expected to fail in that interval. It is a rate and may have a value greater than 1.

- *Standard Error of the Cumulative Proportion Surviving* is an estimate of the variability of the cumulative proportion surviving.

- *Standard Error of the Probability Density* is an estimate of the variability of the probability density.

- *Standard Error of the Hazard Rate* is an estimate of the variability of the hazard rate.

The **median survival time** is the time at which half of the cases experience the terminal event. This is the time when the cumulative proportion surviving is 0.50. Referring to the *Cumulative Proportion Surviving at End* in Figure 17-3, it can be seen that the proportion is 0.6210 at the end of interval 4 (the beginning of the fifth year) and 0.3752 at the end of interval 5 (the beginning of the sixth year); so the median, 0.5, is reached between years 5 and 6. Linear interpolation yields a more accurate estimate. The cumulative proportion surviving reaches 0.50 at 5.49 years. The median is included between the two parts of the table shown in Figure 17-3. It may be roughly estimated from plots of the cumulative proportion surviving against time.

Survival and Hazard Functions

The *Cumulative Proportion Surviving* in Figure 17-3 is an estimate of the **survival function** or **survivorship function** $S(t)$. It is defined as the proportion of cases surviving longer than a specified time t. For example, 37.52% of the cases survive longer than the start of interval 5 (the beginning of the sixth year).

The **hazard function** is a rate—a conditional probability of failure divided by a time interval. The symbol $h(t)$ is used to represent the hazard function. It indicates the expectation that a case will terminate at any particular time period. A high hazard function indicates a high probability of mortality. It can be derived from the survival function $S(t)$ and can take on any value from 0 to infinity.

Survival Function Plots

Figure 17-4 shows a plot of survival (the cumulative proportion surviving at the end of the interval) against the interval start times.

To produce this plot, recall the dialog box and choose:

Options...

☑ Survival

Figure 17-4
Survival plotted against interval start times

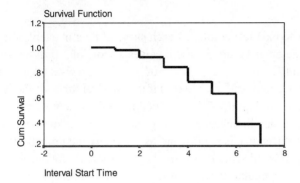

Comparing Groups

Frequently, survival analysis is performed to determine whether one treatment or condition results in longer survival times than another. In the current example, a third column was added to the data called *edu*. It is coded 0 if the renter has no college degree and 1 if the renter has a college degree. The two resulting survival functions are compared using Gehan's generalized Wilcoxon test. Figure 17-5 shows the result of this test for the current example.

To produce this table, recall the dialog box and choose:

▶ Factor: edu

Define Range...
   Minimum 0 Maximum 1

Options...

   Compare Levels of First Factor
   ⊙ Overall

Figure 17-5

Gehan's generalized Wilcoxon test for education level

```
Comparison of survival experience using the Wilcoxon (Gehan) statistic
    Survival Variable   INTERVAL   Interval Start Time
          grouped by   EDU        Education
   Overall comparison   statistic       9.361  D.F.     1   Prob.    .0022
   Group  label                Total N   Uncen   Cen  Pct Cen  Mean Score
      0   No College               57      43    14    24.56     13.8596
      1   College                  43      28    15    34.88    -18.3721
```

Gehan's generalized Wilcoxon test compares each survival time in each group with every survival time in the other group. A case receives a score of 1 if its survival time exceeds that of a case in the other group, a score of −1 if its survival time is less than that of a case in the other group, and a score of 0 if the survival times of the two cases are equal. The *Mean Score* in Figure 17-5 is derived from these scores. The positive value for the *No College* group indicates that this group has longer survival times than the *College* group. This difference is significant, as shown by the probability 0.0022.

The procedure also produced separate survival tables for each condition. From these, it can be seen that the median survival time was greater for the no college group (5.88) than for the college group (4.38).

If a plot is requested, a separate curve is drawn for each level of education. The curve for the no college group, which has the longer survival times, descends more gradually than the curve for the college group. The median for each group can be estimated from these curves.

Figure 17-6

Comparison of survival curves for two levels of education

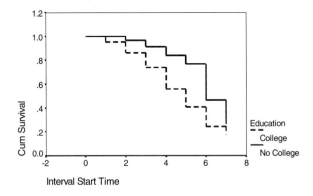

Kaplan-Meier
Survival Analysis Examples

Contributed by Milton Steinberg, Marymount College.

Survival analysis is concerned with the time to occurrence of a critical **event** of interest, such as death, tumor growth, or discharge from employment. The event need not be adverse. It can be an event with a happy outcome, such as time to remission of symptoms or time until finding employment. The time until the event is the **survival time**. Cases can enter a study at various times. Survival time is measured from the time that the case enters the study, not from the beginning of the study itself.

Censored Observations

Survival analysis techniques are unique in that they use information from cases that have not experienced the terminal event during the time of observation. In a study on remission of symptoms, some cases will not show remission during the time of the study. Some job seekers will not find employment during the time of observation. The terminal remission status or employment status of these cases is hidden from view; hence, the term **censored** is applied to them.

When to Use Kaplan-Meier Estimators

In Chapter 17, life tables are constructed for situations in which event times are specified only to an interval. More precise estimates are available when you know exact times by using the **Kaplan-Meier** method. The probability of a terminal event is calculated at every occurrence of the event. This makes Kaplan-Meier techniques useful for studies with few cases where the survival intervals are variable.

Use **life tables** if survival times have been categorized into time intervals such as days, months, or years. Life table techniques determine the probability of the terminal event for each interval by dividing the number of cases experiencing the terminal event during the interval by the number of cases entering the interval alive (after the denominator is adjusted for censored observations).

An Example Using Chemotherapy to Treat Leukemia

Miller, Gong, and Munoz (1981) describe a data set from a paper by Ebury et al. (1977) in which patients suffering from acute myelogenous leukemia (AML) were brought to remission with chemotherapy. They were then divided into two groups. The experimental group continued to receive maintenance doses of chemotherapy. The control group did not. Did the maintenance doses of chemotherapy increase the number of weeks of remission time?

The data were stored in a file with three columns. Figure 18-1 shows the first five entries.

Figure 18-1
First five cases of AML data file

Chemo	Time	Status
1	9.00	1
1	13.00	1
1	13.00	0
1	18.00	1
1	23.00	1

In the column *Chemo*, a case is coded 1 if subjects received maintenance doses of chemotherapy and 0 if they did not. *Time* is the survival time in weeks. *Status* is coded 1 if the case relapsed and 0 if the case had not relapsed by the end of the study (censored).

Computing Cumulative Survival

We will begin by computing cumulative survival for the experimental subjects who received maintenance doses of chemotherapy. These are the cases for which the *Chemo* column is coded 1. Figure 18-2 contains the *Time* and *Status* columns for all of these cases, just as they appear in Figure 18-1. The other columns in Figure 18-2 are computed from the *Time* and *Status* columns.

Figure 18-2
Time (in weeks) to relapse for AML patients in remission

Time	Status	Prior Number in Remission	Number Remaining	Proportion in Remission	Cumulative Survival
9	1	11	10	10/11	10/11=0.9091
13	1	10	9	9/10	0.9091x(9/10)=0.8182
13	0	9	8		
18	1	8	7	7/8	0.8182x(7/8)=0.7159
23	1	7	6	6/7	0.7159x(6/7)=0.6136
28	0	6	5		
31	1	5	4	4/5	0.6136x(4/5)=0.4909
34	1	4	3	3/4	0.4909x(3/4)=0.3682
45	0	3	2		
48	1	2	1	1/2	0.37x(1/2)=0.1841
161	0	1			

The *Time* column indicates the survival time in weeks to relapse. Any convenient unit of time can be used here. The *Status* column indicates whether the subject has experienced the terminal event or whether the observation is censored. The Kaplan-Meier procedure will accept numbers or string identifiers as definers of status.

The first event occurred nine weeks after the maintenance doses began. One patient relapsed. *Prior Number in Remission* is the number of cases alive prior to the event time. It is 11 prior to the first event time because 11 subjects began the study in remission. Since one subject has relapsed, the *Number Remaining* in remission after the first event is 10. The probability of surviving nine weeks is *Proportion in Remission*, which is *Number Remaining* divided by *Prior Number in Remission*. The next event occurred at 13 weeks. *Prior Number in Remission* is decreased to 10 because of the previous relapse. *Number Remaining* is decreased to 9 because of the current relapse.

The probability of remaining in remission for 13 weeks given that the subject was in remission at 9 weeks is the product of the two probabilities as shown in the *Cumulative Survival* column.

Using Censored Observations

Not all subjects experience relapse at the end of the observation period. The third subject joined the study 13 weeks before its end and was still in remission when the study ended. One strategy would be to drop such subjects from consideration because their outcome is unknown, but this would result in estimated survival probabilities that are too low. This subject provides information about surviving in remission for 13 weeks. Although the probability is not estimated for the third subject, that subject contributes to the total number of subjects, and the number of subjects is decremented for the next event. Decrementing the number of subjects decreases the denominator of *Proportion in Remission* and increases the estimated survival probability.

SPSS Kaplan-Meier Procedure

Figure 18-3 shows part of the output that results from submitting the AML data to the SPSS Kaplan-Meier procedure. The procedure produces a separate survival table for the experimental group that received maintenance doses of chemotherapy and the control group that did not. The separate tables were produced because *chemo* was declared as a factor. If no factor had been declared, the procedure would have produced one survival table for all subjects as though they were from the same group. Only the survival table for the experimental group is shown in Figure 18-3; it is similar to the calculated table in Figure 18-2. To produce the output, from the menus choose:

Analyze
  Survival
    Kaplan-Meier...

▶ Time: time

▶ Status: status

Define Event...
    Single value: 1

▶ Factor: chemo

Figure 18-3
Kaplan-Meier table

```
Survival Analysis for TIME      Time (weeks)

Factor CHEMO = Yes

   Time      Status      Cumulative     Standard     Cumulative     Number
                         Survival       Error        Events         Remaining

    9.00     Relapsed    .9091          .0867         1             10
   13.00     Relapsed    .8182          .1163         2              9
   13.00     Censored                                 2              8
   18.00     Relapsed    .7159          .1397         3              7
   23.00     Relapsed    .6136          .1526         4              6
   28.00     Censored                                 4              5
   31.00     Relapsed    .4909          .1642         5              4
   34.00     Relapsed    .3682          .1627         6              3
   45.00     Censored                                 6              2
   48.00     Relapsed    .1841          .1535         7              1
  161.00     Censored                                 7              0

Number of Cases:  11      Censored:   4      ( 36.36%)    Events: 7

             Survival Time    Standard Error    95% Confidence Interval

Mean:          52.65             19.83        (    13.78,      91.51 )
(Limited to   161.00 )
Median:        31.00              7.36        (    16.58,      45.42 )
```

This table presents the following information:

- *Time* is the time of occurrence of the terminal event of interest or the time at which the subject was withdrawn while still in remission (withdrawn alive or censored).

- *Status* indicates whether the subject has experienced the terminal event or has been censored. It contains values or labels, depending on how you have the options set for output labels.

- *Cumulative Survival* is an estimate of the probability of surviving longer than the time listed in the *Time* column. It is not computed for censored events.

- *Standard Error* is the standard error of the *Cumulative Survival* estimate.

- *Cumulative Events* is a count of terminal events that have occurred up to and including the current time. It is not incremented for censored events.

- *Number Remaining* is the number of patients still in remission after the specified time. It is decremented for censored events.

- *Mean Survival Time* is not the arithmetic mean. It is equal to the area under the survival curve for the uncensored cases (Lee, 1992). The survival curve is shown in Figure 18-4.

- *Median Survival Time* is the first event at which cumulative survival reaches 0.5 (50%) or less. It can be estimated more exactly by interpolation within the table.

The mean survival time has been designated as *Limited to 161*. If the cases with the longest survival times are censored, the mean that is calculated using the uncensored cases may be an underestimate. The case with the longest survival time is figured into the calculation, and the mean is reported to be **limited** to the survival time of that censored case (Lee, 1992).

The standard error of the cumulative proportion surviving is calculated as

$$\text{se}(t_k) = S(t_k)\sqrt{\sum_{i=1}^{k} \frac{d_i}{n_i(n_i - d_i)}}$$

where k is the specific event time, $S(t_k)$ is cumulative survival, d_i is the number of events at time t_i, and n_i is the number of cases still in remission (not experiencing the event or censored) prior to time t_i.

Comparing Cumulative Survival Functions: Means and Medians

Did the experimental group that received maintenance doses of chemotherapy have longer survival times in remission than the control group? The output that produced the mean and median for the experimental group, as shown in Figure 18-3, also produced a mean and median for the control group. The mean and median for the experimental group are 52.56 and 31.00, respectively. The mean and median for the control group are 22.71 and 23.00. The larger mean and median for the chemotherapy maintenance group suggests longer survival times for the experimental group.

Comparing Cumulative Survival Functions: Survival Curves

The difference in the two survival functions can be inspected graphically. Figure 18-4 shows a plot with two cumulative survival curves, one for each group in the AML data. Two separate curves were obtained because *chemo* was declared as a factor. If no factor had been declared, one survival function would have been produced, representing all of the cases as though they were from a single group. To obtain this plot from the menu system, use the Dialog Recall button to recall the Kaplan-Meier dialog box and choose:

Options...
   Plots: Survival

Figure 18-4
Cumulative survival function

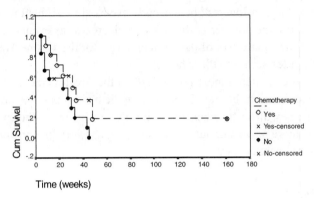

Time (weeks)

The chart in Figure 18-4 was modified in the Chart Editor for presentation in black and white. The default plus signs were changed to X's, and marker display was turned on. The X markers indicate censored cases. The circles represent terminal events (relapse). The curves are step functions because the survival function changes only at terminal events. The survival functions descend because the probability of survival decreases as the pool of survivors decreases (the number of relapses increases). The survival function for the experimental group that received maintenance doses of chemotherapy (*chemo* = 1) descends more gradually than the survival function for the control group. This is consistent with the greater mean and median (longer survival time) for this group.

Comparing Cumulative Survival Functions: Tests of Statistical Significance

In many cases, a researcher wants to be able to make an inference about the population from which the samples are drawn. The Kaplan-Meier procedure provides three statistical tests: the **log rank** (or Mantel-Cox) test, the **Breslow** (or generalized Wilcoxon) test, and the **Tarone-Ware** test. Each of these tests compares the number of terminal events actually observed (D_i) to the number of expected terminal events (E_i), which is calculated from the number at risk and the number of deaths at each event time in the study. The sum of the resulting differences is then calculated:

$$U = \sum_{i=1}^{k} w_i(D_i - E_i)$$

The only difference among the tests is the *w,* or weight, factor. The *w* factor is 1 for the log rank test; hence, all events are weighted equally. The *w* factor is the number at risk at each time point for the Breslow test; hence, early events are weighted more heavily than later events because the number in the risk pool decreases as events occur over time. The *w* factor is the square root of the number at risk for the Tarone-Ware test, so that it weights early cases somewhat less heavily.

The log rank test is considered more powerful than the Breslow test under the special condition that the mortality rate in each group being compared is proportional to that of the others (they differ by a constant multiple). If this is *not* the case, the Breslow test may be more powerful, but the Breslow test has very low power when the percentage of censored cases is large.

Producing Statistical Tests

Figure 18-5 shows the results of three statistical tests performed on the AML data with *chemo* as the factor. The procedure produces complete survival tables for each level of chemo and standard errors and confidence limits for the mean and median of each level of *chemo.* Only the summary comparisons for the two levels of *chemo* and the results of the statistical tests have been reproduced in Figure 18-5. To produce this output, recall the Kaplan-Meier dialog box and select:

Compare Factor...

Test Statistics:
☑ Log rank   ☑ Breslow   ☑ Tarone-Ware

Figure 18-5

Summary statistics and statistical tests for two levels of chemotherapy

```
Survival Analysis for TIME      Time (weeks)
                           Total      Number       Number        Percent
                                      Events      Censored       Censored
     CHEMO       No          12        11             1            8.33
     CHEMO       Yes         11         7             4           36.36
Overall                      23        18             5           21.74
   Test Statistics for Equality of Survival Distributions for CHEMO
                  Statistic       df      Significance
Log Rank            3.40           1          .0653
Breslow             2.72           1          .0989
Tarone-Ware         2.98           1          .0842
```

Since the significance levels for each of the three tests are larger than 0.05, the treatments were not significantly different. We cannot conclude that maintenance doses of chemotherapy would increase survival times in the population.

Stratification: The Interaction of Two Variables

More than one factor may be present, which, in combination with other factors, might affect survival time. In a cancer study, a stratification technique might be used to separate different stages of disease or different histologic groups. Or a researcher might expect that both the presence or absence of positive axillary lymph nodes and the pathologic tumor size would affect survival times. In other words, does tumor size determine survival time, whether or not a patient has lymph node involvement? A study of breast cancer patients at the University of Chicago (Heimann, unpublished) contains data on overall survival times, tumor size, and lymph nodes. A subset of the data was used for this example.

To answer the question, a Kaplan-Meier analysis was performed on overall survival time (*time*) with pathologic tumor size categories (*pathscat*) as the factor and the presence of lymph nodes (*ln_yesno*) as the strata. To produce the output, from the menus choose:

Analyze
  Survival
    Kaplan-Meier...

▶ Time: time
▶ Status: status

Define Event...
  Single value: 1

▶ Factor: pathscat
▶ Strata: ln_yesno

Compare Factor...

  Test Statistics:
  ☑ Log rank
  ⊙ For each stratum

Options...

  ☐ Survival table(s) (deselect)
  Plots:
  ☑ Survival

Figure 18-6 and Figure 18-7 show the descriptive statistics for each level of *pathscat* when *ln_yesno* is *No* or *Yes*. The output has been condensed to facilitate relevant comparisons.

Figure 18-6

Mean survival times for pathologic tumor sizes for patients with no positive lymph nodes

```
Survival Analysis for TIME       Time (months)
Strata LN_YESNO = No
Factor PATHSCAT = <= 2 cm
           Survival Time    Standard Error    95% Confidence Interval
Mean:         127.56               1.40       (   124.82,     130.30 )
(Limited to    133.80 )
Median:           .                  .        (      .  ,         .  )

Strata LN_YESNO = No
Factor PATHSCAT = 2-5 cm
           Survival Time    Standard Error    95% Confidence Interval
Mean:         113.19               3.51       (   106.32,     120.07 )
(Limited to    128.57 )
Median:           .                  .        (      .  ,         .  )

Strata LN_YESNO = No
Factor PATHSCAT = > 5 cm
           Survival Time    Standard Error    95% Confidence Interval
Mean:          42.21               8.35       (    25.85,      58.57 )
(Limited to     52.43 )
Median:           .                  .        (      .  ,         .  )
```

When there is no lymph node involvement, the mean survival times for the different tumor sizes get smaller as the tumor size gets larger. The mean survival times are 127.56, 113.19, and 42.21 months when the tumor size goes from small to large.

Figure 18-7

Mean survival times for pathologic tumor sizes in patients with positive lymph nodes

```
Survival Analysis for TIME       Time (months)
Strata LN_YESNO = Yes
Factor PATHSCAT = <= 2 cm
           Survival Time    Standard Error    95% Confidence Interval
Mean:         119.47               2.88       (   113.81,     125.12 )
(Limited to    129.03 )
Median:           .                  .        (      .  ,         .  )

Strata LN_YESNO = Yes
Factor PATHSCAT = 2-5 cm
           Survival Time    Standard Error    95% Confidence Interval
Mean:          89.99               5.87       (    78.48,     101.49 )
(Limited to    117.23 )
Median:           .                  .        (      .  ,         .  )

Strata LN_YESNO = Yes
Factor PATHSCAT = > 5 cm
           Survival Time    Standard Error    95% Confidence Interval
Mean:          62.57              12.33       (    38.41,      86.73 )
(Limited to     80.00 )
Median:        45.13                  .        (      .  ,         .  )
```

Similarly, in Figure 18-7, when the patients do have positive lymph nodes, the mean survival time also gets shorter as the tumor size gets larger. The mean is again limited to the last censored case (as in Figure 18-3).

The median survival time cannot be calculated for most groups here because less than 50% of the at risk cases in the group experienced the terminal event. See Chapter 17 for a discussion of the median. Figure 18-8 shows summaries of the number of events, number censored (alive), and percentage censored in each combination of categories.

Figure 18-8
Summaries of lymph node involvement and pathologic tumor size

```
Survival Analysis for TIME       Time (months)
                        Total      Number      Number      Percent
                                   Events      Censored     Censored
LN_YESNO      No         860         39          821         95.47
  PATHSCAT  <= 2 cm      666         21          645         96.85
  PATHSCAT  2-5 cm       190         17          173         91.05
  PATH      > 5 cm         4          1            3         75.00
LN_YESNO      Yes        261         27          234         89.66
  PATHSCAT  <= 2 cm      160         10          150         93.75
  PATHSCAT  2-5 cm        93         16           77         82.80
  PATHSCAT  > 5 cm         8          1            7         87.50

Overall                 1121         66         1055         94.11
```

Figure 18-9 shows that the survival times for different categories of pathologic tumor size were significantly different, both for patients with no positive lymph nodes and for patients having positive lymph nodes. The significance is well under the conventional value of $p = 0.05$.

Figure 18-9
Test statistics

```
Test Statistics for Equality of Survival Distributions for PATHSCAT
  For LN_YESNO = No
                  Statistic       df       Significance
  Log Rank          20.50          2           .0000
Test Statistics for Equality of Survival Distributions for PATHSCAT
  For LN_YESNO = Yes
                  Statistic       df       Significance
  Log Rank          14.02          2           .0009
```

These statistics are for each stratum. Since the conclusion is the same in both strata, *Pooled over strata* could be used. If the conclusions for the separate strata are not the same, then do not pool. These tests indicate only that the pathologic tumor size categories are different from one another, but not which specific categories are different. For comparing all distinct pairs of factor categories, select pairwise statistics.

Separate charts for each level of lymph node involvement with survival functions for each category of tumor size are shown in Figure 18-10. In each chart, the curves representing the larger size categories descend more rapidly than the curve for the smallest category. The longer survival for smaller tumor sizes is apparent. For the largest size category (> 5 cm), there is only a small number of steps in each chart, reflecting the small number of cases in this category.

Figure 18-10
Comparison of the survival functions for pathologic tumor sizes with no lymph node involvement

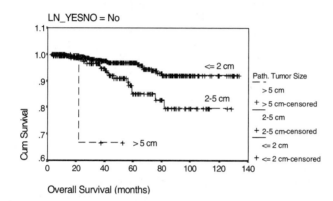

Cox Regression Examples

Contributed by Milton Steinberg, Marymount College.

A series of measurements was taken at the University of Chicago (Heimann, unpublished) on more than 1000 conservatively treated breast cancer cases. Among the measurements were pathologic tumor size, estrogen receptor status, and number of positive axillary lymph nodes. Can any of these factors be used to predict the risk of death from breast cancer? What is the relative risk of death for breast cancer patients who have a positive estrogen receptor status as compared with breast cancer patients who have a negative estrogen receptor status? Do cases with positive estrogen receptor status survive longer than those with negative estrogen receptor status?

As described in the *SPSS Base Applications Guide*, multiple linear regression is a technique used to determine the influence of predictor variables on a dependent variable. However, linear regression has no mechanism for handling censored cases. A nonlinear model is also more reasonable as an approximation for a variable, such as survival time or hazard rate, that cannot take on negative values.

The Cox Regression Model

As explained more fully in Chapter 17, some observations in survival studies are commonly censored. Censored cases do not experience the event of interest in the study, such as death from cancer or recovery from depression, before the end of the study. Cox Regression, like other survival techniques, makes use of the contribution of censored cases.

The Cox **proportional hazards** regression model is popular in part because it requires fewer assumptions than some other survival models. However, it should be used only if the assumption of proportional hazards is met (see "Checking for Proportional Hazards" on p. 270). If the proportional hazards assumption is violated, an extended version of the Cox model must be used.

The Hazard Function

Cox Regression uses the **hazard function** to estimate the relative risk of failure. The hazard function, *h(t)*, is a rate. It is an estimate of the potential for death per unit time at a particular instant, given that the case has survived until that instant (see Kleinbaum, 1996). A high hazard function indicates a high rate of mortality. For example, the hazard function representing the risk of human mortality is high during the first days of life, becomes low and stable through the middle years, and begins to increase with advancing age. Note that the hazard function is not a probability and can therefore exceed 1. It can take on any value from 0 to infinity.

The **survival function** or **survivorship function**, *S(t)*, was introduced in Chapter 17. It is an estimate of the probability of surviving longer than a specified time. The **cumulative hazard function**, *H(t)*, is related to the survival function and can be derived from the survival function (see Lee, 1992: $H(t) = -\ln S(t)$).

The Cox Regression model used to determine the influence of predictor variables on a dependent variable is most simply expressed in terms of the hazard function. Predictor variables are termed **covariates** in this model. A simple model comparing treatment to control, or condition to no condition, can be written as

$$h(t) = [h_0(t)]e^{(BX)}$$
Equation 19-1

Here *X* is a dichotomous covariate that takes the value 0 for control or no condition and the value 1 for treatment or condition. *B* is a regression coefficient, *e* is the base of the natural logarithm (about 2.718), and $h_0(t)$ is the **baseline hazard function** when *X* is set to 0 (the expected risk without the treatment or condition). The expected risk of death for a particular case with condition *X* is equal to the risk of death without condition *X* multiplied by the quantity *e* raised to the power (*BX*). In the breast cancer example, the expected risk of death from cancer in a patient who has a positive estrogen receptor status *h(t)* is equal to the expected risk of death for a patient who has a negative estrogen receptor status $h_0(t)$ multiplied by *e* raised to the power *(BX)*. In this example, *X* takes the value of 0 for negative or 1 for positive receptor status, and *B* is the regression coefficient. It is estimated by maximizing a partial likelihood (Cox and Oakes, 1984; Kalbfleisch and Prentice, 1980).

There are other ways to express Equation 19-1 that are helpful in interpreting the output from Cox Regression. If both sides of Equation 19-1 are divided by $h_0(t)$, the result is

$$h(t)/h_0(t) = e^{(BX)}$$

Equation 19-2

The quantity $h(t)/h_0(t)$ is called the **relative hazard** or the **hazard ratio**. It indicates the increase (or decrease) in risk incurred by applying the treatment or condition.

If the natural log is taken of both sides of Equation 19-2, the result is

$$\ln[h(t)/(h_0(t))] = BX$$

Equation 19-3

The quantity $\ln[h(t)/(h_0(t))]$ is the log relative hazard, which can be used to compare the relative risk for patients with and without the treatment. If the quantity $\ln[h(t)/(h_0(t))]$ is set equal to Y, then Equation 19-3 becomes $Y = BX$. This closely resembles an ordinary regression equation.

A subset of the cases in the original breast cancer data was used for the examples in this chapter. In order to submit the data to the Cox Regression procedure, the file must contain at least two variables: a survival time indicator (the dependent variable) and a status indicator that records whether the event has occurred for the case or if the case is censored. Usually a third, predictor (independent), variable is also entered. In this example, the dependent variable, *time*, indicates months of survival of breast cancer cases. The status indicator variable, *status*, is coded 0 for censored cases and 1 for cases that have died of breast cancer. The predictor variable, estrogen receptor status (*er*), is coded 0 for negative status and 1 for positive status. To produce the output, from the menus choose:

Analyze
  Survival
    Cox Regression...

▶ Time: time

▶ Status: status

Define Event...
  Single value: 1

▶ Covariates: er

Figure 19-1
Statistics for estrogen receptor status

```
------------------ Variables in the Equation --------------------
Variable        B       S.E.      Wald  df      Sig        R     Exp(B)
ER           -.6507     .2814    5.3455   1    .0208    -.0739    .5217
```

The table in Figure 19-1 presents the following information:

- *B* is the estimated coefficient. It is interpreted as the predicted change in log hazard for a unit increase in the predictor.

- *S.E.* is the standard error of the estimated coefficient, *B*.

- *Wald* is the Wald statistic. If $df = 1$, the Wald statistic can be calculated as $(B/S.E.)^2$. It is used to test whether the estimated coefficient *B* is different from 0 in the population. It is distributed as chi-square.

- *df* is degrees of freedom for the Wald statistic. The degrees of freedom for the Wald statistic is 1 except for categorical variables. While the degrees of freedom for each category is 1, the degrees of freedom for the overall test of the categorical variable is the number of categories minus 1.

- *Sig* is the significance level for the Wald statistic.

- *R* is an estimate of the partial correlation of the dependent variable with the covariate.

- *Exp(B)* is $e^{(B)}$ as in Equation 19-2, $h(t)/h_0(t) = e^{(BX)}$. For a dichotomous variable in which there are two levels, 0 and 1, *Exp(B)* is the **relative risk**, which is the ratio of the risk with *X* at 0 compared to the risk with *X* at 1.

R is calculated from the Wald statistic:

$$R = \sqrt{\frac{\text{Wald} - (2 \times df)}{-2LL_0}}$$

Equation 19-4

where $-2LL_0$ = minus 2 times the log likelihood for the initial baseline model. *R* is set to 0 if $2 \times df \geq \text{Wald}$.

Is estrogen receptor status an effective predictor that can be used to predict the risk of death from breast cancer? The negative value of the regression coefficient means that as the value of *er* increases, the risk decreases. Since *er* is coded 0 for negative and 1 for positive, it means that the death rate is expected to be less when estrogen receptor status is positive. This estimated coefficient is significantly different from 0; the Wald statistic is large, and the significance level is small. Estrogen receptor status does appear to be an effective predictor variable in this model where no other variables are considered. Since *Exp(B)* is less than 1, it indicates that there is a decreased relative risk when estrogen receptor status is positive. The hazard from breast cancer with positive estrogen receptor status is about 52% that of the hazard with negative estrogen receptor status, when no other variables are considered. An increased risk would have been indicated by a number greater than 1.

The hazard function for estrogen receptor status can be written as

$$h(t) = [h_0(t)]e^{(-0.6507X)}$$

where X is 0 or 1 (negative or positive receptor status) and $h_0(t)$ is the baseline hazard function.

The difference in risk of breast cancer death between negative and positive estrogen receptor status can be seen graphically. Figure 19-2 shows cumulative hazard functions for positive and negative estrogen status (*er*). To produce the output, recall the dialog box and choose:

Categorical...
▶ Categorical Covariates: er (Indicator(first))

Plots...
Hazard
▶ Separate Lines for: er(Cat)

Figure 19-2
Cumulative hazard function for positive and negative estrogen receptor status

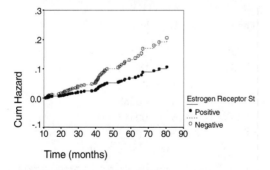

Note: Charts in this chapter have been modified in the Chart Editor for black and white presentation.

In Figure 19-2, the line representing the cumulative hazard function for negative estrogen receptor status is above the line representing positive estrogen receptor status. This shows a higher hazard for cases with negative estrogen receptor status.

Declaring the estrogen receptor status variable categorical has divided it into two patterns because there are two levels of the variable, 0 and 1, and it is categorical. The Cox Regression procedure can also produce plots for more than two patterns.

Generating Cumulative Hazard and Survival Estimates for Individual Cases

The hazard function and the survival function are closely related, and both can be calculated by the Cox Regression procedure. To add cumulative hazard and survival functions to the data, recall the dialog box and choose:

Save...
  Survival:
  ☑ Function
  Diagnostics:
  ☑ Hazard function

Two new variables appear in the Data Editor, *sur_1* and *haz_1*. Figure 19-3 shows values for six uncensored cases, three with negative and three with positive estrogen receptor status.

Figure 19-3
Cumulative hazard and survival estimates for a few selected cases

ID	Estrogen Receptor Status	Time	sur_1	haz_1
1182	Negative	11.03	.99818	.00182
1103	Negative	12.00	.99635	.00366
1153	Negative	13.10	.98891	.01115
1180	Positive	12.20	.99713	.00288
1169	Positive	12.43	.99616	.00385
1155	Positive	13.03	.99518	.00483

The cumulative hazard for case 1153 (with negative estrogen receptor status and surviving for 13.10 months) is 0.01115. The cumulative hazard for the case 1155 (surviving for 13.03 months with positive estrogen receptor status) is 0.00483. The smaller hazard reflects the lesser risk expected for the positive status. Similarly, from the survival column *sur_1*, 99.64% of the cases continue alive after the event at 12.00

months *(er* negative*)* and 99.71% of the cases continue alive after the event at 12.20 months *(er* positive*)*. This reflects the higher survival rate expected for positive status as compared with negative status.

Plotting Survival Functions

Just as the overall differences in risk for estrogen receptor positivity and negativity are clarified by a graph of the cumulative hazard function, the answer to the question of whether cases with positive estrogen receptor status survive longer than those with negative estrogen receptor status is clarified by viewing the survival functions.

To plot the survival functions, recall the dialog box and from the menus choose:

Plots...

☑ Survival
Separate Lines for: er(Cat)

The plot is shown in Figure 19-4. The curve for estrogen receptor positivity is higher than the curve for estrogen receptor negativity. It reflects an expectation of longer survival times with estrogen receptor positive status.

Figure 19-4
Survival curves for estrogen receptor status data

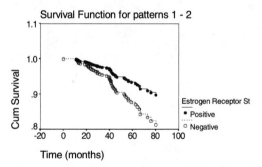

A regression equation can be written for *S(t)* similar to that for *h(t)*:

$$S(t) = [S_0(t)]^p$$

Equation 19-5

where $p = e^{(BX)}$. Instead of $S_0(t)$ being multiplied by $e^{(BX)}$, it is raised to the power $e^{(BX)}$. This creates a more complicated function than that for *h(t)* in Equation 19-1.

Multiple Covariates

As with multiple linear regression, the model for Cox Regression can be expanded to include more than one covariate:

$$h(t) = [h_0(t)]e^{(B_1X_1 + B_2X_2 + ... + B_pX_p)}$$

Equation 19-6

where $X_1...X_p$ are the covariates. The covariates can be continuous or categorical. Dichotomous covariates, such as estrogen receptor status, can be treated as categorical or continuous on an interval scale, since the single interval between 0 and 1 must be an "equal" interval. See the appendix for more information on coding schemes and their interpretation. The Cox Regression procedure automatically codes any variables designated as categorical and permits inclusion of interaction terms in the model.

Suppose the variable representing estrogen receptor status (*er*) is joined in the model with two other variables, one representing the number of positive axillary lymph nodes (*lnpos*) and another representing pathologic tumor size (*pathsize*). The variable *er* is dichotomous and can be considered continuous or categorical. *Lnpos* and *pathsize* are continuous variables.

Figure 19-5 shows the Cox Regression output from the model with three variables included. To produce the output, from the menus choose:

Analyze
  Survival
    Cox Regression...

▶ Time: time
▶ Status: status

Define Event...
  Single value: 1

▶ Covariates: er lnpos pathsize

Figure 19-5
Statistics for model with three variables

```
-------------------- Variables in the Equation --------------------
Variable        B       S.E.     Wald   df     Sig      R      Exp(B)
ER           -.5647    .2955    3.6527   1    .0560   -.0527    .5686
LNPOS         .1453    .0360   16.2735   1    .0001    .1547   1.1563
PATHSIZE      .3999    .1168   11.7168   1    .0006    .1277   1.4917
```

The interpretation is similar to that for Figure 19-1. There are now three estimated coefficients (*B* values), one for each variable. The regression equation can now be written as

$$h(t) = [h_0(t)]e^{((-0.5647 \times er) + (0.1453 \times lnpos) + (0.3999 \times pathsize))}$$

Notice that the estimated coefficient for *er* is not the same as in Figure 19-1. The contribution of each variable to the regression model is considered in the light of the contribution of all the other variables in the model. The value of *B* for *er* was computed as a partial weight after partialing out the influence of the other two variables. This *B* is no longer significant at the 0.05 level. Should *er* be removed from the model?

For multiple level variables, *Exp(B)* estimates the percentage change in risk with each unit change in the covariate. Each unit increase in the number of positive lymph nodes (*lnpos*) is expected to increase the risk of death about 16%, since $Exp(B) = 1.1563$. For the dichotomous variable *er,* the percentage change in risk with each unit change in the covariate can be interpreted as the relative risk, since the covariate takes only the values 0 and 1.

Testing the Overall Model

Does the inclusion of any of the three predictors *er, lnpos,* and *pathsize* do a better job of predicting the hazard rate than a baseline model in which each *B* is set to 0 (the covariates are ignored)? This question is answered by testing whether any of the population *B* values are nonzero. In Cox Regression, coefficients are estimated by maximizing the partial likelihood function, *L.* The partial likelihood is determined by finding the risk of failure at each failure point and taking the product of all of these risks. The natural log of *L* is called the log likelihood, *LL.* Minus 2 times the log likelihood ($-2LL$) for the model of interest can be compared with $-2LL$ for the baseline model in which all *B*'s are set to 0 to test whether all population *B*'s are 0.

Figure 19-6
Comparing regression models

```
Beginning Block Number 0.  Initial Log Likelihood Function
-2 Log Likelihood    596.064
Beginning Block Number 1.  Method:  Enter
Variable(s) Entered at Step Number 1..
   ER         Estrogen Receptor Status
   LNPOS      Positive Axillary Lymph Nodes
   PATHSIZE   Pathologic Tumor Size (cm)
Log likelihood converged after 4 iterations.
-2 Log Likelihood    560.175
                  Chi-Square   df   Sig
Overall (score)      56.953     3   .0000
Change (-2LL) from
 Previous Block      35.888     3   .0000
 Previous Step       35.888     3   .0000
```

The output in Figure 19-6 presents the following information:

■ *Block Number 0* refers to the baseline model with all *B*'s set to 0.

■ *Block Number 1* refers to the model with the predictor variables included. A list of the variables and $-2LL$ is given for this model.

■ *Change (−2LL) from Previous Block* is the difference between $-2LL$ for block 0 and $-2LL$ for block 1. This is the **likelihood-ratio (LR)** test.

■ *Change (−2LL) from Previous Step* refers to stepwise regression procedures (see below).

■ *Overall (score)* is another test of whether all of the coefficients (*B*) in the model are 0 in the population. It is distributed as chi-square and is an approximation to *LR*. This test is also called the **global chi-square** or **overall chi-square**.

■ *df* is the number of variables in the present model minus the number of variables in the previous model.

■ *Sig* is based on the chi-square test. Both the score and $-2LL$ are distributed as chi-square for large samples.

In the current model, the change in $-2LL$ from the previous block, in which all *B*'s were set to 0, is $590.06 - 560.18 = 35.88$. Since $p < 0.0001$, the inference is that at least one population *B* is nonzero. The score agrees with the likelihood ratio.

Finding a Good Model

Does the model using *er*, *lnpos*, and *pathsize* include the best predictors of survival? The estimated coefficient *B* for *er* is no longer significantly different from 0 when *lnpos* and *pathsize* are added to the model. Should *er* be removed from the model? The basic strategy for answering such questions involves adding various combinations of variables to the model and then testing each model to determine which has the best predictive power. But be aware that determination of a best model is not a purely mechanical procedure. The model that best fits the present data was specifically constructed to do so for the sample being used. It may not be the same as the one that best fits other samples from the same population. Practical and theoretical considerations also play a part in choosing a model. Some variables or interactions that seem to be part of the optimal model may be difficult to interpret or hard or expensive to measure.

Methods for Selecting Models

The coefficient for *er* changed when *lnpos* and *pathsize* were added to the model. It no longer made a significant contribution to the prediction of risk. But, the contribution of any one variable is determined in the context of the contribution of all other variables in the model. If other variables were included in the model, *er* might be found to make a significant contribution. Several methods are available for adding and deleting variables from the model. The method used so far has been **forced entry**. All of the variables have been forced into the model in one step. Two stepwise methods are available, **forward selection** and **backward selection,** in which variables are entered and deleted according to specified criteria.

In forward selection, the model begins as the baseline model without any variables in it. Variables are considered one at a time. They are added to the model if they meet the selection criterion based on the *p* value for the score statistic. The default value for inclusion is 0.05. As each new variable is added, the variables already present are evaluated for removal. One of three criteria for removal can be selected: the likelihood-ratio statistic based on the maximum partial likelihood estimates $(-2LL)$, the likelihood-ratio statistic based on conditional parameter estimates, and the Wald statistic. The default for removal from the model is a *p* value of 0.10 for the selected statistic. The maximum partial likelihood estimates criterion may be superior to the others, but it requires recomputation of the model after each variable is deleted in turn. The conditional parameter estimates criterion does not require recomputation of the model and usually gives results similar to those for the maximum partial likelihood estimates criterion. When no more variables meet entry or removal criteria, or when the last model is identical to a prior model, the algorithm stops.

In backward selection, all of the selected variables are entered into the model at the first step. Each variable is then considered for removal. All of the variables that meet removal criteria are removed. Then the excluded variables are reconsidered for inclusion. When no more variables can be entered or removed, the algorithm stops.

Stepwise Regression: Forward Selection Example

For this section, two other variables, age and histologic grade (*histgrad*) have been added to the model. Histologic grade has been treated as a categorical variable with three levels coded as indicator or dummy variables and with the first category as the reference category. A forward selection procedure with removal based on conditional parameter estimates has been selected.

Figure 19-7 shows Cox Regression output using forward selection. To produce the output, from the menus choose:

Analyze
 Survival
  Cox Regression...

▶ Time: time
▶ Status: status

Define Event...
  Single value: 1

▶ Covariates: er lnpos pathsize age histgrad

 Method: Forward:Conditional

Categorical: histgrad (Indicator(first))

(Deselect any Plots or Save variables)

Figure 19-7
Forward selection: Block 0

```
Beginning Block Number 0.  Initial Log Likelihood Function
-2 Log Likelihood    463.880
---------- Variables not in the Equation ----------
Residual Chi Square = 43.49 with 6 df   Sig = .0000
Variable         Score  df   Sig       R
ER               3.6433  1  .0563    .0595
LNPOS           21.8473  1  .0000    .2068
PATHSIZE        24.6556  1  .0000    .2210
AGE              9.3049  1  .0023    .1255
HISTGRAD         5.5342  2  .0628    .0575
  HISTGRAD(1)    1.4984  1  .2209    .0000
  HISTGRAD(2)    4.5858  1  .0322    .0747
```

The forward selection statistics contain the following information:

- *Block Number 0* is the baseline model with all variables excluded.

- *Variables not in the Equation* includes all of the variables in the model because forward selection begins with all of the variables excluded.

- *Residual Chi Square* tests whether all of the coefficients for the variables not in the equation are 0.

- *Score* statistic is used to determine inclusion in the model. For categorical variables, an overall score statistic and score statistics for each of the components are printed. The significance of the overall score statistic determines inclusion.

- *df* for the score statistic is 1 except for categorical variables and interaction terms with two or more components. In that case, the degrees of freedom is the number of components. In a categorical variable, this is one less than the number of levels.

- *Sig* of the score statistic is the criterion for inclusion in the model. The default value for inclusion is 0.05.

- *R* is calculated as previously described, but the score statistic replaces the Wald statistic in the calculation.

The categorical variable, *histgrad*, has an overall score statistic and a statistic for each of its components. The overall score determines whether *histgrad* is included in the model. The degrees of freedom for *histgrad*, overall, is 2. It has three levels that are reduced to two components by the coding scheme.

Because the residual chi-square is significant ($p < 0.0001$), at least one coefficient is implied to be nonzero in the population. The variables *lnpos*, *pathsize*, and *age* all meet the criteria for inclusion at this stage because significance of the chi-squares for their score statistics is less than 0.05. The variable with the lowest *Sig* level will be added at the next step. Figure 19-8 shows the model after the addition of *pathsize*, the variable with the lowest p value (*Sig*) for its score statistic.

Figure 19-8
Block 1, step 1

```
Beginning Block Number 1.  Method:  Forward Stepwise (Conditional LR)
Variable(s) Entered at Step Number 1..
    PATHSIZE  pathologic Tumor Size (cm)
Log likelihood converged after 4 iterations.
-2 Log Likelihood    444.685
                     Chi-Square    df    Sig
Overall (score)        24.656      1   .0000
Change (-2LL) from
 Previous Block         19.195      1   .0000
 Previous Step          19.195      1   .0000

-------------------- Variables in the Equation --------------------
Variable            B       S.E.     Wald   df    Sig      R     Exp(B)
PATHSIZE          .6052    .1229   24.2412   1   .0000   .2190   1.8316

---------- Variables not in the Equation ----------
Residual Chi Square = 13.11 with 5 df   Sig = .0224
Variable          Score   df    Sig      R
ER               1.7005    1   .1922   .0000
LNPOS            8.0718    1   .0045   .1144
AGE              4.4419    1   .0351   .0726
HISTGRAD         3.0975    2   .2125   .0000
 HISTGRAD(1)      .7861    1   .3753   .0000
 HISTGRAD(2)     2.3808    1   .1228   .0287

------Model if Term Removed------
Based on conditional coefficients
Term            Loss
Removed     Chi-square  df    Sig
PATHSIZE       19.1951   1   .0000
```

With *pathsize* entered into the model, $-2LL$ is calculated and compared with $-2LL$ for the baseline model. The likelihood-ratio chi-square is significant, as is the chi-square for the score statistic. The variable *pathsize* has a positive coefficient (*B*), so the larger the pathologic tumor size, the greater the hazard. Examination of *Exp(B)* shows that there is approximately an 83% increase in hazard for each unit increase in *pathsize*.

The *Model if Term Removed* column helps test *pathsize* for removal using the *conditional* criterion requested as Method in the dialog box. Since the *p* value for the chi-square is less than the 0.10 exclusion criterion, *pathsize* is retained in the model.

The residual chi-square for the variables not in the equation is significant. The variable *lnpos* now has the smallest *p* value. It will be selected in the next step.

Figure 19-9 shows step 2.

Figure 19-9
Block 1, step 2

```
Variable(s) Entered at Step Number 2..
    LNPOS      Positive Axillary Lymph Nodes
Coefficients converged after 4 iterations.
-2 Log Likelihood     438.522
                    Chi-Square    df     Sig
Overall (score)       38.818      2    .0000
Change (-2LL) from
 Previous Block        25.358      2    .0000
 Previous Step          6.163      1    .0130

-------------------- Variables in the Equation --------------------
Variable            B       S.E.     Wald  df     Sig      R     Exp(B)
LNPOS             .1253    .0449    7.7982   1    .0052   .1118   1.1335
PATHSIZE          .5031    .1293   15.1403   1    .0001   .1683   1.6538

---------- Variables not in the Equation ----------
Residual Chi Square = 5.964 with 4 df   Sig = .2019
Variable          Score  df    Sig       R
ER               2.1438   1   .1431    .0176
AGE              4.0916   1   .0431    .0671
HISTGRAD         2.6123   2   .2709    .0000
 HISTGRAD(1)      .8418   1   .3589    .0000
 HISTGRAD(2)     2.0770   1   .1495    .0129

------Model if Term Removed------
Based on conditional coefficients
Term           Loss
Removed      Chi-square  df    Sig
LNPOS          6.2162     1   .0127
PATHSIZE      12.9159     1   .0003
```

Change (−2LL) from Previous Step shows the difference between −2*LL* for the model constructed at step 1 and −2*LL* for the model constructed at step 2. *Change (−2LL) from Previous Block* shows the difference between −2*LL* for the baseline model constructed in block 0 and −2*LL* for the model constructed in step 2. Both likelihood ratios show a significant improvement in the model. The model is then reevaluated with both *pathsize* and *lnpos*. Both variables make significant contributions.

Of the variables not in the equation, only *age* has a *p* value that falls below the 0.05 cutoff. It will be selected in the next step. Both *pathsize* and *lnpos* are below criteria for removal from the model, and therefore they are retained in the next step.

Figure 19-10 shows step 3 of the forward selection process.

Figure 19-10
Block 1, step 3

```
Variable(s) Entered at Step Number 3..
    AGE        Age (years)
Log likelihood converged after 4 iterations.
-2 Log Likelihood      434.321
                   Chi-Square    df    Sig
Overall (score)       41.232     3   .0000
Change (-2LL) from
 Previous Block        29.558     3   .0000
 Previous Step          4.200     1   .0404

-------------------- Variables in the Equation --------------------
Variable          B        S.E.      Wald  df    Sig       R    Exp(B)
LNPOS          .1266      .0474    7.1365   1   .0076   .1052   1.1349
PATHSIZE       .4369      .1353   10.4288   1   .0012   .1348   1.5480
AGE           -.0269      .0134    4.0399   1   .0444  -.0663    .9735

---------- Variables not in the Equation ----------
Residual Chi Square = 1.937 with 3 df   Sig = .5855
Variable      Score  df   Sig      R
ER            .8510   1  .3563   .0000
HISTGRAD     1.5352   2  .4641   .0000
 HISTGRAD(1)  .4202   1  .5168   .0000
 HISTGRAD(2) 1.1021   1  .2938   .0000

------Model if Term Removed------
Based on conditional coefficients
Term         Loss
Removed    Chi-square  df    Sig
LNPOS         5.8377   1  .0157
PATHSIZE      9.1787   1  .0024
AGE           4.2026   1  .0404
No more variables can be added or deleted.
```

When the model with *lnpos*, *pathsize*, and *age* is reevaluated, each has a loss chi-square *p* value below the 0.10 cutoff, and all three variables make a significant contribution to predicting hazard or survival. Since *age* has a negative coefficient, increases in age lead to decreases in hazard.

The variables not in the equation, *er* and *histgrad*, have score statistics with *p* values that exceed the 0.05 cutoff criterion. *No more variables can be added or deleted*, and the algorithm stops.

Checking for Proportional Hazards

The proportional hazards model assumes that the hazard function $h(t)$ for the model that includes a particular covariate is proportionally related to the baseline hazard, $h_0(t)$. This expectation is implied in Equation 19-2, where $h(t)$ and $h_0(t)$ are in constant proportion to one another; that is, they are related to one another as a power of e. To see what this means, observe plots of the baseline hazard functions for estrogen receptor positive status and negative status (*er*) in Figure 19-11. To produce the output, from the menus choose:

Analyze
　Survival
　　Cox Regression...

▶ Time: time

▶ Status: status

Define Event...
　　Single value: 1

▶ Strata: er

Plots...
　　Plot Type:
　　☑ Hazard
　　☑ Log minus log

Figure 19-11
Baseline hazard functions for estrogen receptor status data

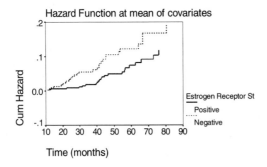

The variable *er* was declared as *strata* rather than as a covariate. This caused baseline hazard functions to be calculated for each level of the variable. Although the coefficients of the hazard functions are different for the baselines of estrogen receptor positivity and negativity, the proportions are approximately the same throughout.

Estrogen receptor negative diverges from estrogen receptor positive at a nearly constant rate so that the difference between the two curves remains proportional over time.

Another useful plot for determining whether the assumption of proportional hazards is met is the **log-minus-log** (LML) plot of the survival function. If the hazards are proportional, the curves generated by LML should be parallel. The curves in Figure 19-12 seem sufficiently parallel to confirm that the proportional hazards assumption is met.

Figure 19-12

Log-minus-log plot for two levels of estrogen receptor response

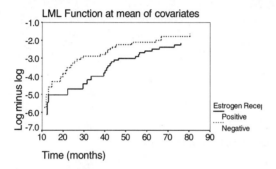

Nonproportional Hazards

Carter, Wampler, and Stablein (1983) reproduced a data set published from Stablein, Carter, and Wampler (1980) that demonstrates a model that violates the assumption of proportional hazards. Mice were injected with leukemia cells and then treated with different doses of the drug ICRF-159. Figure 19-13 compares baseline cumulative hazard functions for two dose strata, 0.0 mg/kg and 112.5 mg/kg.

Figure 19-13

Baseline hazard functions for two doses of ICRF-159

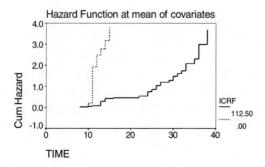

The two curves do not appear to increase proportionally. They diverge radically. The LML plot for the same data in Figure 19-8 confirms this departure from proportionality, since the plotted curves are not parallel.

Figure 19-14
Log-minus-log plot for two doses of ICRF-159

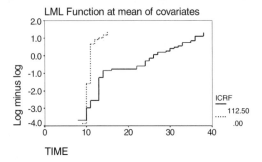

Cox Regression with Time-Dependent Covariates

Since the proportional hazards model implies that the effect of the covariate on the relative hazard is constant over time, it cannot be used to determine the efficacy of ICRF-159; its hazard function was determined to be nonproportional over time. But the covariate can be combined in a product with the survival time variable, or some function of the survival time variable, to create a **time-dependent covariate**. The time-dependent covariate can then be used to fit a nonproportional hazards model in which time is included as a predictor. It can also be used to check on the assumption of proportional hazards. The relative hazard function in such a model is free to vary with time.

$$h(t) = [h_0(t)]e^{(B_1 X_1 + B_2 X_1 * \text{T\_COV\_})}$$

Equation 19-7

In Equation 19-7, B_2 is the coefficient of a compound covariate formed by the product of X_1 with a variable called *T_COV_*, which is some function of the survival time variable for the model that includes X_1. SPSS provides a separate dialog box for calculating Cox Regression with time-dependent covariates. Both Cox Regression and its variant, Cox Time-Dependent, use the Newton-Raphson method, a numerical iterative procedure for solving nonlinear equations, in order to estimate parameters. However, the Cox Regression dialog box also permits saving diagnostics and graph generation.

To set up a Cox time-dependent analysis, from the menus choose:

Analyze
  Survival
    Cox w/ Time-Dep Cov...

At the top of the variables list on the left of the dialog box, a new variable, called $T\_$, has been inserted. The inserted variable, $T\_$, was generated by the time-dependent procedure. It assumes the same values as the variable in the database that is designated as the survival *time* indicator. $T\_$ can be transformed in many ways. For example, if $T\_$ is in months, $T\_ / 12$ would measure years. After you enter the information in the dialog box, the transformed version is stored in a variable called $T\_COV\_$. The strategy is to use $T\_COV\_$ as a covariate in interaction with other variables to generate a regression equation in which variables are free to change as a function of time.

    Figure 19-15 shows output for the model that includes *icrf* and the interaction T_COV_*icrf. To produce the output, from the menus choose:

Analyze
  Survival
    Cox w/ Time-Dep Cov...

Expression for T_COV_: T_

Model...

▶ Time: time

▶ Status: status

Define Event...
  Single value: 1

▶ Covariates: icrf, T_COV_*icrf

Figure 19-15
Cox Regression with a time-dependent covariate

```
--------------------- Variables in the Equation --------------------
Variable          B        S.E.      Wald   df      Sig        R    Exp(B)
ICRF           -.0254      .0038   44.9321    1    .0000    -.1503    .9749
T_COV_*ICRF  8.445E-04  1.700E-04  24.6750    1    .0000     .1092   1.0008
```

The Time-Dependent procedure calculates the values of the covariates at each event time for each case still at risk at that time. In this example, $T\_COV\_$ has been assigned the value of $T\_$, which is nothing more than the survival times in the time *variable*. The *icrf* coefficient gives the per unit change log hazard for time equal to 0. The coefficient for the product T_COV_*icrf is also significant. The significant interaction term indicates that the model that includes *icrf* does indeed violate the proportional hazards assumption and that the creation of the time-dependent variable *T_COV_*icrf* was necessary in order to evaluate *icrf* using Cox Regression.

Segmented Time-Dependent Covariates

The time-dependent covariate, *T_COV_*icrf,* was specifically created as an interaction term to permit the modeling of nonproportional hazards. Another type of time-dependent covariate, the **segmented time-dependent covariate,** is a variable that *intrinsically* varies with time (for example, blood pressure measurements that are taken more than once during a study). Crowley and Hu (1977) provide an example of the analysis of a heart transplant study in which the survival times of transplant patients were compared to those of nontransplant patients. In the version reported here, the covariates placed in the model are *waittime* (waiting time until transplant), *age* (at time of transplant), and *mismatch* (a tissue mismatch score). The transplant patients are not equivalent to the nontransplant patients. Only those who survive long enough to receive a heart can become recipients, so those with longer survival times are more likely to receive a heart. A time-dependent variable is therefore set up as an indicator. It has the value 0 before transplant and assumes the value 1 at the time of transplant (see Cox and Oakes, 1984). The syntax commands for the three time-dependent variables are as follows:

```
TIME PROGRAM.
COMPUTE xplant = (T_ >= waittime).
If missing(waittime) xplant=0.
COMPUTE xplntage = (T_ >= waittime) * age .
If missing(waittime) xplntage=0.
COMPUTE score = (T_ >= waittime) * mismatch .
If missing(waittime) score=0.
COXREG
   survival  /STATUS=followup(1)
  /METHOD=ENTER   xplant xplntage score
  /CRITERIA=PIN(.05) POUT(.10) ITERATE(20)  .
```

The variable *waittime* indicates when transplant has occurred. In the first transformation,

COMPUTE xplant = (T_ >= waittime)

the covariate *xplant* assumes a value of 0 if survival time is shorter than the waiting time until transplant, and *xplant* assumes a value of 1 if survival time is equal to or exceeds the waiting time until transplant. The 1 and 0 are results of true or false evaluation of the logical expression in parentheses. In the second transformation,

If missing(waittime) xplant = 0

all missing values of *xplant* are set to 0. All elements of the variable must have some value or the coefficients will not converge. Similarly, the values of the variable *xplntage* will be 0 for all times less than *waittime* (before transplant), and the values of *xplantage* will be the same as the values for *age* for all times greater than or equal to *waittime*. Finally, *score* has the value 0 before transplant and the value of *mismatch* after transplant.

The COXREG portion of the commands produced the table in Figure 19-16. (The CRITERIA subcommand contains default values, which are listed if you paste the syntax from the dialog box.)

Figure 19-16
Cox Regression with time-dependent covariates for heart transplant data

```
-------------------- Variables in the Equation --------------------
Variable         B       S.E.      Wald  df     Sig        R    Exp(B)
XPLANT      -3.1781     1.1861    7.1790   1   .0074   -.0960    .0417
XPLNTAGE      .0552      .0226    5.9651   1   .0146    .0840   1.0567
SCORE         .4442      .2803    2.5125   1   .1129    .0302   1.5593
```

More Than Two Segments

It is possible to construct segmented covariates with more than two segments. Suppose radiation treatments are administered at the start of each of three months, and tumor size is assessed at the end of each month. A time-dependent covariate might be defined as

$$(T\_ > 1) * size1 + (T\_ >= 1 \& T\_ < 2) * size2 + (T\_ >= 2 \& T\_ < 3) * size3$$

If the survival time is between zero and one month (but not including one month), then *T_COV_* will have the values for *size1*. If survival time is between one and two months (but not including two months), then *T_COV_* will have the values for *size2*, and, similarly, for a survival time between two and three months, the values of *size3*.

Diagnostics

Graphic displays can be used to test whether the assumption of proportional hazards in Cox Regression is met, whether the **log relative hazard** (Equation 19-3) is linear as is assumed in Cox Regression, or whether cases in the data set may have an excessive influence on the outcome of the Cox Regression. The Cox Regression procedure permits you to save the cumulative hazard function (which is also called the **Cox-Snell**

residual), **partial residuals**, **DfBeta**, and **X'Beta** to assist in making these determinations.

Cox Regression was performed for the breast cancer example with *age* as the only covariate. To produce the output, from the menus choose:

Analyze
  Survival
    Cox Regression...

▶ Time: time

▶ Status: status

Define Event...

Single value: 1

▶ Covariates: age

Save...

Diagnostics: ☑ Hazard function ☑ Partial residuals ☑ DfBeta(s)

☑ X*Beta

The Save options each add a new variable to the data: *haz_1*, *pr1_1*, *dfb1_1*, and *xbe_1*, respectively. These new variables can be saved with the data file. If there had been more than one covariate, a complete set of new variables would have been added to the data file for each covariate and named uniquely, as in *haz_2*, *pr1_2*, etc.

Using the Partial Residual for Checking Proportional Hazards

Partial residuals (Schoenfeld residuals) do not depend on time; hence, they may be plotted against time to test for violations of the proportional hazards assumption (Hess, 1995). Figure 19-17 shows a simple scatterplot of the partial residuals for *age* against survival time in the breast cancer data.

Figure 19-17
Plot of partial residuals for age against survival time

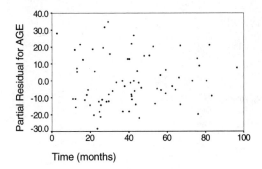

The partial residuals are calculated for uncensored cases only; they can be used for covariates that are not time-dependent. The partial residual for each case is the difference between the observed value of the case and its expected value. The expected value is calculated from all of the cases still at risk when the current case fails. The difference between a case and its expected value should be approximately 0 if proportionality holds. Figure 19-17 shows that the partial residuals are distributed fairly evenly in a band around 0, which is expected if the assumption of proportional hazards is met.

Linearity of the Log Hazard Function

Equation 19-3 defines the log relative hazard. It indicates that the log of the relative hazard is expected to be linearly related to the predictors.

At one time, the Cox-Snell residual (cumulative hazard function) was used to assess linearity. It is now standard practice to use the cumulative hazard function to construct **martingale residuals**. If the status indicator is coded 0 for censored cases and 1 for uncensored cases, martingale residuals are simply the hazard function subtracted from the status indicator. However, the following routine will work in all situations: if the case is censored, use Compute on the Transform menu to set *martgale = –(haz_1)*. If the case is uncensored, then the transformation is *martgale = 1 – haz_1*. Plots of martingale residuals against the covariate (Figure 19-18) or against the linear predictor *X'Beta* (Figure 19-19) should be linear. To find *X'Beta*, multiply each mean-corrected case value by each of its coefficient values (*B*), and add these products together. In this example, there is only one covariate and one coefficient.

Figure 19-18
Plot of martingale residuals against age

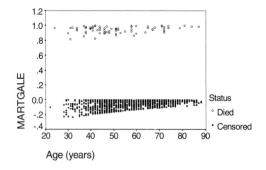

Figure 19-19
Plot of martingale residuals against X'Beta

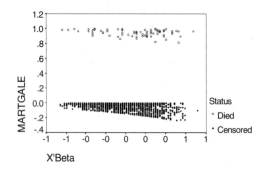

Since the martingale transformation treats censored and uncensored cases differently, it tends to separate them in the plot. In this data, there are many more censored cases than uncensored cases. They have been represented with closed and open circles, respectively, to clearly differentiate them. The censored cases form a fairly straight line around 0, and the uncensored cases form a fairly straight line around 1.

Influential Cases

Influential cases are those that have a disproportionate effect on the result of Cox Regression. The estimates for the regression coefficients are markedly different when such cases are included in the model and when they are removed from the model. DfBetas for each case can be calculated by performing the regression with and without each case in the model and finding the difference between the resulting coefficients for the predictor. This procedure is estimated by an approximation in Cox Regression. Figure 19-20 shows DfBeta for age plotted against the identification number (*id*) for each case.

Figure 19-20
Plot of DfBeta for age by id for each case

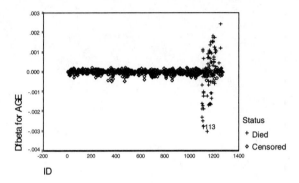

The censored cases are represented by open circles, and the uncensored cases, by plus signs. The uncensored cases seem to have a greater influence than the censored cases. Cases with little influence should form a band around 0. The DfBetas in this example are quite small. No case is outstanding. Extreme cases can be marked with the case number, using the Chart Editor. Case 1113 is the most extreme case in this data set.

Figure 19-21 shows that case 1113 is the oldest uncensored case in the data set. The censored cases in this chart have been hidden in the Chart Editor by making them tiny and white.

Figure 19-21
Plot of survival time against age

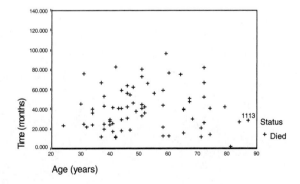

Syntax Reference

Introduction

This Syntax Reference section describes the SPSS command language underlying SPSS Advanced Models. Most of the features of these commands are implemented in the dialog boxes and can be used directly from the dialog boxes. Or you can paste the syntax to a syntax window and edit it or build a command file, which you can save and reuse. The features that are available only in command syntax are summarized following the discussion of the dialog box interface in the corresponding chapter on each statistical procedure.

This introduction to the Syntax Reference section provides basic rules for specifying command syntax and shows how to edit and run syntax in a syntax window. For more information about SPSS command syntax, see the *SPSS Base Syntax Reference Guide*. For more information about running commands in SPSS, see the *SPSS Base User's Guide*.

A Few Useful Terms

All terms in the SPSS command language fall into one or more of the following categories:

- **Keyword.** A word already defined by SPSS to identify a command, subcommand, or specification. Most keywords are, or resemble, common English words.

- **Command.** A specific instruction that controls the execution of SPSS.

- **Subcommand.** Additional instructions for SPSS commands. A command can contain more than one subcommand, each with its own specifications.

- **Specifications.** Instructions added to a command or subcommand. Specifications can include subcommands, keywords, numbers, arithmetic operators, variable names, special delimiters, and so on.

Each command begins with a command keyword (which may contain more than one word). The command keyword is followed by at least one blank space and then any additional specifications. Each command ends with a command terminator, which is a period. For example,

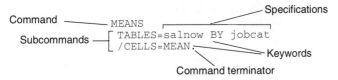

Syntax Diagrams

Each SPSS command described in this manual includes a syntax diagram that shows all of the subcommands, keywords, and specifications allowed for that command. These syntax diagrams are also available in the online Help system for easy reference when entering commands in a syntax window. By remembering the following rules, you can use the syntax diagram as a quick reference for any command:

- Elements shown in all capital letters are keywords defined by SPSS to identify commands, subcommands, functions, operators, and other specifications.

- Elements in lower case describe specifications you supply.
- Elements in bold type are defaults. A default indicated with ** is in effect when the keyword is not specified. (Bold type is not used in the online Help system syntax diagrams.)
- Parentheses, apostrophes, and quotation marks are required where indicated.
- Elements enclosed in square brackets ([ ]) are optional.
- Braces ({ }) indicate a choice among elements. You can specify any one of the elements enclosed within the aligned braces.
- Ellipses indicate that an element can be repeated.
- Most abbreviations are obvious; for example, varname stands for variable name and varlist stands for a list of variables.
- The command terminator is not shown in the syntax diagrams.

Syntax Rules

Keep in mind the following simple rules when writing and editing commands in a syntax window:

- Each command must begin on a new line and end with a period.
- Subcommands are separated by slashes. The slash before the first subcommand in a command is optional in most commands.
- SPSS keywords are not case sensitive, and three-letter abbreviations can be used for most keywords.
- Variable names must be spelled out in full.
- You can use as many lines as you want to specify a single command. However, text included within apostrophes or quotation marks must be contained on a single line.
- You can add space or break lines at almost any point where a single blank is allowed, such as around slashes, parentheses, arithmetic operators, or between variable names.
- Each line of syntax cannot exceed 80 characters.
- The period must be used as the decimal indicator.

For example,

```
FREQUENCIES
 VARIABLES=JOBCAT SEXRACE
 /PERCENTILES=25 50 75
 /BARCHART.
```

and

```
freq var=jobcat sexrace /percent=25 50 75 /bar.
```

are both acceptable alternatives that generate the same results. The second example uses three-letter abbreviations and lower case, and the command is on one line.

INCLUDE Files

If your SPSS commands are contained in a command file that is specified on the SPSS INCLUDE command, the syntax rules are slightly different:

- Each command must begin in the first column of a new line.
- Continuation lines within a command must be indented at least one space.
- The period at the end of the command is optional.

If you generate command syntax by pasting dialog box choices into a syntax window, the format of the commands is suitable for both INCLUDE files and commands run in a syntax window.

Using Command Syntax in a Syntax Window

To edit and run command syntax in a syntax window:

▶ From the menus choose:

File
  New
    Syntax

This opens a syntax window.

▶ Enter the commands in the syntax window. For example, the MANOVA specifications shown in Figure 1 produce a repeated measures analysis of variance.

Figure 1   MANOVA commands in a syntax window

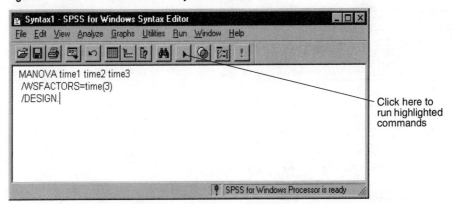

Click here to
run highlighted
commands

▶ Highlight the commands you want to run and click on the Run Current syntax tool (▶). Output is displayed in an output window. If your command syntax generates any error messages, you can edit the syntax and rerun it from the syntax window.

Running an Existing Command File

To run an existing command file:

▶ From the menus choose:
File
  Open...

▶ Select the file you want from the Open File dialog box (see the *SPSS Base User's Guide* for information on how to locate and open syntax files).

▶ Highlight the commands you want to run and click on the Run Current syntax tool (▶).

Online Syntax Help

Syntax diagrams for the SPSS command language are available to assist you when you work with command syntax in a syntax window.

▶ In a syntax window, type the name of the command you want to use. For example, to obtain the syntax chart for the KM command, type km or kaplan-meier. (SPSS commands are not case sensitive.)

▶ With the cursor on the same line, click on the Syntax Help tool (🔧). This opens the Syntax Help window containing the syntax diagram for the command, as shown in Figure 2.

Figure 2   Syntax Help window for the KM command

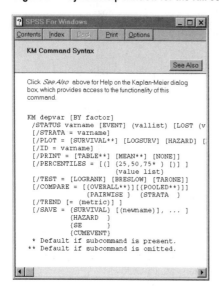

To see the syntax diagram as you work in a syntax window, reduce the main SPSS application window so that the Help window fits beside it or below it.

Copying Syntax from the Help Window to the Syntax Window

You can copy the syntax diagram to a syntax window and edit it.

▶ From the Help window's menu bar, choose:

Options
  Copy

▶ Activate the Syntax Window by clicking on it. From the menus choose:

Edit
  Paste

▶ Edit the command, deleting unnecessary subcommands and keywords and adding required specifications.

COXREG

```
[TIME PROGRAM]*
[commands to compute time dependent covariates]

[CLEAR TIME PROGRAM]

COXREG [VARIABLES =] survival varname [WITH varlist]
     / STATUS = varname [EVENT] (vallist) [LOST (vallist)]
    [/STRATA  = varname]
    [/CATEGORICAL = varname]
    [/CONTRAST (varname) = {DEVIATION (refcat)}]
                          {SIMPLE (refcat)    }
                          {DIFFERENCE         }
                          {HELMERT            }
                          {REPEATED           }
                          {POLYNOMIAL(metric) }
                          {SPECIAL (matrix)   }
                          {INDICATOR (refcat) }

    [/METHOD = {ENTER**          }   [{varlist}]]
               {BSTEP [{COND}]}      {ALL     }
                      {LR  }
                      {WALD}
               {FSTEP [{COND}]}
                      {LR  }
                      {WALD}

    [/MISSING = {EXCLUDE**}]
                {INCLUDE  }

    [/PRINT = [{DEFAULT**}]  [CI ({95})]]
              {SUMMARY  }        {n }
              {BASELINE }
              {CORR     }
              {ALL      }

    [/CRITERIA = [{BCON}({1E-4**})]   [LCON({1E-5**})]
                  {PCON} { n    }         { n      }
                 [ITERATE({20**})]
                         { n  }
                 [PIN({0.05**})]       [POUT({0.1**})]]
                     { n     }             { n   }

    [/PLOT = [NONE**] [SURVIVAL] [HAZARD] [LML] [OMS]]
    [/PATTERN = [varname(value)...] [BY varname]]
    [/OUTFILE = [COEFF(file)] [TABLE(file)]]
    [/SAVE = tempvar [(newvarname)],tempvar ...]
    [/EXTERNAL]
```

* **TIME PROGRAM** is required to generate time-dependent covariates.

**Default if subcommand or keyword is omitted.

Temporary variables created by COXREG are:

SURVIVAL
SE
HAZARD
RESID
LML
DFBETA
PRESID
XBETA

Example:

```
TIME PROGRAM.
COMPUTE Z=AGE + T_.

COXREG SURVIVAL WITH Z
  /STATUS SURVSTA EVENT(1).
```

Overview

COXREG applies Cox proportional hazards regression to analysis of survival times—that is, the length of time before the occurrence of an event. COXREG supports continuous and categorical independent variables (covariates), which can be time-dependent. Unlike SURVIVAL and KM, which compare only distinct subgroups of cases, COXREG provides an easy way of considering differences in subgroups as well as analyzing effects of a set of covariates.

Options

Processing of Independent Variables. You can specify which of the independent variables are categorical with the CATEGORICAL subcommand and control treatment of these variables with the CONTRAST subcommand. You can select one of seven methods for entering independent variables into the model using the METHOD subcommand. You can also indicate interaction terms using the keyword BY between variable names on either the VARIABLES subcommand or the METHOD subcommand.

Specifying Termination and Model-Building Criteria. You can specify the criteria for termination of iteration and control variable entry and removal with the CRITERIA subcommand.

Adding New Variables to Working Data File. You can use the SAVE subcommand to save the cumulative survival, standard error, cumulative hazard, log-minus-log-of-survival function, residuals, XBeta, and, wherever available, partial residuals and DfBeta.

Output. You can print optional output using the PRINT subcommand, suppress or request plots with the PLOT subcommand, and, with the OUTFILE subcommand, write SPSS data files containing coefficients from the final model or a survival table. When only time-constant covariates are used, you can use the PATTERN subcommand to specify a pattern of covariate values in addition to the covariate means to use for the plots and the survival table.

Basic Specification

- The minimum specification on COXREG is a dependent variable with the STATUS subcommand.
- To analyze the influence of time-constant covariates on the survival times, the minimum specification requires either the WITH keyword followed by at least one covariate (independent variable) on the VARIABLES subcommand or a METHOD subcommand with at least one independent variable.
- To analyze the influence of time-dependent covariates on the survival times, the TIME PROGRAM command and transformation language are required to define the functions for the time-dependent covariate(s).

Subcommand Order

- The VARIABLES subcommand must be specified first; the subcommand keyword is optional.
- Remaining subcommands can be named in any order.

Syntax Rules

- Only one dependent variable can be specified for each COXREG command.
- Any number of covariates (independent variables) can be specified. The dependent variable cannot appear on the covariate list.
- The covariate list is required if any of the METHOD subcommands are used without a variable list or if the METHOD subcommand is not used.
- Only one status variable can be specified on the STATUS subcommand. If multiple STATUS subcommands are specified, only the last specification is in effect.
- You can use the BY keyword to specify interaction between covariates.

Operations

- TIME PROGRAM computes the values for time-dependent covariates.
- COXREG replaces covariates specified on CATEGORICAL with sets of contrast variables. In stepwise analyses, the set of contrast variables associated with one categorical variable is entered or removed from the model as a block.
- Covariates are screened to detect and eliminate redundancies.
- COXREG deletes all cases that have negative values for the dependent variable.

Limitations

- Only one dependent variable is allowed.
- Maximum 100 covariates in a single interaction term.
- Maximum 35 levels for a BY variable on PATTERN.

Example

```
TIME PROGRAM.
COMPUTE Z=AGE + T_.

COXREG SURVIVAL WITH Z
   /STATUS SURVSTA EVENT (1).
```

- TIME PROGRAM defines the time-dependent covariate *Z* as the current age. *Z* is then specified as a covariate.
- The dependent variable *SURVIVAL* contains the length of time to the terminal event or to censoring.
- A value of 1 on the variable *SURVSTA* indicates an event.

TIME PROGRAM Command

TIME PROGRAM is required to define time-dependent covariates. These are covariates whose values change during the course of the study.

- TIME PROGRAM and the transformations that define the time-dependent covariate(s) must precede the COXREG command.

- A time-dependent covariate is a function of the current time, which is represented by the special variable $T\_$.

- The working data file must not have a variable named $T\_$. If it does, rename the variable before you run the COXREG command. Otherwise, you will trigger an error.

- $T\_$ cannot be specified as a covariate. Any other variable in the TIME PROGRAM can be specified on the covariate list.

- For every time-dependent covariate, values are generated for each valid case for all un-censored times in the same stratum that occur before the observed time. If no STRATA subcommand is specified, all cases are considered to belong to one stratum.

- If any function defined by the time program results in a missing value for a case that has no missing values for any other variable used in the procedure, COXREG terminates with an error.

CLEAR TIME PROGRAM Command

CLEAR TIME PROGRAM deletes all time-dependent covariates created in the previous time program. It is primarily used in interactive mode to remove temporary variables associated with the time program so that you can redefine time-dependent covariates for the Cox Regression procedure. It is not necessary to use this command if you have already executed COXREG. All temporary variables created by the time program are automatically deleted.

VARIABLES Subcommand

VARIABLES identifies the dependent variable and the covariates to be included in the analysis.

- The minimum specification is the dependent variable. The subcommand keyword is optional.

- You must specify the keyword WITH and a list of all covariates if no METHOD subcommand is specified or if a METHOD subcommand is specified without naming the variables to be used.

- If the covariate list is not specified on VARIABLES but one or more METHOD subcommands are used, the covariate list is assumed to be the union of the sets of variables listed on all the METHOD subcommands.

- You can specify an interaction of two or more covariates using the keyword BY. For example, A B BY C D specifies the three terms *A*, *B*C*, and *D*.

- The keyword TO can be used to specify a list of covariates. The implied variable order is the same as in the working data file.

STATUS Subcommand

To determine whether the event has occurred for a particular observation, COXREG checks the value of a status variable. STATUS lists the status variable and the code for the occurrence of the event.

- Only one status variable can be specified. If multiple STATUS subcommands are specified, COXREG uses the last specification and displays a warning.
- The keyword EVENT is optional, but the value list in parentheses must be specified.
- The value list must be enclosed in parentheses. All cases with non-negative times that do not have a code within the range specified after EVENT are classified as **censored cases**— that is, cases for which the event has not yet occurred.
- The value list can be one value, a list of values separated by blanks or commas, a range of values using the keyword THRU, or a combination.
- If missing values occur within the specified ranges, they are ignored if MISSING=EXCLUDE (the default) is specified, but they are treated as valid values for the range if MISSING=INCLUDE is specified.
- The status variable can be either numeric or string. If a string variable is specified, the EVENT values must be enclosed in apostrophes and the keyword THRU cannot be used.

Example

```
COXREG SURVIVAL WITH GROUP
  /STATUS SURVSTA (3 THRU 5, 8 THRU 10).
```

- STATUS specifies that *SURVSTA* is the status variable.
- A value between either 3 and 5, or 8 and 10, inclusive, means that the terminal event occurred.
- Values outside the specified ranges indicate censored cases.

STRATA Subcommand

STRATA identifies a stratification variable. A different baseline survival function is computed for each stratum.

- The only specification is the subcommand keyword with one, and only one, variable name.
- If you have more than one stratification variable, create a new variable that corresponds to the combination of categories of the individual variables before invoking the COXREG command.
- There is no limit to the number of levels for the strata variable.

Example

```
COXREG SURVIVAL WITH GROUP
 /STATUS SURVSTA (1)
 /STRATA=LOCATION.
```

- STRATA specifies *LOCATION* as the strata variable.
- Different baseline survival functions are computed for each value of *LOCATION*.

CATEGORICAL Subcommand

CATEGORICAL identifies covariates that are nominal or ordinal. Variables that are declared to be categorical are automatically transformed to a set of contrast variables (see "CONTRAST Subcommand" below). If a variable coded as $0 - 1$ is declared as categorical, by default, its coding scheme will be changed to deviation contrasts.

- Covariates not specified on CATEGORICAL are assumed to be at least interval, except for strings.
- Variables specified on CATEGORICAL but not on VARIABLES or any METHOD subcommand are ignored.
- Variables specified on CATEGORICAL are replaced by sets of contrast variables. If the categorical variable has n distinct values, there will be $n - 1$ contrast variables generated. The set of contrast variables associated with one categorical variable are entered or removed from the model together.
- If any one of the variables in an interaction term is specified on CATEGORICAL, the interaction term is replaced by contrast variables.
- All string variables are categorical. Only the first eight characters of each value of a string variable are used in distinguishing among values. Thus, if two values of a string variable are identical for the first eight characters, the values are treated as though they were the same.

CONTRAST Subcommand

CONTRAST specifies the type of contrast used for categorical covariates. The interpretation of the regression coefficients for categorical covariates depends on the contrasts used. The default is DEVIATION. For illustration of contrast types, see the appendix.

- The categorical covariate is specified in parentheses following CONTRAST.
- If the categorical variable has n values, there will be $n - 1$ rows in the contrast matrix. Each contrast matrix is treated as a set of independent variables in the analysis.
- Only one variable can be specified per CONTRAST subcommand, but multiple CONTRAST subcommands can be specified.
- You can specify one of the contrast keywords in the parentheses after the variable specification to request a specific contrast type.

The following contrast types are available:

DEVIATION(refcat)   *Deviations from the overall effect.* This is the default. The effect for each category of the independent variable except one is compared to the overall effect. Refcat is the category for which parameter estimates are not displayed (they must be calculated from the others). By default, refcat is the last category. To omit a category other than the last, specify the sequence number of the omitted category (which is not necessarily the same as its value) in parentheses after the keyword DEVIATION.

SIMPLE(refcat)   *Each category of the independent variable except the last is compared to the last category.* To use a category other than the last as the omitted reference category, specify its sequence number (which is not necessarily the same as its value) in parentheses following the keyword SIMPLE.

DIFFERENCE   *Difference or reverse Helmert contrasts.* The effects for each category of the covariate except the first are compared to the mean effect of the previous categories.

HELMERT   *Helmert contrasts.* The effects for each category of the independent variable except the last are compared to the mean effects of subsequent categories.

POLYNOMIAL(metric)   *Polynomial contrasts.* The first degree of freedom contains the linear effect across the categories of the independent variable, the second contains the quadratic effect, and so on. By default, the categories are assumed to be equally spaced; unequal spacing can be specified by entering a metric consisting of one integer for each category of the independent variable in parentheses after the keyword POLYNOMIAL. For example, `CONTRAST (STIMULUS) = POLYNOMIAL(1,2,4)` indicates that the three levels of *STIMULUS* are actually in the proportion 1:2:4. The default metric is always $(1,2,...,k)$, where k categories are involved. Only the relative differences between the terms of the metric matter: (1,2,4) is the same metric as (2,3,5) or (20,30,50) because, in each instance, the difference between the second and third numbers is twice the difference between the first and second.

REPEATED   *Comparison of adjacent categories.* Each category of the independent variable except the first is compared to the previous category.

SPECIAL(matrix)   *A user-defined contrast.* After this keyword, a matrix is entered in parentheses with $k-1$ rows and k columns, where k is the number of categories of the independent variable. The rows of the contrast matrix contain the special contrasts indicating the desired comparisons between categories. If the special contrasts are linear combinations of each other, COXREG reports the linear dependency and stops processing. If k rows are entered, the first row is discarded and only the last $k-1$ rows are used as the contrast matrix in the analysis.

INDICATOR(refcat)   *Indicator variables.* Contrasts indicate the presence or absence of category membership. By default, refcat is the last category (represented in the contrast matrix as a row of zeros). To omit a category other than the last, specify the sequence number of the category (which is not necessarily the same as its value) in parentheses after keyword INDICATOR.

Example

```
COXREG SURVIVAL WITH GROUP
 /STATUS SURVSTA (1)
 /STRATA=LOCATION
 /CATEGORICAL = GROUP
 /CONTRAST(GROUP)=SPECIAL(2 -1 -1
                          0  1 -1).
```

- The specification of *GROUP* on CATEGORICAL replaces the variable with a set of contrast variables.
- *GROUP* identifies whether a case is in one of the three treatment groups.
- A SPECIAL type contrast is requested. A three-column, two-row contrast matrix is entered in parentheses.

METHOD Subcommand

METHOD specifies the order of processing and the manner in which the covariates enter the model. If no METHOD subcommand is specified, the default method is ENTER.

- The subcommand keyword METHOD can be omitted.

- You can list all covariates to be used for the method on a variable list. If no variable list is specified, the default is ALL: all covariates named after WITH on the VARIABLES subcommand are used for the method.

- The keyword BY can be used between two variable names to specify an interaction term.

- Variables specified on CATEGORICAL are replaced by sets of contrast variables. The contrast variables associated with a categorical variable are entered or removed from the model together.

Three keywords are available to specify how the model is to be built:

ENTER   *Forced entry.* All variables are entered in a single step. This is the default if the METHOD subcommand is omitted.

FSTEP   *Forward stepwise.* The covariates specified on FSTEP are tested for entry into the model one by one based on the significance level of the score statistic. The variable with the smallest significance less than PIN is entered into the model. After each entry, variables that are already in the model are tested for possible removal based on the significance of the Wald statistic, likelihood ratio, or conditional criterion. The variable with the largest probability greater than the specified POUT value is removed and the model is reestimated. Variables in the model are then again evaluated for removal. Once no more variables satisfy the removal criteria, covariates not in the model are evaluated for entry. Model building stops when no more variables meet entry or removal criteria, or when the current model is the same as a previous one.

BSTEP   *Backward stepwise.* As a first step, the covariates specified on BSTEP are entered into the model together and are tested for removal one by one. Stepwise removal and entry then follow the same process as described for FSTEP until no more variables meet entry and removal criteria, or when the current model is the same as a previous one.

- Multiple METHOD subcommands are allowed and are processed in the order in which they are specified. Each method starts with the results from the previous method. If BSTEP is used, all eligible variables are entered at the first step. All variables are then eligible for entry and removal unless they have been excluded from the METHOD variable list.

The statistic used in the test for removal can be specified by an additional keyword in parentheses following FSTEP or BSTEP. If FSTEP or BSTEP is specified by itself, the default is COND.

COND   *Conditional statistic.* This is the default if FSTEP or BSTEP is specified by itself.

WALD   *Wald statistic.* The removal of a covariate from the model is based on the significance of the Wald statistic.

LR   *Likelihood ratio.* The removal of a covariate from the model is based on the significance of the change in the log-likelihood. If LR is specified, the model must be reestimated without each of the variables in the model. This can substantially increase computational time. However, the likelihood-ratio statistic is better than the Wald statistic for deciding which variables are to be removed.

Example

```
COXREG SURVIVAL WITH GROUP SMOKE DRINK
 /STATUS SURVSTA (1)
 /CATEGORICAL = GROUP SMOKE DRINK
 /METHOD ENTER GROUP
 /METHOD BSTEP (LR) SMOKE DRINK SMOKE BY DRINK.
```

- *GROUP*, *SMOKE*, and *DRINK* are specified as covariates and as categorical variables.
- The first METHOD subcommand enters GROUP into the model.
- Variables in the model at the termination of the first METHOD subcommand are included in the model at the beginning of the second METHOD subcommand.
- The second METHOD subcommand adds *SMOKE*, *DRINK*, and the interaction of *SMOKE* with *DRINK* to the previous model.
- Backward stepwise regression analysis is then done using the likelihood-ratio statistic as the removal criterion. The variable *GROUP* is not eligible for removal because it was not specified on the BSTEP subcommand.
- The procedure continues until the removal of a variable will result in a decrease in the log-likelihood with a probability smaller than POUT.

MISSING Subcommand

MISSING controls missing value treatments. If MISSING is omitted, the default is EXCLUDE.

- Cases with negative values on the dependent variable are automatically treated as missing and are excluded.
- To be included in the model, a case must have nonmissing values for the dependent, status, strata, and all independent variables specified on the COXREG command.

EXCLUDE   *Exclude user-missing values.* User-missing values are treated as missing. This is the default if MISSING is omitted.

INCLUDE   *Include user-missing values.* User-missing values are included in the analysis.

PRINT Subcommand

By default, COXREG prints a full regression report for each step. You can use the PRINT subcommand to request specific output. If PRINT is not specified, the default is DEFAULT.

DEFAULT   *Full regression output including overall model statistics and statistics for variables in the equation and variables not in the equation.* This is the default when PRINT is omitted.

SUMMARY   *Summary information.* The output includes -2 log-likelihood for the initial model, one line of summary for each step, and the final model printed with full detail.

CORR   *Correlation/covariance matrix of parameter estimates for the variables in the model.*

| BASELINE | *Baseline table.* For each stratum, a table is displayed showing the baseline cumulative hazard, as well as survival, standard error, and cumulative hazard evaluated at the covariate means for each observed time point in that stratum. |

| CI (value) | *Confidence intervals for e^β.* Specify the confidence level in parentheses. The requested intervals are displayed whenever a variables-in-equation table is printed. The default is 95%. |

| ALL | *All available output.* |

- Estimation histories showing the last 10 iterations are printed if the solution fails to converge.

Example

```
COXREG SURVIVAL WITH GROUP
 /STATUS = SURVSTA (1)
 /STRATA = LOCATION
 /CATEGORICAL = GROUP
 /METHOD = ENTER
 /PRINT ALL.
```

- PRINT requests summary information, a correlation matrix for parameter estimates, a baseline survival table for each stratum, and confidence intervals for e^β with each variables-in-equation table, in addition to the default output.

CRITERIA Subcommand

CRITERIA controls the statistical criteria used in building the Cox Regression models. The way in which these criteria are used depends on the method specified on the METHOD subcommand. The default criteria are noted in the description of each keyword below. Iterations will stop if any of the criteria for BCON, LCON, or ITERATE are satisfied.

| BCON(value) | *Change in parameter estimates for terminating iteration.* Alias PCON. Iteration terminates when the parameters change by less than the specified value. BCON defaults to $1E-4$. To eliminate this criteria, specify a value of 0. |

| ITERATE(value) | *Maximum number of iterations.* If a solution fails to converge after the maximum number of iterations has been reached, COXREG displays an iteration history showing the last 10 iterations and terminates the procedure. The default for ITERATE is 20. |

| LCON(value) | *Percentage change in the log-likelihood ratio for terminating iteration.* If the log-likelihood decreases by less than the specified value, iteration terminates. LCON defaults to $1E-5$. To eliminate this criterion, specify a value of 0. |

| PIN(value) | *Probability of score statistic for variable entry.* A variable whose significance level is greater than PIN cannot enter the model. The default for PIN is 0.05. |

| POUT(value) | *Probability of Wald, LR, or conditional LR statistic to remove a variable.* A variable whose significance is less than POUT cannot be removed. The default for POUT is 0.1. |

Example

```
COXREG SURVIVAL WITH GROUP AGE BP TMRSZ
 /STATUS = SURVSTA (1)
 /STRATA = LOCATION
 /CATEGORICAL = GROUP
 /METHOD BSTEP
 /CRITERIA BCON(0) ITERATE(10) PIN(0.01) POUT(0.05).
```

- A backward stepwise Cox Regression analysis is performed.

- CRITERIA alters four of the default statistical criteria that control the building of a model.

- Zero specified on BCON indicates that change in parameter estimates is not a criterion for termination. BCON can be set to 0 if only LCON and ITER are to be used.

- ITERATE specifies that the maximum number of iterations is 10. LCON is not changed and the default remains in effect. If either ITERATE or LCON is met, iterations will terminate.

- POUT requires that the probability of the statistic used to test whether a variable should remain in the model be smaller than 0.05. This is more stringent than the default value of 0.1.

- PIN requires that the probability of the score statistic used to test whether a variable should be included be smaller than 0.01. This makes it more difficult for variables to be included in the model than does the default PIN, which has a value of 0.05.

PLOT Subcommand

You can request specific plots to be produced with the PLOT subcommand. Each requested plot is produced once for each pattern specified on the PATTERN subcommand. If PLOT is not specified, the default is NONE (no plots are printed). Requested plots are displayed at the end of the final model.

- The set of plots requested is displayed for the functions at the mean of the covariates and at each combination of covariate values specified on PATTERN.

- If time-dependent covariates are included in the model, no plots are produced.

- Lines on a plot are connected as step functions.

NONE   *Do not display plots.*

SURVIVAL   *Plot the cumulative survival distribution.*

HAZARD   *Plot the cumulative hazard function.*

LML   *Plot the log-minus-log-of-survival function.*

OMS   *Plot the one-minus-survival function.*

PATTERN Subcommand

PATTERN specifies the pattern of covariate values to be used for the requested plots and coefficient tables.

- A value must be specified for each variable specified on PATTERN.

- Continuous variables that are included in the model but not named on PATTERN are evaluated at their means.
- Categorical variables that are included in the model but not named on PATTERN are evaluated at the means of the set of contrasts generated to replace them.
- You can request separate lines for each category of a variable that is in the model. Specify the name of the categorical variable after the keyword BY. The BY variable must be a categorical covariate. You cannot specify a value for the BY covariate.
- Multiple PATTERN subcommands can be specified. COXREG produces a set of requested plots for each specified pattern.
- PATTERN cannot be used when time-dependent covariates are included in the model.

OUTFILE Subcommand

OUTFILE writes an external SPSS data file. COXREG writes two types of data files. You can specify the file type to be created with one of the two keywords, followed by the file specification in parentheses.

COEFF   *Write an SPSS data file containing the coefficients from the final model.*

TABLE   *Write the survival table to an SPSS data file.* The file contains cumulative survival, standard error, and cumulative hazard statistics for each uncensored time within each stratum evaluated at the baseline and at the mean of the covariates. Additional covariate patterns can be requested on PATTERN.

- The specified SPSS data file must be an external file. You cannot specify an asterisk (*) to identify the working data file.
- The variables saved in the external file are listed in the output.

SAVE Subcommand

SAVE saves the temporary variables created by COXREG. The temporary variables include:

SURVIVAL   *Survival function evaluated at the current case.*

SE   *Standard error of the survival function.*

HAZARD   *Cumulative hazard function evaluated at the current case.* Alias RESID.

LML   *Log-minus-log-of-survival function.*

DFBETA   *Change in the coefficient if the current case is removed.* There is one *DFBETA* for each covariate in the final model. If there are time-dependent covariates, only *DFBETA* can be requested. Requests for any other temporary variable are ignored.

PRESID   *Partial residuals.* There is one residual variable for each covariate in the final model. If a covariate is not in the final model, the corresponding new variable has the system-missing value.

XBETA   *Linear combination of mean corrected covariates times regression coefficients from the final model.*

- To specify variable names for the new variables, assign the new names in parentheses following each temporary variable name.

- Assigned variable names must be unique in the working data file. Scratch or system variable names cannot be used (that is, the variable names cannot begin with # or $).

- If new variable names are not specified, COXREG generates default names. The default name is composed of the first three characters of the name of the temporary variable (two for *SE*), followed by an underscore and a number to make it unique.

- A temporary variable can be saved only once on the same SAVE subcommand.

Example

```
COXREG SURVIVAL WITH GROUP
 /STATUS = SURVSTA (1)
 /STRATA = LOCATION
 /CATEGORICAL = GROUP
 /METHOD = ENTER
 /SAVE SURVIVAL HAZARD.
```

- COXREG saves cumulative survival and hazard in two new variables, *SUR_1* and *HAZ_1*, provided that neither of the two names exists in the working data file. If one does, the numeric suffixes will be incremented to make a distinction.

EXTERNAL Subcommand

EXTERNAL specifies that the data for each split-file group should be held in an external scratch file during processing. This helps conserve working space when running analyses with large data sets.

- The EXTERNAL subcommand takes no other keyword and is specified by itself.

- If time-dependent covariates exist, external data storage is unavailable, and EXTERNAL is ignored.

GENLOG

```
GENLOG varlist[BY] varlist [WITH covariate varlist]

[/CSTRUCTURE=varname]

[/GRESID=varlist]

[/GLOR=varlist]

[/MODEL={POISSON**   }]
        {MULTINOMIAL}

[/CRITERIA=[CONVERGE({0.001**})][ITERATE({20**})][DELTA({0.5**})]
                    {n       }          {n   }         {n    }

           [CIN({95**})] [EPS({1E-8**})]
                {n    }        {n      }

           [DEFAULT]

[/PRINT=[FREQ**][RESID**][ADJRESID**][DEV**]
        [ZRESID][ITERATE][COV][DESIGN][ESTIM][COR]
        [ALL] [NONE]
        [DEFAULT]]

[/PLOT={DEFAULT**                  }]
       {RESID([ADJRESID][DEV])     }
       {NORMPROB([ADJRESID][DEV])  }
       {NONE                       }

[/SAVE=tempvar (newvar)[tempvar (newvar)...]]

[/MISSING=[{EXCLUDE**}]]
           {INCLUDE  }

[/DESIGN=effect[(n)] effect[(n)]... effect {BY} effect...]
                                           {* }
```

**Default if subcommand or keyword is omitted.

Overview

GENLOG is a general procedure for model fitting, hypothesis testing, and parameter estimation for any model that has categorical variables as its major components. As such, GENLOG
subsumes a variety of related techniques, including general models of multiway contingency
tables, logit models, logistic regression on categorical variables, and quasi-independence
models.

GENLOG, following the regression approach, uses dummy coding to construct a design
matrix for estimation and produces maximum likelihood estimates of parameters by means of
the Newton-Raphson algorithm. Since the regression approach uses the original parameter
spaces, the parameter estimates correspond to the original levels of the categories and are
therefore easier to interpret.

HILOGLINEAR, which uses an iterative proportional-fitting algorithm, is more efficient
for hierarchical models and useful in model building, but it cannot produce parameter estimates for unsaturated models, does not permit specification of contrasts for parameters, and
does not display a correlation matrix of the parameter estimates.

The General Loglinear Analysis and Logit Loglinear Analysis dialog boxes are both associated with the GENLOG command. In previous releases of SPSS, these dialog boxes were associated with the LOGLINEAR command. The LOGLINEAR command is now available only as a syntax command. The differences are described in the discussion of the LOGLINEAR command.

Options

Cell Weights. You can specify cell weights (such as structural zero indicators) for the model with the CSTRUCTURE subcommand.

Linear Combinations. You can compute linear combinations of observed cell frequencies, expected cell frequencies, and adjusted residuals using the GRESID subcommand.

Generalized Log-Odds Ratios. You can specify contrast variables on the GLOR subcommand and test whether the generalized log-odds ratio equals 0.

Model Assumption. You can specify POISSON or MULTINOMIAL on the MODEL subcommand to request the Poisson loglinear model or the product multinomial loglinear model.

Tuning the Algorithm. You can control the values of algorithm-tuning parameters with the CRITERIA subcommand.

Output Display. You can control the output display with the PRINT subcommand.

Optional Plots. You can request plots of adjusted or deviance residuals against observed and expected counts, or normal plots and detrended normal plots of adjusted or deviance residuals using the PLOT subcommand.

Basic Specification

The basic specification is one or more factor variables that define the tabulation. By default, GENLOG assumes a Poisson distribution and estimates the saturated model. Default output includes the factors or effects, their levels, and any labels; observed and expected frequencies and percentages for each factor and code; and residuals, adjusted residuals, and deviance residuals.

Limitations

- Maximum 10 factor variables (dependent *and* independent).
- Maximum 200 covariates.

Subcommand Order

- The variable specification must come first.
- Subcommands can be specified in any order.
- When multiple subcommands are specified, only the last specification takes effect.

Example

```
GENLOG DPREF RACE CAMP.
```

- *DPREF*, *RACE*, and *CAMP* are categorical variables.
- This is a general loglinear model because no BY keyword appears.
- The design defaults to a saturated model that includes all main effects and two-way and three-way interaction effects.

Example

```
GENLOG GSLEVEL EDUC SEX
  /DESIGN=GSLEVEL EDUC SEX.
```

- *GSLEVEL*, *EDUC*, and *SEX* are categorical variables.
- DESIGN specifies a model with main effects only.

Variable List

The variable list specifies the variables to be included in the model. GENLOG analyzes two classes of variables—categorical and continuous. Categorical variables are used to define the cells of the table. Continuous variables are used as cell covariates.

- The list of categorical variables must be specified first. Categorical variables must be numeric.
- Continuous variables can be specified only after the WITH keyword following the list of categorical variables.
- To specify a logit model, use the keyword BY (see "Logit Model" below). A variable list without the keyword BY generates a general loglinear model.
- A variable can be specified only once in the variable list—as a dependent variable immediately following GENLOG, as an independent variable following the keyword BY, or as a covariate following the keyword WITH.
- No range needs to be specified for categorical variables.

Logit Model

The logit model examines the relationships between dependent and independent factor variables.

- To separate the independent variables from the dependent variables in a logit model, use the keyword BY. The categorical variables preceding BY are the dependent variables; the categorical variables following BY are the independent variables.
- Up to 10 variables can be specified, including both dependent and independent variables.
- For the logit model, you must specify MULTINOMIAL on the MODEL subcommand.
- GENLOG displays an analysis of dispersion and two measures of association—entropy and concentration. These measures are discussed in Haberman (1982) and can be used

to quantify the magnitude of association among the variables. Both are proportional-reduction-in-error measures. The entropy statistic is analogous to Theil's entropy measure, while the concentration statistic is analogous to Goodman and Kruskal's tau-*b*. Both statistics measure the strength of association between the dependent variable and the independent variable set.

Example

```
GENLOG  GSLEVEL BY EDUC SEX
  /MODEL=MULTINOMIAL
  /DESIGN=GSLEVEL, GSLEVEL BY EDUC, GSLEVEL BY SEX.
```

- The keyword BY on the variable list specifies a logit model in which *GSLEVEL* is the dependent variable and *EDUC* and *SEX* are the independent variables.
- A logit model is multinomial.
- DESIGN specifies a model that can test for the absence of the joint effect of *SEX* and *EDUC* on *GSLEVEL*.

Cell Covariates

- Continuous variables can be used as covariates. When used, the covariates must be specified after the WITH keyword following the list of categorical variables.
- A variable cannot be named as both a categorical variable and a cell covariate.
- To enter cell covariates into a model, the covariates must be specified on the DESIGN subcommand.
- Cell covariates are not applied on a case-by-case basis. The weighted covariate mean for a cell is applied to that cell.

Example

```
GENLOG DPREF RACE CAMP WITH X
  /DESIGN=DPREF RACE CAMP X.
```

- The variable *X* is a continuous variable specified as a cell covariate. Cell covariates must be specified after the keyword WITH following the variable list. No range is defined for cell covariates.
- To include the cell covariate in the model, the variable *X* is specified on DESIGN.

CSTRUCTURE Subcommand

CSTRUCTURE specifies the variable that contains values for computing cell weights, such as structural zero indicators. By default, cell weights are equal to 1.

- The specification must be a numeric variable.
- Variables specified as dependent or independent variables in the variable list cannot be specified on CSTRUCTURE.
- Cell weights are not applied on a case-by-case basis. The weighted mean for a cell is applied to that cell.

- CSTRUCTURE can be used to impose structural, or *a priori*, zeros on the model. This feature is useful in specifying a quasi-symmetry model and in excluding cells from entering into estimation.
- If multiple CSTRUCTURE subcommands are specified, the last specification takes effect.

Example

```
COMPUTE  CWT=(HUSED NE WIFED).
GENLOG HUSED WIFED WITH DISTANCE
  /CSTRUCTURE=CWT
  /DESIGN=HUSED WIFED DISTANCE.
```

- The Boolean expression assigns *CWT* the value of 1 when *HUSED* is not equal to *WIFED*, and the value of 0 otherwise.
- CSTRUCTURE imposes structural zeros on the diagonal of the symmetric crosstabulation.

GRESID Subcommand

GRESID (Generalized Residual) calculates linear combinations of observed and expected cell frequencies as well as simple, standardized, and adjusted residuals.

- The variables specified must be numeric, and they must contain coefficients of the desired linear combinations.
- Variables specified as dependent or independent variables in the variable list cannot be specified on GRESID.
- The generalized residual coefficient is not applied on a case-by-case basis. The weighted coefficient mean of the value for all cases in a cell is applied to that cell.
- Each variable specified on the GRESID subcommand contains a single linear combination.
- If multiple GRESID subcommands are specified, the last specification takes effect.

Example

```
COMPUTE GR_1=(MONTH LE 6).
COMPUTE GR_2=(MONTH GE 7).
GENLOG  MONTH WITH Z
 /GRESID=GR_1 GR_2
 /DESIGN=Z.
```

- The first variable, *GR_1*, combines the first six months into a single effect; the second variable, *GR_2*, combines the rest of the months.
- For each effect, GENLOG displays the observed and expected counts as well as the simple, standardized, and adjusted residuals.

GLOR Subcommand

GLOR (Generalized Log-Odds Ratio) specifies the population contrast variable(s). For each variable specified, GENLOG tests the null hypothesis that the generalized log-odds ratio equals 0 and displays the Wald statistic and the confidence interval. You can specify the level of the confidence interval using the CIN significance level keyword on CRITERIA. By default, the confidence level is 95%.

- The variable sum is 0 for the loglinear model and for each combined level of independent variables for the logit model.
- Variables specified as dependent or independent variables in the variable list cannot be specified on GLOR.
- The coefficient is not applied on a case-by-case basis. The weighted mean for a cell is applied to that cell.
- If multiple GLOR subcommands are specified, the last specification takes effect.

Example

```
GENLOG A B
 /GLOR=COEFF
 /DESIGN=A B.
```

- Variable *COEFF* contains the coefficients of two dichotomous factors *A* and *B*.
- If the weighted cell mean for *COEFF* is 1 when *A* equals *B* and −1 otherwise, this example tests whether the log-odds ratio equals 0, or in this case, whether variables *A* and *B* are independent.

MODEL Subcommand

MODEL specifies the assumed distribution of your data.

- You can specify only one keyword on MODEL. The default is POISSON.
- If more than one MODEL subcommand is specified, the last specification takes effect.

POISSON   *The Poisson distribution.* This is the default.

MULTINOMIAL   *The multinomial distribution.* For the logit model, you must specify MULTINOMIAL.

CRITERIA Subcommand

CRITERIA specifies the values used in tuning the parameters for the Newton-Raphson algorithm.

- If multiple CRITERIA subcommands are specified, the last specification takes effect.

CONVERGE(n)   *Convergence criterion.* Specify a positive value for the convergence criterion. The default is 0.001.

ITERATE(n)   *Maximum number of iterations.* Specify an integer. The default number is 20.

DELTA(n)   *Cell delta value.* Specify a non-negative value to add to each cell frequency for the first iteration. (For the saturated model, the delta value is added for all iterations.) The default is 0.5. The delta value is used to solve mathematical problems created by 0 observations; if all of your observations are greater than 0, we recommend that you set DELTA to 0.

CIN(n)   *Level of confidence interval.* Specify the percentage interval used in the test of generalized log-odds ratios and parameter estimates. The value must be between 50 and 99.99, inclusive. The default is 95.

EPS(n)   *Epsilon value used for redundancy checking in design matrix.* Specify a positive value. The default is 0.00000001.

DEFAULT   *Default values are used.* DEFAULT can be used to reset all criteria to default values.

Example

```
GENLOG  DPREF BY RACE ORIGIN CAMP
 /MODEL=MULTINOMIAL
 /CRITERIA=ITERATION(50) CONVERGE(.0001).
```

- ITERATION increases the maximum number of iterations to 50.
- CONVERGE lowers the convergence criterion to 0.0001.

PRINT Subcommand

PRINT controls the display of statistics.

- By default, GENLOG displays the frequency table and simple, adjusted, and deviance residuals.
- When PRINT is specified with one or more keywords, only the statistics requested by these keywords are displayed.
- When multiple PRINT subcommands are specified, the last specification takes effect.

The following keywords can be used on PRINT:

FREQ   *Observed and expected cell frequencies and percentages.* This is displayed by default.

RESID   *Simple residuals.* This is displayed by default.

ZRESID   *Standardized residuals.*

ADJRESID *Adjusted residuals.* This is displayed by default.

DEV   *Deviance residuals.* This is displayed by default.

DESIGN   *The design matrix of the model.* The design matrix corresponding to the specified model is displayed.

ESTIM   *The parameter estimates of the model.* The parameter estimates refer to the original categories.

COR   *The correlation matrix of the parameter estimates.*

COV   *The covariance matrix of the parameter estimates.*

ALL   *All available output.*

DEFAULT   *FREQ, RESID, ADJRESID, and DEV.* This keyword can be used to reset PRINT to its default setting.

NONE   *The design and model information with goodness-of-fit statistics only.* This option overrides all other specifications on the PRINT subcommand.

Example

```
GENLOG A B
 /PRINT=ALL
 /DESIGN=A B.
```

- The DESIGN subcommand specifies a main-effects model, which tests the hypothesis of no interaction. The PRINT subcommand displays all available output for this model.

PLOT Subcommand

PLOT specifies what plots you want displayed. Plots of adjusted residuals against observed and expected counts, and normal and detrended normal plots of the adjusted residuals are displayed if PLOT is not specified or is specified without a keyword. When multiple PLOT subcommands are specified, only the last specification is executed.

DEFAULT   *RESID (ADJRESID) and NORMPROB (ADJRESID).* This is the default if PLOT is not specified or is specified with no keyword.

RESID (type)   *Plots of residuals against observed and expected counts.* You can specify the type of residuals to plot. ADJRESID plots adjusted residuals; DEV plots deviance residuals. ADJRESID is the default if you do not specify a type.

NORMPROB (type)   *Normal and detrended normal plots of the residuals.* You can specify the type of residuals to plot. ADJRESID plots adjusted residuals; DEV plots deviance residuals. ADJRESID is the default if you do not specify a type.

NONE   *No plots.*

Example

```
GENLOG  RESPONSE BY SEASON
  /MODEL=MULTINOMIAL
  /PLOT=RESID(ADJRESID,DEV)
  /DESIGN=RESPONSE SEASON(1) BY RESPONSE.
```

- This example requests plots of adjusted and deviance residuals against observed and expected counts.
- Note that if you specify /PLOT=RESID(ADJRESID) RESID(DEV), only the deviance residuals are plotted. The first keyword specification, RESID(ADJRESID), is ignored.

MISSING Subcommand

MISSING controls missing values. By default, GENLOG excludes all cases with system- or user-missing values for any variable. You can specify INCLUDE to include user-missing values.

EXCLUDE   *Delete cases with user-missing values.* This is the default if the subcommand is omitted. You can also specify the keyword DEFAULT.

INCLUDE   *Include cases with user-missing values.* Only cases with system-missing values are deleted.

Example

```
MISSING VALUES A(0).
GENLOG A B
 /MISSING=INCLUDE
 /DESIGN=B.
```

- Even though 0 was specified as missing, it is treated as a nonmissing category of *A* in this analysis.

SAVE Subcommand

SAVE saves specified temporary variables into the working data file. You can assign a new name to each temporary variable saved.

- The temporary variables you can save include *RESID* (raw residual), *ZRESID* (standardized residual), *ADJRESID* (adjusted residual), *DEV* (deviance residual), and *PRED* (predicted cell frequency). An explanatory label is assigned to each saved variable.

- A temporary variable can be saved only once on a SAVE subcommand.

- To assign a name to a saved temporary variable, specify the new name in parentheses following that temporary variable. The new name must conform to SPSS naming conventions and must be unique in the working data file. The names cannot begin with # or $.

- If you do not specify a variable name in parentheses, GENLOG assigns default names to the saved temporary variables. A default name starts with the first three characters of the name of the saved temporary variable, followed by an underscore and a unique number. For example, *RESID* will be saved as *RES_n*, where *n* is a number incremented each time a default name is assigned to a saved *RESID*.

- The saved variables are pertinent to cells in the contingency table, *not* to individual observations. In the Data Editor, all cases that define one cell receive the same value. To make sense of these values, you need to aggregate the data to obtain cell counts.

Example

```
GENLOG A B
 /SAVE PRED (PREDA_B)
 /DESIGN = A, B.
```

- SAVE saves the predicted values for two independent variables *A* and *B*.
- The saved variable is renamed *PREDA_B* and added to the working data file.

DESIGN Subcommand

DESIGN specifies the model to be fit. If DESIGN is omitted or used with no specifications, the saturated model is produced. The saturated model fits all main effects and all interaction effects.

- Only one design can be specified on the subcommand.
- To obtain main-effects models, name all of the variables listed on the variables specification.
- To obtain interactions, use the keyword BY or an asterisk (*) to specify each interaction, for example, A BY B or C*D. To obtain the single-degree-of-freedom partition of a specified factor, specify the partition in parentheses following the factor (see the example below).
- To include cell covariates in the model, first identify them on the variable list by naming them after the keyword WITH, and then specify the variable names on DESIGN.
- Effects that involve only independent variables result in redundancy. GENLOG removes these effects from the model.
- If your variable list includes a cell covariate (identified by the keyword WITH), you cannot imply the saturated model by omitting DESIGN or specifying it alone. You need to request the model explicitly by specifying all main effects and interactions on DESIGN.

Example

```
COMPUTE X=MONTH.
GENLOG MONTH WITH X
   /DESIGN X.
```

- This example tests the linear effect of the dependent variable.
- The variable specification identifies *MONTH* as a categorical variable. The keyword WITH identifies *X* as a covariate.
- DESIGN tests the linear effect of *MONTH*.

Example

```
GENLOG A B
   /DESIGN=A.

GENLOG A B
   /DESIGN=A,B.
```

- Both designs specify main-effects models.
- The first design tests the homogeneity of category probabilities for *B*; it fits the marginal frequencies on *A* but assumes that membership in any of the categories of *B* is equiprobable.
- The second design tests the independence of *A* and *B*. It fits the marginals on both *A* and *B*.

Example

```
GENLOG A  B  C
   /DESIGN=A,B,C, A BY B.
```

- This design consists of the *A* main effect, the *B* main effect, the *C* main effect, and the interaction of *A* and *B*.

Example

```
GENLOG A BY B
 /MODEL=MULTINOMIAL
 /DESIGN=A,A BY B(1).
```

- This example specifies single-degree-of-freedom partitions.
- The value 1 following *B* refers to the first category of *B*.

Example

```
GENLOG HUSED WIFED WITH DISTANCE
  /DESIGN=HUSED WIFED DISTANCE.
```

- The continuous variable *DISTANCE* is identified as a cell covariate by the keyword WITH. The cell covariate is then included in the model by naming it on DESIGN.

Example

```
COMPUTE  X=1.
GENLOG  MONTH WITH X
  /DESIGN=X.
```

- This example specifies an equiprobability model.
- The design tests whether the frequencies in the table are equal by using a constant of 1 as a cell covariate.

GLM: Overview

```
GLM dependent varlist [BY factor list [WITH covariate list]]

[/WSFACTOR=name levels [{DEVIATION [(refcat)]      }] name...
                       {SIMPLE [(refcat)]          }
                       {DIFFERENCE                 }
                       {HELMERT                    }
                       {REPEATED                   }
                       {POLYNOMIAL [({1,2,3...})]]**}
                       {            {metric }      }
                       {SPECIAL (matrix)           }

[/MEASURE=newname newname...]

[/WSDESIGN=effect effect...]†

[/RANDOM=factor factor...]

[/REGWGT=varname]

[/METHOD=SSTYPE({1  })]
               {2  }
               {3**}
               {4  }

[/INTERCEPT=[INCLUDE**] [EXCLUDE]]

[/MISSING=[INCLUDE] [EXCLUDE**]]

[/CRITERIA=[EPS({1E-8**})][ALPHA({0.05**})]
               {a     }          {a      }

[/PRINT  = [DESCRIPTIVE] [HOMOGENEITY] [PARAMETER][ETASQ] [RSSCP]
           [GEF] [LOF] [OPOWER] [TEST [([SSCP] [LMATRIX] [MMATRIX])]]]

[/PLOT=[SPREADLEVEL] [RESIDUALS]
       [PROFILE (factor factor*factor factor*factor*factor ...)]]

[/TEST=effect VS {linear combination [DF(df)]}]
                 {value DF (df)              }

[/LMATRIX={["label"] effect list effect list ...;...}]
          {["label"] effect list effect list ...    }
          {["label"] ALL list; ALL...               }
          {["label"] ALL list                       }

[/CONTRAST (factor name)={DEVIATION[(refcat)]** ‡  }]
                         {SIMPLE [(refcat)]        }
                         {DIFFERENCE               }
                         {HELMERT                  }
                         {REPEATED                 }
                         {POLYNOMIAL  [({1,2,3...})]]}
                         {            {metric }    }
                         {SPECIAL (matrix)         }

[/MMATRIX= {["label"] depvar value depvar value ...;["label"]...}]
           {["label"] depvar value depvar value ...             }
           {["label"] ALL list; ["label"] ...                   }
           {["label"] ALL list                                  }

[/KMATRIX= {list of numbers    }]
           {list of numbers;...}

[/POSTHOC = effect [effect...]
```

```
           ([SNK] [TUKEY] [BTUKEY][DUNCAN]
            [SCHEFFE] [DUNNETT(refcat)] [DUNNETTL(refcat)]
            [DUNNETTR(refcat)] [BONFERRONI] [LSD] [SIDAK]
            [GT2] [GABRIEL] [FREGW] [QREGW] [T2] [T3] [GH][C]
            [WALLER ({100** })]]
                     {kratio}
            [VS effect]

[/EMMEANS=TABLES({OVERALL          }})] [COMPARE ADJ(LSD(none)) (BONFERRONI) (SIDAK)]
                {factor            }
                {factor*factor...  }
                {wsfactor          }
                {wsfactor*wsfactor ... }
                {factor*...wsfactor*...}

[/SAVE=[tempvar [(list of names)]] [tempvar [(list of names)]]...]
       [DESIGN]

[/OUTFILE= [{COVB (filename)}] [EFFECT(filename)] [DESIGN(filename)]
            {CORB (filename)}

[/DESIGN={[INTERCEPT...]    }]
         {[effect effect...]}
```

† WSDESIGN uses the same specification as DESIGN, with only within-subjects factors.

‡ DEVIATION is the default for between-subjects factors, while POLYNOMIAL is the default for within-subjects factors.

** Default if subcommand or keyword is omitted.

Temporary variables (tempvar) are:

PRED, WPRED, RESID, WRESID, DRESID, ZRESID, SRESID, SEPRED, COOK, LEVER

Overview

GLM (general linear model) is a general procedure for analysis of variance and covariance, as well as regression. GLM is the most versatile of the analysis-of-variance procedures in SPSS and can be used for both univariate and multivariate designs. GLM allows you to:

- Include interaction and nested effects in your design model. Multiple nesting is allowed; for example, *A* within *B* within *C* is specified as *A(B(C))*.

- Include covariates in your design model. GLM also allows covariate-by-covariate and covariate-by-factor interactions such as *X* by *X* (or *X*X*), *X* by *A* (or *X*A*), and *X* by *A* within *B* (or *X*A(B)*). Thus, polynomial regression or a test of the homogeneity of regressions can be performed.

- Select appropriate sums-of-squares hypothesis tests for effects in balanced design models, unbalanced all-cells-filled design models, and some-cells-empty design models. The estimable functions corresponding to the hypothesis test for each effect in the model can also be displayed.

- Display the general form of estimable functions.

- Display expected mean squares, automatically detecting and using the appropriate error term for testing each effect in mixed- and random-effects models.

- Select commonly used contrasts or specify custom contrasts to perform hypothesis tests.
- Customize hypothesis testing, based on the null hypothesis **LBM = K**, where **B** is the parameter vector or matrix.
- Display a variety of post hoc tests for multiple comparisons.
- Display estimates of population marginal cell means for both between-subjects factors and within-subjects factors, adjusted for covariates.
- Perform multivariate analysis of variance and covariance.
- Estimate parameters using the method of weighted least squares and a generalized inverse technique.
- Compare graphically the levels in a model by displaying plots of estimated marginal cell means for each level of a factor, with separate lines for each level of another factor in the model.
- Display a variety of estimates and measures useful for diagnostic checking. All of these estimates and measures can be saved in a data file for use by another SPSS procedure.
- Perform repeated measures analysis of variance.
- Display homogeneity tests for testing underlying assumptions in multivariate and univariate analyses.

General Linear Model (GLM) and MANOVA

MANOVA, the other generalized procedure for analysis of variance and covariance in SPSS, is available only in syntax. The major distinction between GLM and MANOVA in terms of statistical design and functionality is that GLM uses a non-full-rank, or overparameterized, indicator variable approach to parameterization of linear models, instead of the full-rank reparameterization approach used in MANOVA. The generalized inverse approach and the aliasing of redundant parameters to zero employed by GLM allow greater flexibility in handling a variety of messy data situations, particularly those involving empty cells. GLM offers a variety of features unavailable in MANOVA:

- Identification of the general forms of estimable functions.
- Identification of forms of estimable functions specific to four types of sums of squares (Types I–IV).
- Tests using the four types of sums of squares, including Type IV, specifically designed for situations involving empty cells.
- Flexible specification of general comparisons among parameters, using the syntax subcommands LMATRIX, MMATRIX and KMATRIX; sets of contrasts can be specified that involve any number of orthogonal or nonorthogonal linear combinations.
- Nonorthogonal contrasts for within-subjects factors (using the syntax subcommand WSFACTORS).
- Tests against nonzero null hypotheses can be specified using the syntax subcommand KMATRIX.
- Estimated marginal means (EMMEANS) and standard errors adjusted for other factors and covariates are available for all between- and within-subjects factor combinations in the original variable metrics.
- Uncorrected pairwise comparisons among estimated marginal means for any main effect in the model, for both between- and within-subjects factors.

- Post hoc or multiple comparison tests for unadjusted one-way factor means are available for between-subjects factors in ANOVA designs; 20 different types of comparisons are offered.
- Weighted least squares (WLS) estimation, including saving of weighted predicted values and residuals.
- Automatic handling of random effects in random-effects models and mixed models, including generation of expected mean squares and automatic assignment of proper error terms.
- Specification of several types of nested models via dialog boxes with proper use of the interaction operator (*), due to the nonreparameterized approach.
- Univariate homogeneity-of-variance assumption tested using the Levene test.
- Between-subjects factors do not require specification of levels.
- Profile (interaction) plots of estimated marginal means for visual exploration of interactions involving combinations of between- and/or within-subjects factors.
- Saving of casewise temporary variables for model diagnosis:
  - Predicted values—unstandardized (raw), weighted unstandardized.
  - Residuals—unstandardized, weighted unstandardized, standardized, Studentized, deleted.
  - Standard error of prediction.
  - Cook's distance.
  - Leverage.
- Saving of an SPSS file with parameter estimates and their degrees of freedom, significance level.

To simplify the presentation, reference material on GLM is divided into three sections: *univariate* designs with one dependent variable, *multivariate* designs with several interrelated dependent variables, and *repeated measures* designs, in which the dependent variables represent the same types of measurements taken at more than one time.

The full syntax diagram for GLM is presented here. The GLM sections that follow include partial syntax diagrams showing the subcommands and specifications discussed in that section. Individually, those diagrams are incomplete. Subcommands listed for univariate designs are available for any analysis, and subcommands listed for multivariate designs can be used in any multivariate analysis, including repeated measures.

Models

The following are examples of models that can be specified using GLM:

Model 1: Univariate or multivariate simple and multiple regression

```
GLM Y WITH X1 X2.
GLM Y1 Y2 WITH X1 X2 X3.
```

Model 2: Fixed-effects ANOVA and MANOVA

```
GLM Y1 Y2 by B.
```

Model 3: ANCOVA and multivariate ANCOVA (MANCOVA)

```
GLM Y1 Y2 BY B WITH X1 X2 X3.
```

Model 4: Random-effects ANOVA and ANCOVA

```
GLM Y1 BY C WITH X1 X2
 /RANDOM = C.
```

Model 5: Mixed-model ANOVA and ANCOVA

```
GLM Y1 BY B, C WITH X1 X2
 /RANDOM = C.
```

Model 6: Repeated measures analysis using a split-plot design

```
(Univariate mixed models approach with subject as a random effect)
```

If *drug* is a between-subjects factor and *time* is a within-subjects factor,

```
GLM Y BY DRUG SUBJECT TIME
 /RANDOM = SUBJECT
 /DESIGN = DRUG SUBJECT*DRUG TIME DRUG*TIME.
```

Model 7: Repeated measures using the WSFACTOR subcommand

Use this model only when there is no random between-subjects effect in the model. For example, if *Y1*, *Y2*, *Y3*, and *Y4* are the dependent variables measured at times 1 to 4,

```
GLM Y1 Y2 Y3 Y4 BY DRUG
 /WSFACTOR = TIME 4
 /DESIGN.
```

Model 8: Repeated measures doubly multivariate model

Repeated measures fixed-effects MANOVA is also called a doubly multivariate model. Varying or time-dependent covariates are not available. This model can be used only when there is no random between-subjects effect in the model.

```
GLM X11 X12 X13 X21 X22 X23
    Y11 Y12 Y13 Y21 Y22 Y23 BY C D
/MEASURE = X Y
/WSFACTOR = A 2 B 3
/WSDESIGN = A B A*B
/DESIGN = C D.
```

Model 9: Means model for ANOVA and MANOVA

This model takes only fixed-effect factors (no random effects and covariates) and always assumes the highest order of the interactions among the factors. For example, *B*, *D*, and *E* are fixed factors, and *Y1* and *Y2* are two dependent variables. You can specify a means model by suppressing the intercept effect and specifying the highest order of interaction on the DESIGN subcommand.

```
GLM Y1 Y2 BY B, D, E
/INTERCEPT = EXCLUDE
/DESIGN = B*D*E.
```

Custom Hypothesis Specifications

GLM provides a flexible way for you to customize hypothesis testing based on the general linear hypothesis **LBM** = **K**, where **B** is the parameter vector or matrix. You can specify a customized linear hypothesis by using one or a combination of the subcommands LMATRIX, MMATRIX, KMATRIX, and CONTRAST.

LMATRIX, MMATRIX, and KMATRIX Subcommands

- The **L** matrix is called the **contrast coefficients matrix**. This matrix specifies coefficients of contrasts, which can be used for studying the between-subjects effects in the model. One way to define the **L** matrix is by specifying the CONTRAST subcommand, on which you select a type of contrast. Another way is to specify your own **L** matrix directly by using the LMATRIX subcommand. For details, see the syntax rules for these two subcommands in GLM: Univariate.

- The **M** matrix is called the **transformation coefficients matrix**. This matrix provides a transformation for the dependent variables. This transformation can be used to construct contrasts among the dependent variables in the model. The **M** matrix can be specified on the MMATRIX subcommand. For details, see the syntax rule for this subcommand in GLM: Multivariate.

- The **K** matrix is called the **contrast results matrix**. This matrix specifies the results matrix in the general linear hypothesis. To define your own **K** matrix, the KMATRIX subcommand can be used. For details, see the syntax rules for this subcommand in GLM: Univariate.

For univariate and multivariate models, you can specify one, two, or all three of the **L**, **M**, and **K** matrices. If only one or two types are specified, the unspecified matrices use the defaults shown in Table 1 (read across the rows).

Table 1   Default matrices for univariate and multivariate models if one matrix is specified

L matrix	M matrix	K matrix
If LMATRIX is used to specify the **L** matrix	Default = identity matrix[*]	Default = zero matrix
Default = intercept matrix[†]	If MMATRIX is used to specify the **M** matrix	Default = zero matrix
Default = intercept matrix[†]	Default = identity matrix[*]	If KMATRIX is used to specify the **K** matrix

[*] The dimension of the identity matrix is the same as the number of dependent variables being studied.

[†] The intercept matrix is the matrix corresponding to the estimable function for the intercept term in the model, provided that the intercept term is included in the model. If the intercept term is not included in the model, the **L** matrix is not defined and this custom hypothesis test cannot be performed.

Example

```
GLM Y1 Y2 BY A B
 /LMATRIX = A 1 -1
 /DESIGN A B.
```

Assume that factor *A* has two levels.

- Since there are two dependent variables, this is a multivariate model with two main factor effects, *A* and *B*.

- A custom hypothesis test is requested by the LMATRIX subcommand.

- Since no MMATRIX or KMATRIX is specified. The **M** matrix is the default two-dimensional identity matrix, and the **K** matrix is a zero-row vector (0, 0).

For a repeated measures model, you can specify one, two, or all three of the **L**, **M**, and **K** matrices. If only one or two types are specified, the unspecified matrices use the defaults shown in Table 2 (read across the rows).

Table 2   Default matrices for repeated measures models if only one matrix is specified

L matrix	M matrix	K matrix
If LMATRIX is used to specify the **L** matrix	Default = average matrix[*]	Default = zero matrix
Default = intercept matrix[†]	If MMATRIX is used to specify the **M** matrix	Default = zero matrix
Default = intercept matrix[†]	Default = average matrix[*]	If KMATRIX is used to specify the **K** matrix

* The average matrix is the transformation matrix that corresponds to the transformation for the between-subjects test. The dimension is the number of measures.

† The intercept matrix is the matrix corresponding to the estimable function for the intercept term in the model, provided that the intercept term is included in the model. If the intercept term is not included in the model, the **L** matrix is not defined and this custom hypothesis test cannot be performed.

Example

```
GLM Y1 Y2 BY A B
 /WSFACTOR TIME (2)
 /MMATRIX Y1 1 Y2 1; Y1 1 Y2 -1
 /DESIGN A B.
```

- Since WSFACTOR is specified, this is a repeated measures model with two between-subjects factors *A* and *B*, and a within-subjects factor, *TIME*.

- A custom hypothesis is requested by the MMATRIX subcommand. The **M** matrix is a 2×2 matrix:

$$
\begin{matrix}
1 & 1 \\
1 & -1
\end{matrix}
$$

- Since the **L** matrix and the **K** matrix are not specified, their defaults are used. The default for the **L** matrix is the matrix corresponding to the estimable function for the intercept term in the between-subjects model, and the default for the **K** matrix is a zero-row vector (0, 0).

CONTRAST Subcommand

When the CONTRAST subcommand is used, an **L** matrix, which is used in custom hypothesis testing, is generated according to the contrast chosen. The **K** matrix is always taken to be the zero matrix. If the model is univariate or multivariate, the **M** matrix is always the identity matrix and its dimension is equal to the number of dependent variables. For a repeated measures model, the **M** matrix is always the average matrix that corresponds to the average transformation for the dependent variable.

GLM: Univariate

```
GLM dependent var [BY factor list [WITH covariate list]]

[/RANDOM=factor factor...]

[/REGWGT=varname]

[/METHOD=SSTYPE({1  })]
                {2  }
                {3**}
                {4  }

[/INTERCEPT=[INCLUDE**] [EXCLUDE]]

[/MISSING=[INCLUDE] [EXCLUDE**]]

[/CRITERIA=[EPS({1E-8**})][ALPHA({0.05**})]
               {a    }         {a      }

[/PRINT = [DESCRIPTIVE] [HOMOGENEITY] [PARAMETER][ETASQ]
          [GEF] [LOF] [OPOWER] [TEST(LMATRIX)]]

[/PLOT=[SPREADLEVEL] [RESIDUALS]
       [PROFILE (factor factor*factor factor*factor*factor ...)]

[/TEST=effect VS {linear combination [DF(df)]}]
                 {value DF (df)               }

[/LMATRIX={["label"] effect list effect list ...;...}]
          {["label"] effect list effect list ...    }
          {["label"] ALL list; ALL...               }
          {["label"] ALL list                       }

[/KMATRIX= {number    }]
           {number;...}

[/CONTRAST (factor name)={DEVIATION[(refcat)]**      }]
                         {SIMPLE [(refcat)]          }
                         {DIFFERENCE                 }
                         {HELMERT                    }
                         {REPEATED                   }
                         {POLYNOMIAL  [({1,2,3...})]]}
                         {                {metric  } }
                         {SPECIAL (matrix)           }

[/POSTHOC =effect [effect...]
          ([SNK] [TUKEY] [BTUKEY][DUNCAN]
          [SCHEFFE] [DUNNETT(refcat)] [DUNNETTL(refcat)]
          [DUNNETTR(refcat)] [BONFERRONI] [LSD] [SIDAK]
          [GT2] [GABRIEL] [FREGW] [QREGW]  [T2] [T3] [GH] [C]
          [WALLER ({100** })])]]
                  {kratio}
          [VS effect]

[/EMMEANS=TABLES({OVERALL        })]  [COMPARE ADJ(LSD(none)) (BONFERRONI) (SIDAK)]
                {factor          }
                {factor*factor...}

 [/SAVE=[tempvar [(name)]] [tempvar [(name)]]...]

 [/OUTFILE= [{COVB (filename)}] [EFFECT(filename)] [DESIGN(filename)]
            {CORB (filename)}


 [/DESIGN={[INTERCEPT...]   }]
          {[effect effect...]}
```

** Default if subcommand or keyword is omitted.

Temporary variables (tempvar) are:

PRED, WPRED, RESID, WRESID, DRESID, ZRESID, SRESID, SEPRED, COOK, LEVER

Example:

```
GLM YIELD BY SEED FERT
  /DESIGN.
```

Overview

This section describes the use of GLM for univariate analyses. However, most of the subcommands described here can be used in any type of analysis with GLM. For additional subcommands used in those types of analysis, see GLM: Multivariate and GLM: Repeated Measures. For basic specification, syntax rules, and limitations of the GLM procedures, see GLM: Overview. For examples, see the *SPSS Base Applications Guide*.

Options

Design Specification. You can specify which terms to include in the design on the DESIGN subcommand. This allows you to estimate a model other than the default full factorial model, incorporate factor-by-covariate interactions or covariate-by-covariate interactions, and indicate nesting of effects.

Contrast Types. You can specify contrasts other than the default deviation contrasts on the CONTRAST subcommand.

Optional Output. You can choose from a wide variety of optional output on the PRINT subcommand. Output appropriate to univariate designs includes descriptive statistics for each cell, parameter estimates, Levene's test for equality of variance across cells, partial eta-squared for each effect and each parameter estimate, the general estimable function matrix, and a contrast coefficients table (**L'** matrix). The OUTFILE subcommand allows you to write out the covariance or correlation matrix, the design matrix, or the statistics from the between-subjects ANOVA table into a separate SPSS data file.

Using the EMMEANS subcommand, you can request tables of estimated marginal means of the dependent variable and their standard deviations. The SAVE subcommand allows you to save predicted values and residuals in weighted or unweighted and standardized or unstandardized forms. You can specify different means comparison tests for comparing all possible pairs of cell means using the POSTHOC subcommand. In addition, you can specify your own hypothesis tests by specifying an **L** matrix and a **K** matrix to test the univariate hypothesis **LB** = **K**.

Basic Specification

- The basic specification is a variable list identifying the dependent variable, the factors (if any), and the covariates (if any).
- By default, GLM uses a model that includes the intercept term, the covariate (if any), and the full factorial model, which includes all main effects and all possible interactions among factors. The intercept term is excluded if it is excluded in the model by specifying the keyword EXCLUDE on the INTERCEPT subcommand. Sums of squares are calculated and hypothesis tests are performed using type-specific estimable functions. Parameters are estimated using the normal equation and a generalized inverse of the SSCP matrix.

Subcommand Order

- The variable list must be specified first.
- Subcommands can be used in any order.

Syntax Rules

- For many analyses, the GLM variable list and the DESIGN subcommand are the only specifications needed.
- If you do not enter a DESIGN subcommand, GLM will use a full factorial model, with main effects of covariates, if any.
- Minimum syntax—at least one dependent variable must be specified, and at least one of the following must be specified: INTERCEPT, a between-subjects factor, or a covariate. The design contains the intercept by default.
- If more than one DESIGN subcommand is specified, only the last one is in effect.
- Dependent variables and covariates must be numeric, but factors can be numeric or string variables.
- If a string variable is specified as a factor, only the first eight characters of each value are used in distinguishing among values.
- If more than one MISSING subcommand is specified, only the last one is in effect.
- The following words are reserved as keywords or internal commands in the GLM procedure:

  INTERCEPT, BY, WITH, ALL, OVERALL, WITHIN

  Variable names that duplicate these words should be changed before you run GLM.

Limitations

- Any number of factors can be specified, but if the number of between-subjects factors plus the number of split variables exceeds 18, the Descriptive Statistics table is not printed even when you request it.
- Memory requirements depend primarily on the number of cells in the design. For the default full factorial model, this equals the product of the number of levels or categories in each factor.

Example

```
GLM YIELD BY SEED FERT WITH RAINFALL
  /PRINT=DESCRIPTIVE PARAMETER
  /DESIGN.
```

- *YIELD* is the dependent variable; *SEED* and *FERT* are factors; *RAINFALL* is a covariate.
- The PRINT subcommand requests the descriptive statistics for the dependent variable for each cell and the parameter estimates, in addition to the default tables Between-Subjects Factors and Univariate Tests.

- The DESIGN subcommand requests the default design, a full factorial model with a covariate. This subcommand could have been omitted or could have been specified in full as

    `/DESIGN = INTERCEPT RAINFALL, SEED, FERT, SEED BY FERT.`

GLM Variable List

The variable list specifies the dependent variable, the factors, and the covariates in the model.

- The dependent variable must be the first specification on GLM.
- The names of the factors follow the dependent variable. Use the keyword BY to separate the factors from the dependent variable.
- Enter the covariates, if any, following the factors. Use the keyword WITH to separate covariates from factors (if any) and the dependent variable.

Example

`GLM DEPENDNT BY FACTOR1 FACTOR2, FACTOR3.`

- In this example, three factors are specified.
- A default full factorial model is used for the analysis.

Example

```
GLM Y BY A WITH X
   /DESIGN.
```

- In this example, the DESIGN subcommand requests the default design, which includes the intercept term, the covariate *X* and the factor *A*.

RANDOM Subcommand

RANDOM allows you to specify which effects in your design are random. When the RANDOM subcommand is used, a table of expected mean squares for all effects in the design is displayed, and an appropriate error term for testing each effect is calculated and used automatically.

- Random always implies a univariate mixed-model analysis.
- If you specify an effect on RANDOM, higher-order effects containing the specified effect (excluding any effects containing covariates) are automatically treated as random effects.
- The keyword INTERCEPT and effects containing covariates are not allowed on this subcommand.
- The RANDOM subcommand cannot be used if there is any within-subjects factor in the model (that is, RANDOM cannot be specified if WSFACTOR is specified).
- When the RANDOM subcommand is used, the appropriate error terms for the hypothesis testing of all effects in the model are automatically computed and used.
- More than one RANDOM subcommand is allowed. The specifications are accumulated.

Example

```
GLM DEP BY A B
   /RANDOM = B
   /DESIGN = A,B, A*B.
```

- In the example, effects *B* and *A*B* are considered as random effects. Notice that if only effect *B* is specified in the RANDOM subcommand, *A*B* is automatically considered as a random effect.

- The hypothesis testing for each effect (*A*, *B*, and *A*B*) in the design will be carried out using the appropriate error term, which is calculated automatically.

REGWGT Subcommand

The only specification on REGWGT is the name of the variable containing the weights to be used in estimating a weighted least-squares model.

- Specify a numeric weight variable name following the REGWGT subcommand. Only observations with positive values in the weight variable will be used in the analysis.

- If more than one REGWGT subcommand is specified, only the last one is in effect.

Example

```
GLM OUTCOME BY TREATMNT
   /REGWGT WT.
```

- The procedure performs a weighted least-squares analysis. The variable *WT* is used as the weight variable.

METHOD Subcommand

METHOD controls the computational aspects of the GLM analysis. You can specify one of four different methods for partitioning the sums of squares. If more than one METHOD subcommand is specified, only the last one is in effect.

SSTYPE(1)   *Type I sum-of-squares method.* The Type I sum-of-squares method is also known as the hierarchical decomposition of the sum-of-squares method. Each term is adjusted only for the terms that precede it on the DESIGN subcommand. Under a balanced design, it is an orthogonal decomposition, and the sums of squares in the model add up to the total sum of squares.

SSTYPE(2)   *Type II sum-of-squares method.* This method calculates the sum of squares of an effect in the model adjusted for all other "appropriate" effects. An appropriate effect is one that corresponds to all effects that do not *contain* the effect being examined.

For any two effects *F1* and *F2* in the model, *F1* is said to be **contained** in *F2* under the following three conditions:
- Both effects *F1* and *F2* have the same covariate, if any.
- *F2* consists of more factors than *F1*.
- All factors in *F1* also appear in *F2*.

The intercept effect is treated as contained in all the pure factor effects. However, it is not contained in any effect involving a covariate. No effect is contained in the intercept effect. Thus, for any one effect *F* of interest, all other effects in the model can be classified as in one of the following two groups: the effects that do not contain *F* or the effects that contain *F*.

If the model is a main-effects design (that is, only main effects are in the model), the Type II sum-of-squares method is equivalent to the regression approach sums of squares. This means that each main effect is adjusted for every other term in the model.

SSTYPE(3)   *Type III sum-of-squares method.* This is the default. This method calculates the sum of squares of an effect *F* in the design as the sum of squares adjusted for any other effects that do not contain it, and *orthogonal* to any effects (if any) that contain it. The Type III sums of squares have one major advantage—they are invariant with respect to the cell frequencies as long as the general form of estimability remains constant. Hence, this type of sums of squares is often used for an unbalanced model with no missing cells. In a factorial design with no missing cells, this method is equivalent to the Yates' weighted squares of means technique, and it also coincides with the overparameterized Σ-restricted model.

SSTYPE(4)   *Type IV sum-of-squares method.* This method is designed for a situation in which there are missing cells. For any effect *F* in the design, if *F* is not contained in any other effect, then Type IV = Type III = Type II. When *F* is contained in other effects, then Type IV distributes the contrasts being made among the parameters in *F* to all higher-level effects equitably.

Example

```
GLM DEP BY A B C
  /METHOD=SSTYPE(3)
  /DESIGN=A, B, C.
```

- The design is a main-effects model.
- The METHOD subcommand requests that the model be fitted with Type III sums of squares.

INTERCEPT Subcommand

INTERCEPT controls whether an intercept term is included in the model. If more than one INTERCEPT subcommand is specified, only the last one is in effect.

INCLUDE   *Include the intercept term.* The intercept (constant) term is included in the model. This is the default.

EXCLUDE   *Exclude the intercept term.* The intercept term is excluded from the model. Specification of the keyword INTERCEPT on the DESIGN subcommand overrides INTERCEPT = EXCLUDE.

MISSING Subcommand

By default, cases with missing values for any of the variables on the GLM variable list are excluded from the analysis. The MISSING subcommand allows you to include cases with user-missing values.

- If MISSING is not specified, the default is EXCLUDE.
- Pairwise deletion of missing data is not available in GLM.
- Keywords INCLUDE and EXCLUDE are mutually exclusive.
- If more than one MISSING subcommand is specified, only the last one is in effect.

EXCLUDE   *Exclude both user-missing and system-missing values.* This is the default when MISSING is not specified.

INCLUDE   *User-missing values are treated as valid.* System-missing values cannot be included in the analysis.

CRITERIA Subcommand

CRITERIA controls the statistical criteria used to build the models.

- More than one CRITERIA subcommand is allowed. The specifications are accumulated. Conflicts across CRITERIA subcommands are resolved using the conflicting specification given on the last CRITERIA subcommand.
- The keyword must be followed by a positive number in parentheses.

EPS(n)   *The tolerance level in redundancy detection.* This value is used for redundancy checking in the design matrix. The default value is 1E-8.

ALPHA(n)   *The alpha level.* This keyword has two functions. First, it gives the alpha level at which the power is calculated for the F test. Once the noncentrality parameter for the alternative hypothesis is estimated from the data, then the power is the probability that the test statistic is greater than the critical value under the alternative hypothesis. (The observed power is displayed by default for GLM.) The second function of alpha is to specify the level of the confidence interval. If the alpha level specified is n, the value $(1 - n) \times 100$ indicates the level of confidence for all individual and simultaneous confidence intervals generated for the specified model. The value of n must be between 0 and 1, exclusive. The default value of alpha is 0.05. This means that the default power calculation is at the 0.05 level, and the default level of the confidence intervals is 95%, since $(1 - 0.05) \times 100 = 95$.

PRINT Subcommand

PRINT controls the display of optional output.

- Some PRINT output applies to the entire GLM procedure and is displayed only once.
- Additional output can be obtained on the EMMEANS, PLOT, and SAVE subcommands.
- Some optional output may greatly increase the processing time. Request only the output you want to see.
- If no PRINT command is specified, default output for a univariate analysis includes a factor information table and a Univariate Tests table (ANOVA) for all effects in the model.
- If more than one PRINT subcommand is specified, only the last one is in effect.

The following keywords are available for GLM univariate analyses. For information on PRINT specifications appropriate for other GLM models, see GLM: Multivariate and GLM: Repeated Measures.

DESCRIPTIVES   *Basic information about each cell in the design.* Observed means, standard deviations, and counts for the dependent variable in all cells. The cells are constructed from the highest-order crossing of the between-subjects factors. For a multivariate model, statistics are given for each dependent variable. If the number of between-subjects factors plus the number of split variables exceeds 18, the Descriptive Statistics table is not printed.

HOMOGENEITY   *Tests of homogeneity of variance.* Levene's test for equality of variances for the dependent variable across all level combinations of the between-subjects factors. If there are no between-subjects factors, this keyword is not valid. For a multivariate model, tests are displayed for each dependent variable.

PARAMETER   *Parameter estimates.* Parameter estimates, standard errors, *t* tests, and confidence intervals.

ETASQ   *Partial eta-squared (η^2).* This value is an overestimate of the actual effect size in an *F* test. It is defined as

$$\text{partial eta-squared} \ = \ \frac{dfh \times F}{dfh \times F + dfe}$$

where *F* is the test statistic and *dfh* and *dfe* are its degrees of freedom and degrees of freedom for error. The keyword EFSIZE can be used in place of ETASQ.

GEF   *General estimable function table.* This table shows the general form of the estimable functions.

LOF   *Perform a lack-of-fit test (which requires at least one cell to have multiple observations).* If the test is rejected, it implies that the current model cannot adequately account for the relationship between the response variable and the predictors. Either a variable is omitted or extra terms are needed in the model.

OPOWER   *Observed power for each test.* The observed power gives the probability that the *F* test would detect a population difference between groups equal to that implied by the sample difference.

TEST(LMATRIX)   *Set of contrast coefficients (L) matrices.* The transpose of the **L** matrix (**L'**) is displayed. This set always includes one matrix displaying the estimable function for each between-subjects effect appearing or implied in the DESIGN subcommand. Also, any **L** matrices generated by the LMATRIX or CONTRAST subcommands are displayed. TEST(ESTIMABLE) can be used in place of TEST(LMATRIX).

Example

```
GLM DEP BY A B WITH COV
  /PRINT=DESCRIPTIVE, TEST(LMATRIX), PARAMETER
  /DESIGN.
```

- Since the design in the DESIGN subcommand is not specified, the default design is used. In this case, the design includes the intercept term, the covariate *COV*, and the full factorial terms of *A* and *B*, which are *A*, *B*, and *A*B*.

- For each combination of levels of *A* and *B*, SPSS displays the descriptive statistics of *DEP*.

- The set of **L** matrices that generates the sums of squares for testing each effect in the design is displayed.

- The parameter estimates, their standard errors, *t* tests, confidence intervals, and the observed power for each test are displayed.

PLOT Subcommand

PLOT provides a variety of plots useful in checking the assumptions needed in the analysis. The PLOT subcommand can be specified more than once. All of the plots requested on each PLOT subcommand are produced.

Use the following keywords on the PLOT subcommand to request plots:

SPREADLEVEL   *Spread-versus-level plots.* Plots of observed cell means versus standard deviations, and versus variances.

RESIDUALS   *Observed by predicted by standardized residuals plot.* A plot is produced for each dependent variable. In a univariate analysis, a plot is produced for the single dependent variable.

PROFILE   *Line plots of dependent variable means for one-way, two-way, or three-way crossed factors.* The PROFILE keyword must be followed by parentheses containing a list of one or more factor combinations. All factors specified (either individual or crossed) must be made up of only valid factors on the factor list. Factor combinations on the PROFILE keyword may use an asterisk (*) or the keyword BY to specify crossed factors. A factor cannot occur in a single factor combination more than once.

The order of factors in a factor combination is important, and there is no restriction on the order of factors. If a single factor is specified after the PROFILE keyword, a line plot of estimated means at each level of the factor is produced. If a two-way crossed factor combination is specified, the output includes a multiple-line plot of estimated means at each level of the first specified factor, with a separate line drawn for each level of the second specified factor. If a three-way crossed factor combination is specified, the output includes multiple-line plots of estimated means at each level of the first specified factor, with separate lines for each level of the second factor, and separate plots for each level of the third factor.

Example

```
GLM DEP BY A B
  /PLOT = SPREADLEVEL PROFILE(A A*B A*B*C)
  /DESIGN.
```

Assume each of the factors A, B, and C has three levels.

- Spread-versus-level plots are produced showing observed cell means versus standard deviations and observed cell means versus variances.

- Five profile plots are produced. For factor A, a line plot of estimated means at each level of A is produced (one plot). For the two-way crossed factor combination A*B, a multiple-line plot of estimated means at each level of A, with a separate line for each level of B, is produced (one plot). For the three-way crossed factor combination A*B*C, a multiple-line plot of estimated means at each level of A, with a separate line for each level of B, is produced for each of the three levels of C (three plots).

TEST Subcommand

The TEST subcommand allows you to test a hypothesis term against a specified error term.

- TEST is valid only for univariate analyses. Multiple TEST subcommands are allowed, each executed independently.

- You must specify both the hypothesis term and the error term. There is no default.

- The hypothesis term is specified before the keyword VS. It must be a valid effect specified or implied on the DESIGN subcommand.

- The error term is specified after the keyword VS. You can specify either a linear combination or a value. The linear combination of effects takes the general form: `coefficient*effect +/- coefficient*effect ...`

- All effects in the linear combination must be specified or implied on the DESIGN subcommand. Effects specified or implied on DESIGN but not listed after VS are assumed to have a coefficient of 0.

- Duplicate effects are allowed. GLM adds coefficients associated with the same effect before performing the test. For example, the linear combination `5*A-0.9*B-A` will be combined to `4*A-0.9B`.

- A coefficient can be specified as a fraction with a positive denominator—for example, 1/3 or –1/3, but 1/–3 is invalid.
- If you specify a value for the error term, you must specify the degrees of freedom after the keyword DF. The degrees of freedom must be a positive real number. DF and the degrees of freedom are optional for a linear combination.

Example

```
GLM DEP BY A B
  /TEST = A VS B + A*B
  /DESIGN = A, B, A*B.
```

- *A* is tested against the pooled effect of *B* + *A*B*.

LMATRIX Subcommand

The LMATRIX subcommand allows you to customize your hypotheses tests by specifying the **L** matrix (contrast coefficients matrix) in the general form of the linear hypothesis **LB = K**, where **K = 0** if it is not specified on the KMATRIX subcommand. The vector **B** is the parameter vector in the linear model.

- The basic format for the LMATRIX subcommand is an optional label in quotes, an effect name or the keyword ALL, and a list of real numbers. There can be multiple effect names (or the keyword ALL) and number lists.
- The optional label is a string with a maximum length of 255 characters. Only one label can be specified.
- Only valid effects appearing or implied on the DESIGN subcommand can be specified on the LMATRIX subcommand.
- The length of the list of real numbers must be equal to the number of parameters (including the redundant ones) corresponding to that effect. For example, if the effect *A*B* takes up six columns in the design matrix, then the list after *A*B* must contain exactly six numbers.
- A number can be specified as a fraction with a positive denominator—for example, 1/3 or –1/3, but 1/–3 is invalid.
- A semicolon (;) indicates the end of a row in the **L** matrix.
- When ALL is specified, the length of the list that follows ALL is equal to the total number of parameters (including the redundant ones) in the model.
- Effects appearing or implied on the DESIGN subcommand but not specified here are assumed to have entries of 0 in the corresponding columns of the **L** matrix.
- Multiple LMATRIX subcommands are allowed. Each is treated independently.

Example

```
GLM DEP BY A B
  /LMATRIX = "B1 vs B2 at A1"
              B 1 -1 0 A*B 1 -1
  /LMATRIX = "Effect A"
              A 1 0 -1
              A*B 1/3  1/3  1/3
                    0    0    0
                  -1/3 -1/3 -1/3;
              A 0 1 -1
              A*B 0    0    0
                  1/3  1/3  1/3
                 -1/3 -1/3 -1/3
  /LMATRIX = "B1 vs B2 at A2"
              ALL  0
                   0  0  0
                   1 -1  0
                   0  0  0  1 -1  0  0  0  0
  /DESIGN = A, B, A*B.
```

Assume that factors *A* and *B* each have three levels. There are three LMATRIX subcommands; each is treated independently.

- **B1 versus B2 at A1.** In the first LMATRIX subcommand, the difference is tested between levels 1 and 2 of effect *B* when effect *A* is fixed at level 1. Since there are three levels each in effects *A* and *B*, the interaction effect *A*B* should take up nine columns in the design matrix. Notice that only the first two columns of *A*B* are specified with values 1 and –1; the rest are all assumed to be 0. Columns corresponding to effect *B* are all assumed to be 0.

- **Effect A.** In the second LMATRIX subcommand, effect *A* is tested. Since there are three levels in effect *A*, at most two independent contrasts can be formed; thus, there are two rows in the **L** matrix, which are separated by a semicolon (;). The first row tests the difference between levels 1 and 3 of effect *A*, while the second row tests the difference between levels 2 and 3 of effect *A*.

- **B1 versus B2 at A2.** In the last LMATRIX subcommand, the keyword ALL is used. The first 0 corresponds to the intercept effect; the next three zeros correspond to effect *A*.

KMATRIX Subcommand

The KMATRIX subcommand allows you to customize your hypothesis tests by specifying the **K** matrix (contrast results matrix) in the general form of the linear hypothesis **LB** = **K**. The vector **B** is the parameter vector in the linear model.

- The default **K** matrix is a zero matrix; that is, **LB** = 0 is assumed.

- For the KMATRIX subcommand to be valid, at least one of the following subcommands must be specified: the LMATRIX subcommand or the INTERCEPT = INCLUDE subcommand.

- If KMATRIX is specified but LMATRIX is not specified, the LMATRIX is assumed to take the row vector corresponding to the intercept in the estimable function, provided the subcommand INTERCEPT = INCLUDE is specified. In this case, the **K** matrix can be only a scalar matrix.

- If KMATRIX and LMATRIX are specified, then the number of rows in the requested **K** and **L** matrices must be equal. If there are multiple LMATRIX subcommands, then all requested **L** matrices must have the same number of rows, and **K** must have the same number of rows as these **L** matrices.

- A semicolon (;) can be used to indicate the end of a row in the **K** matrix.
- If more than one KMATRIX subcommand is specified, only the last one is in effect.

Example

```
GLM DEP BY A B
  /LMATRIX = "Effect A"
             A 1  0 -1; A 1 -1  0
  /LMATRIX = "Effect B"
             B 1  0 -1; B 1 -1  0
  /KMATRIX = 0; 0
  /DESIGN = A B.
```

In this example, assume that factors *A* and *B* each have three levels.

- There are two LMATRIX subcommands; both have two rows.
- The first LMATRIX subcommand tests whether the effect of *A* is 0, while the second LMATRIX subcommand tests whether the effect of *B* is 0.
- The KMATRIX subcommand specifies that the **K** matrix also has two rows, each with value 0.

CONTRAST Subcommand

CONTRAST specifies the type of contrast desired among the levels of a factor. For a factor with k levels or values, the contrast type determines the meaning of its $k-1$ degrees of freedom.

- Specify the factor name in parentheses following the subcommand CONTRAST.
- You can specify only one factor per CONTRAST subcommand, but you can enter multiple CONTRAST subcommands.
- After closing the parentheses, enter an equals sign followed by one of the contrast keywords.
- This subcommand creates an **L** matrix such that the columns corresponding to the factor match the contrast given. The other columns are adjusted so that the **L** matrix is estimable.

The following contrast types are available:

DEVIATION   *Deviations from the grand mean.* This is the default for between-subjects factors. Each level of the factor except one is compared to the grand mean. One category (by default, the last) must be omitted so that the effects will be independent of one another. To omit a category other than the last, specify the number of the omitted category (which is not necessarily the same as its value) in parentheses after the keyword DEVIATION. For example,

```
GLM Y BY B
  /CONTRAST(B)=DEVIATION(1).
```

Suppose factor *B* has three levels, with values 2, 4, and 6. The specified contrast omits the first category, in which *B* has the value 2. Deviation contrasts are not orthogonal.

POLYNOMIAL   *Polynomial contrasts.* This is the default for within-subjects factors. The first degree of freedom contains the linear effect across the levels of the factor, the second contains the quadratic effect, and so on. In a balanced design, polynomial contrasts are orthogonal. By default, the levels are assumed to be equally spaced; you can specify unequal spacing by entering a metric consisting of one integer for each level of the factor in parentheses after the keyword POLYNOMIAL. (All metrics specified cannot be equal; thus, (1, 1, . . . 1) is not valid.) For example,

```
GLM RESPONSE BY STIMULUS
   /CONTRAST(STIMULUS) = POLYNOMIAL(1,2,4).
```

Suppose that factor *STIMULUS* has three levels. The specified contrast indicates that the three levels of *STIMULUS* are actually in the proportion 1:2:4. The default metric is always (1, 2, . . . *k*), where *k* levels are involved. Only the relative differences between the terms of the metric matter (1, 2, 4) is the same metric as (2, 3, 5) or (20, 30, 50) because, in each instance, the difference between the second and third numbers is twice the difference between the first and second.

DIFFERENCE   *Difference or reverse Helmert contrasts.* Each level of the factor except the first is compared to the mean of the previous levels. In a balanced design, difference contrasts are orthogonal.

HELMERT   *Helmert contrasts.* Each level of the factor except the last is compared to the mean of subsequent levels. In a balanced design, Helmert contrasts are orthogonal.

SIMPLE   *Each level of the factor except the last is compared to the last level.* To use a category other than the last as the omitted reference category, specify its number (which is not necessarily the same as its value) in parentheses following the keyword SIMPLE. For example,

```
GLM Y BY B
   /CONTRAST(B)=SIMPLE(1).
```

Suppose that factor *B* has three levels with values 2, 4, and 6. The specified contrast compares the other levels to the first level of *B*, in which *B* has the value 2. Simple contrasts are not orthogonal.

REPEATED   *Comparison of adjacent levels.* Each level of the factor except the first is compared to the previous level. Repeated contrasts are not orthogonal.

SPECIAL   *A user-defined contrast.* Values specified after this keyword are stored in a matrix in column major order. For example, if factor *A* has three levels, then CONTRAST(A)= SPECIAL(1 1 1 -1 0 0 1 -1) produces the following contrast matrix:

```
1   1    0
1  -1    1
1   0   -1
```

Orthogonal contrasts are particularly useful. In a balanced design, contrasts are orthogonal if the sum of the coefficients in each contrast row is 0 and if, for any pair of contrast rows, the products of corresponding coefficients sum to 0. DIFFERENCE, HELMERT, and POLYNOMIAL contrasts always meet these criteria in balanced designs. For illustration of contrast types, see the appendix.

Example

```
GLM DEP BY FAC
  /CONTRAST(FAC)=DIFFERENCE
  /DESIGN.
```

- Suppose that the factor *FAC* has five categories and therefore four degrees of freedom.
- CONTRAST requests DIFFERENCE contrasts, which compare each level (except the first) with the mean of the previous levels.

POSTHOC Subcommand

POSTHOC allows you to produce multiple comparisons between means of a factor. These comparisons are usually not planned at the beginning of the study but are suggested by the data in the course of study.

- Post hoc tests are computed for the dependent variable. The alpha value used in the tests can be specified by using the keyword ALPHA on the CRITERIA subcommand. The default alpha value is 0.05. The confidence level for any confidence interval constructed is $(1 - \alpha) \times 100$. The default confidence level is 95. For a multivariate model, tests are computed for all dependent variables specified.
- Only between-subjects factors appearing in the factor list are valid in this subcommand. Individual factors can be specified.
- You can specify one or more effects to be tested. Only fixed main effects appearing or implied on the DESIGN subcommand are valid test effects.
- Optionally, you can specify an effect defining the error term following the keyword VS after the test specification. The error effect can be any single effect in the design that is not the intercept or a main effect named on a POSTHOC subcommand.
- A variety of multiple comparison tests are available. Some tests are designed for detecting homogeneity subsets among the groups of means, some are designed for pairwise comparisons among all means, and some can be used for both purposes.
- For tests that are used for detecting homogeneity subsets of means, non-empty group means are sorted in ascending order. Means that are not significantly different are included together to form a homogeneity subset. The significance for each homogeneity subset of means is displayed. In a case where the numbers of valid cases are not equal in all groups, for most post hoc tests, the harmonic mean of the group sizes is used as the sample size in the calculation. For QREGW or FREGW, individual sample sizes are used.
- For tests that are used for pairwise comparisons, the display includes the difference between each pair of compared means, the confidence interval for the difference, and the significance. The sample sizes of the two groups being compared are used in the calculation.

- Output for tests specified on the POSTHOC subcommand are available according to their statistical purposes. The following table illustrates the statistical purpose of the post hoc tests:

Post Hoc Tests	Statistical Purpose	
Keyword	Homogeneity Subsets Detection	Pairwise Comparison and Confidence Interval
LSD		Yes
SIDAK		Yes
BONFERRONI		Yes
GH		Yes
T2		Yes
T3		Yes
C		Yes
DUNNETT		Yes*
DUNNETTL		Yes*
DUNNETTR		Yes*
SNK	Yes	
BTUKEY	Yes	
DUNCAN	Yes	
QREGW	Yes	
FREGW	Yes	
WALLER	Yes[†]	
TUKEY	Yes	Yes
SCHEFFE	Yes	Yes
GT2	Yes	Yes
GABRIEL	Yes	Yes

* Only C.I.'s for differences between test group means and control group means are given.

† No significance for Waller test is given.

- Tests that are designed for homogeneity subset detection display the detected homogeneity subsets and their corresponding significances.
- Tests that are designed for both homogeneity subset detection and pairwise comparisons display both kinds of output.
- For the DUNNETT, DUNNETTL, and DUNNETTR keywords, only individual factors can be specified.
- The default reference category for DUNNETT, DUNNETTL, and DUNNETTR is the last category. An integer greater than 0 within parentheses can be used to specify a different reference category. For example, POSTHOC = A (DUNNETT(2)) requests a DUNNETT test for factor *A*, using the second level of *A* as the reference category.

- The keywords DUNCAN, DUNNETT, DUNNETTL, and DUNNETTR must be spelled out in full; using the first three characters alone is not sufficient.
- If the REGWGT subcommand is specified, weighted means are used in performing post hoc tests.
- Multiple POSTHOC subcommands are allowed. Each specification is executed independently so that you can test different effects against different error terms.

SNK
Student-Newman-Keuls procedure based on the Studentized range test.

TUKEY
Tukey's honestly significant difference. This test uses the Studentized range statistic to make all pairwise comparisons between groups.

BTUKEY
Tukey's b. Multiple comparison procedure based on the average of Studentized range tests.

DUNCAN
Duncan's multiple comparison procedure based on the Studentized range test.

SCHEFFE
Scheffé's multiple comparison t test.

DUNNETT(refcat)
Dunnett's two-tailed t test. Each level of the factor is compared to a reference category. A reference category can be specified in parentheses. The default reference category is the last category. This keyword must be spelled out in full.

DUNNETTL(refcat)
Dunnett's one-tailed t test. This test indicates whether the mean at any level (except the reference category) of the factor is *smaller* than that of the reference category. A reference category can be specified in parentheses. The default reference category is the last category. This keyword must be spelled out in full.

DUNNETTR(refcat)
Dunnett's one-tailed t test. This test indicates whether the mean at any level (except the reference category) of the factor is *larger* than that of the reference category. A reference category can be specified in parentheses. The default reference category is the last category. This keyword must be spelled out in full.

BONFERRONI
Bonferroni t test. This test is based on Student's *t* statistic and adjusts the observed significance level for the fact that multiple comparisons are made.

LSD
Least significant difference t test. Equivalent to multiple *t* tests between all pairs of groups. This test does not control the overall probability of rejecting the hypotheses that some pairs of means are different, while in fact they are equal.

SIDAK
Sidak t test. This test provides tighter bounds than the Bonferroni test.

GT2
Hochberg's GT2. Pairwise comparisons test based on the Studentized maximum modulus test. Unless the cell sizes are extremely unbalanced, this test is fairly robust even for unequal variances.

GABRIEL	*Gabriel's pairwise comparisons test based on the Studentized maximum modulus test.*
FREGW	*Ryan-Einot-Gabriel-Welsch's multiple stepdown procedure based on an F test.*
QREGW	*Ryan-Einot-Gabriel-Welsch's multiple stepdown procedure based on the Studentized range test.*
T2	*Tamhane's T2.* Tamhane's pairwise comparisons test based on a *t* test. This test can be applied in situations where the variances are unequal.
T3	*Dunnett's T3.* Pairwise comparisons test based on the Studentized maximum modulus. This test is appropriate when the variances are unequal.
GH	*Games and Howell's pairwise comparisons test based on the Studentized range test.* This test can be applied in situations where the variances are unequal.
C	*Dunnett's C.* Pairwise comparisons based on the weighted average of Studentized ranges. This test can be applied in situations where the variances are unequal.
WALLER(kratio)	*Waller-Duncan* t *test.* This test uses a Bayesian approach. It is restricted to cases with equal sample sizes. For cases with unequal sample sizes, the harmonic mean of the sample size is used. The kratio is the Type 1/Type 2 error seriousness ratio. The default value is 100. You can specify an integer greater than 1 within parentheses.

EMMEANS Subcommand

EMMEANS displays estimated marginal means of the dependent variable in the cells (with covariates held at their overall mean value) and their standard errors for the specified factors. Note that these are predicted, not observed, means. The estimated marginal means are calculated using a modified definition by Searle, Speed, and Milliken (1980).

- TABLES, followed by an option in parentheses, is required. COMPARE is optional; if specified, it must follow TABLES.

- Multiple EMMEANS subcommands are allowed. Each is treated independently.

- If redundant EMMEANS subcommands are specified, only the last redundant subcommand is in effect. EMMEANS subcommands are redundant if the option specified on TABLES is the same (including redundant crossed factor combinations—for example, *A*B* and *B*A*).

TABLES(option)   *Table specification.* Valid options are the keyword OVERALL, factors appearing on the factor list, and crossed factors constructed of factors on the factor list. Crossed factors can be specified using an asterisk (*) or the keyword BY. All factors in a crossed factor specification must be unique.

If OVERALL is specified, the estimated marginal means of the dependent variable are displayed, collapsing over between-subjects factors.

If a between-subjects factor, or a crossing of between-subjects factors, is specified on the TABLES keyword, GLM collapses over any other between-subjects factors before computing the estimated marginal means for the dependent variable. For a multivariate model, GLM collapses over any other between- or within-subjects factors.

COMPARE(factor) ADJ(method)

Main- or simple-main-effects omnibus tests and pairwise comparisons of the dependent variable. This option gives the mean difference, standard error, significance, and confidence interval for each pair of levels for the effect specified in the TABLES command, as well as an omnibus test for that effect. If only one factor is specified on TABLES, COMPARE can be specified by itself; otherwise, the factor specification is required. In this case, levels of the specified factor are compared with each other for each level of the other factors in the interaction.

The optional ADJ keyword allows you to apply an adjustment to the confidence intervals and significance values to account for multiple comparisons. Methods available are LSD (no adjustment), BONFERRONI, or SIDAK.

Example

```
GLM DEP BY A B
  /EMMEANS = TABLES(A*B)COMPARE(A)
  /DESIGN.
```

- The output of this analysis includes a pairwise comparisons table for the dependent variable *DEP*.
- Assume that *A* has three levels and *B* has two levels. The first level of *A* is compared with the second and third levels, the second level with the first and third levels, and the third level with the first and second levels. The pairwise comparison is repeated for the two levels of *B*.

SAVE Subcommand

Use SAVE to add one or more residual or fit values to the working data file.

- Specify one or more temporary variables, each followed by an optional new name in parentheses. For a multivariate model, you can optionally specify a new name for the temporary variable related to each dependent variable.
- WPRED and WRESID can be saved only if REGWGT has been specified.

- Specifying a temporary variable on this subcommand results in a variable being added to the active data file for each dependent variable.
- You can specify variable names for the temporary variables. These names must be unique, valid variable names. For a multivariate model, there should be as many variable names specified as there are dependent variables, listed in the order of the dependent variables as specified on the GLM command. If you do not specify enough variable names, default variable names are used for any remaining variables.
- If new names are not specified, GLM generates a rootname using a shortened form of the temporary variable name with a suffix. For a multivariate model, the suffix _n is added to the temporary variable name, where n is the ordinal number of the dependent variable as specified on the GLM command.
- If more than one SAVE subcommand is specified, only the last one is in effect.

PRED   *Unstandardized predicted values.*

WPRED   *Weighted unstandardized predicted values.* Available only if REGWGT has been specified.

RESID   *Unstandardized residuals.*

WRESID   *Weighted unstandardized residuals.* Available only if REGWGT has been specified.

DRESID   *Deleted residuals.*

ZRESID   *Standardized residuals.*

SRESID   *Studentized residuals.*

SEPRED   *Standard errors of predicted value.*

COOK   *Cook's distances.*

LEVER   *Uncentered leverage values.*

OUTFILE Subcommand

The OUTFILE subcommand writes an SPSS data file that can be used in other procedures.
- You must specify a keyword on OUTFILE. There is no default.
- You must specify a filename in parentheses after a keyword. A filename with a path must be enclosed within quotation marks. The asterisk (*) is not allowed.
- If you specify more than one keyword, a different filename is required for each.
- If more than one OUTFILE subcommand is specified, only the last one is in effect.
- For COVB or CORB, the output will contain, in addition to the covariance or correlation matrix, three rows for each dependent variable: a row of parameter estimates, a row of residual degrees of freedom, and a row of significance values for the *t* statistics corresponding to the parameter estimates. All statistics are displayed separately by split.

COVB (filename)	*Writes the parameter covariance matrix.*
CORB (filename)	*Writes the parameter correlation matrix.*
EFFECT (filename)	*Writes the statistics from the between-subjects ANOVA table.* Invalid for repeated measures analyses.
DESIGN (filename)	*Writes the design matrix.* The number of rows equals the number of cases, and the number of columns equals the number of parameters. The variable names are *DES_1*, *DES_2*, ..., *DES_p*, where *p* is the number of the parameters.

DESIGN Subcommand

DESIGN specifies the effects included in a specific model. The cells in a design are defined by all of the possible combinations of levels of the factors in that design. The number of cells equals the product of the number of levels of all the factors. A design is *balanced* if each cell contains the same number of cases. GLM can analyze both balanced and unbalanced designs.

- Specify a list of terms to be included in the model, separated by spaces or commas.
- The default design, if the DESIGN subcommand is omitted or is specified by itself, is a design consisting of the following terms in order: the intercept term (if INTERCEPT=INCLUDE is specified), next the covariates given in the covariate list, and then the full factorial model defined by all factors on the factor list and excluding the intercept.
- To include a term for the main effect of a factor, enter the name of the factor on the DESIGN subcommand.
- To include the intercept term in the design, use the keyword INTERCEPT on the DESIGN subcommand. If INTERCEPT is specified on the DESIGN subcommand, the subcommand INTERCEPT=EXCLUDE is overridden.
- To include a term for an interaction between factors, use the keyword BY or the asterisk (*) to join the factors involved in the interaction. For example, *A*B* means a two-way interaction effect of *A* and *B*, where *A* and *B* are factors. *A*A* is not allowed because factors inside an interaction effect must be distinct.
- To include a term for nesting one effect within another, use the keyword WITHIN or a pair of parentheses on the DESIGN subcommand. For example, *A(B)* means that *A* is nested within *B*. The expression *A(B)* is equivalent to the expression *A WITHIN B*. When more than one pair of parentheses is present, each pair of parentheses must be enclosed or nested within another pair of parentheses. Thus, *A(B)(C)* is not valid.
- Multiple nesting is allowed. For example, *A(B(C))* means that *B* is nested within *C*, and *A* is nested within *B(C)*.
- Interactions between nested effects are not valid. For example, neither *A(C)*B(C)* nor *A(C)*B(D)* is valid.
- To include a covariate term in the design, enter the name of the covariate on the DESIGN subcommand.

- Covariates can be connected, but not nested, through the * operator to form another covariate effect. Therefore, interactions among covariates such as *X1*X1* and *X1*X2* are valid, but not *X1(X2)*. Using covariate effects such as *X1*X1*, *X1*X1*X1*, *X1*X2*, and *X1*X1*X2*X2* makes fitting a polynomial regression model easy in GLM.

- Factor and covariate effects can be connected only by the * operator. Suppose *A* and *B* are factors, and *X1* and *X2* are covariates. Examples of valid factor-by-covariate interaction effects are *A*X1*, *A*B*X1*, *X1*A(B)*, *A*X1*X1*, and *B*X1*X2*.

- If more than one DESIGN subcommand is specified, only the last one is in effect.

Example

```
GLM Y BY A B C WITH X
  /DESIGN A B(A) X*A.
```

- In this example, the design consists of a main effect *A*, a nested effect *B* within *A*, and an interaction effect of a covariate *X* with a factor *A*.

GLM: Multivariate

```
GLM dependent varlist [BY factor list [WITH covariate list]]

[/REGWGT=varname]

[/METHOD=SSTYPE({1  })]
              {2  }
              {3**}
              {4  }

[/INTERCEPT=[INCLUDE**] [EXCLUDE]]

[/MISSING=[INCLUDE] [EXCLUDE**]]

[/CRITERIA=[EPS({1E-8**})] [ALPHA({0.05**})]
              {a      }          {a     }

[/PRINT  = [DESCRIPTIVE] [HOMOGENEITY] [PARAMETER][ETASQ] [RSSCP]
           [GEF] [LOF] [OPOWER] [TEST [([SSCP] [LMATRIX] [MMATRIX])]]

[/PLOT=[SPREADLEVEL] [RESIDUALS]
       [PROFILE (factor factor*factor factor*factor*factor ...)]

[/LMATRIX={["label"] effect list effect list ...;...}]
          {["label"] effect list effect list ...    }
          {["label"] ALL list; ALL...               }
          {["label"] ALL list                       }

[/MMATRIX= {["label"] depvar value depvar value ...;["label"]...}]
           {["label"] depvar value depvar value ...            }
           {["label"] ALL list; ["label"] ...                  }
           {["label"] ALL list                                 }

[/KMATRIX= {list of numbers     }]
           {list of numbers;...}

[/SAVE=[tempvar [(list of names)]] [tempvar [(list of names)]]...]
       [DESIGN]

[/OUTFILE= [{COVB (filename)}] [EFFECT(filename)] [DESIGN(filename)]
            {CORB (filename)}

[/DESIGN={[INTERCEPT...]    }]
         {[effect effect...]}
```

** Default if subcommand or keyword is omitted.

Temporary variables (tempvar) are:

PRED, WPRED, RESID, WRESID, DRESID, ZRESID, SRESID, SEPRED, COOK, LEVER

Example:

```
GLM SCORE1 TO SCORE4 BY METHOD(1,3).
```

Overview

This section discusses the subcommands that are used in multivariate general linear models and covariance designs with several interrelated dependent variables. The discussion focuses on subcommands and keywords that do not apply, or apply in different manners, to univariate analyses. It does not contain information on all of the subcommands you will need to specify the design. For subcommands not covered here, see GLM: Univariate.

Options

Optional Output. In addition to the output described in GLM: Univariate, you can have both multivariate and univariate F tests. Using the PRINT subcommand, you can request the hypothesis and error sums-of-squares and cross-product matrices for each effect in the design, the transformation coefficient table (**M** matrix), Box's M test for equality of covariance matrices, and Bartlett's test of sphericity.

Basic Specification

- The basic specification is a variable list identifying the dependent variables, with the factors (if any) named after BY and the covariates (if any) named after WITH.
- By default, GLM uses a model that includes the intercept term, the covariates (if any), and the full factorial model, which includes all main effects and all possible interactions among factors. The intercept term is excluded if it is excluded in the model by specifying EXCLUDE on the INTERCEPT subcommand. GLM produces multivariate and univariate F tests for each effect in the model. It also calculates the power for each test based on the default alpha value.

Subcommand Order

- The variable list must be specified first.
- Subcommands can be used in any order.

Syntax Rules

- The syntax rules applicable to univariate analysis, in "Syntax Rules" on p. 322 in GLM: Univariate, also apply to multivariate analysis.
- If you enter one of the multivariate specifications in a univariate analysis, GLM ignores it.

Limitations

- Any number of factors can be specified, but if the number of between-subjects factors plus the number of split variables exceeds 18, the Descriptive Statistics table is not printed even when you request it.
- Memory requirements depend primarily on the number of cells in the design. For the default full factorial model, this equals the product of the number of levels or categories in each factor.

GLM Variable List

- Multivariate GLM calculates statistical tests that are valid for analyses of dependent variables that are correlated with one another. The dependent variables must be specified first.
- The factor and covariate lists follow the same rules as in univariate analyses.
- If the dependent variables are uncorrelated, the univariate significance tests have greater statistical power.

PRINT Subcommand

By default, if no PRINT subcommand is specified, multivariate GLM produces multivariate tests (MANOVA) and univariate tests (ANOVA) for all effects in the model. All of the PRINT specifications described in GLM: Univariate are available in multivariate analyses. The following additional output can be requested:

TEST(SSCP)   *Sums-of-squares and cross-product matrices.* Hypothesis (HSSCP) and error (ESSCP) sums-of-squares and cross-product matrices for each effect in the design are displayed. Each between-subjects effect has a different HSSCP matrix, but there is a single ESSCP matrix for all between-subjects effects. For a repeated measures design, each within-subjects effect has an HSSCP matrix and an ESSCP matrix. If there are no within-subjects effects, the ESSCP matrix for the between-subjects effects is the same as the RSSCP matrix.

TEST(MMATRIX)   *Set of transformation coefficients (M) matrices.* Any **M** matrices generated by the MMATRIX subcommand are displayed. If no **M** matrix is specified on the MMATRIX subcommand, this specification will be skipped, unless you are using a repeated measures design. In a repeated measures design, this set always includes the **M** matrix determined by the WSFACTOR subcommand. The specification TEST(TRANSFORM) is equivalent to TEST(MMATRIX).

HOMOGENEITY   *Tests of homogeneity of variance.* In addition to Levene's test for equality of variances for each dependent variable, the display includes Box's *M* test of homogeneity of the covariance matrices of the dependent variables across all level combinations of the between-subjects factors.

RSSCP   *Sums of squares and cross-products of residuals.* Three matrices are displayed:

Residual SSCP matrix. A square matrix of sums of squares and cross-products of residuals. The dimension of this matrix is the same as the number of dependent variables in the model.

Residual covariance matrix. The residual SSCP matrix divided by the degrees of freedom of the residual.

Residual correlation matrix. The standardized form of the residual covariance matrix.

Example:

```
GLM Y1 Y2 Y3 BY A B
 /PRINT = HOMOGENEITY RSSCP
 /DESIGN.
```

- Since there are three dependent variables, this is a multivariate model.
- The keyword RSSCP produces three matrices of sums of squares and cross-products of residuals. The output also contains the result of Bartlett's test of the sphericity of the residual covariance matrix.
- In addition to the Levene test for each dependent variable, the keyword HOMOGENEITY produces the result of Box's M test of homogeneity in the multivariate model.

MMATRIX Subcommand

The MMATRIX subcommand allows you to customize your hypothesis tests by specifying the **M** matrix (transformation coefficients matrix) in the general form of the linear hypothesis **LBM** = **K**, where **K** = **0** if it is not specified on the KMATRIX subcommand. The vector **B** is the parameter vector in the linear model.

- Specify an optional label in quotes. Then either list dependent variable names, each followed by a real number, or specify the keyword ALL followed by a list of real numbers. Only variable names that appear on the dependent variable list can be specified on the MMATRIX subcommand.
- You can specify one label for each column in the **M** matrix.
- If you specify ALL, the length of the list that follows ALL should be equal to the number of dependent variables.
- There is no limit on the length of the label.
- For the MMATRIX subcommand to be valid, at least one of the following must be specified: the LMATRIX subcommand or INTERCEPT=INCLUDE. (Either of these specifications defines an **L** matrix.)
- If both LMATRIX and MMATRIX are specified, the **L** matrix is defined by the LMATRIX subcommand.
- If MMATRIX or KMATRIX is specified but LMATRIX is not specified, the **L** matrix is defined by the estimable function for the intercept effect, provided that the intercept effect is included in the model.
- If LMATRIX is specified, but MMATRIX is not specified, the **M** matrix is assumed to be an $r \times r$ identity matrix, where r is the number of dependent variables.
- A semicolon (;) indicates the end of a column in the **M** matrix.
- Dependent variables not appearing on a list of dependent variable names and real numbers are assigned a value of 0.
- Dependent variables not appearing in the MMATRIX subcommand will have a row of zeros in the **M** matrix.
- A number can be specified as a fraction with a positive denominator—for example, 1/3 or –1/3, but 1/–3 is invalid.

- The number of columns must be greater than 0. You can specify as many columns as you need.
- If more than one MMATRIX subcommand is specified, only the last one is in effect.

Example:

```
GLM Y1 Y2 Y3 BY A B
 /MMATRIX = "Y1-Y2" Y1 1 Y2 -1; "Y1-Y3" Y1 1 Y3 -1
            "Y2-Y3" Y2 1 Y3 -1
 /DESIGN.
```

- In the above example, *Y1*, *Y2*, and *Y3* are the dependent variables.
- The MMATRIX subcommand requests all pairwise comparisons among the dependent variables.
- Since LMATRIX was not specified, the **L** matrix is defined by the estimable function for the intercept effect.

GLM: Repeated Measures

```
GLM dependent varlist [BY factor list [WITH covariate list]]

/WSFACTOR=name levels [{DEVIATION [(refcat)]      }] name...
                       {SIMPLE [(refcat)]          }
                       {DIFFERENCE                 }
                       {HELMERT                    }
                       {REPEATED                   }
                       {POLYNOMIAL [(({1,2,3...})]**}
                       {               {metric }   }
                       {SPECIAL (matrix)           }

[/MEASURE=newname newname...]

[/WSDESIGN=effect effect...]

[/REGWGT=varname]

[/METHOD=SSTYPE({1  })]
               {2  }
               {3**}
               {4  }

[/INTERCEPT=[INCLUDE**] [EXCLUDE]]

[/MISSING=[INCLUDE] [EXCLUDE**]]

[/PRINT  = [DESCRIPTIVE] [HOMOGENEITY] [PARAMETER][ETASQ] [RSSCP]
           [GEF] [LOF] [OPOWER] [TEST [([SSCP] [LMATRIX] [MMATRIX])]]]

[/SAVE=[tempvar [(list of names)]] [tempvar [(list of names)]]...]
       [DESIGN]

[/EMMEANS=TABLES({OVERALL            }]) [COMPARE ADJ(LSD(none)(BONFERRONI)(SIDAK))]
                {factor              }
                {factor*factor...    }
                {wsfactor            }
                {wsfactor*wsfactor...}
                {factor*...wsfactor*...}
                {factor*factor...    }

[/DESIGN={[INTERCEPT...]    }]*
         {[effect effect...]}
```

* The **DESIGN** subcommand has the same syntax as is described in GLM: Univariate.

** Default if subcommand or keyword is omitted.

Example:
```
GLM Y1 TO Y4 BY GROUP
  /WSFACTOR=YEAR 4.
```

Overview

This section discusses the subcommands that are used in repeated measures designs, in which the dependent variables represent measurements of the same variable (or variables) taken repeatedly. This section does not contain information on all of the subcommands that you will need to specify the design. For some subcommands or keywords not covered here, such as

DESIGN, see GLM: Univariate. For information on optional output and the multivariate significance tests available, see GLM: Multivariate.

- In a simple repeated measures analysis, all dependent variables represent different measurements of the same variable for different values (or levels) of a within-subjects factor. Between-subjects factors and covariates can also be included in the model, just as in analyses not involving repeated measures.

- A **within-subjects factor** is simply a factor that distinguishes measurements made on the same subject or case, rather than distinguishing different subjects or cases.

- GLM permits more complex analyses, in which the dependent variables represent levels of two or more within-subjects factors.

- GLM also permits analyses in which the dependent variables represent measurements of several variables for the different levels of the within-subjects factors. These are known as **doubly multivariate designs**.

- A repeated measures analysis includes a within-subjects design describing the model to be tested with the within-subjects factors, as well as the usual between-subjects design describing the effects to be tested with between-subjects factors. The default for the within-subjects factors design is a full factorial model which includes the main within-subjects factor effects and all their interaction effects.

- If a custom hypothesis test is required (defined by the CONTRAST, LMATRIX, or KMATRIX subcommands), the default transformation matrix (**M** matrix) is taken to be the average transformation matrix, which can be displayed by using the keyword TEST(MMATRIX) on the PRINT subcommand. The default contrast result matrix (**K** matrix) is the zero matrix.

- If the contrast coefficient matrix (**L** matrix) is not specified, but a custom hypothesis test is required by the MMATRIX or the KMATRIX subcommand, the contrast coefficient matrix (**L** matrix) is taken to be the **L** matrix which corresponds to the estimable function for the intercept in the between-subjects model. This matrix can be displayed by using the keyword TEST(LMATRIX) on the PRINT subcommand.

Basic Specification

- The basic specification is a variable list followed by the WSFACTOR subcommand.

- Whenever WSFACTOR is specified, GLM performs special repeated measures processing. The multivariate and univariate tests are provided. In addition, for any within-subjects effect involving more than one transformed variable, the Mauchly test of sphericity is displayed to test the assumption that the covariance matrix of the transformed variables is constant on the diagonal and zero off the diagonal. The Greenhouse-Geisser epsilon and the Huynh-Feldt epsilon are also displayed for use in correcting the significance tests in the event that the assumption of sphericity is violated.

Subcommand Order

- The list of dependent variables, factors, and covariates must be first.

Syntax Rules

- The WSFACTOR (within-subjects factors), WSDESIGN (within-subjects design), and MEASURE subcommands are used only in repeated measures analysis.
- WSFACTOR is required for any repeated measures analysis.
- If WSDESIGN is not specified, a full factorial within-subjects design consisting of all main effects and all interactions among within-subjects factors is used by default.
- The MEASURE subcommand is used for doubly multivariate designs, in which the dependent variables represent repeated measurements of more than one variable.

Limitations

- Any number of factors can be specified, but if the number of between-subjects factors plus the number of split variables exceeds 18, the Descriptive Statistics table is not printed even when you request it.
- Maximum 18 within-subjects factors.
- Memory requirements depend primarily on the number of cells in the design. For the default full factorial model, this equals the product of the number of levels or categories in each factor.

Example

```
GLM Y1 TO Y4 BY GROUP
  /WSFACTOR=YEAR 4 POLYNOMIAL
  /WSDESIGN=YEAR
  /PRINT=PARAMETER
  /DESIGN=GROUP.
```

- WSFACTOR specifies a repeated measures analysis in which the four dependent variables represent a single variable measured at four levels of the within-subjects factor. The within-subjects factor is called *YEAR* for the duration of the GLM procedure.
- POLYNOMIAL requests polynomial contrasts for the levels of *YEAR*. Because the four variables, *Y1*, *Y2*, *Y3*, and *Y4*, in the working data file represent the four levels of *YEAR*, the effect is to perform an orthonormal polynomial transformation of these variables.
- PRINT requests that the parameter estimates be displayed.
- WSDESIGN specifies a within-subjects design that includes only the effect of the *YEAR* within-subjects factor. Because *YEAR* is the only within-subjects factor specified, this is the default design, and WSDESIGN could have been omitted.
- DESIGN specifies a between-subjects design that includes only the effect of the *GROUP* between-subjects factor. This subcommand could have been omitted.

GLM Variable List

The list of dependent variables, factors, and covariates must be specified first.

- WSFACTOR determines how the dependent variables on the GLM variable list will be interpreted.

- The number of dependent variables on the GLM variable list must be a multiple of the number of cells in the within-subjects design. If there are six cells in the within-subjects design, each group of six dependent variables represents a single within-subjects variable that has been measured in each of the six cells.

- Normally, the number of dependent variables should equal the number of cells in the within-subjects design multiplied by the number of variables named on the MEASURE subcommand (if one is used). If you have more groups of dependent variables than are accounted for by the MEASURE subcommand, GLM will choose variable names to label the output, which may be difficult to interpret.

- Covariates are specified after keyword WITH. You can specify constant covariates. Constant covariates represent variables whose values remain the same at each within-subjects level.

Example

```
GLM MATH1 TO MATH4 BY METHOD WITH SES
  /WSFACTOR=SEMESTER 4.
```

- The four dependent variables represent a score measured four times (corresponding to the four levels of *SEMESTER*).

- *SES* is a constant covariate. Its value does not change over the time covered by the four levels of *SEMESTER*.

- Default contrast (POLYNOMIAL) is used.

WSFACTOR Subcommand

WSFACTOR names the within-subjects factors, specifies the number of levels for each, and specifies the contrast for each.

- Presence of the WSFACTOR subcommand implies that the repeated measures model is being used.

- Mauchly's test of sphericity is automatically performed when WSFACTOR is specified.

- Names and number levels for the within-subjects factors are specified on the WSFACTOR subcommand. Factor names must not duplicate any of the dependent variables, factors, or covariates named on the GLM variable list. A type of contrast can also be specified for each within-subjects factor in order to perform comparisons among its levels. This contrast amounts to a transformation on the dependent variables.

- If there are more than one within-subjects factors, they must be named in the order corresponding to the order of the dependent variables on the GLM variable list. GLM varies the levels of the last-named within-subjects factor most rapidly when assigning dependent variables to within-subjects cells (see the example below).

- The number of cells in the within-subjects design is the product of the number of levels for all within-subjects factors.

- Levels of the factors must be represented in the data by the dependent variables named on the GLM variable list.
- The number of levels of each factor must be at least two. Enter an integer equal to or greater than 2 after each factor to indicate how many levels the factor has. Optionally, you can enclose the number of levels in parentheses.
- Enter only the *number of levels* for within-subjects factors, not a range of values.
- If more than one WSFACTOR subcommand is specified, only the last one is in effect.

Contrasts for WSFACTOR

The levels of a within-subjects factor are represented by different dependent variables. Therefore, contrasts between levels of such a factor compare these dependent variables. Specifying the type of contrast amounts to specifying a transformation to be performed on the dependent variables.

- In testing the within-subjects effects, an orthonormal transformation is automatically performed on the dependent variables in a repeated measures analysis.
- The contrast for each within-subjects factor is entered after the number of levels. If no contrast keyword is specified, POLYNOMIAL(1,2,3...) is the default. This contrast is used in comparing the levels of the within-subjects factors. Intrinsically orthogonal contrast types are recommended for within-subjects factors if you wish to examine each degree-of-freedom test, provided compound symmetry is assumed within each within-subjects factor. Other orthogonal contrast types are DIFFERENCE and HELMERT.
- If there are more than one within-subjects factors, the transformation matrix (**M** matrix) is computed as the Kronecker product of the matrices generated by the contrasts specified.
- The transformation matrix (**M** matrix) generated by the specified contrasts can be displayed by using the keyword TEST(MMATRIX) on the subcommand PRINT.
- The contrast types available for within-subjects factors are the same as those on the CONTRAST subcommand for between-subjects factors, described in "CONTRAST Subcommand" on p. 332 in GLM: Univariate. See the appendix also.

The following contrast types are available:

DEVIATION   *Deviations from the grand mean.* This is the default for between-subjects factors. Each level of the factor except one is compared to the grand mean. One category (by default the last) must be omitted so that the effects will be independent of one another. To omit a category other than the last, specify the number of the omitted category in parentheses after the keyword DEVIATION. For example,

```
GLM Y1 Y2 Y3 BY GROUP
 /WSFACTOR = Y 3 DEVIATION (1)
```

Deviation contrasts are not orthogonal.

POLYNOMIAL   *Polynomial contrasts.* This is the default for within-subjects factors. The first degree of freedom contains the linear effect across the levels of the factor, the second contains the quadratic effect, and so on. In a balanced design, polynomial contrasts are orthogonal. By default, the levels are assumed to be equally spaced; you can specify unequal spacing by entering a metric consisting of one integer for each level of the factor in parentheses after the keyword POLYNOMIAL. (All metrics specified cannot be equal; thus $(1, 1, ..., 1)$ is not valid.) For example,

```
/WSFACTOR=D 3 POLYNOMIAL(1,2,4).
```

Suppose that factor D has three levels. The specified contrast indicates that the three levels of D are actually in the proportion 1:2:4. The default metric is always $(1,2,...,k)$, where k levels are involved. Only the relative differences between the terms of the metric matter (1,2,4) is the same metric as (2,3,5) or (20,30,50) because, in each instance, the difference between the second and third numbers is twice the difference between the first and second.

DIFFERENCE   *Difference or reverse Helmert contrasts.* Each level of the factor except the first is compared to the mean of the previous levels. In a balanced design, difference contrasts are orthogonal.

HELMERT   *Helmert contrasts.* Each level of the factor except the last is compared to the mean of subsequent levels. In a balanced design, Helmert contrasts are orthogonal.

SIMPLE   *Each level of the factor except the last is compared to the last level.* To use a category other than the last as the omitted reference category, specify its number in parentheses following keyword SIMPLE. For example,

```
/WSFACTOR=B 3 SIMPLE (1).
```

Simple contrasts are not orthogonal.

REPEATED   *Comparison of adjacent levels.* Each level of the factor except the first is compared to the previous level. Repeated contrasts are not orthogonal.

SPECIAL   *A user-defined contrast.* Values specified after this keyword are stored in a matrix in column major order. For example, if factor A has three levels, then WSFACTOR(A)= SPECIAL(1 1 1 -1 0 0 1 -1) produces the following contrast matrix:

$$
\begin{array}{rrr}
1 & 1 & 0 \\
1 & -1 & 1 \\
1 & 0 & -1
\end{array}
$$

Example

```
GLM X1Y1 X1Y2 X2Y1 X2Y2 X3Y1 X3Y2 BY TREATMNT GROUP
  /WSFACTOR=X 3 Y 2
  /DESIGN.
```

- The GLM variable list names six dependent variables and two between-subjects factors, *TREATMNT* and *GROUP*.

- WSFACTOR identifies two within-subjects factors whose levels distinguish the six dependent variables. *X* has three levels and *Y* has two. Thus, there are $3 \times 2 = 6$ cells in the within-subjects design, corresponding to the six dependent variables.

- Variable *X1Y1* corresponds to levels 1,1 of the two within-subjects factors; variable *X1Y2* corresponds to levels 1,2; *X2Y1* to levels 2,1; and so on up to *X3Y2*, which corresponds to levels 3,2. The first within-subjects factor named, *X*, varies most slowly, and the last within-subjects factor named, *Y*, varies most rapidly on the list of dependent variables.

- Because there is no WSDESIGN subcommand, the within-subjects design will include all main effects and interactions: *X*, *Y*, and *X* by *Y*.

- Likewise, the between-subjects design includes all main effects and interactions (*TREATMNT*, *GROUP*, and *TREATMNT* by *GROUP*) plus the intercept.

- In addition, a repeated measures analysis always includes interactions between the within-subjects factors and the between-subjects factors. There are three such interactions for each of the three within-subjects effects.

Example

```
GLM SCORE1 SCORE2 SCORE3 BY GROUP
  /WSFACTOR=ROUND 3 DIFFERENCE
  /CONTRAST(GROUP)=DEVIATION
  /PRINT=PARAMETER TEST(LMATRIX).
```

- This analysis has one between-subjects factor, *GROUP*, and one within-subjects factor, *ROUND*, with three levels that are represented by the three dependent variables.

- The WSFACTOR subcommand also specifies difference contrasts for *ROUND*, the within-subjects factor.

- There is no WSDESIGN subcommand, so a default full factorial within-subjects design is assumed. This could also have been specified as `WSDESIGN=ROUND`, or simply `WSDESIGN`.

- The CONTRAST subcommand specifies deviation contrasts for *GROUP*, the between-subjects factor. This subcommand could have been omitted because deviation contrasts are the default.

- PRINT requests the display of the parameter estimates for the model and the **L** matrix.

- There is no DESIGN subcommand, so a default full factorial between-subjects design is assumed. This could also have been specified as `DESIGN=GROUP`, or simply `DESIGN`.

WSDESIGN Subcommand

WSDESIGN specifies the design for within-subjects factors. Its specifications are like those of the DESIGN subcommand, but it uses the within-subjects factors rather than the between-subjects factors.

- The default WSDESIGN is a full factorial design, which includes all main effects and all interactions for within-subjects factors. The default is in effect whenever a design is processed without a preceding WSDESIGN or when the preceding WSDESIGN subcommand has no specifications.

- A WSDESIGN specification cannot include between-subjects factors or terms based on them, nor does it accept interval-level variables.

- The keyword INTERCEPT is not allowed on WSDESIGN.

- Nested effects are not allowed. Therefore, the symbols ( ) are not allowed here.
- If more than one WSDESIGN subcommand is specified, only the last one is in effect.

Example

```
GLM JANLO,JANHI,FEBLO,FEBHI,MARLO,MARHI BY SEX
  /WSFACTOR MONTH 3 STIMULUS 2
  /WSDESIGN MONTH, STIMULUS
  /DESIGN SEX.
```

- There are six dependent variables, corresponding to three months and two different levels of stimulus.
- The dependent variables are named on the GLM variable list in an order such that the level of stimulus varies more rapidly than the month. Thus, *STIMULUS* is named last on the WSFACTOR subcommand.
- The WSDESIGN subcommand specifies only the main effects for within-subjects factors. There is no *MONTH* by *STIMULUS* interaction term.

MEASURE Subcommand

In a doubly multivariate analysis, the dependent variables represent multiple variables measured under the different levels of the within-subjects factors. Use MEASURE to assign names to the variables that you have measured for the different levels of within-subjects factors.

- Specify a list of one or more variable names to be used in labeling the averaged results. If no within-subjects factor has more than two levels, MEASURE has no effect. You can use up to 255 characters for each name.
- The number of dependent variables in the dependent variables list should equal the product of the number of cells in the within-subjects design and the number of names on MEASURE.
- If you do not enter a MEASURE subcommand and there are more dependent variables than cells in the within-subjects design, GLM assigns names (normally *MEASURE_1*, *MEASURE_2*, etc.) to the different measures.
- All of the dependent variables corresponding to each measure should be listed together and ordered so that the within-subjects factor named last on the WSFACTORS subcommand varies most rapidly.

Example

```
GLM TEMP11 TEMP12 TEMP21 TEMP22 TEMP31 TEMP32,
  WEIGHT11 WEIGHT12 WEIGHT21 WEIGHT22 WEIGHT31 WEIGHT32 BY GROUP
  /WSFACTOR=DAY 3 AMPM 2
  /MEASURE=TEMP WEIGHT
  /WSDESIGN=DAY, AMPM, DAY BY AMPM
  /DESIGN.
```

- There are 12 dependent variables: 6 temperatures and 6 weights, corresponding to morning and afternoon measurements on three days.
- WSFACTOR identifies the two factors (*DAY* and *AMPM*) that distinguish the temperature and weight measurements for each subject. These factors define six within-subjects cells.
- MEASURE indicates that the first group of six dependent variables correspond to *TEMP* and the second group of six dependent variables correspond to *WEIGHT*.

- These labels, *TEMP* and *WEIGHT*, are used on the output as the measure labels.
- WSDESIGN requests a full factorial within-subjects model. Because this is the default, WSDESIGN could have been omitted.

EMMEANS Subcommand

EMMEANS displays estimated marginal means of the dependent variables in the cells, adjusted for the effects of covariates at their overall means, for the specified factors. Note that these are predicted, not observed, means. The standard errors are also displayed. For a detailed description of the EMMEANS subcommand, see "EMMEANS Subcommand" on p. 337 in GLM: Univariate.

- For the TABLES and COMPARE keywords, valid options include the within-subjects factors specified in the WSFACTOR subcommand, crossings among them, and crossings among factors specified in the factor list and factors specified on the WSFACTOR subcommand.
- All factors in a crossed-factors specification must be unique.
- If a between- or within-subjects factor, or a crossing of between- or within-subjects factors, is specified on the TABLES keyword, then GLM will collapse over any other between- or within-subjects factors before computing the estimated marginal means for the dependent variables.

HILOGLINEAR

```
HILOGLINEAR {varlist} (min,max) [varlist ...]
            {ALL     }

 [/METHOD [= BACKWARD]]

 [/MAXORDER = k]

 [/CRITERIA = [CONVERGE({0.25**})] [ITERATE({20**})] [P({0.05**})]
                       {n      }            {n   }      {prob  }
              [DELTA({0.5**})] [MAXSTEPS({10**})]
                    {d      }            {n   }
              [DEFAULT] ]

 [/CWEIGHT = {varname }]
            {(matrix)}

 [/PRINT = {[FREQ**] [RESID**] [ESTIM**][ASSOCIATION**]}]
           {DEFAULT**                                  }
           {ALL                                        }
           {NONE                                       }

 [/PLOT = [{NONE**            } ]
          {DEFAULT           }
          {[RESID] [NORMPROB]}
          {ALL               }

 [/MISSING = [{EXCLUDE**}]]
             {INCLUDE  }

 [/DESIGN = effectname effectname*effectname ...]
```

** Default if subcommand or keyword is omitted.

Example

```
HILOGLINEAR V1(1,2) V2(1,2)
  /DESIGN=V1*V2.
```

Overview

HILOGLINEAR fits hierarchical loglinear models to multidimensional contingency tables using an iterative proportional-fitting algorithm. HILOGLINEAR also estimates parameters for saturated models. These techniques are described in Everitt (1977), Bishop et al. (1975), and Goodman (1978). HILOGLINEAR is much more efficient for these models than the LOG-LINEAR procedure because HILOGLINEAR uses an iterative proportional-fitting algorithm rather than the Newton-Raphson method used in LOGLINEAR.

Options

Design Specification. You can request automatic model selection using backward elimination with the METHOD subcommand. You can also specify any hierarchical design and request multiple designs using the DESIGN subcommand.

Design Control. You can control the criteria used in the iterative proportional-fitting and model-selection routines with the CRITERIA subcommand. You can also limit the order of effects in the model with the MAXORDER subcommand and specify structural zeros for cells in the tables you analyze with the CWEIGHT subcommand.

Display and Plots. You can select the display for each design with the PRINT subcommand. For saturated models, you can request tests for different orders of effects as well. With the PLOT subcommand, you can request residuals plots or normal probability plots of residuals.

Basic Specification

- The basic specification is a variable list with at least two variables followed by their minimum and maximum values.
- HILOGLINEAR estimates a saturated model for all variables in the analysis.
- By default, HILOGLINEAR displays parameter estimates, measures of partial association, goodness of fit, and frequencies for the saturated model.

Subcommand Order

- The variable list must be specified first.
- Subcommands affecting a given DESIGN must appear before the DESIGN subcommand. Otherwise, subcommands can appear in any order.
- MISSING can be placed anywhere after the variable list.

Syntax Rules

- DESIGN is optional. If DESIGN is omitted or the last specification is not a DESIGN subcommand, a default saturated model is estimated.
- You can specify multiple PRINT, PLOT, CRITERIA, MAXORDER, and CWEIGHT subcommands. The last of each type specified is in effect for subsequent designs.
- PRINT, PLOT, CRITERIA, MAXORDER, and CWEIGHT specifications remain in effect until they are overridden by new specifications on these subcommands.
- You can specify multiple METHOD subcommands, but each one affects only the next design.
- MISSING can be specified only once.

Operations

- HILOGLINEAR builds a contingency table using all variables on the variable list. The table contains a cell for each possible combination of values within the range specified for each variable.
- HILOGLINEAR assumes that there is a category for every integer value in the range of each variable. Empty categories waste space and can cause computational problems. If there

are empty categories, use the RECODE command to create consecutive integer values for categories.

- Cases with values outside the range specified for a variable are excluded.
- If the last subcommand is not a DESIGN subcommand, HILOGLINEAR displays a warning and generates the default model. This is the saturated model unless MAXORDER is specified. This model is in addition to any that are explicitly requested.
- If the model is not saturated (for example, when MAXORDER is less than the number of factors), only the goodness of fit and the observed and expected frequencies are given.
- The display uses the WIDTH subcommand defined on the SET command. If the defined width is less than 132, some portions of the display may be deleted.

Limitations

The HILOGLINEAR procedure cannot estimate all possible frequency models, and it produces limited output for unsaturated models.

- It can estimate only hierarchical loglinear models.
- It treats all table variables as nominal. (You can use LOGLINEAR to fit nonhierarchical models to tables involving variables that are ordinal.)
- It can produce parameter estimates for saturated models only (those with all possible main-effect and interaction terms).
- It can estimate partial associations for saturated models only.
- It can handle tables with no more than 10 factors.

Example

```
HILOGLINEAR V1(1,2) V2(1,2) V3(1,3) V4(1,3)
   /DESIGN=V1*V2*V3, V4.
```

- HILOGLINEAR builds a $2 \times 2 \times 3 \times 3$ contingency table for analysis.
- DESIGN specifies the generating class for a hierarchical model. This model consists of main effects for all four variables, two-way interactions among *V1*, *V2*, and *V3*, and the three-way interaction term *V1* by *V2* by *V3*.

Variable List

The required variable list specifies the variables in the analysis. The variable list must precede all other subcommands.

- Variables must be numeric and have integer values. If a variable has a fractional value, the fractional portion is truncated.
- Keyword ALL can be used to refer to all user-defined variables in the working data file.
- A range must be specified for each variable, with the minimum and maximum values separated by a comma and enclosed in parentheses.

- If the same range applies to several variables, the range can be specified once after the last variable to which it applies.
- If ALL is specified, all variables must have the same range.

METHOD Subcommand

By default, HILOGLINEAR tests the model specified on the DESIGN subcommand (or the default model) and does not perform any model selection. All variables are entered and none are removed. Use METHOD to specify automatic model selection using backward elimination for the next design specified.

- You can specify METHOD alone or with the keyword BACKWARD for an explicit specification.
- When the backward-elimination method is requested, a step-by-step output is displayed regardless of the specification on the PRINT subcommand.
- METHOD affects only the next design.

BACKWARD   *Backward elimination.* Perform backward elimination of terms in the model. All terms are entered. Those that do not meet the P criterion specified on the CRITERIA subcommand (or the default P) are removed one at a time.

MAXORDER Subcommand

MAXORDER controls the maximum order of terms in the model estimated for subsequent designs. If MAXORDER is specified, HILOGLINEAR tests a model only with terms of that order or less.

- MAXORDER specifies the highest-order term that will be considered for the next design. MAXORDER can thus be used to abbreviate computations for the BACKWARD method.
- If the integer on MAXORDER is less than the number of factors, parameter estimates and measures of partial association are not available. Only the goodness of fit and the observed and expected frequencies are displayed.
- You can use MAXORDER with backward elimination to find the best model with terms of a certain order or less. This is computationally much more efficient than eliminating terms from the saturated model.

Example

```
HILOGLINEAR V1 V2 V3(1,2)
    /MAXORDER=2
    /DESIGN=V1 V2 V3
    /DESIGN=V1*V2*V3 .
```

- HILOGLINEAR builds a $2 \times 2 \times 2$ contingency table for *V1*, *V2*, and *V3*.
- MAXORDER has no effect on the first DESIGN subcommand because the design requested considers only main effects.
- MAXORDER restricts the terms in the model specified on the second DESIGN subcommand to two-way interactions and main effects.

CRITERIA Subcommand

Use the CRITERIA subcommand to change the values of constants in the iterative proportional-fitting and model-selection routines for subsequent designs.

- The default criteria are in effect if the CRITERIA subcommand is omitted (see below).
- You cannot specify the CRITERIA subcommand without any keywords.
- Specify each CRITERIA keyword followed by a criterion value in parentheses. Only those criteria specifically altered are changed.
- You can specify more than one keyword on CRITERIA, and they can be in any order.

DEFAULT *Reset parameters to their default values.* If you have specified criteria other than the defaults for a design, use this keyword to restore the defaults for subsequent designs.

CONVERGE(n) *Convergence criterion.* The default is 10^{-3} times the largest cell size, or 0.25, whichever is larger.

ITERATE(n) *Maximum number of iterations.* The default is 20.

P(n) *Probability for change in chi-square if term is removed.* Specify a value between (but not including) 0 and 1 for the significance level. The default is 0.05. P is in effect only when you request BACKWARD on the METHOD subcommand.

MAXSTEPS(n) *Maximum number of steps for model selection.* Specify an integer between 1 and 99, inclusive. The default is 10.

DELTA(d) *Cell delta value.* The value of delta is added to each cell frequency for the first iteration. It is left in the cells for saturated models only. The default value is 0.5. You can specify any decimal value between 0 and 1 for *d*. HILOGLINEAR does not display parameter estimates or the covariance matrix of parameter estimates if any zero cells (either structural or sampling) exist in the expected table after delta is added.

CWEIGHT Subcommand

CWEIGHT specifies cell weights for a model. CWEIGHT is typically used to specify structural zeros in the table. You can also use CWEIGHT to adjust tables to fit new margins.

- You can specify the name of a variable whose values are cell weights, or provide a matrix of cell weights enclosed in parentheses.
- If you use a variable to specify cell weights, you are allowed only one CWEIGHT subcommand.
- If you specify a matrix, you must provide a weight for every cell in the contingency table, where the number of cells equals the product of the number of values of all variables.
- Cell weights are indexed by the values of the variables in the order in which they are specified on the variable list. The index values of the rightmost variable change the most quickly.
- You can use the notation *n**cw to indicate that cell weight *cw* is repeated *n* times in the matrix.

Example

```
HILOGLINEAR V1(1,2) V2(1,2) V3(1,3)
 /CWEIGHT=CELLWGT
 /DESIGN=V1*V2, V2*V3, V1*V3.
```

- This example uses the variable *CELLWGT* to assign cell weights for the table. Only one CWEIGHT subcommand is allowed.

Example

```
HILOGLINEAR V4(1,3) V5(1,3)
 /CWEIGHT=(0 1 1  1 0 1  1 1 0)
 /DESIGN=V4, V5.
```

- The HILOGLINEAR command sets the diagonal cells in the model to structural zeros. This type of model is known as a **quasi-independence model**.
- Because both *V4* and *V5* have three values, weights must be specified for nine cells.
- The first cell weight is applied to the cell in which *V4* is 1 and *V5* is 1; the second weight is applied to the cell in which *V4* is 1 and *V5* is 2; and so on.

Example

```
HILOGLINEAR V4(1,3) V5(1,3)
 /CWEIGHT=(0 3*1 0 3*1 0)
 /DESIGN=V4,V5.
```

- This example is the same as the previous example except that the *n*cw* notation is used.

Example

```
* An Incomplete Rectangular Table

DATA LIST FREE / LOCULAR RADIAL FREQ.
WEIGHT BY FREQ.
BEGIN DATA
1 1 462
1 2 130
1 3 2
1 4 1
2 1 103
2 2 35
2 3 1
2 4 0
3 5 614
3 6 138
3 7 21
3 8 14
3 9 1
4 5 443
4 6 95
4 7 22
4 8 8
4 9 5
END DATA.
HILOGLINEAR LOCULAR (1,4) RADIAL (1,9)
 /CWEIGHT=(4*1 5*0   4*1 5*0   4*0 5*1   4*0 5*1)
 /DESIGN LOCULAR RADIAL.
```

- This example uses aggregated table data as input.
- The DATA LIST command defines three variables. The values of *LOCULAR* and *RADIAL* index the levels of those variables, so that each case defines a cell in the table. The values of *FREQ* are the cell frequencies.
- The WEIGHT command weights each case by the value of the variable *FREQ*. Because each case represents a cell in this example, the WEIGHT command assigns the frequencies for each cell.
- The BEGIN DATA and END DATA commands enclose the inline data.
- The HILOGLINEAR variable list specifies two variables. *LOCULAR* has values 1, 2, 3, and 4. *RADIAL* has integer values 1 through 9.
- The CWEIGHT subcommand identifies a block rectangular pattern of cells that are logically empty. There is one weight specified for each cell of the 36-cell table.
- In this example, the matrix form needs to be used in CWEIGHT because the structural zeros do not appear in the actual data. (For example, there is no case corresponding to *LOCULAR*=1, *RADIAL*=5.)
- The DESIGN subcommand specifies main effects only for *LOCULAR* and *RADIAL*. Lack of fit for this model indicates an interaction of the two variables.
- Because there is no PRINT or PLOT subcommand, HILOGLINEAR produces the default output for an unsaturated model.

PRINT Subcommand

PRINT controls the display produced for the subsequent designs.

- If PRINT is omitted or included with no specifications, the default display is produced.
- If any keywords are specified on PRINT, only output specifically requested is displayed.
- HILOGLINEAR displays Pearson and likelihood-ratio chi-square goodness-of-fit tests for models. For saturated models, it also provides tests that the k-way effects and the k-way and higher-order effects are 0.
- Both adjusted and unadjusted degrees of freedom are displayed for tables with sampling or structural zeros. K-way and higher-order tests use the unadjusted degrees of freedom.
- The unadjusted degrees of freedom are not adjusted for zero cells, and they estimate the upper bound of the true degrees of freedom. These are the same degrees of freedom you would get if all cells were filled.
- The adjusted degrees of freedom are calculated from the number of non-zero-fitted cells minus the number of parameters that would be estimated if all cells were filled (that is, unadjusted degrees of freedom minus the number of zero-fitted cells). This estimate of degrees of freedom may be too low if some parameters do not exist because of zeros.

DEFAULT   *Default displays.* This option includes FREQ and RESID output for nonsaturated models, and FREQ, RESID, ESTIM, and ASSOCIATION output for saturated models. For saturated models, the observed and expected frequencies are equal, and the residuals are zeros.

FREQ   *Observed and expected cell frequencies.*

RESID	*Raw and standardized residuals.*
ESTIM	*Parameter estimates for a saturated model.*
ASSOCIATION	*Partial associations.* You can request partial associations of effects only when you specify a saturated model. This option is computationally expensive for tables with many factors.
ALL	*All available output.*
NONE	*Design information and goodness-of-fit statistics only.* Use of this option overrides all other specifications on PRINT.

PLOT Subcommand

Use PLOT to request residuals plots.

- If PLOT is included without specifications, standardized residuals and normal probability plots are produced.
- No plots are displayed for saturated models.
- If PLOT is omitted, no plots are produced.

RESID	*Standardized residuals by observed and expected counts.*
NORMPLOT	*Normal probability plots of adjusted residuals.*
NONE	*No plots.* Specify NONE to suppress plots requested on a previous PLOT subcommand. This is the default if PLOT is omitted.
DEFAULT	*Default plots.* Includes RESID and NORMPLOT. This is the default when PLOT is specified without keywords.
ALL	*All available plots.*

MISSING Subcommand

By default, a case with either system-missing or user-missing values for any variable named on the HILOGLINEAR variable list is omitted from the analysis. Use MISSING to change the treatment of cases with user-missing values.

- MISSING can be named only once and can be placed anywhere following the variable list.
- MISSING cannot be used without specifications.
- A case with a system-missing value for any variable named on the variable list is always excluded from the analysis.

EXCLUDE	*Delete cases with missing values.* This is the default if the subcommand is omitted. You can also specify keyword DEFAULT.
INCLUDE	*Include user-missing values as valid.* Only cases with system-missing values are deleted.

DESIGN Subcommand

By default, HILOGLINEAR uses a saturated model that includes all variables on the variable list. The model contains all main effects and interactions for those variables. Use DESIGN to specify a different generating class for the model.

- If DESIGN is omitted or included without specifications, the default model is estimated. When DESIGN is omitted, SPSS issues a warning message.

- To specify a design, list the highest-order terms, using variable names and asterisks (*) to indicate interaction effects.

- In a hierarchical model, higher-order interaction effects imply lower-order interaction and main effects. V1*V2*V3 implies the three-way interaction *V1* by *V2* by *V3*, two-way interactions *V1* by *V2*, *V1* by *V3*, and *V2* by *V3*, and main effects for *V1*, *V2*, and *V3*. The highest-order effects to be estimated are the generating class.

- Any PRINT, PLOT, CRITERIA, METHOD, and MAXORDER subcommands that apply to a DESIGN subcommand must appear before it.

- All variables named on DESIGN must be named or implied on the variable list.

- You can specify more than one DESIGN subcommand. One model is estimated for each DESIGN subcommand.

- If the last subcommand on HILOGLINEAR is not DESIGN, the default model will be estimated in addition to models explicitly requested. SPSS issues a warning message for a missing DESIGN subcommand.

KM

```
KM varname [BY factor varname]

   /STATUS = varname [EVENT](vallist) [LOST(vallist)]

   [/STRATA = varname]

   [/PLOT = {NONE**                          }]
            {[SURVIVAL][LOGSURV][HAZARD][OMS]}

   [/ID  = varname]

   [/PRINT = [TABLE**][MEAN**][NONE]]

   [/PERCENTILE = [(]{25, 50, 75 }[)]]
                     {value list }

   [/TEST = [LOGRANK**][BRESLOW][TARONE]]

   [/COMPARE = [{OVERALL**}][{POOLED**}]]
               {PAIRWISE } {STRATA  }

   [/TREND = [(METRIC)]]

   [/SAVE = tempvar[(newvar)],...]
```

**Default if subcommand or keyword is omitted.

Temporary variables created by Kaplan-Meier are:

SURVIVAL
HAZARD
SE
CUMEVENT

Example:

```
KM LENGTH BY SEXRACE
 /STATUS=EMPLOY  EVENT (1) LOST (2)
 /STRATA=LOCATION.
```

Overview

KM (alias K-M) uses the Kaplan-Meier (product-limit) technique to describe and analyze the length of time to the occurrence of an event, often known as **survival time**. KM is similar to SURVIVAL in that it produces nonparametric estimates of the survival functions. However, instead of dividing the period of time under examination into arbitrary intervals, KM evaluates the survival function at the observed event times. For analysis of survival times with covariates, including time-dependent covariates, see the COXREG command.

Options

KM Tables. You can include one factor variable on the KM command. A KM table is produced for each level of the factor variable. You can also suppress the KM tables in the output with the PRINT subcommand.

Survival Status. You can specify the code(s) indicating that an event has occurred as well as code(s) for cases lost to follow-up using the STATUS subcommand.

Plots. You can plot the survival functions on a linear or log scale or plot the hazard function for each combination of factor and stratum with the PLOT subcommand.

Test Statistics. When a factor variable is specified, you can specify one or more tests of equality of survival distributions for the different levels of the factor using the TEST subcommand. You can also specify a trend metric for the requested tests with the TREND subcommand.

Display ID and Percentiles. You can specify an ID variable on the ID subcommand to identify each case. You can also request display of percentiles in the output with the PERCENTILES subcommand.

Comparisons. When a factor variable is specified, you can use the COMPARE subcommand to compare the different levels of the factor, either pairwise or across all levels, and either pooled across all strata or within a stratum.

Add New Variables to Working Data File. You can save new variables appended to the end of the working data file with the SAVE subcommand.

Basic Specification

- The basic specification requires a survival variable and the STATUS subcommand naming a variable that indicates whether the event occurred.
- The basic specification prints one survival table followed by the mean and median survival time with standard errors and 95% confidence intervals.

Subcommand Order

- The survival variable and the factor variable (if there is one) must be specified first.
- Remaining subcommands can be specified in any order.

Syntax Rules

- Only one survival variable can be specified. To analyze multiple survival variables, use multiple KM commands.
- Only one factor variable can be specified following the BY keyword. If you have multiple factors, use the transformation language to create a single factor variable before invoking KM.

- Only one status variable can be listed on the STATUS subcommand. You must specify the value(s) indicating that the event occurred.

- Only one variable can be specified on the STRATA subcommand. If you have more than one stratum, use the transformation language to create a single variable to specify on the STRATA subcommand.

Operations

- KM deletes all cases that have negative values for the survival variable.

- KM estimates the survival function and associated statistics for each combination of factor and stratum.

- Three statistics can be computed to test the equality of survival functions across factor levels within a stratum or across all factor levels while controlling for strata. The statistics are the log rank (Mantel-Cox), the generalized Wilcoxon (Breslow), and the Tarone-Ware tests.

- When the PLOTS subcommand is specified, KM produces one plot of survival functions for each stratum, with all factor levels represented by different symbols or colors.

Limitations

- Maximum 35 factor levels (symbols) can appear in a plot.

Example

```
KM LENGTH BY SEXRACE
 /STATUS=EMPLOY EVENT (1) LOST (2)
 /STRATA=LOCATION.
```

- Survival analysis is used to examine the length of unemployment. The survival variable *LENGTH* contains the number of months a subject is unemployed. The factor variable *SEXRACE* combines sex and race factors.

- A value of 1 on the variable *EMPLOY* indicates the occurrence of the event (employment). All other observed cases are censored. A value of 2 on *EMPLOY* indicates cases lost to follow-up. Cases with other values for *EMPLOY* are known to have remained unemployed during the course of the study. KM separates the two types of censored cases in the KM table if LOST is specified.

- For each combination of *SEXRACE* and *LOCATION,* one KM table is produced, followed by the mean and median survival time with standard errors and confidence intervals.

Survival and Factor Variables

You must identify the survival and factor variables for the analysis.

- The minimum specification is one, and only one, survival variable.

- Only one factor variable can be specified using the BY keyword. If you have more than one factor, create a new variable combining all factors. There is no limit to the factor levels.

Example

```
DO IF SEX = 1.
+ COMPUTE SEXRACE = RACE.
ELSE.
+ COMPUTE SEXRACE = RACE + SEX.
END IF.
KM LENGTH BY SEXRACE
 /STATUS=EMPLOY EVENT (1) LOST (2).
```

- The two control variables, *SEX* and *RACE*, each with two values, 1 and 2, are combined into one factor variable, *SEXRACE*, with four values, 1 to 4.
- KM specifies *LENGTH* as the survival variable and *SEXRACE* as the factor variable.
- One KM table is produced for each factor level.

STATUS Subcommand

To determine whether the terminal event has occurred for a particular observation, KM checks the value of a status variable. STATUS lists the status variable and the code(s) for the occurrence of the event. The code(s) for cases lost to follow-up can also be specified.

- Only one status variable can be specified. If multiple STATUS subcommands are specified, KM uses the last specification and displays a warning.
- The keyword EVENT is optional, but the value list in parentheses must be specified. Use EVENT for clarity's sake, especially when LOST is specified.
- The value list must be enclosed in parentheses. All cases with non-negative times that do not have a code within the range specified after EVENT are classified as **censored cases**— that is, cases for which the event has not yet occurred.
- The keyword LOST and the following value list are optional. LOST cannot be omitted if the value list for lost cases is specified.
- When LOST is specified, all cases with non-negative times that have a code within the specified value range are classified as lost to follow-up. Cases lost to follow-up are treated as censored in the analysis, and the statistics do not change, but the two types of censored cases are listed separately in the KM table.
- The value lists on EVENT or LOST can be one value, a list of values separated by blanks or commas, a range of values using the keyword THRU, or a combination.
- The status variable can be either numeric or string. If a string variable is specified, the EVENT or LOST values must be enclosed in apostrophes, and the keyword THRU cannot be used.

Example

```
KM LENGTH BY SEXRACE
 /STATUS=EMPLOY  EVENT (1) LOST (3,5 THRU 8).
```

- STATUS specifies that *EMPLOY* is the status variable.
- A value of 1 for *EMPLOY* means that the event (employment) occurred for the case.
- Values of 3 and 5 through 8 for *EMPLOY* mean that contact was lost with the case. The different values code different causes for the loss of contact.
- The summary table in the output includes columns for number lost and percentage lost, as well as for number censored and percentage censored.

STRATA Subcommand

STRATA identifies a **stratification variable**—that is, a variable whose values are used to form subgroups (strata) within the categories of the factor variable. Analysis is done within each level of the strata variable for each factor level, and estimates are pooled over strata for an overall comparison of factor levels.

- The minimum specification is the subcommand keyword with one, and only one, variable name.
- If you have more than one strata variable, create a new variable to combine the levels on separate variables before invoking the KM command.
- There is no limit to the number of levels for the strata variable.

Example

```
KM LENGTH BY SEXRACE
 /STATUS=EMPLOY EVENT (1) LOST (3,5 THRU 8)
 /STRATA=LOCATION.
```

- STRATA specifies *LOCATION* as the stratification variable. Analysis of the length of unemployment is done for each location within each sex and race subgroup.

PLOT Subcommand

PLOT plots the cumulative survival distribution on a linear or logarithmic scale or plots the cumulative hazard function. A separate plot with all factor levels is produced for each stratum. Each factor level is represented by a different symbol or color. Censored cases are indicated by markers.

- When PLOT is omitted, no plots are produced. The default is NONE.
- When PLOT is specified without a keyword, the default is SURVIVAL. A plot of survival functions for each stratum is produced.
- To request specific plots, specify, following the PLOT subcommand, any combination of the keywords defined below.
- Multiple keywords can be used on the PLOT subcommand, each requesting a different plot. The effect is cumulative.

NONE   *Suppress all plots.* NONE is the default if PLOT is omitted.

SURVIVAL   *Plot the cumulative survival distribution on a linear scale.* SURVIVAL is the default when PLOT is specified without a keyword.

LOGSURV   *Plot the cumulative survival distribution on a logarithmic scale.*

HAZARD   *Plot the cumulative hazard function.*

OMS   *Plot the one-minus-survival function.*

Example

```
KM LENGTH BY SEXRACE
 /STATUS=EMPLOY EVENT (1) LOST (3,5 THRU 8)
 /STRATA=LOCATION
 /PLOT = SURVIVAL HAZARD.
```

- PLOT produces one plot of the cumulative survival distribution on a linear scale and one plot of the cumulative hazard rate for each value of *LOCATION*.

ID Subcommand

ID specifies a variable used for labeling cases. If the ID variable is a string, KM uses the string values as case identifiers in the KM table. If the ID variable is numeric, KM uses value labels or numeric values if value labels are not defined.

- ID is the first column of the KM table displayed for each combination of factor and stratum.
- If a string value or a value label exceeds 20 characters in width, KM truncates the case identifier and displays a warning.

PRINT Subcommand

By default, KM prints survival tables and the mean and median survival time with standard errors and confidence intervals if PRINT is omitted. If PRINT is specified, only the specified keyword is in effect. Use PRINT to suppress tables or the mean statistics.

TABLE   *Print the KM tables.* If PRINT is not specified, TABLE, together with MEAN, is the default. Specify TABLE on PRINT to suppress the mean statistics.

MEAN   *Print the mean statistics.* KM prints the mean and median survival time with standard errors and confidence intervals. If PRINT is not specified, MEAN, together with TABLE, is the default. Specify MEAN on PRINT to suppress the KM tables.

NONE   *Suppress both the KM tables and the mean statistics.* Only plots and comparisons are printed.

Example

```
KM LENGTH BY SEXRACE
 /STATUS=EMPLOY EVENT (1) LOST (3,5 THRU 8)
 /STRATA=LOCATION
 /PLOT=SURVIVAL HAZARD
 /PRINT=NONE.
```

- PRINT=NONE suppresses both the KM tables and the mean statistics.

PERCENTILES Subcommand

PERCENTILES displays percentiles for each combination of factor and stratum. Percentiles are not displayed without the PERCENTILES subcommand. If the subcommand is specified without a value list, the default is 25, 50, and 75 for quartile display. You can specify any values between 0 and 100.

TEST Subcommand

TEST specifies the test statistic to use for testing the equality of survival distributions for the different levels of the factor.

- TEST is valid only when a factor variable is specified. If no factor variable is specified, KM issues a warning and TEST is not executed.
- If TEST is specified without a keyword, the default is LOGRANK. If a keyword is specified on TEST, only the specified test is performed.
- Each of the test statistics has a chi-square distribution with one degree of freedom.

LOGRANK   *Perform the log rank (Mantel-Cox) test.*

BRESLOW   *Perform the Breslow (generalized Wilcoxon) test.*

TARONE   *Perform the Tarone-Ware test.*

COMPARE Subcommand

COMPARE compares the survival distributions for the different levels of the factor. Each of the keywords specifies a different method of comparison.

- COMPARE is valid only when a factor variable is specified. If no factor variable is specified, KM issues a warning and COMPARE is not executed.
- COMPARE uses whatever tests are specified on the TEST subcommand. If no TEST subcommand is specified, the log rank test is used.
- If COMPARE is not specified, the default is OVERALL and POOLED. All factor levels are compared across strata in a single test. The test statistics are displayed after the summary table at the end of output.
- Multiple COMPARE subcommands can be specified to request different comparisons.

OVERALL   *Compare all factor levels in a single test.* OVERALL, together with POOLED, is the default when COMPARE is not specified.

PAIRWISE   *Compare each pair of factor levels.* KM compares all distinct pairs of factor levels.

POOLED   *Pool the test statistics across all strata.* The test statistics are displayed after the summary table for all strata. POOLED, together with OVERALL, is the default when COMPARE is not specified.

STRATA   *Compare the factor levels for each stratum.* The test statistics are displayed for each stratum separately.

- If a factor variable has different levels across strata, you cannot request a pooled comparison. If you specify POOLED on COMPARE, KM displays a warning and ignores the request.

Example

```
KM LENGTH BY SEXRACE
 /STATUS=EMPLOY EVENT (1) LOST (3,5 THRU 8)
 /STRATA=LOCATION
 /TEST = BRESLOW
 /COMPARE = PAIRWISE.
```

- TEST specifies the Breslow test.
- COMPARE uses the Breslow test statistic to compare all distinct pairs of *SEXRACE* values and pools the test results over all strata defined by *LOCATION*.
- Test statistics are displayed at the end of output for all strata.

TREND Subcommand

TREND specifies that there is a trend across factor levels. This information is used when computing the tests for equality of survival functions specified on the TEST subcommand.

- The minimum specification is the subcommand keyword by itself. The default metric is chosen as follows:

  if *g* is even,

  $$(-(g-1), ..., -3, -1, 1, 3, ..., (g-1))$$

  otherwise,

  $$\left(-\frac{(g-1)}{2}, ..., -1, 0, 1, ..., \frac{(g-1)}{2}\right)$$

  where *g* is the number of levels for the factor variable.

- If TREND is specified but COMPARE is not, KM performs the default log rank test with the trend metric for an OVERALL POOLED comparison.
- If the metric specified on TREND is longer than required by the factor levels, KM displays a warning and ignores extra values.

Example

```
KM LENGTH BY SEXRACE
 /STATUS=EMPLOY EVENT (1) LOST (3,5 THRU 8)
 /STRATA=LOCATION
 /TREND.
```

- TREND is specified by itself. KM uses the default metric. Since *SEXRACE* has four levels, the default is (–3,–1, 1, 3).
- Even though no TEST or COMPARE subcommand is specified, KM performs the default log rank test with the trend metric and does a default OVERALL POOLED comparison.

SAVE Subcommand

SAVE saves the temporary variables created by KM. The following temporary variables can be saved:

SURVIVAL *Survival function evaluated at current case.*

SE *Standard error of the survival function.*

HAZARD *Cumulative hazard function evaluated at current case.*

CUMEVENT *Cumulative number of events.*

- To specify variable names for the new variables, assign the new names in parentheses following each temporary variable name.

- Assigned variable names must be unique in the working data file. Scratch or system variable names cannot be used (that is, variable names cannot begin with # or $).

- If new variable names are not specified, KM generates default names. The default name is composed of the first three characters of the name of the temporary variable (two for *SE*), followed by an underscore and a number to make it unique.

- A temporary variable can be saved only once on the same SAVE subcommand.

Example

```
KM LENGTH BY SEXRACE
 /STATUS=EMPLOY EVENT (1) LOST (3,5 THRU 8)
 /STRATA=LOCATION
 /SAVE SURVIVAL HAZARD.
```

- KM saves cumulative survival and cumulative hazard rates in two new variables, *SUR_1* and *HAZ_1*, provided that neither name exists in the working data file. If one does, the numeric suffixes will be incremented to make a distinction.

LOGLINEAR

The syntax for **LOGLINEAR** is available only in a syntax window, not from the dialog box interface. See GENLOG for information on the **LOGLINEAR** command available from the dialog box interface.

```
LOGLINEAR varlist(min,max)...[BY] varlist(min,max)

        [WITH covariate varlist]

 [/CWEIGHT={varname }] [/CWEIGHT=(matrix)...]
          {(matrix)}

 [/GRESID={varlist }]  [/GRESID=(matrix)...]
          {(matrix)}

 [/CONTRAST (varname)={DEVIATION [(refcat)]      } [/CONTRAST...]]
                      {DIFFERENCE              }
                      {HELMERT                 }
                      {SIMPLE [(refcat)]       }
                      {REPEATED                }
                      {POLYNOMIAL [({1,2,3,...})]}
                      {           {metric  }  }
                      {[BASIS] SPECIAL(matrix) }

 [/CRITERIA=[CONVERGE({0.001**})] [ITERATE({20**})] [DELTA({0.5**})]
                     {n       }            {n  }          {n     }
            [DEFAULT]]

 [/PRINT={[FREQ**][RESID**][DESIGN][ESTIM][COR]}]
         {DEFAULT                              }
         {ALL                                  }
         {NONE                                 }

 [/PLOT={NONE**  }]
        {DEFAULT }
        {RESID   }
        {NORMPROB}

 [/MISSING=[{EXCLUDE**}]]
           {INCLUDE  }

 [/DESIGN=effect[(n)] effect[(n)]... effect BY effect...] [/DESIGN...]
```

**Default if subcommand or keyword is omitted.

Example:

```
LOGLINEAR JOBSAT (1,2) ZODIAC (1,12) /DESIGN=JOBSAT.
```

Overview

LOGLINEAR is a general procedure for model fitting, hypothesis testing, and parameter estimation for any model that has categorical variables as its major components. As such, LOGLINEAR subsumes a variety of related techniques, including general models of multiway contingency tables, logit models, logistic regression on categorical variables, and quasi-independence models.

LOGLINEAR models cell frequencies using the multinomial response model and produces maximum likelihood estimates of parameters by means of the Newton-Raphson algorithm (Haberman, 1978). HILOGLINEAR, which uses an iterative proportional-fitting algorithm, is more efficient for hierarchical models, but it cannot produce parameter estimates for unsaturated models, does not permit specification of contrasts for parameters, and does not display a correlation matrix of the parameter estimates.

Comparison of the GENLOG and LOGLINEAR Commands

The General Loglinear Analysis and Logit Loglinear Analysis dialog boxes are both associated with the GENLOG command. In previous releases of SPSS, these dialog boxes were associated with the LOGLINEAR command. The LOGLINEAR command is now available only as a syntax command. The differences are described below.

Distribution assumptions

- GENLOG can handle both Poisson and multinomial distribution assumptions for observed cell counts.

- LOGLINEAR assumes only multinomial distribution.

Approach

- GENLOG uses a regression approach to parameterize a categorical variable in a design matrix.

- LOGLINEAR uses contrasts to reparameterize a categorical variable. The major disadvantage of the reparameterization approach is in the interpretation of the results when there is a redundancy in the corresponding design matrix. Also, the reparameterization approach may result in incorrect degrees of freedom for an incomplete table, leading to incorrect analysis results.

Contrasts and generalized log-odds ratios (GLOR)

- GENLOG doesn't provide contrasts to reparameterize the categories of a factor. However, it offers generalized log-odds ratios (GLOR) for cell combinations. Often, comparisons among categories of factors can be derived from GLOR.

- LOGLINEAR offers contrasts to reparameterize the categories of a factor.

Deviance residual

- GENLOG calculates and displays the deviance residual and its normal probability plot, in addition to the other residuals.

- LOGLINEAR does not calculate the deviance residual.

Factor-by-covariate design

- When there is a factor-by-covariate term in the design, GENLOG generates one regression coefficient of the covariate for each combination of factor values. The estimates of these regression coefficients are calculated and displayed.

- LOGLINEAR estimates and displays the contrasts of these regression coefficients.

Partition effect

- In GENLOG, the term *partition effect* refers to the category of a factor.

- In LOGLINEAR, the term *partition effect* refers to a particular contrast.

Options

Model Specification. You can specify the model or models to be fit using the DESIGN subcommand.

Cell Weights. You can specify cell weights, such as structural zeros, for the model with the CWEIGHT subcommand.

Output Display. You can control the output display with the PRINT subcommand.

Optional Plots. You can produce plots of adjusted residuals against observed and expected counts, normal plots, and detrended normal plots with the PLOT subcommand.

Linear Combinations. You can calculate linear combinations of observed cell frequencies, expected cell frequencies, and adjusted residuals using the GRESID subcommand.

Contrasts. You can indicate the type of contrast desired for a factor using the CONTRAST subcommand.

Criteria for Algorithm. You can control the values of algorithm-tuning parameters with the CRITERIA subcommand.

Basic Specification

The basic specification is two or more variables that define the crosstabulation. The minimum and maximum values for each variable must be specified in parentheses after the variable name.

By default, LOGLINEAR estimates the saturated model for a multidimensional table. Output includes the factors or effects, their levels, and any labels; observed and expected frequencies and percentages for each factor and code; residuals, standardized residuals, and adjusted residuals; two goodness-of-fit statistics (the likelihood-ratio chi-square and Pearson's chi-square); and estimates of the parameters with accompanying z values and 95% confidence intervals.

Limitations

- Maximum 10 independent (factor) variables.

- Maximum 200 covariates.

Subcommand Order

- The variables specification must come first.

- The subcommands that affect a specific model must be placed before the DESIGN subcommand specifying the model.

- All subcommands can be used more than once and, with the exception of the DESIGN subcommand, are carried from model to model unless explicitly overridden.
- If the last subcommand is not DESIGN, LOGLINEAR generates a saturated model in addition to the explicitly requested model(s).

Example

```
LOGLINEAR JOBSAT (1,2) ZODIAC (1,12) /DESIGN=JOBSAT, ZODIAC.
```

- The variable list specifies two categorical variables, *JOBSAT* and *ZODIAC*. *JOBSAT* has values 1 and 2. *ZODIAC* has values 1 through 12.
- DESIGN specifies a model with main effects only.

Example

```
LOGLINEAR DPREF (2,3) RACE CAMP (1,2).
```

- *DPREF* is a categorical variable with values 2 and 3. *RACE* and *CAMP* are categorical variables with values 1 and 2.
- This is a general loglinear model because no BY keyword appears. The design defaults to a saturated model that includes all main effects and interaction effects.

Example

```
LOGLINEAR GSLEVEL (4,8) EDUC (1,4) SEX (1,2)
   /DESIGN=GSLEVEL EDUC SEX.
```

- *GSLEVEL* is a categorical variable with values 4 through 8. *EDUC* is a categorical variable with values 1 through 4. *SEX* has values 1 and 2.
- DESIGN specifies a model with main effects only.

Example

```
LOGLINEAR GSLEVEL (4,8) BY EDUC (1,4) SEX (1,2)
   /DESIGN=GSLEVEL, GSLEVEL BY EDUC, GSLEVEL BY SEX.
```

- The keyword BY on the variable list specifies a logit model in which *GSLEVEL* is the dependent variable and *EDUC* and *SEX* are the independent variables.
- DESIGN specifies a model that can test for the absence of joint effect of *SEX* and *EDUC* on *GSLEVEL*.

Variable List

The variable list specifies the variables to be included in the model. LOGLINEAR analyzes two classes of variables: categorical and continuous. Categorical variables are used to define the cells of the table. Continuous variables are used as cell covariates. Continuous variables can be specified only after the keyword WITH following the list of categorical variables.

- The list of categorical variables must be specified first. Categorical variables must be numeric and integer.

- A range must be defined for each categorical variable by specifying, in parentheses after each variable name, the minimum and maximum values for that variable. Separate the two values with at least one space or a comma.

- To specify the same range for a list of variables, specify the list of variables followed by a single range. The range applies to all variables on the list.

- To specify a logit model, use the keyword BY (see "Logit Model" below). A variable list without the keyword BY generates a general loglinear model.

- Cases with values outside the specified range are excluded from the analysis. Non-integer values within the range are truncated for the purpose of building the table.

Logit Model

- To segregate the independent (factor) variables from the dependent variables in a logit model, use the keyword BY. The categorical variables preceding BY are the dependent variables; the categorical variables following BY are the independent variables.

- A total of 10 categorical variables can be specified. In most cases, one of them is dependent.

- A DESIGN subcommand should be used to request the desired logit model.

- LOGLINEAR displays an analysis of dispersion and two measures of association: entropy and concentration. These measures are discussed in Haberman (1982) and can be used to quantify the magnitude of association among the variables. Both are proportional reduction in error measures. The entropy statistic is analogous to Theil's entropy measure, while the concentration statistic is analogous to Goodman and Kruskal's tau-*b*. Both statistics measure the strength of association between the dependent variable and the predictor variable set.

Cell Covariates

- Continuous variables can be used as covariates. When used, the covariates must be specified after the keyword WITH following the list of categorical variables. Ranges are not specified for the continuous variables.

- A variable cannot be named as both a categorical variable and a cell covariate.

- To enter cell covariates into a model, the covariates must be specified on the DESIGN sub-command.
- Cell covariates are not applied on a case-by-case basis. The mean covariate value for a cell in the contingency table is applied to that cell.

Example

```
LOGLINEAR DPREF(2,3) RACE CAMP (1,2) WITH CONSTANT
 /DESIGN=DPREF RACE CAMP CONSTANT.
```

- Variable *CONSTANT* is a continuous variable specified as a cell covariate. Cell covariates must be specified after the keyword WITH following the variable list. No range is defined for cell covariates.
- To include the cell covariate in the model, variable *CONSTANT* is specified on DESIGN.

CWEIGHT Subcommand

CWEIGHT specifies cell weights, such as structural zeros, for a model. By default, cell weights are equal to 1.

- The specification is either one numeric variable or a matrix of weights enclosed in parentheses.
- If a matrix of weights is specified, the matrix must contain the same number of elements as the product of the levels of the categorical variables. An asterisk can be used to signify repetitions of the same value.
- If weights are specified for a multiple-factor model, the index value of the rightmost factor increments the most rapidly.
- If a numeric variable is specified, only one CWEIGHT subcommand can be used on LOGLINEAR.
- To use multiple cell weights on the same LOGLINEAR command, specify all weights in matrix format. Each matrix must be specified on a separate CWEIGHT subcommand, and each CWEIGHT specification remains in effect until explicitly overridden by another CWEIGHT subcommand.
- CWEIGHT can be used to impose structural, or *a priori*, zeros on the model. This feature is useful in the analysis of symmetric tables.

Example

```
COMPUTE  CWT=1.
IF (HUSED EQ WIFED) CWT=0.
LOGLINEAR HUSED WIFED(1,4) WITH DISTANCE
  /CWEIGHT=CWT
  /DESIGN=HUSED WIFED DISTANCE.
```

- COMPUTE initially assigns *CWT* the value 1 for all cases.
- IF assigns *CWT* the value 0 when *HUSED* equals *WIFED*.

- CWEIGHT imposes structural zeros on the diagonal of the symmetric crosstabulation. Because a variable name is specified, only one CWEIGHT can be used.

Example

```
LOGLINEAR  HUSED WIFED(1,4) WITH DISTANCE
 /CWEIGHT=(0, 4*1, 0, 4*1, 0, 4*1, 0)
 /DESIGN=HUSED WIFED DISTANCE
 /CWEIGHT=(16*1)
 /DESIGN=HUSED WIFED DISTANCE.
```

- The first CWEIGHT matrix specifies the same values as variable *CWT* provided in the first example. The specified matrix is as follows:

```
0 1 1 1
1 0 1 1
1 1 0 1
1 1 1 0
```

- The same matrix can be specified in full as (0 1 1 1 1 0 1 1 1 1 0 1 1 1 1 0).

- By using the matrix format on CWEIGHT rather than a variable name, a different CWEIGHT subcommand can be used for the second model.

GRESID Subcommand

GRESID (Generalized Residual) calculates linear combinations of observed cell frequencies, expected cell frequencies, and adjusted residuals.

- The specification is either a numeric variable or a matrix whose contents are coefficients of the desired linear combinations.

- If a matrix of coefficients is specified, the matrix must contain the same number of elements as the number of cells implied by the variables specification. An asterisk can be used to signify repetitions of the same value.

- Each GRESID subcommand specifies a single linear combination. Each matrix or variable must be specified on a separate GRESID subcommand. All GRESID subcommands specified are displayed for each design.

Example

```
LOGLINEAR  MONTH(1,18) WITH Z
 /GRESID=(6*1,12*0)
 /GRESID=(6*0,6*1,6*0)
 /GRESID=(12*0,6*1)
 /DESIGN=Z.
```

- The first GRESID subcommand combines the first six months into a single effect. The second GRESID subcommand combines the second six months, and the third GRESID subcommand combines the last six months.

- For each effect, LOGLINEAR displays the observed and expected counts, the residual, and the adjusted residual.

CONTRAST Subcommand

CONTRAST indicates the type of contrast desired for a factor, where a factor is any categorical dependent or independent variable. The default contrast is DEVIATION for each factor.

- The specification is CONTRAST, which is followed by a variable name in parentheses and the contrast-type keyword.

- To specify a contrast for more than one factor, use a separate CONTRAST subcommand for each specified factor. Only one contrast can be in effect for each factor on each DESIGN.

- A contrast specification remains in effect for subsequent designs until explicitly overridden by another CONTRAST subcommand.

- The design matrix used for the contrasts can be displayed by specifying keyword DESIGN on the PRINT subcommand. However, this matrix is the basis matrix that is used to determine contrasts; it is not the contrast matrix itself.

- CONTRAST can be used for a multinomial logit model, in which the dependent variable has more than two categories.

- CONTRAST can be used for fitting linear logit models. The keyword BASIS is not appropriate for such models.

- In a logit model, CONTRAST is used to transform the independent variable into a metric variable. Again, the keyword BASIS is not appropriate.

The following contrast types are available. For illustration of contrast types, see the appendix.

DEVIATION(refcat)   *Deviations from the overall effect.* DEVIATION is the default contrast if the CONTRAST subcommand is not used. Refcat is the category for which parameter estimates are not displayed (they are the negative of the sum of the others). By default, refcat is the last category of the variable.

DIFFERENCE   *Levels of a factor with the average effect of previous levels of a factor.* Also known as reverse Helmert contrasts.

HELMERT   *Levels of a factor with the average effect of subsequent levels of a factor.*

SIMPLE(refcat)   *Each level of a factor to the reference level.* By default, LOGLINEAR uses the last category of the factor variable as the reference category. Optionally, any level can be specified as the reference category enclosed in parentheses after the keyword SIMPLE. The sequence of the level, not the actual value, must be specified.

REPEATED   *Adjacent comparisons across levels of a factor.*

POLYNOMIAL(metric)   *Orthogonal polynomial contrasts.* The default is equal spacing. Optionally, the coefficients of the linear polynomial can be specified in parentheses, indicating the spacing between levels of the treatment measured by the given factor.

[BASIS]SPECIAL(matrix) *User-defined contrast.* As many elements as the number of categories squared must be specified. If BASIS is specified before SPECIAL, a basis matrix is generated for the special contrast, which makes the coefficients of the contrast equal to the special matrix. Otherwise, the matrix specified is transposed and then used as the basis matrix to determine coefficients for the contrast matrix.

Example

```
LOGLINEAR  A(1,4) BY B(1,4)
 /CONTRAST(B)=POLYNOMIAL
 /DESIGN=A A BY B(1)
 /CONTRAST(B)=SIMPLE
 /DESIGN=A A BY B(1).
```

- The first CONTRAST subcommand requests polynomial contrasts of *B* for the first design.

- The second CONTRAST subcommand requests the simple contrast of *B*, with the last category (value 4) used as the reference category for the second DESIGN subcommand.

Example

```
* Multinomial logit model

LOGLINEAR  PREF(1,5) BY RACE ORIGIN CAMP(1,2)
  /CONTRAST(PREF)=SPECIAL(5*1, 1 1 1 1 -4, 3 -1 -1 -1 0,
      0 1 1 -2 0, 0 1 -1 0 0).
```

- LOGLINEAR builds special contrasts among the five categories of the dependent variable *PREF*, which measures preference for training camps among Army recruits. For *PREF*, 1=stay, 2=move to north, 3=move to south, 4=move to unnamed camp, and 5=undecided.

- The four contrasts are: (1) move or stay versus undecided, (2) stay versus move, (3) named camp versus unnamed, and (4) northern camp versus southern. Because these contrasts are orthogonal, SPECIAL and BASIS SPECIAL produce equivalent results.

Example

```
* Contrasts for a linear logit model

LOGLINEAR RESPONSE(1,2) BY YEAR(0,20)
 /PRINT=DEFAULT ESTIM
 /CONTRAST(YEAR)=SPECIAL(21*1, -10, -9, -8, -7, -6, -5, -4,
                        -3, -2, -1, 0, 1, 2, 3, 4, 5, 6, 7,
                        8, 9, 10, 399*1)
 /DESIGN=RESPONSE RESPONSE BY YEAR(1).
```

- *YEAR* measures years of education and ranges from 0 through 20. Therefore, allowing for the constant effect, *YEAR* has 20 estimable parameters associated with it.

- The SPECIAL contrast specifies the constant—that is, 21*1—and the linear effect of *YEAR*—that is, –10 to 10. The other 399 1's fill out the 21*21 matrix.

Example

```
* Contrasts for a logistic regression model

LOGLINEAR RESPONSE(1,2) BY TIME(1,4)
  /CONTRAST(TIME) = SPECIAL(4*1, 7 14 27 51, 8*1)
  /PRINT=ALL /PLOT=DEFAULT
  /DESIGN=RESPONSE, TIME(1) BY RESPONSE.
```

- CONTRAST is used to transform the independent variable into a metric variable.

- *TIME* represents elapsed time in days. Therefore, the weights in the contrast represent the metric of the passage of time.

CRITERIA Subcommand

CRITERIA specifies the values of some constants in the Newton-Raphson algorithm. Defaults or specifications remain in effect until overridden with another CRITERIA subcommand.

CONVERGE(n)   *Convergence criterion.* Specify a value for the convergence criterion. The default is 0.001.

ITERATE(n)   *Maximum number of iterations.* Specify the maximum number of iterations for the algorithm. The default number is 20.

DELTA(n)   *Cell delta value.* The value of delta is added to each cell frequency for the first iteration. For saturated models, it remains in the cell. The default value is 0.5. LOGLINEAR does not display parameter estimates or correlation matrices of parameter estimates if any sampling zero cells exist in the expected table after delta is added. Parameter estimates and correlation matrices can be displayed in the presence of structural zeros.

DEFAULT   *Default values are used.* DEFAULT can be used to reset the parameters to the default.

Example

```
LOGLINEAR  DPREF(2,3) BY RACE ORIGIN CAMP(1,2)
 /CRITERIA=ITERATION(50) CONVERGE(.0001).
```

- ITERATION increases the maximum number of iterations to 50.

- CONVERGE lowers the convergence criterion to 0.0001.

PRINT Subcommand

PRINT requests statistics that are not produced by default.

- By default, LOGLINEAR displays the frequency table and residuals. The parameter estimates of the model are also displayed if DESIGN is not used.

- Multiple PRINT subcommands are permitted. The specifications are cumulative.

The following keywords can be used on PRINT:

FREQ   *Observed and expected cell frequencies and percentages.* This is displayed by default.

RESID   *Raw, standardized, and adjusted residuals.* This is displayed by default.

DESIGN   *The design matrix of the model, showing the basis matrix corresponding to the contrasts used.*

ESTIM   *The parameter estimates of the model.* If you do not specify a design on the DESIGN subcommand, LOGLINEAR generates a saturated model and displays the parameter estimates for the saturated model. LOGLINEAR does not display parameter estimates or correlation matrices of parameter estimates if any sampling zero cells exist in the expected table after delta is added. Parameter estimates and a correlation matrix are displayed when structural zeros are present.

COR   *The correlation matrix of the parameter estimates.* Alias COV.

ALL   *All available output.*

DEFAULT   *FREQ and RESID.* ESTIM is also displayed by default if the DESIGN subcommand is not used.

NONE   *The design information and goodness-of-fit statistics only.* This option overrides all other specifications on the PRINT subcommand. The NONE option applies only to the PRINT subcommand.

Example

```
LOGLINEAR A(1,2) B(1,2)
 /PRINT=ESTIM
 /DESIGN=A,B,A BY B
 /PRINT=ALL
 /DESIGN=A,B.
```

- The first design is the saturated model. The parameter estimates are displayed with ESTIM specified on PRINT.

- The second design is the main-effects model, which tests the hypothesis of no interaction. The second PRINT subcommand displays all available display output for this model.

PLOT Subcommand

PLOT produces optional plots. No plots are displayed if PLOT is not specified or is specified without any keyword. Multiple PLOT subcommands can be used. The specifications are cumulative.

RESID   *Plots of adjusted residuals against observed and expected counts.*

NORMPROB   *Normal and detrended normal plots of the adjusted residuals.*

NONE   *No plots.*

DEFAULT   *RESID and NORMPROB.* Alias ALL.

Example

```
LOGLINEAR  RESPONSE(1,2) BY TIME(1,4)
 /CONTRAST(TIME)=SPECIAL(4*1, 7 14 27 51, 8*1)
 /PLOT=DEFAULT
 /DESIGN=RESPONSE TIME(1) BY RESPONSE
 /PLOT=NONE
 /DESIGN.
```

- RESID and NORMPROB plots are displayed for the first design.

- No plots are displayed for the second design.

MISSING Subcommand

MISSING controls missing values. By default, LOGLINEAR excludes all cases with system- or user-missing values on any variable. You can specify INCLUDE to include user-missing values. If INCLUDE is specified, user-missing values must also be included in the value range specification.

EXCLUDE *Delete cases with user-missing values.* This is the default if the subcommand is omitted. You can also specify the keyword DEFAULT.

INCLUDE *Include user-missing values.* Only cases with system-missing values are deleted.

Example

```
MISSING VALUES A(0).
LOGLINEAR A(0,2) B(1,2) /MISSING=INCLUDE
 /DESIGN=B.
```

- Even though 0 was specified as missing, it is treated as a nonmissing category of *A* in this analysis.

DESIGN Subcommand

DESIGN specifies the model or models to be fit. If DESIGN is omitted or used with no specifications, the saturated model is produced. The saturated model fits all main effects and all interaction effects.

- To specify more than one model, use more than one DESIGN subcommand. Each DESIGN specifies one model.

- To obtain main-effects models, name all the variables listed on the variables specification.

- To obtain interactions, use the keyword BY to specify each interaction, as in A BY B and C BY D. To obtain the single-degree-of-freedom partition of a specified contrast, specify the partition in parentheses following the factor (see the example below).

- To include cell covariates in the model, first identify them on the variable list by naming them after the keyword WITH, and then specify the variable names on DESIGN.

- To specify an equiprobability model, name a cell covariate that is actually a constant of 1.

Example

```
* Testing the linear effect of the dependent variable

COMPUTE X=MONTH.
LOGLINEAR MONTH (1,12) WITH X
  /DESIGN X.
```

- The variable specification identifies *MONTH* as a categorical variable with values 1 through 12. The keyword WITH identifies *X* as a covariate.

- DESIGN tests the linear effect of *MONTH*.

Example

```
* Specifying main effects models

LOGLINEAR A(1,4) B(1,5)
  /DESIGN=A
  /DESIGN=A,B.
```

- The first design tests the homogeneity of category probabilities for *B*; it fits the marginal frequencies on *A*, but assumes that membership in any of the categories of *B* is equiprobable.

- The second design tests the independence of *A* and *B*. It fits the marginals on both *A* and *B*.

Example

```
* Specifying interactions

LOGLINEAR A(1,4) B(1,5) C(1,3)
  /DESIGN=A,B,C, A BY B.
```

- This design consists of the *A* main effect, the *B* main effect, the *C* main effect, and the interaction of *A* and *B*.

Example

```
* Single-degree-of-freedom partitions

LOGLINEAR A(1,4) BY B(1,5)
  /CONTRAST(B)=POLYNOMIAL
  /DESIGN=A,A BY B(1).
```

- The value 1 following *B* refers to the first partition of *B*, which is the linear effect of *B*; this follows from the contrast specified on the CONTRAST subcommand.

Example

```
* Specifying cell covariates

LOGLINEAR HUSED WIFED(1,4) WITH DISTANCE
   /DESIGN=HUSED WIFED DISTANCE.
```

- The continuous variable *DISTANCE* is identified as a cell covariate by specifying it after WITH on the variable list. The cell covariate is then included in the model by naming it on DESIGN.

Example

```
* Equiprobability model

COMPUTE  X=1.
LOGLINEAR  MONTH(1,18) WITH X
   /DESIGN=X.
```

- This model tests whether the frequencies in the 18-cell table are equal by using a cell covariate that is a constant of 1.

MANOVA: Overview

```
MANOVA dependent varlist [BY factor list (min,max)[factor list...]
                         [WITH covariate list]]

[/WSFACTORS=varname (levels) [varname...] ]

[/WSDESIGN]*

[/TRANSFORM [(dependent varlist [/dependent varlist])]=
                   [ORTHONORM] [{CONTRAST}] {DEVIATION (refcat)   } ]
                              {BASIS   }  {DIFFERENCE          }
                                          {HELMERT             }
                                          {SIMPLE (refcat)     }
                                          {REPEATED            }
                                          {POLYNOMIAL [({1,2,3...})]}
                                          {          {metric }  }
                                          {SPECIAL (matrix)    }

[/MEASURE=newname newname...]

[/RENAME={newname} {newname}...]
         {*      } {*       }

[/ERROR={WITHIN          } ]
        {RESIDUAL        }
        {WITHIN + RESIDUAL}
        {n               }

[/CONTRAST (factorname)={DEVIATION** [(refcat)]   }] †
                       {POLYNOMIAL**[({1,2,3...})]}]
                       {          {metric }  }
                       {SIMPLE [(refcat)]        }
                       {DIFFERENCE               }
                       {HELMERT                  }
                       {REPEATED                 }
                       {SPECIAL (matrix)         }

[/PARTITION (factorname)[=({1,1...  })]]]
                          {n1,n2...}

[/METHOD=[{UNIQUE**  }]  [{CONSTANT**}]  [{QR**    }]]
         {SEQUENTIAL}    {NOCONSTANT}   {CHOLESKY}

[/{PRINT  }= [CELLINFO [([MEANS] [SSCP] [COV] [COR] [ALL])]]
   {NOPRINT}  [HOMOGENEITY [(([ALL] [BARTLETT] [COCHRAN] [BOXM])]]]
              [DESIGN [([OVERALL] [ONEWAY] [DECOMP] [BIAS] [SOLUTION]
                       [REDUNDANCY] [COLLINEARITY] [ALL])]]
              [PARAMETERS [([ESTIM] [ORTHO][COR][NEGSUM][EFSIZE][OPTIMAL][ALL])]]
              [SIGNIF [[(SINGLEDF)]
                      [(MULTIV**)] [(EIGEN)] [(DIMENR)]
                      [(UNIV**)] [(HYPOTH)][(STEPDOWN)] [(BRIEF)]
                      [{(AVERF**)}] [(HF)] [(GG)] [(EFSIZE)]]
                      {(AVONLY) }
              [ERROR[(STDDEV)][(COR)][(COV)][(SSCP)]]

[/OMEANS =[VARIABLES(varlist)] [TABLES ({factor name    }] ]
                                       {factor BY factor}
                                       {CONSTANT        }

[/PMEANS =[VARIABLES(varlist)] [TABLES ({factor name    })] [PLOT]] ]
                                       {factor BY factor}
                                       {CONSTANT        }

[/RESIDUALS=[CASEWISE] [PLOT] ]

[/POWER=[T({.05**})] [F({.05**})] [{APPROXIMATE}]]
           {a    }     {a    }    {EXACT      }
```

```
[/CINTERVAL=[{INDIVIDUAL}][({.95}) ]
             {JOINT    }  {a  }
             [UNIVARIATE ({SCHEFFE})]
                         {BONFER }
             [MULTIVARIATE  ({ROY      })]  ]
                            {PILLAI   }
                            {BONFER   }
                            {HOTELLING}
                            {WILKS    }
[/PCOMPS [COR] [COV] [ROTATE(rottype)]
         [NCOMP(n)] [MINEIGEN(eigencut)] [ALL] ]

[/PLOT=[BOXPLOTS] [CELLPLOTS] [NORMAL]  [ALL] ]

[/DISCRIM [RAW] [STAN] [ESTIM] [COR] [ALL]
          [ROTATE(rottype)] [ALPHA({.25**})]]
                                   {a    }

[/MISSING=[LISTWISE**] [{EXCLUDE**}] ]
                        {INCLUDE  }

[/MATRIX=[IN({file})]  [OUT({file})]]
            {[*] }         {[*] }

[/ANALYSIS [({UNCONDITIONAL**})]=[()dependent varlist
             {CONDITIONAL    }      [WITH covariate varlist]
                                      [/dependent varlist...][)][WITH varlist] ]

[/DESIGN={factor [(n)]  }[BY factor[(n)]] [WITHIN factor[(n)]][WITHIN...]
         {[POOL(varlist)}

         [+ {factor [(n)] }...]
            {POOL(varlist)}

         [[= n] {AGAINST} {WITHIN  }
                {VS     } {RESIDUAL}
                          {WR      }
                          {n       }

         [{factor [(n)] } ... ]
          {POOL(varlist)}

         [MWITHIN factor(n)]
         [MUPLUS]
         [CONSTANT [=n] ]
```

* WSDESIGN uses the same specification as DESIGN, with only within-subjects factors.

† DEVIATION is the default for between-subjects factors, while POLYNOMIAL is the default for within-subjects factors.

** Default if subcommand or keyword is omitted.

Example 1:

```
* Analysis of Variance

MANOVA RESULT BY TREATMNT(1,4) GROUP(1,2).
```

Example 2:

```
* Analysis of Covariance

MANOVA RESULT BY TREATMNT(1,4) GROUP(1,2) WITH RAINFALL.
```

Example 3:

```
* Repeated Measures Analysis

MANOVA SCORE1 TO SCORE4 BY CLASS(1,2)
  /WSFACTORS=MONTH(4).
```

Example 4:

```
* Parallelism Test with Crossed Factors

MANOVA YIELD BY PLOT(1,4) TYPEFERT(1,3) WITH FERT
  /ANALYSIS YIELD
  /DESIGN FERT, PLOT, TYPEFERT, PLOT BY TYPEFERT,
  FERT BY PLOT + FERT BY TYPEFERT
  + FERT BY PLOT BY TYPEFERT.
```

Overview

MANOVA (multivariate analysis of variance) is a generalized procedure for analysis of variance and covariance. MANOVA is a powerful analysis-of-variance procedure and can be used for both univariate and multivariate designs. MANOVA allows you to perform the following tasks:

- Specify nesting of effects.
- Specify individual error terms for effects in mixed-model analyses.
- Estimate covariate-by-factor interactions to test the assumption of homogeneity of regressions.
- Obtain parameter estimates for a variety of contrast types, including irregularly spaced polynomial contrasts with multiple factors.
- Test user-specified special contrasts with multiple factors.
- Partition effects in models.
- Pool effects in models.

MANOVA and General Linear Model (GLM)

MANOVA is available only in syntax. GLM (general linear model), the other generalized procedure for analysis of variance and covariance in SPSS, is available both in syntax and via the dialog boxes. The major distinction between GLM and MANOVA in terms of statistical design and functionality is that GLM uses a non-full-rank, or overparameterized, indicator variable approach to parameterization of linear models instead of the full-rank reparameterization approach used in MANOVA. The generalized inverse approach and the aliasing of redundant parameters to zero used by GLM allow greater flexibility in handling a variety of data situations, particularly those involving empty cells. For features provided by GLM but unavailable in MANOVA, refer to "General Linear Model (GLM) and MANOVA" on p. 314.

To simplify the presentation, reference material on MANOVA is divided into three sections: *univariate* designs with one dependent variable; *multivariate* designs with several interrelated dependent variables; and *repeated measures* designs in which the dependent variables represent the same types of measurements taken at more than one time.

The full syntax diagram for MANOVA is presented here. The MANOVA sections that follow include partial syntax diagrams showing the subcommands and specifications discussed in that section. Individually, those diagrams are incomplete. Subcommands listed for univariate designs are available for any analysis, and subcommands listed for multivariate designs can be used in any multivariate analysis, including repeated measures.

MANOVA was designed and programmed by Philip Burns of Northwestern University.

MANOVA: Univariate

```
MANOVA dependent var [BY factor list (min,max)][factor list...]
                     [WITH covariate list]
 [/ERROR={WITHIN            } ]
         {RESIDUAL          }
         {WITHIN + RESIDUAL}
         {n                 }
 [/CONTRAST (factor name)={DEVIATION** [(refcat)]      }]
                          {POLYNOMIAL  [({1,2,3...})]}}
                          {            {metric  }  }
                          {SIMPLE [(refcat)]          }
                          {DIFFERENCE                 }
                          {HELMERT                    }
                          {REPEATED                   }
                          {SPECIAL (matrix)           }
 [/PARTITION (factor name)[=({1,1...  })]]
                             {n1,n2...}
 [/METHOD=[{UNIQUE**  }]  [{CONSTANT**}] [{QR**     }]]
           {SEQUENTIAL}    {NOCONSTANT}   {CHOLESKY}
 [/{PRINT  } = [CELLINFO [(([MEANS] [SSCP] [COV] [COR] [ALL])]]
   {NOPRINT}  [HOMOGENEITY [(([ALL] [BARTLETT] [COCHRAN])]]
              [DESIGN [([OVERALL] [ONEWAY] [DECOMP] [BIAS] [SOLUTION]
                        [REDUNDANCY] [COLLINEARITY])]]
              [PARAMETERS [(([ESTIM][ORTHO][COR][NEGSUM][EFSIZE][OPTIMAL][ALL])]]
              [SIGNIF[({SINGLEDF})]]
              [ERROR[({STDDEV})]]                                          ]
 [/OMEANS =[VARIABLES(varlist)] [TABLES ({factor name    }] ]
                                         {factor BY factor}
                                         {CONSTANT        }
 [/PMEANS =[TABLES ({factor name   })] [PLOT]] ]
                    {factor BY factor}
                    {CONSTANT        }
 [/RESIDUALS=[CASEWISE] [PLOT] ]
 [/POWER=[T({.05**})] [F({.05**})]] [{APPROXIMATE}]]
          {a   }     {a   }       {EXACT      }
 [/CINTERVAL=[{INDIVIDUAL}][({.95}) ]] [UNIVARIATE ({SCHEFFE})]
             {JOINT     }  {  a}                  {BONFER }
 [/PLOT=[BOXPLOTS] [CELLPLOTS] [NORMAL]  [ALL] ]
 [/MISSING=[LISTWISE**] [{EXCLUDE**}] ]
                        {INCLUDE   }
 [/MATRIX=[IN({file})]  [OUT({file})]]
          {[*] }        {[*] }
 [/ANALYSIS=dependent var [WITH covariate list]]
 [/DESIGN={factor [(n)]  }[BY factor[(n)]] [WITHIN factor[(n)]][WITHIN...]
          {[POOL(varlist)}
          [+ {factor [(n)] }...]
             {POOL(varlist)}
          [[= n] {AGAINST} {WITHIN  }
                 {VS     } {RESIDUAL}
                           {WR      }
                           {n       }
          [{factor [(n)] } ... ]
           {POOL(varlist)}
          [MUPLUS]
          [MWITHIN factor(n)]
          [CONSTANT [=n] ]
```

** Default if subcommand or keyword is omitted.

Example:

```
MANOVA YIELD BY SEED(1,4) FERT(1,3)
   /DESIGN.
```

Overview

This section describes the use of MANOVA for univariate analyses. However, the subcommands described here can be used in any type of analysis with MANOVA. For additional subcommands used in those types of analysis, see MANOVA: Multivariate and MANOVA: Repeated Measures. For basic specification, syntax rules, and limitations of the MANOVA procedures, see MANOVA: Overview.

Options

Design Specification. You can specify which terms to include in the design on the DESIGN subcommand. This allows you to estimate a model other than the default full factorial model, incorporate factor-by-covariate interactions, indicate nesting of effects, and indicate specific error terms for each effect in mixed models. You can specify a different continuous variable as a dependent variable or work with a subset of the continuous variables with the ANALYSIS subcommand.

Contrast Types. You can specify contrasts other than the default deviation contrasts on the CONTRAST subcommand. You can also subdivide the degrees of freedom associated with a factor using the PARTITION subcommand and test the significance of a specific contrast or group of contrasts.

Optional Output. You can choose from a wide variety of optional output on the PRINT subcommand or suppress output using the NOPRINT subcommand. Output appropriate to univariate designs includes cell means, design or other matrices, parameter estimates, and tests for homogeneity of variance across cells. Using the OMEANS, PMEANS, RESIDUAL, and PLOT subcommands, you can also request tables of observed and/or predicted means, casewise values and residuals for your model, and various plots useful in checking assumptions. In addition, you can request observed power values based on fixed-effect assumptions using the POWER subcommand and request simultaneous confidence intervals for each parameter estimate and regression coefficient using the CINTERVAL subcommand.

Matrix Materials. You can write matrices of intermediate results to a matrix data file, and you can read such matrices in performing further analyses using the MATRIX subcommand.

Basic Specification

- The basic specification is a variable list identifying the dependent variable, the factors (if any), and the covariates (if any).
- By default, MANOVA uses a full factorial model, which includes all main effects and all possible interactions among factors. Estimation is performed using the cell-means model and UNIQUE (regression-type) sums of squares, adjusting each effect for all other effects in the model. Parameters are estimated using DEVIATION contrasts to determine if their categories differ significantly from the mean.

Subcommand Order

- The variable list must be specified first.
- Subcommands applicable to a specific design must be specified before that DESIGN subcommand. Otherwise, subcommands can be used in any order.

Syntax Rules

- For many analyses, the MANOVA variable list and the DESIGN subcommand are the only specifications needed. If a full factorial design is desired, DESIGN can be omitted.
- All other subcommands apply only to designs that follow. If you do not enter a DESIGN subcommand or if the last subcommand is not DESIGN, MANOVA will use a full factorial model.
- Unless replaced, MANOVA subcommands other than DESIGN remain in effect for all subsequent models.
- MISSING can be specified only once.
- The following words are reserved as keywords or internal commands in the MANOVA procedure: AGAINST, CONSPLUS, CONSTANT, CONTIN, MUPLUS, MWITHIN, POOL, R, RESIDUAL, RW, VERSUS, VS, W, WITHIN, and WR. Variable names that duplicate these words should be changed before you invoke MANOVA.
- If you enter one of the multivariate specifications in a univariate analysis, MANOVA will ignore it.

Limitations

- Maximum 20 factors.
- Maximum 200 dependent variables.
- Memory requirements depend primarily on the number of cells in the design. For the default full factorial model, this equals the product of the number of levels or categories in each factor.

Example

```
MANOVA YIELD BY SEED(1,4) FERT(1,3) WITH RAINFALL
   /PRINT=CELLINFO(MEANS) PARAMETERS(ESTIM)
   /DESIGN.
```

- *YIELD* is the dependent variable; *SEED* (with values 1, 2, 3, and 4) and *FERT* (with values 1, 2, and 3) are factors; *RAINFALL* is a covariate.
- The PRINT subcommand requests the means of the dependent variable for each cell and the default deviation parameter estimates.
- The DESIGN subcommand requests the default design, a full factorial model. This subcommand could have been omitted or could have been specified in full as:

```
/DESIGN = SEED, FERT, SEED BY FERT.
```

MANOVA Variable List

The variable list specifies all variables that will be used in any subsequent analyses.

- The dependent variable must be the first specification on MANOVA.
- By default, MANOVA treats a list of dependent variables as jointly dependent, implying a multivariate design. However, you can change the role of a variable or its inclusion status in the analysis on the ANALYSIS subcommand.
- The names of the factors follow the dependent variable. Use the keyword BY to separate the factors from the dependent variable.
- Factors must have adjacent integer values, and you must supply the minimum and maximum values in parentheses after the factor name(s).
- If several factors have the same value range, you can specify a list of factors followed by a single value range in parentheses.
- Certain one-cell designs, such as univariate and multivariate regression analysis, canonical correlation, and one-sample Hotelling's T^2, do not require a factor specification. To perform these analyses, omit the keyword BY and the factor list.
- Enter the covariates, if any, following the factors and their ranges. Use the keyword WITH to separate covariates from factors (if any) and the dependent variable.

Example

```
MANOVA DEPENDNT BY FACTOR1 (1,3) FACTOR2, FACTOR3 (1,2).
```

- In this example, three factors are specified.
- *FACTOR1* has values 1, 2, and 3, while *FACTOR2* and *FACTOR3* have values 1 and 2.
- A default full factorial model is used for the analysis.

Example

```
MANOVA Y BY A(1,3) WITH X
  /DESIGN.
```

- In this example, the *A* effect is tested after adjusting for the effect of the covariate *X*. It is a test of equality of adjusted *A* means.
- The test of the covariate *X* is adjusted for *A*. It is a test of the pooled within-groups regression of *Y* on *X*.

ERROR Subcommand

ERROR allows you to specify or change the error term used to test all effects for which you do not explicitly specify an error term on the DESIGN subcommand. ERROR affects all terms in all subsequent designs, except terms for which you explicitly provide an error term.

WITHIN   *Terms in the model are tested against the within-cell sum of squares.* This specification can be abbreviated to W. This is the default unless there is no variance within cells or unless a continuous variable is named on the DESIGN subcommand.

RESIDUAL	*Terms in the model are tested against the residual sum of squares.* This specification can be abbreviated to R. This includes all terms not named on the DESIGN subcommand.
WITHIN+RESIDUAL	*Terms are tested against the pooled within-cells and residual sum of squares.* This specification can be abbreviated to WR or RW. This is the default for designs in which a continuous variable appears on the DESIGN subcommand.
error number	*Terms are tested against a numbered error term.* The error term must be defined on each DESIGN subcommand (for a discussion of error terms, see the DESIGN subcommand on p. 411).

- If you specify ERROR=WITHIN+RESIDUAL and one of the components does not exist, MANOVA uses the other component alone.

- If you specify your own error term by number and a design does not have an error term with the specified number, MANOVA does not carry out significance tests. It will, however, display hypothesis sums of squares and, if requested, parameter estimates.

Example

```
MANOVA DEP BY A(1,2) B(1,4)
   /ERROR = 1
   /DESIGN = A, B, A BY B = 1 VS WITHIN
   /DESIGN = A, B.
```

- ERROR defines error term 1 as the default error term.

- In the first design, *A* by *B* is defined as error term 1 and is therefore used to test the *A* and *B* effects. The *A* by *B* effect itself is explicitly tested against the within-cells error.

- In the second design, no term is defined as error term 1, so no significance tests are carried out. Hypothesis sums of squares are displayed for *A* and *B*.

CONTRAST Subcommand

CONTRAST specifies the type of contrast desired among the levels of a factor. For a factor with k levels or values, the contrast type determines the meaning of its $k - 1$ degrees of freedom. If the subcommand is omitted or is specified with no keyword, the default is DEVIATION for between-subjects factors.

- Specify the factor name in parentheses following the subcommand CONTRAST.

- You can specify only one factor per CONTRAST subcommand, but you can enter multiple CONTRAST subcommands.

- After closing the parentheses, enter an equals sign followed by one of the contrast keywords.

- To obtain *F* tests for individual degrees of freedom for the specified contrast, enter the factor name followed by a number in parentheses on the DESIGN subcommand. The number refers to a partition of the factor's degrees of freedom. If you do not use the PARTITION subcommand, each degree of freedom is a distinct partition.

The following contrast types are available:

DEVIATION *Deviations from the grand mean.* This is the default for between-subjects factors. Each level of the factor except one is compared to the grand mean. One category (by default the last) must be omitted so that the effects will be independent of one another. To omit a category other than the last, specify the number of the omitted category (which is not necessarily the same as its value) in parentheses after the keyword DEVIATION. For example,

```
MANOVA A BY B(2,4)
    /CONTRAST(B)=DEVIATION(1).
```

The specified contrast omits the first category, in which *B* has the value 2. Deviation contrasts are not orthogonal.

POLYNOMIAL *Polynomial contrasts.* This is the default for within-subjects factors. The first degree of freedom contains the linear effect across the levels of the factor, the second contains the quadratic effect, and so on. In a balanced design, polynomial contrasts are orthogonal. By default, the levels are assumed to be equally spaced; you can specify unequal spacing by entering a metric consisting of one integer for each level of the factor in parentheses after the keyword POLYNOMIAL. For example,

```
MANOVA RESPONSE BY STIMULUS (4,6)
    /CONTRAST(STIMULUS) = POLYNOMIAL(1,2,4).
```

The specified contrast indicates that the three levels of *STIMULUS* are actually in the proportion 1:2:4. The default metric is always $(1,2,...,k)$, where k levels are involved. Only the relative differences between the terms of the metric matter (1,2,4) is the same metric as (2,3,5) or (20,30,50) because, in each instance, the difference between the second and third numbers is twice the difference between the first and second.

DIFFERENCE *Difference or reverse Helmert contrasts.* Each level of the factor except the first is compared to the mean of the previous levels. In a balanced design, difference contrasts are orthogonal.

HELMERT *Helmert contrasts.* Each level of the factor except the last is compared to the mean of subsequent levels. In a balanced design, Helmert contrasts are orthogonal.

SIMPLE *Each level of the factor except the last is compared to the last level.* To use a category other than the last as the omitted reference category, specify its number (which is not necessarily the same as its value) in parentheses following the keyword SIMPLE. For example,

```
MANOVA A BY B(2,4)
     /CONTRAST(B)=SIMPLE(1).
```

The specified contrast compares the other levels to the first level of *B*, in which *B* has the value 2. Simple contrasts are not orthogonal.

REPEATED   *Comparison of adjacent levels.* Each level of the factor except the first is compared to the previous level. Repeated contrasts are not orthogonal.

SPECIAL   *A user-defined contrast.* After this keyword, enter a square matrix in parentheses with as many rows and columns as there are levels in the factor. The first row represents the mean effect of the factor and is generally a vector of 1's. It represents a set of weights indicating how to collapse over the categories of this factor in estimating parameters for other factors. The other rows of the contrast matrix contain the special contrasts indicating the desired comparisons between levels of the factor. If the special contrasts are linear combinations of each other, MANOVA reports the linear dependency and stops processing.

Orthogonal contrasts are particularly useful. In a balanced design, contrasts are orthogonal if the sum of the coefficients in each contrast row is 0 and if, for any pair of contrast rows, the products of corresponding coefficients sum to 0. DIFFERENCE, HELMERT, and POLYNOMIAL contrasts always meet these criteria in balanced designs. For illustration of contrast types, see the appendix.

Example

```
MANOVA DEP BY FAC(1,5)
  /CONTRAST(FAC)=DIFFERENCE
  /DESIGN=FAC(1) FAC(2) FAC(3) FAC(4).
```

- The factor *FAC* has five categories and therefore four degrees of freedom.
- CONTRAST requests DIFFERENCE contrasts, which compare each level (except the first) with the mean of the previous levels.
- Each of the four degrees of freedom is tested individually on the DESIGN subcommand.

PARTITION Subcommand

PARTITION subdivides the degrees of freedom associated with a factor. This permits you to test the significance of the effect of a specific contrast or group of contrasts of the factor instead of the overall effect of all contrasts of the factor. The default is a single degree of freedom for each partition.

- Specify the factor name in parentheses following the PARTITION subcommand.
- Specify an integer list in parentheses after the optional equals sign to indicate the degrees of freedom for each partition.
- Each value in the partition list must be a positive integer, and the sum of the values cannot exceed the degrees of freedom for the factor.
- The degrees of freedom available for a factor are one less than the number of levels of the factor.
- The meaning of each degree of freedom depends upon the contrast type for the factor. For example, with deviation contrasts (the default for between-subjects factors), each degree of freedom represents the deviation of the dependent variable in one level of the factor from its grand mean over all levels. With polynomial contrasts, the degrees of freedom represent the linear effect, the quadratic effect, and so on.

- If your list does not account for all the degrees of freedom, MANOVA adds one final partition containing the remaining degrees of freedom.
- You can use a repetition factor of the form *n** to specify a series of partitions with the same number of degrees of freedom.
- To specify a model that tests only the effect of a specific partition of a factor in your design, include the number of the partition in parentheses on the DESIGN subcommand (see the example below).
- If you want the default single degree-of-freedom partition, you can omit the PARTITION subcommand and simply enter the appropriate term on the DESIGN subcommand.

Example

```
MANOVA OUTCOME BY TREATMNT(1,12)
  /PARTITION(TREATMNT) = (3*2,4)
  /DESIGN TREATMNT(2).
```

- The factor *TREATMNT* has 12 categories, hence 11 degrees of freedom.
- PARTITION divides the effect of *TREATMNT* into four partitions, containing, respectively, 2, 2, 2, and 4 degrees of freedom. A fifth partition is formed to contain the remaining 1 degree of freedom.
- DESIGN specifies a model in which only the second partition of *TREATMNT* is tested. This partition contains the third and fourth degrees of freedom.
- Since the default contrast type for between-subjects factors is DEVIATION, this second partition represents the deviation of the third and fourth levels of *TREATMNT* from the grand mean.

METHOD Subcommand

METHOD controls the computational aspects of the MANOVA analysis. You can specify one of two different methods for partitioning the sums of squares. The default is UNIQUE.

UNIQUE   *Regression approach.* Each term is corrected for every other term in the model. With this approach, sums of squares for various components of the model do not add up to the total sum of squares unless the design is balanced. This is the default if the METHOD subcommand is omitted or if neither of the two keywords is specified.

SEQUENTIAL *Hierarchical decomposition of the sums of squares.* Each term is adjusted only for the terms that precede it on the DESIGN subcommand. This is an orthogonal decomposition, and the sums of squares in the model add up to the total sum of squares.

You can control how parameters are to be estimated by specifying one of the following two keywords available on MANOVA. The default is QR.

QR   *Use modified Givens rotations.* QR bypasses the normal equations and the inaccuracies that can result from creating the cross-products matrix, and it generally results in extremely accurate parameter estimates. This is the default if the METHOD subcommand is omitted or if neither of the two keywords is specified.

CHOLESKY   *Use Cholesky decomposition of the cross-products matrix.* Useful for large data sets with covariates entered on the DESIGN subcommand.

You can also control whether a constant term is included in all models. Two keywords are available on METHOD. The default is CONSTANT.

CONSTANT   *All models include a constant (grand mean) term, even if none is explicitly specified on the DESIGN subcommand.* This is the default if neither of the two keywords is specified.

NOCONSTANT   *Exclude constant terms from models that do not include the keyword CONSTANT on the DESIGN subcommand.*

Example

```
MANOVA DEP BY A B C (1,4)
  /METHOD=NOCONSTANT
  /DESIGN=A, B, C
  /METHOD=CONSTANT SEQUENTIAL
  /DESIGN.
```

- For the first design, a main-effects model, the METHOD subcommand requests the model to be fitted with no constant.
- The second design requests a full factorial model to be fitted with a constant and with a sequential decomposition of sums of squares.

PRINT and NOPRINT Subcommands

PRINT and NOPRINT control the display of optional output.

- Specifications on PRINT remain in effect for all subsequent designs.
- Some PRINT output, such as CELLINFO, applies to the entire MANOVA procedure and is displayed only once.
- You can turn off optional output that you have requested on PRINT by entering a NOPRINT subcommand with the specifications originally used on the PRINT subcommand.
- Additional output can be obtained on the PCOMPS, DISCRIM, OMEANS, PMEANS, PLOT, and RESIDUALS subcommands.
- Some optional output greatly increases the processing time. Request only the output you want to see.

The following specifications are appropriate for univariate MANOVA analyses. For information on PRINT specifications appropriate for other MANOVA models, see MANOVA: Multivariate and MANOVA: Repeated Measures.

CELLINFO   *Basic information about each cell in the design.*

PARAMETERS   *Parameter estimates.*

HOMOGENEITY   *Tests of homogeneity of variance.*

DESIGN   *Design information.*

ERROR   *Error standard deviations.*

CELLINFO Keyword

You can request any of the following cell information by specifying the appropriate keyword(s) in parentheses after CELLINFO. The default is MEANS.

MEANS   *Cell means, standard deviations, and counts for the dependent variable and covariates.* Confidence intervals for the cell means are displayed if you have set a wide width. This is the default when CELLINFO is requested with no further specification.

SSCP   *Within-cell sum-of-squares and cross-products matrices for the dependent variable and covariates.*

COV   *Within-cell variance-covariance matrices for the dependent variable and covariates.*

COR   *Within-cell correlation matrices, with standard deviations on the diagonal, for the dependent variable and covariates.*

ALL   *MEANS, SSCP, COV, and COR.*

- Output from CELLINFO is displayed once before the analysis of any particular design. Specify CELLINFO only once.
- When you specify SSCP, COV, or COR, the cells are numbered for identification, beginning with cell 1.
- The levels vary most rapidly for the factor named last on the MANOVA variables specification.
- Empty cells are neither displayed nor numbered.
- A table showing the levels of each factor corresponding to each cell number is displayed at the beginning of MANOVA output.

Example

```
MANOVA DEP BY A(1,4) B(1,2) WITH COV
  /PRINT=CELLINFO(MEANS COV)
  /DESIGN.
```

- For each combination of levels of *A* and *B*, MANOVA displays separately the means and standard deviations of *DEP* and *COV*. Beginning with cell 1, it will then display the variance-covariance matrix of *DEP* and *COV* within each non-empty cell.
- A table of cell numbers will be displayed to show the factor levels corresponding to each cell.
- The keyword COV, as a parameter of CELLINFO, is not confused with the variable *COV*.

PARAMETERS Keyword

The keyword PARAMETERS displays information relating to the estimated size of the effects in the model. You can specify any of the following keywords in parentheses on PARAMETERS. The default is ESTIM.

ESTIM   *The estimated parameters themselves, along with their standard errors, t tests, and confidence intervals.* Only nonredundant parameters are displayed. This is the default if PARAMETERS is requested without further specification.

NEGSUM   *The negative of the sum of parameters for each effect.* For DEVIATION main effects, this equals the parameter for the omitted (redundant) contrast. NEGSUM is displayed along with the parameter estimates.

ORTHO   *The orthogonal estimates of parameters used to produce the sums of squares.*

COR   *Covariance factors and correlations among the parameter estimates.*

EFSIZE   *The effect size values.*

OPTIMAL   *Optimal Scheffé contrast coefficients.*

ALL   *ESTIM, NEGSUM, ORTHO, COR, EFSIZE, and OPTIMAL.*

SIGNIF Keyword

SIGNIF requests special significance tests, most of which apply to multivariate designs (see MANOVA: Multivariate). The following specification is useful in univariate applications of MANOVA:

SINGLEDF   *Significance tests for each single degree of freedom making up each effect for analysis-of-variance tables.*

- When non-orthogonal contrasts are requested or when the design is unbalanced, the SINGLEDF effects will differ from single degree-of-freedom partitions. SINGLEDF effects are orthogonal within an effect; single degree-of-freedom partitions are not.

Example

```
MANOVA DEP BY FAC(1,5)
  /CONTRAST(FAC)=POLY
  /PRINT=SIGNIF(SINGLEDF)
  /DESIGN.
```

- POLYNOMIAL contrasts are applied to *FAC*, testing the linear, quadratic, cubic, and quartic components of its five levels. POLYNOMIAL contrasts are orthogonal in balanced designs.

- The SINGLEDF specification on SIGNIF requests significance tests for each of these four components.

HOMOGENEITY Keyword

HOMOGENEITY requests tests for the homogeneity of variance of the dependent variable across the cells of the design. You can specify one or more of the following specifications in parentheses. If HOMOGENEITY is requested without further specification, the default is ALL.

BARTLETT   *Bartlett-Box* F *test.*

COCHRAN   *Cochran's* C.

ALL   *Both BARTLETT and COCHRAN.* This is the default.

DESIGN Keyword

You can request the following by entering one or more of the specifications in parentheses following the keyword DESIGN. If DESIGN is requested without further specification, the default is OVERALL.

The DECOMP and BIAS matrices can provide valuable information on the confounding of the effects and the estimability of the chosen contrasts. If two effects are confounded, the entry corresponding to them in the BIAS matrix will be nonzero; if they are orthogonal, the entry will be zero. This is particularly useful in designs with unpatterned empty cells. For further discussion of the matrices, see Bock (1985).

OVERALL   *The overall reduced-model design matrix (not the contrast matrix).* This is the default.

ONEWAY   *The one-way basis matrix (not the contrast matrix) for each factor.*

DECOMP   *The upper triangular QR/CHOLESKY decomposition of the design.*

BIAS   *Contamination coefficients displaying the bias present in the design.*

SOLUTION   *Coefficients of the linear combinations of the cell means used in significance testing.*

REDUNDANCY   *Exact linear combinations of parameters that form a redundancy.* This keyword displays a table only if QR (the default) is the estimation method.

COLLINEARITY *Collinearity diagnostics for design matrices.* These diagnostics include the singular values of the normalized design matrix (which are the same as those of the normalized decomposition matrix), condition indexes corresponding to each singular value, and the proportion of variance of the corresponding parameter accounted for by each principal component. For greatest accuracy, use the QR method of estimation whenever you request collinearity diagnostics.

ALL   *All available options.*

ERROR Keyword

Generally, the keyword ERROR on PRINT produces error matrices. In univariate analyses, the only valid specification for ERROR is STDDEV, which is the default if ERROR is specified by itself.

STDDEV *The error standard deviation.* Normally, this is the within-cells standard deviation of the dependent variable. If you specify multiple error terms on DESIGN, this specification will display the standard deviation for each.

OMEANS Subcommand

OMEANS (observed means) displays tables of the means of continuous variables for levels or combinations of levels of the factors.

- Use the keywords VARIABLES and TABLES to indicate which observed means you want to display.
- With no specifications, the OMEANS subcommand is equivalent to requesting `CELLINFO (MEANS)` on PRINT.
- OMEANS displays confidence intervals for the cell means if you have set the width to 132.
- Output from OMEANS is displayed once before the analysis of any particular design. This subcommand should be specified only once.

VARIABLES   *Continuous variables for which you want means.* Specify the variables in parentheses after the keyword VARIABLES. You can request means for the dependent variable or any covariates. If you omit the VARIABLES keyword, observed means are displayed for the dependent variable and all covariates. If you enter the keyword VARIABLES, you must also enter the keyword TABLES, discussed below.

TABLES   *Factors for which you want the observed means displayed.* List in parentheses the factors, or combinations of factors, separated with BY. Observed means are displayed for each level, or combination of levels, of the factors named (see the example below). Both weighted means and unweighted means (where all cells are weighted equally, regardless of the number of cases they contain) are displayed. If you enter the keyword CONSTANT, the grand mean is displayed.

Example

```
MANOVA DEP BY A(1,3) B(1,2)
  /OMEANS=TABLES(A,B)
  /DESIGN.
```

- Because there is no VARIABLES specification on the OMEANS subcommand, observed means are displayed for all continuous variables. *DEP* is the only dependent variable here, and there are no covariates.
- The TABLES specification on the OMEANS subcommand requests tables of observed means for each of the three categories of *A* (collapsing over *B*) and for both categories of *B* (collapsing over *A*).
- MANOVA displays both weighted means, in which all cases count equally, and unweighted means, in which all cells count equally.

PMEANS Subcommand

PMEANS (predicted means) displays a table of the predicted cell means of the dependent variable, both adjusted for the effect of covariates in the cell and unadjusted for covariates. For comparison, it also displays the observed cell means.

- Output from PMEANS can be computationally expensive.
- PMEANS without any additional specifications displays a table showing for each cell the observed mean of the dependent variable, the predicted mean adjusted for the effect of covariates in that cell (*ADJ. MEAN*), the predicted mean unadjusted for covariates (*EST. MEAN*), and the raw and standardized residuals from the estimated means.

- Cells are numbered in output from PMEANS so that the levels vary most rapidly on the factor named last in the MANOVA variables specification. A table showing the levels of each factor corresponding to each cell number is displayed at the beginning of the MANOVA output.
- Predicted means are suppressed for any design in which the MUPLUS keyword appears.
- Covariates are not predicted.
- In designs with covariates and multiple error terms, use the ERROR subcommand to designate which error term's regression coefficients are to be used in calculating the standardized residuals.

For univariate analysis, the following keywords are available on the PMEANS subcommand:

TABLES   *Additional tables showing adjusted predicted means for specified factors or combinations of factors.* Enter the names of factors or combinations of factors in parentheses after this keyword. For each factor or combination, MANOVA displays the predicted means (adjusted for covariates) collapsed over all other factors.

PLOT   *A plot of the predicted means for each cell.*

Example

```
MANOVA DEP BY A(1,4) B(1,3)
  /PMEANS TABLES(A, B, A BY B)
  /DESIGN = A, B.
```

- PMEANS displays the default table of observed and predicted means for *DEP* and raw and standardized residuals in each of the 12 cells in the model.
- The TABLES specification on PMEANS displays tables of predicted means for *A* (collapsing over *B*), for *B* (collapsing over *A*), and all combinations of *A* and *B*.
- Because *A* and *B* are the only factors in the model, the means for *A* by *B* in the TABLES specification come from every cell in the model. They are identical to the adjusted predicted means in the default PMEANS table, which always includes all non-empty cells.
- Predicted means for *A* by *B* can be requested in the TABLES specification, even though the *A* by *B* effect is not in the design.

RESIDUALS Subcommand

Use RESIDUALS to display and plot casewise values and residuals for your models.

- Use the ERROR subcommand to specify an error term other than the default to be used to standardize the residuals.
- If a designated error term does not exist for a given design, no predicted values or residuals are calculated.
- If you specify RESIDUALS without any keyword, CASEWISE output is displayed.

The following keywords are available:

CASEWISE   *A case-by-case listing of the observed, predicted, residual, and standardized residual values for each dependent variable.*

PLOT   *A plot of observed values, predicted values, and case numbers versus the standardized residuals, plus normal and detrended normal probability plots for the standardized residuals (five plots in all).*

POWER Subcommand

POWER requests observed power values based on fixed-effect assumptions for all univariate and multivariate F tests and t tests. Both approximate and exact power values can be computed, although exact multivariate power is displayed only when there is one hypothesis degree of freedom. If POWER is specified by itself, with no keywords, MANOVA calculates the approximate observed power values of all F tests at 0.05 significance level.

The following keywords are available on the POWER subcommand:

APPROXIMATE   *Approximate power values.* This is the default if POWER is specified without any keyword. Approximate power values for univariate tests are derived from an Edgeworth-type normal approximation to the noncentral beta distribution. Approximate values are normally accurate to three decimal places and are much cheaper to compute than exact values.

EXACT   *Exact power values.* Exact power values for univariate tests are computed from the noncentral incomplete beta distribution.

F(a)   *Alpha level at which the power is to be calculated for* F *tests.* The default is 0.05. To change the default, specify a decimal number between 0 and 1 in parentheses after F. The numbers 0 and 1 themselves are not allowed. F test at 0.05 significance level is the default when POWER is omitted or specified without any keyword.

T(a)   *Alpha level at which the power is to be calculated for* t *tests.* The default is 0.05. To change the default, specify a decimal number between 0 and 1 in parentheses after t. The numbers 0 and 1 themselves are not allowed.

- For univariate F tests and t tests, MANOVA computes a measure of the effect size based on partial η^2:

$$partial\ \eta^2 = (ssh)/(ssh + sse)$$

where *ssh* is the hypothesis sum of squares and *sse* is the error sum of squares. The measure is an overestimate of the actual effect size. However, it is consistent and is applicable to all F tests and t tests. For a discussion of effect size measures, see Cohen (1977) or Hays (1981).

CINTERVAL Subcommand

CINTERVAL requests simultaneous confidence intervals for each parameter estimate and regression coefficient. MANOVA provides either individual or joint confidence intervals at any desired confidence level. You can compute joint confidence intervals using either Scheffé or Bonferroni intervals. Scheffé intervals are based on all possible contrasts, while Bonferroni intervals are based on the number of contrasts actually made. For a large number of contrasts, Bonferroni intervals will be larger than Scheffé intervals. Timm (1975) provides a good discussion of which intervals are best for certain situations. Both Scheffé and Bonferroni intervals are computed separately for each term in the design. You can request only one type of confidence interval per design.

The following keywords are available on the CINTERVAL subcommand. If the subcommand is specified without any keyword, CINTERVAL automatically displays individual univariate confidence intervals at the 0.95 level.

INDIVIDUAL(a)   *Individual confidence intervals.* Specify the desired confidence level in parentheses following the keyword. The desired confidence level can be any decimal number between 0 and 1. When individual intervals are requested, BONFER and SCHEFFE have no effect.

JOINT(a)   *Joint confidence intervals.* Specify the desired confidence level in parentheses after the keyword. The default is 0.95. The desired confidence level can be any decimal number between 0 and 1.

UNIVARIATE(type)   *Univariate confidence interval.* Specify either SCHEFFE for Scheffé intervals or BONFER for Bonferroni intervals in parentheses after the keyword. The default specification is SCHEFFE.

PLOT Subcommand

MANOVA can display a variety of plots useful in checking the assumptions needed in the analysis. Plots are produced only once in the MANOVA procedure, regardless of how many DESIGN subcommands you enter. Use the following keywords on the PLOT subcommand to request plots. If the PLOT subcommand is specified by itself, the default is BOXPLOT.

BOXPLOTS   *Boxplots.* Plots are displayed for each continuous variable (dependent or covariate) named on the MANOVA variable list. Boxplots provide a simple graphical means of comparing the cells in terms of mean location and spread. The data must be stored in memory for these plots; if there is not enough memory, boxplots are not produced and a warning message is issued. This is the default if the PLOT subcommand is specified without a keyword.

CELLPLOTS   *Cell statistics, including a plot of cell means versus cell variances, a plot of cell means versus cell standard deviations, and a histogram of cell means.* Plots are produced for each continuous variable (dependent or covariate) named on the MANOVA variable list. The first two plots aid in detecting heteroscedasticity (nonhomogeneous variances) and in determining an appropriate data transformation if one is needed. The third plot gives distributional information for the cell means.

NORMAL   *Normal and detrended normal plots.* Plots are produced for each continuous variable (dependent or covariate) named on the MANOVA variable list. MANOVA ranks the scores and then plots the ranks against the expected normal deviate, or detrended expected normal deviate, for that rank. These plots aid in detecting non-normality and outlying observations. All data must be held in memory to compute ranks. If not enough memory is available, MANOVA displays a warning and skips the plots.

- ZCORR, an additional plot available on the PLOT subcommand, is described in MANOVA: Multivariate.
- You can request other plots on PMEANS and RESIDUALS (see respective subcommands).

MISSING Subcommand

By default, cases with missing values for any of the variables on the MANOVA variable list are excluded from the analysis. The MISSING subcommand allows you to include cases with user-missing values. If MISSING is not specified, the defaults are LISTWISE and EXCLUDE.

- The same missing-value treatment is used to process all designs in a single execution of MANOVA.
- If you enter more than one MISSING subcommand, the last one entered will be in effect for the entire procedure, including designs specified before the last MISSING subcommand.
- Pairwise deletion of missing data is not available in MANOVA.
- Keywords INCLUDE and EXCLUDE are mutually exclusive; either can be specified with LISTWISE.

LISTWISE   *Cases with missing values for any variable named on the MANOVA variable list are excluded from the analysis.* This is always true in the MANOVA procedure.

EXCLUDE   *Exclude both user-missing and system-missing values.* This is the default when MISSING is not specified.

INCLUDE   *User-missing values are treated as valid.* For factors, you must include the missing-value codes within the range specified on the MANOVA variable list. It may be necessary to recode these values so that they will be adjacent to the other factor values. System-missing values cannot be included in the analysis.

MATRIX Subcommand

MATRIX reads and writes SPSS matrix data files. It writes correlation matrices that can be read by subsequent MANOVA procedures.

- Either IN or OUT is required to specify the matrix file in parentheses. When both IN and OUT are used on the same MANOVA procedure, they can be specified on separate MATRIX subcommands or on the same subcommand.
- The matrix materials include the N, mean, and standard deviation. Documents from the file that form the matrix are not included in the matrix data file.
- MATRIX=IN cannot be used in place of GET or DATA LIST to begin a new SPSS command file. MATRIX is a subcommand on MANOVA, and MANOVA cannot run before a working data file is defined. To begin a new command file and immediately read a matrix, first GET the matrix file, and then specify IN(*) on MATRIX.
- Records in the matrix data file read by MANOVA can be in any order, with the following exceptions: the order of split-file groups cannot be violated, and all *CORR* vectors must appear contiguously within each split-file group.
- When MANOVA reads matrix materials, it ignores the record containing the total number of cases. In addition, it skips unrecognized records. MANOVA does not issue a warning when it skips records.

The following two keywords are available on the MATRIX subcommand:

OUT   *Write an SPSS matrix data file.* Specify either a file or an asterisk, and enclose the specification in parentheses. If you specify a file, the file is stored on disk and can be retrieved at any time. If you specify an asterisk (*) or leave the parentheses empty, the matrix file replaces the working data file but is not stored on disk unless you use SAVE or XSAVE.

IN   *Read an SPSS matrix data file.* If the matrix file *is not* the current working data file, specify a file in parentheses. If the matrix file *is* the current working data file, specify an asterisk (*) or leave the parentheses empty.

Format of the SPSS Matrix Data File

The SPSS matrix data file includes two special variables created by SPSS: *ROWTYPE_* and *VARNAME_*.

- Variable *ROWTYPE_* is a short string variable having values *N, MEAN, CORR* (for Pearson correlation coefficients), and *STDDEV.*
- Variable *VARNAME_* is a short string variable whose values are the names of the variables and covariates used to form the correlation matrix. When *ROWTYPE_* is *CORR*, *VARNAME_* gives the variable associated with that row of the correlation matrix.
- Between *ROWTYPE_* and *VARNAME_* are the factor variables (if any) defined in the BY portion of the MANOVA variable list. (Factor variables receive the system-missing value on vectors that represent pooled values.)
- Remaining variables are the variables used to form the correlation matrix.

Split Files and Variable Order

- When split-file processing is in effect, the first variables in the matrix system file will be the split variables, followed by *ROWTYPE_*, the factor variable(s), *VARNAME_*, and then the variables used to form the correlation matrix.
- A full set of matrix materials is written for each subgroup defined by the split variable(s).
- A split variable cannot have the same variable name as any other variable written to the matrix data file.
- If a split file is in effect when a matrix is written, the same split file must be in effect when that matrix is read into another procedure.

Additional Statistics

In addition to the *CORR* values, MANOVA always includes the following with the matrix materials:

- The total weighted number of cases used to compute each correlation coefficient.
- A vector of *N*'s for each cell in the data.
- A vector of *MEAN*'s for each cell in the data.

- A vector of pooled standard deviations, *STDDEV*. This is the square root of the within-cells mean square error for each variable.

Example

```
GET FILE IRIS.
MANOVA SEPALLEN SEPALWID PETALLEN PETALWID BY TYPE(1,3)
   /MATRIX=OUT(MANMTX).
```

- MANOVA reads data from the SPSS data file *IRIS* and writes one set of matrix materials to the file *MANMTX*.
- The working data file is still *IRIS*. Subsequent commands are executed on the file *IRIS*.

Example

```
GET FILE IRIS.
MANOVA SEPALLEN SEPALWID PETALLEN PETALWID BY TYPE(1,3)
   /MATRIX=OUT(*).
LIST.
```

- MANOVA writes the same matrix as in the example above. However, the matrix file replaces the working data file. The LIST command is executed on the matrix file, not on the file *IRIS*.

Example

```
GET FILE=PRSNNL.
FREQUENCIES VARIABLE=AGE.

MANOVA SEPALLEN SEPALWID PETALLEN PETALWID BY TYPE(1,3)
   /MATRIX=IN(MANMTX).
```

- This example assumes that you want to perform a frequencies analysis on the file *PRSNNL* and then use MANOVA to read a different file. The file you want to read is an existing SPSS matrix data file. The external matrix file *MANMTX* is specified in parentheses after IN on the MATRIX subcommand.
- *MANMTX* does not replace *PRSNNL* as the working file.

Example

```
GET FILE=MANMTX.
MANOVA SEPALLEN SEPALWID PETALLEN PETALWID BY TYPE(1,3)
   /MATRIX=IN(*).
```

- This example assumes that you are starting a new session and want to read an existing SPSS matrix data file. GET retrieves the matrix file *MANMTX*.
- An asterisk is specified in parentheses after IN on the MATRIX subcommand to read the working data file. You can also leave the parentheses empty to indicate the default.
- If the GET command is omitted, SPSS issues an error message.
- If you specify *MANMTX* in parentheses after IN, SPSS issues an error message.

ANALYSIS Subcommand

ANALYSIS allows you to work with a subset of the continuous variables (dependent variable and covariates) you have named on the MANOVA variable list. In univariate analysis of variance, you can use ANALYSIS to allow factor-by-covariate interaction terms in your model (see the DESIGN subcommand below). You can also use it to switch the roles of the dependent variable and a covariate.

- In general, ANALYSIS gives you complete control over which continuous variables are to be dependent variables, which are to be covariates, and which are to be neither.

- ANALYSIS specifications are like the MANOVA variables specification, except that factors are not named. Enter the dependent variable and, if there are covariates, the keyword WITH and the covariates.

- Only variables listed as dependent variables or covariates on the MANOVA variable list can be entered on the ANALYSIS subcommand.

- In a univariate analysis of variance, the most important use of ANALYSIS is to omit covariates altogether from the analysis list, thereby making them available for inclusion on DESIGN (see the example below and the DESIGN subcommand examples).

- For more information on ANALYSIS, refer to MANOVA: Multivariate.

Example

```
MANOVA DEP BY FACTOR(1,3) WITH COV
   /ANALYSIS DEP
   /DESIGN FACTOR, COV, FACTOR BY COV.
```

- *COV*, a continuous variable, is included on the MANOVA variable list as a covariate.

- *COV* is not mentioned on ANALYSIS, so it will not be included in the model as a dependent variable or covariate. It can, therefore, be explicitly included on the DESIGN subcommand.

- DESIGN includes the main effects of *FACTOR* and *COV* and the *FACTOR* by *COV* interaction.

DESIGN Subcommand

DESIGN specifies the effects included in a specific model. It must be the last subcommand entered for any model.

The cells in a design are defined by all of the possible combinations of levels of the factors in that design. The number of cells equals the product of the number of levels of all the factors. A design is *balanced* if each cell contains the same number of cases. MANOVA can analyze both balanced and unbalanced designs.

- Specify a list of terms to be included in the model, separated by spaces or commas.

- The default design, if the DESIGN subcommand is omitted or is specified by itself, is a full factorial model containing all main effects and all orders of factor-by-factor interaction.

- If the last subcommand specified is not DESIGN, a default full factorial design is estimated.

- To include a term for the main effect of a factor, enter the name of the factor on the DESIGN subcommand.

- To include a term for an interaction between factors, use the keyword BY to join the factors involved in the interaction.

- Terms are entered into the model in the order in which you list them on DESIGN. If you have specified SEQUENTIAL on the METHOD subcommand to partition the sums of squares in a hierarchical fashion, this order may affect the significance tests.

- You can specify other types of terms in the model, as described in the following sections.

- Multiple DESIGN subcommands are accepted. An analysis of one model is produced for each DESIGN subcommand.

Example

```
MANOVA Y BY A(1,2) B(1,2) C(1,3)
   /DESIGN
   /DESIGN A, B, C
   /DESIGN A, B, C, A BY B, A BY C.
```

- The first DESIGN produces the default full factorial design, with all main effects and interactions for factors *A*, *B*, and *C*.

- The second DESIGN produces an analysis with main effects only for *A*, *B*, and *C*.

- The third DESIGN produces an analysis with main effects and the interactions between *A* and the other two factors. The interaction between *B* and *C* is not in the design, nor is the interaction between all three factors.

Partitioned Effects: Number in Parentheses

You can specify a number in parentheses following a factor name on the DESIGN subcommand to identify individual degrees of freedom or partitions of the degrees of freedom associated with an effect.

- If you specify PARTITION, the number refers to a partition. Partitions can include more than one degree of freedom (see the PARTITION subcommand on p. 398). For example, if the first partition of *SEED* includes two degrees of freedom, the term SEED(1) on a DESIGN subcommand tests the two degrees of freedom.

- If you do not use PARTITION, the number refers to a single degree of freedom associated with the effect.

- The number refers to an individual level for a factor if that factor follows the keyword WITHIN or MWITHIN (see the sections on nested effects and pooled effects below).

- A factor has one less degree of freedom than it has levels or values.

Example

```
MANOVA YIELD BY SEED(1,4) WITH RAINFALL
   /PARTITION(SEED)=(2,1)
   /DESIGN=SEED(1) SEED(2).
```

- Factor *SEED* is subdivided into two partitions, one containing the first two degrees of freedom and the other the last degree of freedom.

- The two partitions of *SEED* are treated as independent effects.

Nested Effects: WITHIN Keyword

Use the WITHIN keyword (alias W) to nest the effects of one factor within those of another factor or an interaction term.

Example

```
MANOVA YIELD BY SEED(1,4) FERT(1,3) PLOT (1,4)
  /DESIGN = FERT WITHIN SEED BY PLOT.
```

- The three factors in this example are type of seed (*SEED*), type of fertilizer (*FERT*), and location of plots (*PLOT*).
- The DESIGN subcommand nests the effects of *FERT* within the interaction term of *SEED* by *PLOT*. The levels of *FERT* are considered distinct for each combination of levels of *SEED* and *PLOT*.

Simple Effects: WITHIN and MWITHIN Keywords

A factor can be nested within one specific level of another factor by indicating the level in parentheses. This allows you to estimate simple effects or the effect of one factor within only one level of another. Simple effects can be obtained for higher-order interactions as well.
    Use WITHIN to request simple effects of between-subjects factors.

Example

```
MANOVA YIELD BY SEED(2,4) FERT(1,3) PLOT (1,4)
  /DESIGN = FERT WITHIN SEED (1).
```

- This example requests the simple effect of *FERT* within the first level of *SEED*.
- The number (*n*) specified after a WITHIN factor refers to the level of that factor. It is the ordinal position, which is not necessarily the value of that level. In this example, the first level is associated with value 2.
- The number does *not* refer to the number of partitioned effects (see "Partitioned Effects: Number in Parentheses" on p. 412).

Example

```
MANOVA YIELD BY SEED(2,4) FERT(1,3) PLOT (3,5)
  /DESIGN = FERT WITHIN PLOT(1) WITHIN SEED(2)
```

- This example requests the effect of *FERT* within the second *SEED* level of the first *PLOT* level.
- The second *SEED* level is associated with value 3 and the first *PLOT* level is associated with value 3.

Use MWITHIN to request simple effects of within-subjects factors in repeated measures analysis (see MANOVA: Repeated Measures).

Pooled Effects: Plus Sign

To pool different effects for the purpose of significance testing, join the effects with a plus sign (+). A single test is made for the combined effect of the pooled terms.

- The keyword BY is evaluated before effects are pooled together.
- Parentheses are not allowed to change the order of evaluation. For example, it is illegal to specify `(A + B) BY C`. You must specify `/DESIGN=A BY C + B BY C`.

Example

```
MANOVA Y BY A(1,3) B(1,4) WITH X
 /ANALYSIS=Y
 /DESIGN=A, B, A BY B, A BY X + B BY X + A BY B BY X.
```

- This example shows how to test homogeneity of regressions in a two-way analysis of variance.
- The + signs are used to produce a pooled test of all interactions involving the covariate *X*. If this test is significant, the assumption of homogeneity of variance is questionable.

MUPLUS Keyword

MUPLUS combines the constant term (μ) in the model with the term specified after it. The normal use of this specification is to obtain parameter estimates that represent weighted means for the levels of some factor. For example, MUPLUS SEED represents the constant, or overall, mean plus the effect for each level of *SEED*. The significance of such effects is usually uninteresting, but the parameter estimates represent the weighted means for each level of *SEED*, adjusted for any covariates in the model.

- MUPLUS cannot appear more than once on a given DESIGN subcommand.
- MUPLUS is the only way to get standard errors for the predicted mean for each level of the factor specified.
- Parameter estimates are not displayed by default; you must explicitly request them on the PRINT subcommand or via a CONTRAST subcommand.
- You can obtain the unweighted mean by specifying the full factorial model, excluding those terms contained by an effect, and prefixing the effect whose mean is to be found by MUPLUS.

Effects of Continuous Variables

Usually you name factors but not covariates on the DESIGN subcommand. The linear effects of covariates are removed from the dependent variable before the design is tested. However, the design can include variables measured at the interval level and originally named as covariates or as additional dependent variables.

- Continuous variables on a DESIGN subcommand must be named as dependents or covariates on the MANOVA variable list.

- Before you can name a continuous variable on a DESIGN subcommand, you must supply an ANALYSIS subcommand that does *not* name the variable. This excludes it from the analysis as a dependent variable or covariate and makes it eligible for inclusion on DESIGN.

- More than one continuous variable can be pooled into a single effect (provided that they are all excluded on an ANALYSIS subcommand) with the keyword POOL(varlist). For a single continuous variable, `POOL(VAR)` is equivalent to `VAR`.

- The TO convention in the variable list for POOL refers to the order of continuous variables (dependent variables and covariates) on the original MANOVA variable list, which is not necessarily their order on the working data file. This is the only allowable use of the keyword TO on a DESIGN subcommand.

- You can specify interaction terms between factors and continuous variables. If *FAC* is a factor and *COV* is a covariate that has been omitted from an ANALYSIS subcommand, `FAC BY COV` is a valid specification on a DESIGN statement.

- You cannot specify an interaction between two continuous variables. Use the COMPUTE command to create a variable representing the interaction prior to MANOVA.

Example

```
*   This example tests whether the regression of the dependent
    variable Y on the two variables X1 and X2 is the same across
    all the categories of the factors AGE and TREATMNT.

MANOVA Y BY AGE(1,5) TREATMNT(1,3) WITH X1, X2
  /ANALYSIS = Y
  /DESIGN = POOL(X1,X2),
            AGE, TREATMNT, AGE BY TREATMNT,
            POOL(X1,X2) BY AGE + POOL(X1,X2) BY TREATMNT
               + POOL(X1,X2) BY AGE BY TREATMNT.
```

- ANALYSIS excludes *X1* and *X2* from the standard treatment of covariates, so that they can be used in the design.

- DESIGN includes five terms. `POOL(X1,X2)`, the overall regression of the dependent variable on *X1* and *X2*, is entered first, followed by the two factors and their interaction.

- The last term is the test for equal regressions. It consists of three factor-by-continuous-variable interactions pooled together. `POOL(X1,X2) BY AGE` is the interaction between *AGE* and the combined effect of the continuous variables *X1* and *X2*. It is combined with similar interactions between *TREATMNT* and the continuous variables and between the *AGE* by *TREATMNT* interaction and the continuous variables.

- If the last term is not statistically significant, there is no evidence that the regression of *Y* on *X1* and *X2* is different across any combination of the categories of *AGE* and *TREATMNT*.

Error Terms for Individual Effects

The "error" sum of squares against which terms in the design are tested is specified on the ERROR subcommand. For any particular term on a DESIGN subcommand, you can specify a different error term to be used in the analysis of variance. To do so, name the term followed by the keyword VS (or AGAINST) and the error term keyword.

- To test a term against only the within-cells sum of squares, specify the term followed by VS WITHIN on the DESIGN subcommand. For example, GROUP VS WITHIN tests the effect of the factor *GROUP* against only the within-cells sum of squares. For most analyses, this is the default error term.

- To test a term against only the residual sum of squares (the sum of squares for all terms not included in your DESIGN), specify the term followed by VS RESIDUAL.

- To test against the combined within-cells and residual sums of squares, specify the term followed by VS WITHIN+RESIDUAL.

- To test against any other sum of squares in the analysis of variance, include a term corresponding to the desired sum of squares in the design and assign it to an integer between 1 and 10. You can then test against the number of the error term. It is often convenient to test against the term before you define it. This is perfectly acceptable as long as you define the error term on the same DESIGN subcommand.

Example

```
MANOVA DEP BY A, B, C (1,3)
  /DESIGN=A VS 1,
          B WITHIN A = 1 VS 2,
          C WITHIN B WITHIN A = 2 VS WITHIN.
```

- In this example, the factors *A*, *B*, and *C* are completely nested; levels of *C* occur within levels of *B*, which occur within levels of *A*. Each factor is tested against everything within it.

- *A*, the outermost factor, is tested against the *B* within *A* sum of squares, to see if it contributes anything beyond the effects of *B* within each of its levels. The *B* within *A* sum of squares is defined as error term number 1.

- *B* nested within *A*, in turn, is tested against error term number 2, which is defined as the *C* within *B* within *A* sum of squares.

- Finally, *C* nested within *B* nested within *A* is tested against the within-cells sum of squares.

User-defined error terms are specified by simply inserting = n after a term, where *n* is an integer from 1 to 10. The equals sign is required. Keywords used in building a design term, such as BY or WITHIN, are evaluated first. For example, error term number 2 in the above example consists of the entire term C WITHIN B WITHIN A. An error-term *number,* but not an error-term *definition,* can follow the keyword VS.

CONSTANT Keyword

By default, the constant (grand mean) term is included as the first term in the model.

- If you have specified NOCONSTANT on the METHOD subcommand, a constant term will not be included in any design unless you request it with the CONSTANT keyword on DESIGN.

- You can specify an error term for the constant.

- A factor named CONSTANT will not be recognized on the DESIGN subcommand.

MANOVA: Multivariate

```
MANOVA dependent varlist [BY factor list (min,max) [factor list...]]
                         [WITH covariate list]

[/TRANSFORM [(dependent varlist [/dependent varlist])]=
                  [ORTHONORM] [{CONTRAST}] {DEVIATIONS (refcat)     }]
                              {BASIS   }  {DIFFERENCE              }
                                          {HELMERT                 }
                                          {SIMPLE (refcat)         }
                                          {REPEATED                }
                                          {POLYNOMIAL[({1,2,3...})]}]
                                                       {metric  }
                                          {SPECIAL (matrix)        }

[/RENAME={newname} {newname}...]
         {*       } {*      }

[/{PRINT  }=[HOMOGENEITY [({BOXM})]]
  {NOPRINT} [ERROR [(([COV] [COR] [SSCP] [STDDEV])]]
            [SIGNIF [(([MULTIV**] [EIGEN] [DIMENR]
                      [UNIV**] [HYPOTH][STEPDOWN] [BRIEF])]]
            [TRANSFORM]                                          ]

[/PCOMPS=[COR] [COV] [ROTATE(rottype)]
         [NCOMP(n)] [MINEIGEN(eigencut)] [ALL]]

[/PLOT=[ZCORR]]

[/DISCRIM [RAW] [STAN] [ESTIM] [COR] [ALL]
          [ROTATE(rottype)] [ALPHA({.25**})]]
                                   {a    }

[/POWER=[T({.05**})] [F({.05**})] [{APPROXIMATE}]]
           {a   }      {a   }      {EXACT      }

[/CINTERVAL=[MULTIVARIATE  (({ROY     })]]
                            {PILLAI   }
                            {BONFER   }
                            {HOTELLING}
                            {WILKS    }

[/ANALYSIS [({UNCONDITIONAL**})]=[()dependent varlist
            {CONDITIONAL    }     [WITH covariate varlist]
                                  [/dependent varlist...][)][WITH varlist]]

[/DESIGN...]*
```

* The DESIGN subcommand has the same syntax as is described in MANOVA: Univariate.

**Default if subcommand or keyword is omitted.

Example:
```
MANOVA SCORE1 TO SCORE4 BY METHOD(1,3).
```

Overview

This section discusses the subcommands that are used in multivariate analysis of variance and covariance designs with several interrelated dependent variables. The discussion focuses on subcommands and keywords that do not apply, or apply in different manners, to univariate analyses. It does not contain information on all of the subcommands you will need to specify the design. For subcommands not covered here, see MANOVA: Univariate.

Options

Dependent Variables and Covariates. You can specify subsets and reorder the dependent variables and covariates using the ANALYSIS subcommand. You can specify linear transformations of the dependent variables and covariates using the TRANSFORM subcommand. When transformations are performed, you can rename the variables using the RENAME subcommand and request the display of a transposed transformation matrix currently in effect using the PRINT subcommand.

Optional Output. You can request or suppress output on the PRINT and NOPRINT subcommands. Additional output appropriate to multivariate analysis includes error term matrices, Box's M statistic, multivariate and univariate F tests, and other significance analyses. You can also request predicted cell means for specific dependent variables on the PMEANS subcommand, produce a canonical discriminant analysis for each effect in your model with the DISCRIM subcommand, specify a principal components analysis of each error sum-of-squares and cross-product matrix in a multivariate analysis on the PCOMPS subcommand, display multivariate confidence intervals using the CINTERVAL subcommand, and generate a half-normal plot of the within-cells correlations among the dependent variables with the PLOT subcommand.

Basic Specification

- The basic specification is a variable list identifying the dependent variables, with the factors (if any) named after BY and the covariates (if any) named after WITH.
- By default, MANOVA produces multivariate and univariate F tests.

Subcommand Order

- The variable list must be specified first.
- Subcommands applicable to a specific design must be specified before that DESIGN subcommand. Otherwise, subcommands can be used in any order.

Syntax Rules

- All syntax rules applicable to univariate analysis apply to multivariate analysis. See "Syntax Rules" on p. 394 in MANOVA: Univariate.
- If you enter one of the multivariate specifications in a univariate analysis, MANOVA ignores it.

Limitations

- Maximum 20 factors.
- Memory requirements depend primarily on the number of cells in the design. For the default full factorial model, this equals the product of the number of levels or categories in each factor.

MANOVA Variable List

- Multivariate MANOVA calculates statistical tests that are valid for analyses of dependent variables that are correlated with one another. The dependent variables must be specified first.
- The factor and covariate lists follow the same rules as in univariate analyses.
- If the dependent variables are uncorrelated, the univariate significance tests have greater statistical power.

TRANSFORM Subcommand

TRANSFORM performs linear transformations of some or all of the continuous variables (dependent variables and covariates). Specifications on TRANSFORM include an optional list of variables to be transformed, optional keywords to describe how to generate a transformation matrix from the specified contrasts, and a required keyword specifying the transformation contrasts.

- Transformations apply to all subsequent designs unless replaced by another TRANSFORM subcommand.
- TRANSFORM subcommands are not cumulative. Only the transformation specified most recently is in effect at any time. You can restore the original variables in later designs by specifying SPECIAL with an identity matrix.
- You should not use TRANSFORM when you use the WSFACTORS subcommand to request repeated measures analysis; a transformation is automatically performed in repeated measures analysis (see MANOVA: Repeated Measures).
- Transformations are in effect for the duration of the MANOVA procedure only. After the procedure is complete, the original variables remain in the working data file.
- By default, the transformation matrix is not displayed. Specify the keyword TRANSFORM on the PRINT subcommand to see the matrix generated by the TRANSFORM subcommand.
- If you do not use the RENAME subcommand with TRANSFORM, the variables specified on TRANSFORM are renamed temporarily (for the duration of the procedure) as $T1$, $T2$, etc. Explicit use of RENAME is recommended.
- Subsequent references to transformed variables should use the new names. The only exception is when you supply a VARIABLES specification on the OMEANS subcommand after using TRANSFORM. In this case, specify the original names. OMEANS displays observed means of original variables (see the OMEANS subcommand on p. 403 in MANOVA: Univariate).

Variable Lists

- By default, MANOVA applies the transformation you request to all continuous variables (dependent variables and covariates).

- You can enter a variable list in parentheses following the TRANSFORM subcommand. If you do, only the listed variables are transformed.

- You can enter multiple variable lists, separated by slashes, within a single set of parentheses. Each list must have the same number of variables, and the lists must not overlap. The transformation is applied separately to the variables on each list.

- In designs with covariates, transform only the dependent variables, or, in some designs, apply the same transformation separately to the dependent variables and the covariates.

CONTRAST, BASIS, and ORTHONORM Keywords

You can control how the transformation matrix is to be generated from the specified contrasts. If none of these three keywords is specified on TRANSFORM, the default is CONTRAST.

CONTRAST   *Generate the transformation matrix directly from the contrast matrix specified* (see the CONTRAST subcommand on p. 396 in MANOVA: Univariate). This is the default.

BASIS   *Generate the transformation matrix from the one-way basis matrix corresponding to the specified contrast matrix.* BASIS makes a difference only if the transformation contrasts are not orthogonal.

ORTHONORM   *Orthonormalize the transformation matrix by rows before use.* MANOVA eliminates redundant rows. By default, orthonormalization is not done.

- CONTRAST and BASIS are alternatives and are mutually exclusive.

- ORTHONORM is independent of the CONTRAST/BASIS choice; you can enter it before or after either of those keywords.

Transformation Methods

To specify a transformation method, use one of the following keywords available on the TRANSFORM subcommand. Note that these are identical to the keywords available for the CONTRAST subcommand (see the CONTRAST subcommand on p. 396 in MANOVA: Univariate). However, in univariate designs, they are applied to the different levels of a factor. Here they are applied to the continuous variables in the analysis. This reflects the fact that the different dependent variables in a multivariate MANOVA setup can often be thought of as corresponding to different levels of some factor.

- The transformation keyword (and its specifications, if any) must follow all other specifications on the TRANSFORM subcommand.

DEVIATION   *Deviations from the mean of the variables being transformed.* The first transformed variable is the mean of all variables in the transformation. Other transformed variables represent deviations of individual variables from the mean. One of the original variables (by default the last) is omitted as redundant. To omit a variable other than the last, specify the number of the variable to be omitted in parentheses after the DEVIATION keyword. For example,

```
/TRANSFORM (A B C) = DEVIATION(1)
```

omits *A* and creates variables representing the mean, the deviation of *B* from the mean, and the deviation of *C* from the mean. A DEVIATION transformation is not orthogonal.

DIFFERENCE *Difference or reverse Helmert transformation.* The first transformed variable is the mean of the original variables. Each of the original variables except the first is then transformed by subtracting the mean of those (original) variables that precede it. A DIFFERENCE transformation is orthogonal.

HELMERT *Helmert transformation.* The first transformed variable is the mean of the original variables. Each of the original variables except the last is then transformed by subtracting the mean of those (original) variables that follow it. A HELMERT transformation is orthogonal.

SIMPLE *Each original variable, except the last, is compared to the last of the original variables.* To use a variable other than the last as the omitted reference variable, specify its number in parentheses following the keyword SIMPLE. For example,

```
/TRANSFORM(A B C) = SIMPLE(2)
```

specifies the second variable, *B*, as the reference variable. The three transformed variables represent the mean of *A*, *B*, and *C*, the difference between *A* and *B*, and the difference between *C* and *B*. A SIMPLE transformation is not orthogonal.

POLYNOMIAL *Orthogonal polynomial transformation.* The first transformed variable represents the mean of the original variables. Other transformed variables represent the linear, quadratic, and higher-degree components. By default, values of the original variables are assumed to represent equally spaced points. You can specify unequal spacing by entering a metric consisting of one integer for each variable in parentheses after the keyword POLYNOMIAL. For example,

```
/TRANSFORM(RESP1 RESP2 RESP3) = POLYNOMIAL(1,2,4)
```

might indicate that three response variables correspond to levels of some stimulus that are in the proportion 1:2:4. The default metric is always $(1,2,...,k)$, where k variables are involved. Only the relative differences between the terms of the metric matter: (1,2,4) is the same metric as (2,3,5) or (20,30,50) because in each instance the difference between the second and third numbers is twice the difference between the first and second.

REPEATED *Comparison of adjacent variables.* The first transformed variable is the mean of the original variables. Each additional transformed variable is the difference between one of the original variables and the original variable that followed it. Such transformed variables are often called *difference scores.* A REPEATED transformation is not orthogonal.

SPECIAL   *A user-defined transformation.* After the keyword SPECIAL, enter a square matrix in parentheses with as many rows and columns as there are variables to transform. MANOVA multiplies this matrix by the vector of original variables to obtain the transformed variables (see the examples below).

Example

```
MANOVA X1 TO X3 BY A(1,4)
  /TRANSFORM(X1 X2 X3) = SPECIAL( 1  1  1,
                                  1  0 -1,
                                  2 -1 -1)
  /DESIGN.
```

- The given matrix will be post-multiplied by the three continuous variables (considered as a column vector) to yield the transformed variables. The first transformed variable will therefore equal $X1 + X2 + X3$, the second will equal $X1 - X3$, and the third will equal $2X1 - X2 - X3$.

- The variable list is optional in this example since all three interval-level variables are transformed.

- You do not need to enter the matrix one row at a time, as shown above. For example,

```
  /TRANSFORM = SPECIAL(1 1 1 1 0 -1 2 -1 -1)
```

is equivalent to the TRANSFORM specification in the above example.

- You can specify a repetition factor followed by an asterisk to indicate multiple consecutive elements of a SPECIAL transformation matrix. For example,

```
  /TRANSFORM = SPECIAL (4*1 0 -1 2 2*-1)
```

is again equivalent to the TRANSFORM specification above.

Example

```
MANOVA X1 TO X3, Y1 TO Y3 BY A(1,4)
  /TRANSFORM (X1 X2 X3/Y1 Y2 Y3) = SPECIAL( 1  1  1,
                                            1  0 -1,
                                            2 -1 -1)
  /DESIGN.
```

- Here the same transformation shown in the previous example is applied to *X1*, *X2*, *X3* and to *Y1*, *Y2*, *Y3*.

RENAME Subcommand

Use RENAME to assign new names to transformed variables. Renaming variables after a transformation is strongly recommended. If you transform but do not rename the variables, the names *T1*, *T2*,...,*Tn* are used as names for the transformed variables.

- Follow RENAME with a list of new variable names.

- You must enter a new name for each dependent variable and covariate on the MANOVA variable list.

- Enter the new names in the order in which the original variables appeared on the MANOVA variable list.

- To retain the original name for one or more of the interval variables, you can either enter an asterisk or reenter the old name as the new name.

- References to dependent variables and covariates on subcommands following RENAME must use the new names. The original names will not be recognized within the MANOVA procedure. The only exception is the OMEANS subcommand, which displays observed means of the original (untransformed) variables. Use the original names on OMEANS.

- The new names exist only during the MANOVA procedure that created them. They do not remain in the working data file after the procedure is complete.

Example

```
MANOVA A, B, C, V4, V5 BY TREATMNT(1,3)
   /TRANSFORM(A, B, C) = REPEATED
   /RENAME = MEANABC, AMINUSB, BMINUSC, *, *
   /DESIGN.
```

- The REPEATED transformation produces three transformed variables, which are then assigned mnemonic names *MEANABC*, *AMINUSB*, and *BMINUSC*.

- *V4* and *V5* retain their original names.

Example

```
MANOVA WT1, WT2, WT3, WT4 BY TREATMNT(1,3) WITH COV
   /TRANSFORM (WT1 TO WT4) = POLYNOMIAL
   /RENAME = MEAN, LINEAR, QUAD, CUBIC, *
   /ANALYSIS = MEAN, LINEAR, QUAD WITH COV
   /DESIGN.
```

- After the polynomial transformation of the four *WT* variables, RENAME assigns appropriate names to the various trends.

- Even though only four variables were transformed, RENAME applies to all five continuous variables. An asterisk is required to retain the original name for *COV*.

- The ANALYSIS subcommand following RENAME refers to the interval variables by their new names.

PRINT and NOPRINT Subcommands

All of the PRINT specifications described in MANOVA: Univariate are available in multivariate analyses. The following additional output can be requested. To suppress any optional output, specify the appropriate keyword on NOPRINT.

ERROR   *Error matrices.* Three types of matrices are available.

SIGNIF   *Significance tests.*

TRANSFORM   *Transformation matrix.* It is available if you have transformed the dependent variables with the TRANSFORM subcommand.

HOMOGENEITY *Test for homogeneity of variance.* BOXM is available for multivariate analyses.

ERROR Keyword

In multivariate analysis, error terms consist of entire matrices, not single values. You can display any of the following error matrices on a PRINT subcommand by requesting them in parentheses following the keyword ERROR. If you specify ERROR by itself, without further specifications, the default is to display COV and COR.

SSCP   *Error sums-of-squares and cross-products matrix.*

COV   *Error variance-covariance matrix.*

COR   *Error correlation matrix with standard deviations on the diagonal.* This also displays the determinant of the matrix and Bartlett's test of sphericity, a test of whether the error correlation matrix is significantly different from an identity matrix.

SIGNIF Keyword

You can request any of the optional output listed below by entering the appropriate specification in parentheses after the keyword SIGNIF on the PRINT subcommand. Further specifications for SIGNIF are described in MANOVA: Repeated Measures.

MULTIV   *Multivariate F tests for group differences.* MULTIV is always printed unless explicitly suppressed with the NOPRINT subcommand.

EIGEN   *Eigenvalues of the $S_h S_e^{-1}$ matrix.* This matrix is the product of the hypothesis sums-of-squares and cross-products (SSCP) matrix and the inverse of the error SSCP matrix. To print EIGEN, request it on the PRINT subcommand.

DIMENR   *A dimension-reduction analysis.* To print DIMENR, request it on the PRINT subcommand.

UNIV   *Univariate F tests.* UNIV is always printed except in repeated measures analysis. If the dependent variables are uncorrelated, univariate tests have greater statistical power. To suppress UNIV, use the NOPRINT subcommand.

HYPOTH   *The hypothesis SSCP matrix.* To print HYPOTH, request it on the PRINT subcommand.

STEPDOWN   *Roy-Bargmann stepdown F tests.* To print STEPDOWN, request it on the PRINT subcommand.

BRIEF   *Abbreviated multivariate output.* This is similar to a univariate analysis of variance table but with Wilks' multivariate *F* approximation (lambda) replacing the univariate *F*. BRIEF overrides any of the SIGNIF specifications listed above.

SINGLEDF   *Significance tests for the single degree of freedom making up each effect for ANOVA tables.* Results are displayed separately corresponding to each hypothesis degree of freedom. See MANOVA: Univariate.

- If neither PRINT nor NOPRINT is specified, MANOVA displays the results corresponding to MULTIV and UNIV for a multivariate analysis not involving repeated measures.

- If you enter any specification except BRIEF or SINGLEDF for SIGNIF on the PRINT subcommand, the requested output is displayed in addition to the default.
- To suppress the default, specify the keyword(s) on the NOPRINT subcommand.

TRANSFORM Keyword

The keyword TRANSFORM specified on PRINT displays the transposed transformation matrix in use for each subsequent design. This matrix is helpful in interpreting a multivariate analysis in which the interval-level variables have been transformed with either TRANSFORM or WSFACTORS.

- The matrix displayed by this option is the transpose of the transformation matrix.
- Original variables correspond to the rows of the matrix, and transformed variables correspond to the columns.
- A **transformed variable** is a linear combination of the original variables using the coefficients displayed in the column corresponding to that transformed variable.

HOMOGENEITY Keyword

In addition to the BARTLETT and COCHRAN specifications described in MANOVA: Univariate, the following test for homogeneity is available for multivariate analyses:

BOXM   *Box's* M *statistic.* BOXM requires at least two dependent variables. If there is only one dependent variable when BOXM is requested, MANOVA prints Bartlett-Box *F* test statistic and issues a note.

PLOT Subcommand

In addition to the plots described in MANOVA: Univariate, the following is available for multivariate analyses:

ZCORR   *A half-normal plot of the within-cells correlations among the dependent variables.* MANOVA first transforms the correlations using Fisher's Z transformation. If errors for the dependent variables are uncorrelated, the plotted points should lie close to a straight line.

PCOMPS Subcommand

PCOMPS requests a principal components analysis of each error matrix in a multivariate analysis. You can display the principal components of the error correlation matrix, the error variance-covariance matrix, or both. These principal components are corrected for differences due to the factors and covariates in the MANOVA analysis. They tend to be more useful than principal components extracted from the raw correlation or covariance matrix when there are significant group differences between the levels of the factors or when a significant amount of error variance is accounted for by the covariates. You can specify any of the keywords listed below on PCOMPS.

COR   *Principal components analysis of the error correlation matrix.*

COV   *Principal components analysis of the error variance-covariance matrix.*

ROTATE   *Rotate the principal components solution.* By default, no rotation is per-
               formed. Specify a rotation type (either VARIMAX, EQUAMAX, or QUARTIMAX)
               in parentheses after the keyword ROTATE. To cancel a rotation specified for a
               previous design, enter NOROTATE in the parentheses after ROTATE.

NCOMP(n)   *The number of principal components to rotate.* Specify a number in paren-
               theses. The default is the number of dependent variables.

MINEIGEN(n) *The minimum eigenvalue for principal component extraction.* Specify a cut-
               off value in parentheses. Components with eigenvalues below the cutoff
               will not be retained in the solution. The default is 0; all components (or the
               number specified on NCOMP) are extracted.

ALL   *COR, COV, and ROTATE.*

- You must specify either COR or COV (or both). Otherwise, MANOVA will not produce any
  principal components.
- Both NCOMP and MINEIGEN limit the number of components that are rotated.
- If the number specified on NCOMP is less than two, two components are rotated provided that
  at least two components have eigenvalues greater than any value specified on MINEIGEN.
- Principal components analysis is computationally expensive if the number of dependent
  variables is large.

DISCRIM Subcommand

DISCRIM produces a canonical discriminant analysis for each effect in a design. (For covariates,
DISCRIM produces a canonical correlation analysis.) These analyses aid in the interpretation of
multivariate effects. You can request the following statistics by entering the appropriate keywords after the subcommand DISCRIM:

RAW   *Raw discriminant function coefficients.*

STAN   *Standardized discriminant function coefficients.*

ESTIM   *Effect estimates in discriminant function space.*

COR   *Correlations between the dependent variables and the canonical variables defined
             by the discriminant functions.*

ROTATE   *Rotation of the matrix of correlations between dependent and canonical variables.*
             Specify rotation type VARIMAX, EQUAMAX, or QUARTIMAX in parentheses after this
             keyword.

ALL   *RAW, STAN, ESTIM, COR, and ROTATE.*

By default, the significance level required for the extraction of a canonical variable is 0.25.
You can change this value by specifying the keyword ALPHA and a value between 0 and 1 in
parentheses:

ALPHA   *The significance level required before a canonical variable is extracted.* The default is 0.25. To change the default, specify a decimal number between 0 and 1 in parentheses after ALPHA.

- The correlations between dependent variables and canonical functions are not rotated unless at least two functions are significant at the level defined by ALPHA.
- If you set ALPHA to 1.0, all discriminant functions are reported (and rotated, if you so request).
- If you set ALPHA to 0, no discriminant functions are reported.

POWER Subcommand

The following specifications are available for POWER in multivariate analysis. For applications of POWER in univariate analysis, see MANOVA: Univariate.

APPROXIMATE   *Approximate power values.* This is the default. Approximate power values for multivariate tests are derived from procedures presented by Muller and Peterson (1984). Approximate values are normally accurate to three decimal places and are much cheaper to compute than exact values.

EXACT   *Exact power values.* Exact power values for multivariate tests are computed from the noncentral F distribution. Exact multivariate power values will be displayed only if there is one hypothesis degree of freedom, where all the multivariate criteria have identical power.

- For information on the multivariate generalizations of power and effect size, see Muller and Peterson (1984), Green (1978), and Huberty (1972).

CINTERVAL Subcommand

In addition to the specifications described in MANOVA: Univariate, the keyword MULTIVARIATE is available for multivariate analysis. You can specify a type in parentheses after the MULTIVARIATE keyword. The following type keywords are available on MULTIVARIATE:

ROY   *Roy's largest root.* An approximation given by Pillai (1967) is used. This approximation is accurate for upper percentage points (0.95 to 1), but it is not as good for lower percentage points. Thus, for Roy intervals, the user is restricted to the range 0.95 to 1.

PILLAI   *Pillai's trace.* The intervals are computed by approximating the percentage points with percentage points of the F distribution.

WILKS   *Wilks' lambda.* The intervals are computed by approximating the percentage points with percentage points of the F distribution.

HOTELLING   *Hotelling's trace.* The intervals are computed by approximating the percentage points with percentage points of the F distribution.

BONFER   *Bonferroni intervals.* This approximation is based on Student's t distribution.

- The Wilks', Pillai's, and Hotelling's approximate confidence intervals are thought to match exact intervals across a wide range of alpha levels, especially for large sample sizes (Burns, 1984). Use of these intervals, however, has not been widely investigated.

- To obtain multivariate intervals separately for each parameter, choose individual multivariate intervals. For individual multivariate confidence intervals, the hypothesis degree of freedom is set to 1, in which case Hotelling's, Pillai's, Wilks', and Roy's intervals will be identical and equivalent to those computed from percentage points of Hotelling's T^2 distribution. Individual Bonferroni intervals will differ and, for a small number of dependent variables, will generally be shorter.

- If you specify MULTIVARIATE on CINTERVAL, you must specify a type keyword. If you specify CINTERVAL without any keyword, the default is the same as with univariate analysis—CINTERVAL displays individual-univariate confidence intervals at the 0.95 level.

ANALYSIS Subcommand

ANALYSIS is discussed in MANOVA: Univariate as a means of obtaining factor-by-covariate interaction terms. In multivariate analyses, it is considerably more useful.

- ANALYSIS specifies a subset of the continuous variables (dependent variables and covariates) listed on the MANOVA variable list and completely redefines which variables are dependent and which are covariates.

- All variables named on an ANALYSIS subcommand must have been named on the MANOVA variable list. It does not matter whether they were named as dependent variables or as covariates.

- Factors cannot be named on an ANALYSIS subcommand.

- After the keyword ANALYSIS, specify the names of one or more dependent variables and, optionally, the keyword WITH followed by one or more covariates.

- An ANALYSIS specification remains in effect for all designs until you enter another ANALYSIS subcommand.

- Continuous variables named on the MANOVA variable list but omitted from the ANALYSIS subcommand currently in effect can be specified on the DESIGN subcommand. See the DESIGN subcommand on p. 411 in MANOVA: Univariate.

- You can use an ANALYSIS subcommand to request analyses of several groups of variables provided that the groups do not overlap. Separate the groups of variables with slashes and enclose the entire ANALYSIS specification in parentheses.

CONDITIONAL and UNCONDITIONAL Keywords

When several analysis groups are specified on a single ANALYSIS subcommand, you can control how each list is to be processed by specifying CONDITIONAL or UNCONDITIONAL in the parentheses immediately following the ANALYSIS subcommand. The default is UNCONDITIONAL.

UNCONDITIONAL   *Process each analysis group separately, without regard to other lists. This is the default.*

CONDITIONAL   *Use variables specified in one analysis group as covariates in subsequent analysis groups.*

- CONDITIONAL analysis is not carried over from one ANALYSIS subcommand to another.
- You can specify a final covariate list outside the parentheses. These covariates apply to every list within the parentheses, regardless of whether you specify CONDITIONAL or UNCONDITIONAL. The variables on this global covariate list must not be specified in any individual lists.

Example

```
MANOVA A B C BY FAC(1,4) WITH D, E
  /ANALYSIS = (A, B / C / D WITH E)
  /DESIGN.
```

- The first analysis uses *A* and *B* as dependent variables and uses no covariates.
- The second analysis uses *C* as a dependent variable and uses no covariates.
- The third analysis uses *D* as the dependent variable and uses *E* as a covariate.

Example

```
MANOVA A, B, C, D, E BY FAC(1,4) WITH F G
  /ANALYSIS = (A, B / C / D WITH E) WITH F G
  /DESIGN.
```

- A final covariate list `WITH F G` is specified outside the parentheses. The covariates apply to every list within the parentheses.
- The first analysis uses *A* and *B*, with *F* and *G* as covariates.
- The second analysis uses *C*, with *F* and *G* as covariates.
- The third analysis uses *D*, with *E*, *F*, and *G* as covariates.
- Factoring out *F* and *G* is the only way to use them as covariates in all three analyses, since no variable can be named more than once on an ANALYSIS subcommand.

Example

```
MANOVA A B C BY FAC(1,3)
  /ANALYSIS(CONDITIONAL) = (A WITH B / C)
  /DESIGN.
```

- In the first analysis, *A* is the dependent variable, *B* is a covariate, and *C* is not used.
- In the second analysis, *C* is the dependent variable, and both *A* and *B* are covariates.

MANOVA: Repeated Measures

```
MANOVA dependent varlist [BY factor list (min,max)[factor list...]
        [WITH [varying covariate list] [(constant covariate list)]]

  /WSFACTORS = varname (levels) [varname...]

 [/WSDESIGN = [effect effect...]

 [/MEASURE = newname newname...]

 [/RENAME = newname newname...]

 [/{PRINT  }=[SIGNIF({AVERF**}) (HF) (GG) (EFSIZE)]]
   {NOPRINT}         {AVONLY }

 [/DESIGN]*
```

* The DESIGN subcommand has the same syntax as is described in MANOVA: Univariate.

** Default if subcommand or keyword is omitted.

Example:
```
MANOVA Y1 TO Y4 BY GROUP(1,2)
  /WSFACTORS=YEAR(4).
```

Overview

This section discusses the subcommands that are used in repeated measures designs, in which the dependent variables represent measurements of the same variable (or variables) at different times. This section does not contain information on all subcommands you will need to specify the design. For some subcommands or keywords not covered here, such as DE-SIGN, see MANOVA: Univariate. For information on optional output and the multivariate significance tests available, see MANOVA: Multivariate.

- In a simple repeated measures analysis, all dependent variables represent different measurements of the same variable for different values (or levels) of a within-subjects factor. Between-subjects factors and covariates can also be included in the model, just as in analyses not involving repeated measures.

- A **within-subjects factor** is simply a factor that distinguishes measurements made on the same subject or case, rather than distinguishing different subjects or cases.

- MANOVA permits more complex analyses, in which the dependent variables represent levels of two or more within-subjects factors.

- MANOVA also permits analyses in which the dependent variables represent measurements of several variables for the different levels of the within-subjects factors. These are known as **doubly multivariate designs**.

- A repeated measures analysis includes a within-subjects design describing the model to be tested with the within-subjects factors, as well as the usual between-subjects design describing the effects to be tested with between-subjects factors. The default for both types of design is a full factorial model.

- MANOVA always performs an orthonormal transformation of the dependent variables in a repeated measures analysis. By default, MANOVA renames them as *T1*, *T2*, and so forth.

Basic Specification

- The basic specification is a variable list followed by the WSFACTORS subcommand.
- By default, MANOVA performs special repeated measures processing. Default output includes SIGNIF(AVERF) but not SIGNIF(UNIV). In addition, for any within-subjects effect involving more than one transformed variable, the Mauchly test of sphericity is displayed to test the assumption that the covariance matrix of the transformed variables is constant on the diagonal and zero off the diagonal. The Greenhouse-Geiser epsilon and the Huynh-Feldt epsilon are also displayed for use in correcting the significance tests in the event that the assumption of sphericity is violated.

Subcommand Order

- The list of dependent variables, factors, and covariates must be first.
- WSFACTORS must be the first subcommand used after the variable list.

Syntax Rules

- The WSFACTORS (within-subjects factors), WSDESIGN (within-subjects design), and MEASURE subcommands are used only in repeated measures analysis.
- WSFACTORS is required for any repeated measures analysis.
- If WSDESIGN is not specified, a full factorial within-subjects design consisting of all main effects and interactions among within-subjects factors is used by default.
- The MEASURE subcommand is used for doubly multivariate designs, in which the dependent variables represent repeated measurements of more than one variable.
- Do not use the TRANSFORM subcommand with the WSFACTORS subcommand because WSFACTORS automatically causes an orthonormal transformation of the dependent variables.

Limitations

- Maximum 20 between-subjects factors. There is no limit on the number of measures for doubly multivariate designs.
- Memory requirements depend primarily on the number of cells in the design. For the default full factorial model, this equals the product of the number of levels or categories in each factor.

Example

```
MANOVA Y1 TO Y4 BY GROUP(1,2)
  /WSFACTORS=YEAR(4)
  /CONTRAST(YEAR)=POLYNOMIAL
  /RENAME=CONST, LINEAR, QUAD, CUBIC
  /PRINT=TRANSFORM PARAM(ESTIM)
  /WSDESIGN=YEAR
  /DESIGN=GROUP.
```

- WSFACTORS immediately follows the MANOVA variable list and specifies a repeated measures analysis in which the four dependent variables represent a single variable measured at four levels of the within-subjects factor. The within-subjects factor is called *YEAR* for the duration of the MANOVA procedure.

- CONTRAST requests polynomial contrasts for the levels of *YEAR*. Because the four variables, *Y1*, *Y2*, *Y3*, and *Y4*, in the working data file represent the four levels of *YEAR*, the effect is to perform an orthonormal polynomial transformation of these variables.

- RENAME assigns names to the dependent variables to reflect the transformation.

- PRINT requests that the transformation matrix and the parameter estimates be displayed.

- WSDESIGN specifies a within-subjects design that includes only the effect of the *YEAR* within-subjects factor. Because *YEAR* is the only within-subjects factor specified, this is the default design, and WSDESIGN could have been omitted.

- DESIGN specifies a between-subjects design that includes only the effect of the *GROUP* between-subjects factor. This subcommand could have been omitted.

MANOVA Variable List

The list of dependent variables, factors, and covariates must be specified first.

- WSFACTORS determines how the dependent variables on the MANOVA variable list will be interpreted.

- The number of dependent variables on the MANOVA variable list must be a multiple of the number of cells in the within-subjects design. If there are six cells in the within-subjects design, each group of six dependent variables represents a single within-subjects variable that has been measured in each of the six cells.

- Normally, the number of dependent variables should equal the number of cells in the within-subjects design multiplied by the number of variables named on the MEASURE subcommand (if one is used). If you have more groups of dependent variables than are accounted for by the MEASURE subcommand, MANOVA will choose variable names to label the output, which may be difficult to interpret.

- Covariates are specified after the keyword WITH. You can specify either varying covariates or constant covariates, or both. **Varying covariates**, similar to dependent variables in a repeated measures analysis, represent measurements of the same variable (or variables) at different times while **constant covariates** represent variables whose values remain the same at each within-subjects measurement.

- If you use varying covariates, the number of covariates specified must be an integer multiple of the number of dependent variables.

- If you use constant covariates, you must specify them in parentheses. If you use both constant and varying covariates, constant variates must be specified after all varying covariates.

Example

```
MANOVA MATH1 TO MATH4 BY METHOD(1,2) WITH PHYS1 TO PHYS4 (SES)
       /WSFACTORS=SEMESTER(4).
```

- The four dependent variables represent a score measured four times (corresponding to the four levels of *SEMESTER*).
- The four varying covariates *PHYS1* to *PHYS4* represents four measurements of another score.
- *SES* is a constant covariate. Its value does not change over the time covered by the four levels of *SEMESTER*.
- Default contrast (POLYNOMIAL) is used.

WSFACTORS Subcommand

WSFACTORS names the within-subjects factors and specifies the number of levels for each.

- For repeated measures designs, WSFACTORS must be the first subcommand after the MANOVA variable list.
- Only one WSFACTORS subcommand is permitted per execution of MANOVA.
- Names for the within-subjects factors are specified on the WSFACTORS subcommand. Factor names must not duplicate any of the dependent variables, factors, or covariates named on the MANOVA variable list.
- If there are more than one within-subjects factors, they must be named in the order corresponding to the order of the dependent variables on the MANOVA variable list. MANOVA varies the levels of the last-named within-subjects factor most rapidly when assigning dependent variables to within-subjects cells (see the example below).
- Levels of the factors must be represented in the data by the dependent variables named on the MANOVA variable list.
- Enter a number in parentheses after each factor to indicate how many levels the factor has. If two or more adjacent factors have the same number of levels, you can enter the number of levels in parentheses after all of them.
- Enter only the number of levels for within-subjects factors, not a range of values.
- The number of cells in the within-subjects design is the product of the number of levels for all within-subjects factors.

Example

```
MANOVA X1Y1 X1Y2 X2Y1 X2Y2 X3Y1 X3Y2 BY TREATMNT(1,5) GROUP(1,2)
       /WSFACTORS=X(3) Y(2)
       /DESIGN.
```

- The MANOVA variable list names six dependent variables and two between-subjects factors, *TREATMNT* and *GROUP*.

- WSFACTORS identifies two within-subjects factors whose levels distinguish the six dependent variables. *X* has three levels and *Y* has two. Thus, there are $3 \times 2 = 6$ cells in the within-subjects design, corresponding to the six dependent variables.

- Variable *X1Y1* corresponds to levels 1,1 of the two within-subjects factors; variable *X1Y2* corresponds to levels 1,2; *X2Y1* to levels 2,1; and so on up to *X3Y2*, which corresponds to levels 3,2. The first within-subjects factor named, *X*, varies most slowly, and the last within-subjects factor named, *Y*, varies most rapidly on the list of dependent variables.

- Because there is no WSDESIGN subcommand, the within-subjects design will include all main effects and interactions: *X*, *Y*, and *X* by *Y*.

- Likewise, the between-subjects design includes all main effects and interactions: *TREATMNT*, *GROUP*, and *TREATMNT* by *GROUP*.

- In addition, a repeated measures analysis always includes interactions between the within-subjects factors and the between-subjects factors. There are three such interactions for each of the three within-subjects effects.

CONTRAST for WSFACTORS

The levels of a within-subjects factor are represented by different dependent variables. Therefore, contrasts between levels of such a factor compare these dependent variables. Specifying the type of contrast amounts to specifying a transformation to be performed on the dependent variables.

- An orthonormal transformation is automatically performed on the dependent variables in a repeated measures analysis.

- To specify the type of orthonormal transformation, use the CONTRAST subcommand for the within-subjects factors.

- Regardless of the contrast type you specify, the transformation matrix is orthonormalized before use.

- If you do not specify a contrast type for within-subjects factors, the default contrast type is orthogonal POLYNOMIAL. Intrinsically orthogonal contrast types are recommended for within-subjects factors if you wish to examine each degree-of-freedom test. Other orthogonal contrast types are DIFFERENCE and HELMERT. MULTIV and AVERF tests are identical, no matter what contrast was specified.

- To perform non-orthogonal contrasts, you must use the TRANSFORM subcommand instead of CONTRAST. The TRANSFORM subcommand is discussed in MANOVA: Multivariate.

- When you implicitly request a transformation of the dependent variables with CONTRAST for within-subjects factors, the same transformation is applied to any covariates in the analysis. The number of covariates must be an integer multiple of the number of dependent variables.

- You can display the transpose of the transformation matrix generated by your within-subjects contrast using the keyword TRANSFORM on the PRINT subcommand.

Example

```
MANOVA SCORE1 SCORE2 SCORE3 BY GROUP(1,4)
  /WSFACTORS=ROUND(3)
  /CONTRAST(ROUND)=DIFFERENCE
  /CONTRAST(GROUP)=DEVIATION
  /PRINT=TRANSFORM PARAM(ESTIM).
```

- This analysis has one between-subjects factor, *GROUP*, with levels 1, 2, 3, and 4, and one within-subjects factor, *ROUND*, with three levels that are represented by the three dependent variables.

- The first CONTRAST subcommand specifies difference contrasts for *ROUND*, the within-subjects factor.

- There is no WSDESIGN subcommand, so a default full factorial within-subjects design is assumed. This could also have been specified as `WSDESIGN=ROUND`, or simply `WSDESIGN`.

- The second CONTRAST subcommand specifies deviation contrasts for *GROUP*, the between-subjects factor. This subcommand could have been omitted because deviation contrasts are the default.

- PRINT requests the display of the transformation matrix generated by the within-subjects contrast and the parameter estimates for the model.

- There is no DESIGN subcommand, so a default full factorial between-subjects design is assumed. This could also have been specified as `DESIGN=GROUP`, or simply `DESIGN`.

PARTITION for WSFACTORS

The PARTITION subcommand also applies to factors named on WSFACTORS. (See the PARTITION subcommand on p. 398 in MANOVA: Univariate.)

WSDESIGN Subcommand

WSDESIGN specifies the design for within-subjects factors. Its specifications are like those of the DESIGN subcommand, but it uses the within-subjects factors rather than the between-subjects factors.

- The default WSDESIGN is a full factorial design, which includes all main effects and all interactions for within-subjects factors. The default is in effect whenever a design is processed without a preceding WSDESIGN or when the preceding WSDESIGN subcommand has no specifications.

- A WSDESIGN specification can include main effects, factor-by-factor interactions, nested terms (term within term), terms using the keyword MWITHIN, and pooled effects using the plus sign. The specification is the same as on the DESIGN subcommand but involves only within-subjects factors.

- A WSDESIGN specification cannot include between-subjects factors or terms based on them, nor does it accept interval-level variables, the keywords MUPLUS or CONSTANT, or error-term definitions or references.

- The WSDESIGN specification applies to all subsequent within-subjects designs until another WSDESIGN subcommand is encountered.

Example

```
MANOVA JANLO,JANHI,FEBLO,FEBHI,MARLO,MARHI BY SEX(1,2)
  /WSFACTORS MONTH(3) STIMULUS(2)
  /WSDESIGN MONTH, STIMULUS
  /WSDESIGN
  /DESIGN SEX.
```

- There are six dependent variables, corresponding to three months and two different levels of stimulus.
- The dependent variables are named on the MANOVA variable list in such an order that the level of stimulus varies more rapidly than the month. Thus, *STIMULUS* is named last on the WSFACTORS subcommand.
- The first WSDESIGN subcommand specifies only the main effects for within-subjects factors. There is no *MONTH* by *STIMULUS* interaction term.
- The second WSDESIGN subcommand has no specifications and, therefore, invokes the default within-subjects design, which includes the main effects and their interaction.

MWITHIN Keyword for Simple Effects

You can use MWITHIN on either the WSDESIGN or the DESIGN subcommand in a model with both between- and within-subjects factors to estimate simple effects for factors nested within factors of the opposite type.

Example

```
MANOVA WEIGHT1 WEIGHT2 BY TREAT(1,2)
 /WSFACTORS=WEIGHT(2)
 /DESIGN=MWITHIN TREAT(1) MWITHIN TREAT(2)
MANOVA WEIGHT1 WEIGHT2 BY TREAT(1,2)
 /WSFACTORS=WEIGHT(2)
 /WSDESIGN=MWITHIN WEIGHT(1) MWITHIN WEIGHT(2)
 /DESIGN.
```

- The first DESIGN tests the simple effects of *WEIGHT* within each level of *TREAT*.
- The second DESIGN tests the simple effects of *TREAT* within each level of *WEIGHT.*

MEASURE Subcommand

In a doubly multivariate analysis, the dependent variables represent multiple variables measured under the different levels of the within-subjects factors. Use MEASURE to assign names to the variables that you have measured for the different levels of within-subjects factors.

- Specify a list of one or more variable names to be used in labeling the averaged results. If no within-subjects factor has more than two levels, MEASURE has no effect.
- The number of dependent variables on the DESIGN subcommand should equal the product of the number of cells in the within-subjects design and the number of names on MEASURE.
- If you do not enter a MEASURE subcommand and there are more dependent variables than cells in the within-subjects design, MANOVA assigns names (normally *MEAS.1*, *MEAS.2*, etc.) to the different measures.

- All of the dependent variables corresponding to each measure should be listed together and ordered so that the within-subjects factor named last on the WSFACTORS subcommand varies most rapidly.

Example

```
MANOVA TEMP1 TO TEMP6, WEIGHT1 TO WEIGHT6 BY GROUP(1,2)
  /WSFACTORS=DAY(3) AMPM(2)
  /MEASURE=TEMP WEIGHT
  /WSDESIGN=DAY, AMPM, DAY BY AMPM
  /PRINT=SIGNIF(HYPOTH AVERF)
  /DESIGN.
```

- There are 12 dependent variables: 6 temperatures and 6 weights, corresponding to morning and afternoon measurements on three days.

- WSFACTORS identifies the two factors (*DAY* and *AMPM*) that distinguish the temperature and weight measurements for each subject. These factors define six within-subjects cells.

- MEASURE indicates that the first group of six dependent variables correspond to *TEMP* and the second group of six dependent variables correspond to *WEIGHT*.

- These labels, *TEMP* and *WEIGHT*, are used on the output requested by PRINT.

- WSDESIGN requests a full factorial within-subjects model. Because this is the default, WSDESIGN could have been omitted.

RENAME Subcommand

Because any repeated measures analysis involves a transformation of the dependent variables, it is always a good idea to rename the dependent variables. Choose appropriate names depending on the type of contrast specified for within-subjects factors. This is easier to do if you are using one of the orthogonal contrasts. The most reliable way to assign new names is to inspect the transformation matrix.

Example

```
MANOVA LOW1 LOW2 LOW3 HI1 HI2 HI3
  /WSFACTORS=LEVEL(2) TRIAL(3)
  /CONTRAST(TRIAL)=DIFFERENCE
  /RENAME=CONST LEVELDIF TRIAL21 TRIAL312 INTER1 INTER2
  /PRINT=TRANSFORM
  /DESIGN.
```

- This analysis has two within-subjects factors and no between-subjects factors.

- Difference contrasts are requested for *TRIAL*, which has three levels.

- Because all orthonormal contrasts produce the same F test for a factor with two levels, there is no point in specifying a contrast type for *LEVEL*.

- New names are assigned to the transformed variables based on the transformation matrix. These names correspond to the meaning of the transformed variables: the mean or constant, the average difference between levels, the average effect of trial 2 compared to 1, the average effect of trial 3 compared to 1 and 2; and the two interactions between *LEVEL* and *TRIAL*.

- The transformation matrix requested by the PRINT subcommand looks like Figure 1.

Figure 1   Transformation matrix

	CONST	LEVELDIF	TRIAL1	TRIAL2	INTER1	INTER2
LOW1	0.408	0.408	-0.500	-0.289	-0.500	-0.289
LOW2	0.408	0.408	0.500	-0.289	0.500	-0.289
LOW3	0.408	0.408	0.000	0.577	0.000	0.577
HI1	0.408	-0.408	-0.500	-0.289	0.500	0.289
HI2	0.408	-0.408	0.500	-0.289	-0.500	0.289
HI3	0.408	-0.408	0.000	0.577	0.000	-0.577

PRINT Subcommand

The following additional specifications on PRINT are useful in repeated measures analysis:

SIGNIF(AVERF)   *Averaged* F *tests for use with repeated measures.* This is the default display in repeated measures analysis. The averaged F tests in the multivariate setup for repeated measures are equivalent to the univariate (or split-plot or mixed-model) approach to repeated measures.

SIGNIF(AVONLY)   *Only the averaged* F *test for repeated measures.* AVONLY produces the same output as AVERF and suppresses all other SIGNIF output.

SIGNIF(HF)   *The Huynh-Feldt corrected significance values for averaged univariate* F *tests.*

SIGNIF(GG)   *The Greenhouse-Geisser corrected significance values for averaged univariate* F *tests.*

SIGNIF(EFSIZE)   *The effect size for the univariate* F *and* t *tests.*

- The keywords AVERF and AVONLY are mutually exclusive.
- When you request repeated measures analysis with the WSFACTORS subcommand, the default display includes SIGNIF(AVERF) but does not include the usual SIGNIF(UNIV).
- The averaged F tests are appropriate in repeated measures because the dependent variables that are averaged actually represent contrasts of the WSFACTOR variables. When the analysis is not doubly multivariate, as discussed above, you can specify PRINT=SIGNIF(UNIV) to obtain significance tests for each degree of freedom, just as in univariate MANOVA.

SURVIVAL

```
SURVIVAL TABLES=survival varlist
               [BY varlist (min, max)...][BY varlist (min, max)...]

 /INTERVALS=THRU n BY a [THRU m BY b ...]

 /STATUS=status variable({min, max}) FOR {ALL             }
                        {value   }      {survival varlist}
[/STATUS=...]

[/PLOT  ({ALL     })={ALL             } BY {ALL    }    BY {ALL     }]
        {LOGSURV }   {survival varlis}   {varlist}      {varlist}
        {SURVIVAL}
        {HAZARD  }
        {DENSITY }
        {OMS     }

[/PRINT={TABLE**}]
        {NOTABLE}

[/COMPARE={ALL**           } BY {ALL** } BY {ALL** }]
          {survival varlist}   {varlist}   {varlist}

[/CALCULATE=[{EXACT**     }] [PAIRWISE] [COMPARE] ]
             {CONDITIONAL}
             {APPROXIMATE}

[/MISSING={GROUPWISE**}  [INCLUDE] ]
          {LISTWISE   }

[/WRITE=[{NONE**}] ]
        {TABLES}
        {BOTH  }
```

**Default if subcommand or keyword is omitted.

Example:

```
SURVIVAL TABLES=MOSFREE BY TREATMNT(1,3)
 /STATUS = PRISON (1) FOR MOSFREE
 /INTERVAL=THRU 24 BY 3.
```

Overview

SURVIVAL produces actuarial life tables, plots, and related statistics for examining the length of time to the occurrence of an event, often known as **survival time**. Cases can be classified into groups for separate analyses and comparisons. Time intervals can be calculated with the SPSS date- and time-conversion functions—for example, CTIME.DAYS or YRMODA (see the *SPSS Base Syntax Reference Guide*). For a closely related alternative nonparametric analysis of survival times using the product-limit Kaplan-Meier estimator, see the KM command. For an analysis of survival times with covariates, including time-dependent covariates, see the COXREG command.

Options

Life Tables. You can list the variables to be used in the analysis, including any control variables on the TABLES subcommand. You can also suppress the life tables in the output with the PRINT subcommand.

Intervals. SURVIVAL reports the percentage alive at various times after the initial event. You can select the time points for reporting with the INTERVALS subcommand.

Plots. You can plot the survival functions for all cases or separately for various subgroups with the PLOT subcommand.

Comparisons. When control variables are listed on the TABLES subcommand, you can compare groups based on the Wilcoxon (Gehan) statistic using the COMPARE subcommand. You can request pairwise or approximate comparisons with the CALCULATE subcommand.

Writing a File. You can write the life tables, including the labeling information, to a file with the WRITE subcommand.

Basic Specification

- The basic specification requires three subcommands: TABLES, INTERVALS, and STATUS. TABLES identifies at least one survival variable from the working data file, INTERVALS divides the time period into intervals, and STATUS names a variable that indicates whether the event occurred.
- The basic specification prints one or more life tables, depending on the number of survival and control variables specified.

Subcommand Order

- TABLES must be first.
- Remaining subcommands can be named in any order.

Syntax Rules

- Only one TABLES subcommand can be specified, but multiple survival variables can be named. A survival variable cannot be specified as a control variable on any subcommands.
- Only one INTERVALS subcommand can be in effect on a SURVIVAL command. The interval specifications apply to all of the survival variables listed on TABLES. If multiple INTERVALS subcommands are used, the last specification supersedes all previous ones.
- Only one status variable can be listed on each STATUS subcommand. To specify multiple status variables, use multiple STATUS subcommands.
- You can specify multiple control variables on one BY keyword. Use a second BY keyword to specify second-order control variables to interact with the first-order control variables.
- All variables, including survival variables, control variables, and status variables, must be numeric. SURVIVAL does not process string variables.

Operations

- SURVIVAL computes time intervals according to specified interval widths, calculates the survival functions for each interval, and builds one life table for each group of survival variables. The life table is displayed unless explicitly suppressed.
- When the PLOT subcommand is specified, SURVIVAL plots the survival functions for all cases or separately for various groups.
- When the COMPARE subcommand is specified, SURVIVAL compares survival-time distributions of different groups based on the Wilcoxon (Gehan) statistic.

Limitations

- Maximum 20 survival variables.
- Maximum 100 control variables total on the first- and second-order control-variable lists combined.
- Maximum 20 THRU and BY specifications on INTERVALS.
- Maximum 35 values can appear on a plot.

Example

```
SURVIVAL TABLES=MOSFREE BY TREATMNT(1,3)
  /STATUS = PRISON (1) FOR MOSFREE
  /INTERVALS = THRU 24 BY 3.
```

- The survival analysis is used to examine the length of time between release from prison and return to prison for prisoners in three treatment programs. The variable *MOSFREE* is the length of time in months a prisoner stayed out of prison. The variable *TREATMNT* indicates the treatment group for each case.
- A value of 1 on the variable *PRISON* indicates a terminal outcome—that is, cases coded as 1 have returned to prison. Cases with other non-negative values for *PRISON* have not returned. Because we don't know their final outcome, such cases are called censored.
- Life tables are produced for each of the three subgroups. INTERVALS specifies that the survival experience be described every three months for the first two years.

TABLES Subcommand

TABLES identifies the survival and control variables to be included in the analysis.

- The minimum specification is one or more survival variables.
- To specify one or more first-order control (or factor) variables, use the keyword BY followed by the control variable(s). First-order control variables are processed in sequence. For example, BY A(1,3) B(1,2) results in five groups ($A = 1$, $A = 2$, $A = 3$, $B = 1$, and $B = 2$).
- You can specify one or more second-order control variables following a second BY keyword. Separate life tables are generated for each combination of values of the first-order and second-order controls. For example, BY A(1,3) BY B(1,2) results in six groups

($A = 1 \ B = 1, A = 1 \ B = 2, A = 2 \ B = 1, A = 2 \ B = 2, A = 3 \ B = 1$, and $A = 3 \ B = 2$).

- Each control variable must be followed by a value range in parentheses. These values must be integers separated by a comma or a blank. Non-integer values in the data are truncated, and the case is assigned to a subgroup based on the integer portion of its value on the variable. To specify only one value for a control variable, use the same value for the minimum and maximum.

- To generate life tables for all cases combined, as well as for control variables, use COMPUTE to create a variable that has the same value for all cases. With this variable as a control, tables for the entire set of cases, as well as for the control variables, will be produced.

Example

```
SURVIVAL TABLES = MOSFREE BY TREATMNT(1,3) BY RACE(1,2)
  /STATUS = PRISON(1)
  /INTERVAL = THRU 24 BY 3.
```

- *MOSFREE* is the survival variable, and *TREATMNT* is the first-order control variable. The second BY defines *RACE* as a second-order control group having a value of 1 or 2.

- Six life tables with the median survival time are produced, one for each pair of values for the two control variables.

INTERVALS Subcommand

INTERVALS determines the period of time to be examined and how the time will be grouped for the analysis. The interval specifications apply to all of the survival variables listed on TABLES.

- SURVIVAL always uses 0 as the starting point for the first interval. Do not specify the 0. The INTERVALS specification *must* begin with the keyword THRU.

- Specify the terminal value of the time period after the keyword THRU. The final interval includes any observations that exceed the specified terminal value.

- The grouping increment, which follows the keyword BY, must be in the same units as the survival variable.

- The period to be examined can be divided into intervals of varying lengths by repeating the THRU and BY keywords. The period must be divided in ascending order. If the time period is not a multiple of the increment, the endpoint of the period is adjusted upward to the next even multiple of the grouping increment.

- When the period is divided into intervals of varying lengths by repeating the THRU and BY specifications, the adjustment of one period to produce even intervals changes the starting point of subsequent periods. If the upward adjustment of one period completely overlaps the next period, no adjustment is made and the procedure terminates with an error.

Example

```
SURVIVAL TABLES = MOSFREE BY TREATMNT(1,3)
  /STATUS = PRISON(1) FOR MOSFREE
  /INTERVALS = THRU 12 BY 1 THRU 24 BY 3.
```

- INTERVALS produces life tables computed from 0 to 12 months at one-month intervals and from 13 to 24 months at three-month intervals.

Example

```
SURVIVAL  ONSSURV BY TREATMNT (1,3)
 /STATUS = OUTCOME (3,4) FOR ONSSURV
 /INTERVALS = THRU 50 BY 6.
```

- On the INTERVALS subcommand, the value following BY (6) does not divide evenly into the period to which it applies (50). Thus, the endpoint of the period is adjusted upward to the next even multiple of the BY value, resulting in a period of 54 with 9 intervals of 6 units each.

Example

```
SURVIVAL  ONSSURV BY TREATMNT (1,3)
 /STATUS = OUTCOME (3,4) FOR ONSSURV
 /INTERVALS = THRU 50 BY 6 THRU 100 BY 10 THRU 200 BY 20.
```

- Multiple THRU and BY specifications are used on the INTERVAL subcommand to divide the period of time under examination into intervals of different lengths.
- The first THRU and BY specifications are adjusted to produce even intervals as in the previous example. As a result, the following THRU and BY specifications are automatically readjusted to generate 5 intervals of 10 units (through 104), followed by 5 intervals of 20 units (through 204).

STATUS Subcommand

To determine whether the terminal event has occurred for a particular observation, SURVIVAL checks the value of a status variable. STATUS lists the status variable associated with each survival variable and the codes that indicate that a terminal event occurred.

- Specify a status variable followed by a value range enclosed in parentheses. The value range identifies the codes that indicate that the terminal event has taken place. All cases with non-negative times that do not have a code in the value range are classified as **censored cases**, which are cases for which the terminal event has not yet occurred.
- If the status variable does not apply to all the survival variables, specify FOR and the name of the survival variable(s) to which the status variable applies.
- Each survival variable on TABLES must have an associated status variable identified by a STATUS subcommand.
- Only one status variable can be listed on each STATUS subcommand. To specify multiple status variables, use multiple STATUS subcommands.
- If FOR is omitted on the STATUS specification, the status-variable specification applies to all of the survival variables not named on another STATUS subcommand.
- If more than one STATUS subcommand omits the keyword FOR, the final STATUS subcommand without FOR applies to all survival variables not specified by FOR on other STATUS subcommands. No warning is printed.

Example

```
SURVIVAL  ONSSURV BY TREATMNT (1,3)
   /INTERVALS = THRU 50 BY 5, THRU 100 BY 10
   /STATUS = OUTCOME (3,4) FOR ONSSURV.
```

- STATUS specifies that a code of 3 or 4 on *OUTCOME* means that the terminal event for the survival variable *ONSSURV* occurred.

Example

```
SURVIVAL TABLES = NOARREST MOSFREE BY TREATMNT(1,3)
   /STATUS = ARREST (1) FOR NOARREST
   /STATUS = PRISON (1)
   /INTERVAL=THRU 24 BY 3.
```

- STATUS defines the terminal event for *NOARREST* as a value of 1 for *ARREST*. Any other value for *ARREST* is considered censored.
- The second STATUS subcommand defines the value of 1 for *PRISON* as the terminal event. The keyword FOR is omitted. Thus, the status-variable specification applies to *MOSFREE*, which is the only survival variable not named on another STATUS subcommand.

PLOT Subcommand

PLOT produces plots of the cumulative survival distribution, the hazard function, and the probability density function. The PLOT subcommand can plot only the survival functions generated by the TABLES subcommand; PLOT cannot eliminate control variables.

- When specified by itself, the PLOT subcommand produces all available plots for each survival variable. Points on each plot are identified by values of the first-order control variables. If second-order controls are used, a separate plot is generated for every value of the second-order control variables.
- To request specific plots, specify, in parentheses following PLOT, any combination of the keywords defined below.
- Optionally, generate plots for only a subset of the requested life tables. Use the same syntax as used on the TABLES subcommand for specifying survival and control variables, omitting the value ranges. Each survival variable named on PLOT must have as many control levels as were specified for that variable on TABLES. However, only one control variable needs to be present for each level. If a required control level is missing on the PLOT specification, the default BY ALL is used for that level. The keyword ALL can be used to refer to an entire set of survival or control variables.
- To determine the number of plots that will be produced, multiply the number of functions plotted by the number of survival variables times the number of first-order controls times the number of distinct values represented in all of the second-order controls.

ALL   *Plot all available functions.* ALL is the default if PLOT is used without specifications.

LOGSURV   *Plot the cumulative survival distribution on a logarithmic scale.*

SURVIVAL   *Plot the cumulative survival distribution on a linear scale.*

HAZARD   *Plot the hazard function.*

DENSITY   *Plot the density function.*

OMS   *Plot the one-minus-survival function.*

Example

```
SURVIVAL TABLES = NOARREST MOSFREE BY TREATMNT(1,3)
  /STATUS = ARREST (1) FOR NOARREST
  /STATUS = PRISON (1) FOR MOSFREE
  /INTERVALS = THRU 24 BY 3
  /PLOT (SURVIVAL,HAZARD) = MOSFREE.
```

- Separate life tables are produced for each of the survival variables (*NOARREST* and *MOSFREE*) for each of the three values of the control variable *TREATMNT*.
- PLOT produces plots of the cumulative survival distribution and the hazard rate for *MOSFREE* for the three values of *TREATMNT* (even though *TREATMNT* is not included on the PLOT specification).
- Because plots are requested only for the survival variable *MOSFREE*, no plots are generated for the variable *NOARREST*.

PRINT Subcommand

By default, SURVIVAL prints life tables. PRINT can be used to suppress the life tables.

TABLE   *Print the life tables.* This is the default.

NOTABLE   *Suppress the life tables.* Only plots and comparisons are printed. The WRITE subcommand, which is used to write the life tables to a file, can be used when NOTABLE is in effect.

Example

```
SURVIVAL TABLES = MOSFREE BY TREATMNT(1,3)
  /STATUS = PRISON (1) FOR MOSFREE
  /INTERVALS = THRU 24 BY 3
  /PLOT (ALL)
  /PRINT = NOTABLE.
```

- PRINT NOTABLE suppresses the printing of life tables.

COMPARE Subcommand

COMPARE compares the survival experience of subgroups defined by the control variables. At least one first-order control variable is required for calculating comparisons.

- When specified by itself, the COMPARE subcommand produces comparisons using the TABLES variable list.
- Alternatively, specify the survival and control variables for the comparisons. Use the same syntax as used on the TABLES subcommand for specifying survival and control variables, omitting the value ranges. Only variables that appear on the TABLES subcommand

can be listed on COMPARE, and their role as survival, first-order, and second-order control variables cannot be altered. The keyword TO can be used to refer to a group of variables, and the keyword ALL can be used to refer to an entire set of survival or control variables.

- By default, COMPARE calculates exact comparisons between subgroups. Use the CALCULATE subcommand to obtain pairwise comparisons or approximate comparisons.

Example

```
SURVIVAL TABLES = MOSFREE BY TREATMNT(1,3)
  /STATUS = PRISON (1) FOR MOSFREE
  /INTERVAL = THRU 24 BY 3
  /COMPARE.
```

- COMPARE computes the Wilcoxon (Gehan) statistic, degrees of freedom, and observed significance level for the hypothesis that the three survival curves based on the values of *TREATMNT* are identical.

Example

```
SURVIVAL TABLES=ONSSURV,RECSURV BY TREATMNT(1,3)
  /STATUS = RECURSIT(1,9) FOR RECSURV
  /STATUS = STATUS(3,4) FOR ONSSURV
  /INTERVAL = THRU 50 BY 5 THRU 100 BY 10
  /COMPARE = ONSSURV BY TREATMNT.
```

- COMPARE requests a comparison of *ONSSURV* by *TREATMNT*. No comparison is made of *RECSURV* by *TREATMNT*.

CALCULATE Subcommand

CALCULATE controls the comparisons of survival for subgroups specified on the COMPARE subcommand.

- The minimum specification is the subcommand keyword by itself. EXACT is the default.
- Only one of the keywords EXACT, APPROXIMATE, and CONDITIONAL can be specified. If more than one keyword is used, only one is in effect. The order of precedence is APPROXIMATE, CONDITIONAL, and EXACT.
- The keywords PAIRWISE and COMPARE can be used with any of the EXACT, APPROXIMATE, or CONDITIONAL keywords.
- If CALCULATE is used without the COMPARE subcommand, CALCULATE is ignored. However, if the keyword COMPARE is specified on CALCULATE and the COMPARE subcommand is omitted, SPSS generates an error message.
- Data can be entered into SURVIVAL for each individual case or aggregated for all cases in an interval. The way in which data are entered determines whether an exact or an approximate comparison is most appropriate. See "Using Aggregated Data" on p. 447.

EXACT   *Calculate exact comparisons.* This is the default. You can obtain exact comparisons based on the survival experience of each observation with individual data. While this method is the most accurate, it requires that all of the data be in memory simultaneously. Thus, exact comparisons may be impractical for large samples. It is also inappropriate when individual data are not available and data aggregated by interval must be used.

APPROXIMATE   *Calculate approximate comparisons only.* Approximate comparisons are appropriate for aggregated data. The approximate-comparison approach assumes that all events occur at the midpoint of the interval. With exact comparisons, some of these midpoint ties can be resolved. However, if interval widths are not too great, the difference between exact and approximate comparisons should be small.

CONDITIONAL   *Calculate approximate comparisons if memory is insufficient.* Approximate comparisons are produced only if there is insufficient memory available for exact comparisons.

PAIRWISE   *Perform pairwise comparisons.* Comparisons of all pairs of values of the first-order control variable are produced along with the overall comparison.

COMPARE   *Produce comparisons only.* Survival tables specified on the TABLES subcommand are not computed, and requests for plots are ignored. This allows all available workspace to be used for comparisons. The WRITE subcommand cannot be used when this specification is in effect.

Example

```
SURVIVAL TABLES = MOSFREE BY TREATMNT(1,3)
  /STATUS = PRISON (1) FOR MOSFREE
  /INTERVAL = THRU 24 BY 3
  /COMPARE /CALCULATE = PAIRWISE.
```

- PAIRWISE on CALCULATE computes the Wilcoxon (Gehan) statistic, degrees of freedom, and observed significance levels for each pair of values of *TREATMNT*, as well as for an overall comparison of survival across all three *TREATMNT* subgroups: group 1 with group 2, group 1 with group 3, and group 2 with group 3.
- All comparisons are exact comparisons.

Example

```
SURVIVAL TABLES = MOSFREE BY TREATMNT(1,3)
  /STATUS = PRISON (1) FOR MOSFREE
  /INTERVAL = THRU 24 BY 3
  /COMPARE /CALCULATE = APPROXIMATE COMPARE.
```

- APPROXIMATE on CALCULATE computes the Wilcoxon (Gehan) statistic, degrees of freedom, and probability for the overall comparison of survival across all three *TREATMNT* subgroups using the approximate method.
- Because the keyword COMPARE is specified on CALCULATE, survival tables are not computed.

Using Aggregated Data

When aggregated survival information is available, the number of censored and uncensored cases at each time point must be entered. Up to two records can be entered for each interval, one for censored cases and one for uncensored cases. The number of cases included on each record is used as the weight factor. If control variables are used, there will be up to two records (one for censored and one for uncensored cases) for each value of the control variable in each interval. These records must contain the value of the control variable and the number of cases that belong in the particular category as well as values for survival time and status.

Example

```
DATA LIST   / SURVEVAR 1-2 STATVAR 4 SEX 6 COUNT 8.
VALUE LABELS   STATVAR 1 'DECEASED' 2 'ALIVE'
               /SEX 1 'FEMALE' 2 'MALE'.
BEGIN DATA
 1 1 1 6
 1 1 1 1
 1 2 2 2
 1 1 2 1
 2 2 1 1
 2 1 1 2
 2 2 2 1
 2 1 2 3
   ...
END DATA.
WEIGHT COUNT.
SURVIVAL TABLES = SURVEVAR BY SEX (1,2)
  /INTERVALS = THRU 10 BY 1
  /STATUS = STATVAR (1) FOR SURVEVAR.
```

- This example reads aggregated data and performs a SURVIVAL analysis when a control variable with two values is used.

- The first data record has a code of 1 on the status variable *STATVAR*, indicating that it is an uncensored case, and a code of 1 on *SEX*, the control variable. The number of cases for this interval is 6, the value of the variable *COUNT*. Intervals with weights of 0 do not have to be included.

- *COUNT* is not used in SURVIVAL but is the weight variable. In this example, each interval requires four records to provide all of the data for each *SURVEVAR* interval.

MISSING Subcommand

MISSING controls missing-value treatments. The default is GROUPWISE.

- Negative values on the survival variables are automatically treated as missing data. In addition, cases outside the value range on a control variable are excluded.

- GROUPWISE and LISTWISE are mutually exclusive. However, each can be used with INCLUDE.

GROUPWISE   *Exclude missing values groupwise.* Cases with missing values on a variable are excluded from any calculation involving that variable. This is the default.

LISTWISE   *Exclude missing values listwise.* Cases missing on any variables named on TABLES are excluded from the analysis.

INCLUDE   *Include user-missing values.* User-missing values are included in the analysis.

WRITE Subcommand

WRITE writes data in the survival tables to a file. This file can be used for further analyses or to produce graphics displays.

- When WRITE is omitted, the default is NONE. No output file is created.
- When WRITE is used, a PROCEDURE OUTPUT command must precede the SURVIVAL command. The OUTFILE subcommand on PROCEDURE OUTPUT specifies the output file.
- When WRITE is specified without a keyword, the default is TABLES.

NONE   *Do not write procedure output to a file.* This is the default when WRITE is omitted.

TABLES   *Write survival-table data records.* All survival-table statistics are written to a file.

BOTH   *Write out survival-table data and label records.* Variable names, variable labels, and value labels are written out along with the survival table statistics.

Format

WRITE writes five types of records. The keyword TABLES writes record types 30, 31, and 40. The keyword BOTH writes record types 10, 20, 30, 31, and 40. The format of each record type is described in Table 1 through Table 5.

Table 1   Record type 10, produced only by keyword BOTH

Columns	Content	Format
1–2	Record type (10)	F2.0
3–7	Table number	F5.0
8–15	Name of survival variable	A8
16–55	Variable label of survival variable	A40
56	Number of BY's (0, 1, or 2)	F1.0
57–60	Number of rows in current survival table	F4.0

- One type-10 record is produced for each life table.
- Column 56 specifies the number of orders of control variables (0, 1, or 2) that have been applied to the life table.
- Columns 57–60 specify the number of rows in the life table. This number is the number of intervals in the analysis that show subjects entering; intervals in which no subjects enter are not noted in the life tables.

Table 2   Record type 20, produced by keyword BOTH

Columns	Content	Format
1–2	Record type (20)	F2.0
3–7	Table number	F5.0
8–15	Name of control variable	A8
16–55	Variable label of control variable	A40
56–60	Value of control variable	F5.0
61–80	Value label for this value	A20

- One type-20 record is produced for each control variable in each life table.
- If only first-order controls have been placed in the survival analysis, one type-20 record will be produced for each table. If second-order controls have also been applied, two type-20 records will be produced per table.

Table 3   Record type 30, produced by both keywords TABLES and BOTH

Columns	Content	Format
1–2	Record type (30)	F2.0
3–7	Table number	F5.0
8–13	Beginning of interval	F6.2
14–21	Number entering interval	F8.2
22–29	Number withdrawn in interval	F8.2
30–37	Number exposed to risk	F8.2
38–45	Number of terminal events	F8.2

- Information on record type 30 continues on record type 31. Each pair of type-30 and type-31 records contains the information from one line of the life table.

Table 4   Record type 31, continuation of record type 30

Columns	Content	Format
1–2	Record type (31)	F2.0
3–7	Table number	F5.0
8–15	Proportion terminating	F8.6
16–23	Proportion surviving	F8.6
24–31	Cumulative proportion surviving	F8.6
32–39	Probability density	F8.6
40–47	Hazard rate	F8.6
48–54	S.E. of cumulative proportion surviving	F7.4
55–61	S.E. of probability density	F7.4
62–68	S.E. of hazard rate	F7.4

- Record type 31 is a continuation of record type 30.
- As many type-30 and type-31 record pairs are output for a table as it has lines (this number is noted in columns 57–60 of the type-10 record for the table).

Table 5   Record type 40, produced by both keywords TABLES and BOTH

Columns	Content	Format
1–2	Record type (40)	F2.0

- Type-40 records indicate the completion of the series of records for one life table.

Record Order

The SURVIVAL output file contains records for each of the life tables specified on the TABLES subcommand. All records for a given table are produced together in sequence. The records for the life tables are produced in the same order as the tables themselves. All life tables for the first survival variable are written first. The values of the first- and second-order control variables rotate, with the values of the first-order controls changing more rapidly.

Example

```
PROCEDURE OUTPUT OUTFILE = SURVTBL.
SURVIVAL TABLES = MOSFREE BY TREATMNT(1,3)
  /STATUS = PRISON (1) FOR MOSFREE
  /INTERVAL = THRU 24 BY 3
  /WRITE = BOTH.
```

- WRITE generates a procedure output file called *SURVTBL*, containing life tables, variable names and labels, and value labels stored as record types 10, 20, 30, 31, and 40.

VARCOMP

```
VARCOMP dependent variable BY factor list [WITH covariate list]

 /RANDOM = factor [factor ...]

[/METHOD = {MINQUE({1})**}]
                   {0}
           {ML              }
           {REML            }
           {SSTYPE({3})     }
                   {1}

[/INTERCEPT = {INCLUDE**}]
              {EXCLUDE   }

[/MISSING = {EXCLUDE**}]
            {INCLUDE   }

[/REGWGT = varname]

[/CRITERIA = [CONVERGE({1.0E-8**})] [EPS({1.0E-8**})] [ITERATE({50**})]
                      {n        }        {n        }            {n   }

[/PRINT = [EMS] [HISTORY({1**})] [SS]]
                        {n  }

[/OUTFILE = [VAREST] [{COVB}] (filename) ]
                      {CORB}

[/DESIGN = {[INTERCEPT] [effect effect ...]}]
```

** Default if subcommand or keyword is omitted.

Example:

```
VARCOMP Y1 BY B C WITH X1 X2
 /RANDOM = C
 /DESIGN.
```

Overview

The VARCOMP procedure estimates variance components for mixed models. Following the general linear model approach, VARCOMP uses indicator variable coding to construct a design matrix and then uses one of the four available methods to estimate the contribution of each random effect to the variance of the dependent variable.

Options

Regression Weights. You can specify regression weights for the model with the REGWGT subcommand.

Estimation Methods. You can use one of the four methods available for estimating variance components using the METHOD subcommand.

Tuning the Algorithm. You can control the values of algorithm-tuning parameters with the CRITERIA subcommand.

Optional Output. You can request additional output using the PRINT subcommand.

Saving the Results. You can save the variance component estimates and their asymptotic covariance matrix (if produced) to an external data file.

Basic Specification

The basic specification is one dependent variable and one or more factor variables that define the crosstabulation and one or more factor variables on the RANDOM subcommand to classify factors into either fixed or random factors. By default, VARCOMP uses the minimum norm quadratic unbiased estimator with unit prior weights to estimate variance components. Default output includes a factor-level information table and a variance component estimates table.

Subcommand Order

- The variable specification must come first.
- Other subcommands can be specified in any order.

Syntax Rules

- Only one dependent variable can be specified.
- At least one factor must be specified after BY.
- At least one factor must be specified on the RANDOM subcommand.

Variable List

The variable list specifies the dependent variable and the factors in the model.
- The dependent variable must be the first specification on VARCOMP.
- The factors follow the dependent variable and are separated from it by the keyword BY.
- The covariates, if any, follow the factors and are separated from the dependent variable and the factors by the keyword WITH.
- The dependent variable and the covariates must be numeric, but the factor variables can be either numeric or string. If a factor is a long string variable, only the first eight characters of each value are used.

RANDOM Subcommand

The RANDOM subcommand allows you to specify random factors.
- You must specify at least one RANDOM subcommand with one random factor.
- You can specify multiple random factors on a RANDOM subcommand. You can also use multiple RANDOM subcommands. Specifications are accumulative.

- Only factors listed after the keyword BY in the variable list are allowed on the RANDOM subcommand.
- If you specify a factor on RANDOM, all effects containing the factor are automatically declared as random effects.

Example

```
VARCOM Y BY DRUG SUBJECT
 /RANDOM = SUBJECT
 /DESIGN = DRUG DRUG*SUBJECT.
```

- This example specifies a mixed model where *DRUG* is the fixed factor and *SUBJECT* is a random factor.
- The default method MINQUE(1) is used to estimate the contribution of the random effect DRUG*SUBJECT to the variance of the dependent variable.

METHOD Subcommand

The METHOD subcommand offers four different methods for estimating the variances of the random effects. If more than one METHOD subcommand is specified, only the last one is in effect. If the subcommand is not specified, the default method MINQUE(1) is used. METHOD cannot be specified without a keyword.

MINQUE(n)   *Minimum norm quadratic unbiased estimator.* This is the default method. When $n = 0$, zero weight is assigned to the random effects and unit weight is assigned to the residual term. When $n = 1$, unit weight is assigned to both the random effects and the residual term. By default, $n = 1$.

ML   *Maximum likelihood method.* Parameters of the fixed effects and variances of the random effects are estimated simultaneously. However, only the variances are reported.

REML   *Restricted maximum likelihood method.* Variances of the random effects are estimated based on residuals of the model after adjusting for the fixed effects.

SSTYPE(n)   *ANOVA method.* The ANOVA method equates the expected mean squares of the random effects to their observed mean squares. Their variances are then estimated by solving a system of linear equations. The expected mean squares are computed based on the type of sum of squares chosen. Two types are available in VARCOMP: Type I ($n = 1$) and Type III ($n = 3$). Type III is the default option for this method.

INTERCEPT Subcommand

The INTERCEPT subcommand controls whether an intercept term is included in the model. If more than one INTERCEPT subcommand is specified, only the last one is in effect.

INCLUDE   *Include the intercept term.* The intercept (constant) term is included in the model. This is the default when INTERCEPT is not specified.

EXCLUDE   *Exclude the intercept term.* The intercept (constant) term is excluded from the model. EXCLUDE is ignored if you specify the keyword INTERCEPT on the DESIGN subcommand.

MISSING Subcommand

By default, cases with missing values for any of the variables on the VARCOMP variable list are excluded from the analyses. The MISSING subcommand allows you to include cases with user-missing values.

- Pairwise deletion of missing data is not available in VARCOMP.
- If more than one MISSING subcommand is specified, only the last one is in effect.

EXCLUDE   *Exclude both user-missing and system-missing values.* This is the default when MISSING is not specified.

INCLUDE   *User-missing values are treated as valid.* System-missing values cannot be included in the analysis.

REGWGT Subcommand

REGWGT specifies the weight variable. Values of this variable are used as regression weights in a weighted least squares model.

- Specify one numeric variable name on the REGWGT subcommand.
- Cases with nonpositive values in the regression weight variable are excluded from the analyses.
- If more than one variable is specified on the same REGWGT subcommand, only the last variable is in effect.
- If more than one REGWGT subcommand is specified, only the last one is in effect.

CRITERIA Subcommand

The CRITERIA subcommand specifies numerical tolerance for checking singularity and offers control of the iterative algorithm used for ML or REML estimation.

- Multiple CRITERIA subcommands are allowed.
- The last specified value for any keyword takes effect. If none is specified, the default is used.

EPS(n)   *Epsilon value used as tolerance in checking singularity.* n must be a positive value. The default is 1.0E-8.

CONVERGE(n)   *Convergence criterion.* Convergence is assumed if the relative change in the objective function is less than the specified value. n must be a positive value. The default is 1.0E-8. Available only if you specify ML or REML on the METHOD subcommand.

| ITERATE(n) | *Maximum number of iterations. n* must be a positive integer. The default is 50. Available only if you specify ML or REML on the METHOD subcommand. |

PRINT Subcommand

The PRINT subcommand controls the display of optional output. If PRINT is not specified, the default output includes a factor information table and a variance component estimates table.

- For the maximum likelihood (ML) and restricted maximum likelihood (REML) methods, an asymptotic covariance matrix of the variance estimates table is also displayed.
- If more than one PRINT subcommand is specified, the specifications are accumulated. However, if you specify the keyword HISTORY more than once but with different values for *n*, the last specification is in effect

EMS	*Expected mean squares.* Expected mean squares of all of the effects. Available only if you specify SSTYPE(n) on the METHOD subcommand.
HISTORY(n)	*Iteration history.* The table contains the objective function value and variance component estimates at every *n* iteration. *n* must be a positive integer. The default is 1. The last iteration is always printed if HISTORY is specified on PRINT. Available only if you specify ML or REML on the METHOD subcommand.
SS	*Sums of squares.* The table contains sums of squares, degrees of freedom, and mean squares for each source of variation. Available only if you specify SSTYPE(n) on the METHOD subcommand.

OUTFILE Subcommand

The OUTFILE subcommand writes the variance component estimates to a data file that can be used in other procedures. For the ML and REML methods, OUTFILE can also write the asymptotic covariance or correlation matrix to a data file. If more than one OUTFILE subcommand is specified, the last specification is in effect.

- OUTFILE writes an external file. You must specify a valid filename in parentheses.
- COVB and CORB are available only if you specify ML or REML on the METHOD subcommand.
- COVB and CORB are mutually exclusive; only one of them can be specified on an OUTFILE subcommand.

VAREST	*Variance component estimates.* A variable will be created to contain the estimates, and another variable will be created to hold the labels of the variance components.
COVB	*Covariance matrix.* The asymptotic covariance matrix of the variance component estimates. One variable is created for each variance component.
CORB	*Correlation matrix.* The asymptotic correlation matrix of the variance component estimates. One variable is created for each variance component.

(filename)   *Output filename.* Specify one valid filename. The variance component estimates and the asymptotic covariance or correlation matrix (if requested) are
written to the same file.

DESIGN Subcommand

The DESIGN subcommand specifies the effects in a model. DESIGN can be specified anywhere after the variable list. If more than one DESIGN subcommand is specified, only the last
one is in effect.

- Specify a list of effect terms to be included in the design. Each term must be separated
  from the next by a comma or a space. Valid specifications include the keyword
  INTERCEPT, factors, covariates, and interaction or nested terms.
- The factors and covariates must have been specified on the variable list.
- If a factor is specified on the RANDOM subcommand, all effects that include that factor
  are random effects.
- If the DESIGN subcommand is omitted or specified without any term, the default design
  is generated. The default design includes the intercept term (if INTERCEPT=EXCLUDE is
  not specified), the covariates (if any) in the order in which they are specified on the variable list, the main factorial effects, and all orders of factor-by-factor interaction.

INTERCEPT   *Include the intercept term.* Specifying INTERCEPT on DESIGN explicitly includes the intercept term regardless of the specification on the INTERCEPT
subcommand.

BY   *Interaction.* You can also use the asterisk (*). Interaction terms can be formed
among factors, among covariates, and between factors and covariates.

Factors inside an interaction effect must be distinct. For factors *A, B,* and *C,*
expressions like A*C*A or A*A are invalid.

Covariates inside an interaction effect do not have to be distinct. For covariate *X*, X*X is the product of *X* and itself. This is equivalent to a covariate
whose values are the square of those of *X.*

WITHIN   *Nesting.* You can also use a pair of parentheses. Factors and covariates can
be nested within factors but no effects can be nested within covariates. Suppose that *A* and *B* are factors and *X* and *Y* are covariates. Both A(B) and X(B)
are valid, but X(Y) is not.

Factors inside a nested effect must be distinct. Expressions like A(A) are
invalid.

Multiple-level nesting is supported. For example, A(B(C)) or A WITHIN B
WITHIN C means that factor *B* is nested within factor *C,* and factor *A* is nested
within *B(C).* The expression A(B)(C) is invalid.

Nesting within an interaction effect is valid. For example, A(B*C) means that factor *A* is nested within *B*C* while X(A*B) means covariate *X* is nested within *A*B*.

Interactions among nested effects are allowed. For example, A*B(C) means interaction between *A* and *B* within levels of *C*. X*Y(A) means the product of *X* and *Y* nested within levels of *C*. The expression A(C)*B(C) is invalid.

Example

```
VARCOM Y BY DRUG SUBJECT WITH X
 /RANDOM = SUBJECT
 /DESIGN = DRUG SUBJECT DRUG*SUBJECT X*SUBECT.
```

- The DESIGN subcommand specifies two main effects and two interaction terms.
- All effects that involve the factor *SUBJECT* are assumed to be random.

Categorical Variable Coding Schemes

In many SPSS procedures, you can request automatic replacement of a categorical independent variable with a set of contrast variables, which will then be entered or removed from an equation as a block. You can specify how the set of contrast variables is to be coded, usually on the CONTRAST subcommand. This appendix explains and illustrates how different contrast types requested on CONTRAST actually work.

Deviation

Deviation from the grand mean. In matrix terms, these contrasts have the form:

$$
\begin{array}{lccccc}
\text{mean} & (& 1/k & 1/k & \dots & 1/k & 1/k\ ) \\
\text{df(1)} & (& 1-1/k & -1/k & \dots & -1/k & -1/k\ ) \\
\text{df(2)} & (& -1/k & 1-1/k & \dots & -1/k & -1/k\ ) \\
& & \cdot & & & \cdot \\
& & \cdot & & & \cdot \\
\text{df(k--1)} & (& -1/k & -1/k & \dots & 1-1/k & -1/k\ )
\end{array}
$$

where k is the number of categories for the independent variable and the last category is omitted by default. For example, the deviation contrasts for an independent variable with three categories are as follows:

$$
\begin{array}{rrr}
(& 1/3 & 1/3 & 1/3\ ) \\
(& 2/3 & -1/3 & -1/3\ ) \\
(& -1/3 & 2/3 & -1/3\ )
\end{array}
$$

To omit a category other than the last, specify the number of the omitted category in parentheses after the DEVIATION keyword. For example, the following subcommand obtains the deviations for the first and third categories and omits the second:

```
/CONTRAST(FACTOR)=DEVIATION(2)
```

Suppose that *factor* has three categories. The resulting contrast matrix will be

$$
\begin{array}{rrr}
(\ 1/3 & 1/3 & 1/3 \ ) \\
(\ 2/3 & -1/3 & -1/3 \ ) \\
(-1/3 & -1/3 & 2/3 \ )
\end{array}
$$

Simple

Simple contrasts. Compares each level of a factor to the last. The general matrix form is

$$
\begin{array}{lrrrrr}
\text{mean} & (\ 1/k & 1/k & \ldots & 1/k & 1/k \ ) \\
df(1) & (\ 1 & 0 & \ldots & 0 & -1 \ ) \\
df(2) & (\ 0 & 1 & \ldots & 0 & -1 \ ) \\
\cdot & & \cdot & & \\
\cdot & & \cdot & & \\
df(k-1) & (\ 0 & 0 & \ldots & 1 & -1 \ )
\end{array}
$$

where k is the number of categories for the independent variable. For example, the simple contrasts for an independent variable with four categories are as follows:

$$
\begin{array}{rrrr}
(\ 1/4 & 1/4 & 1/4 & 1/4 \ ) \\
(\ 1 & 0 & 0 & -1 \ ) \\
(\ 0 & 1 & 0 & -1 \ ) \\
(\ 0 & 0 & 1 & -1 \ )
\end{array}
$$

To use another category instead of the last as a reference category, specify in parentheses after the SIMPLE keyword the sequence number of the reference category, which is not necessarily the value associated with that category. For example, the following CONTRAST subcommand obtains a contrast matrix that omits the second category:

```
/CONTRAST(FACTOR) = SIMPLE(2)
```

Suppose that *factor* has four categories. The resulting contrast matrix will be

$$
\begin{pmatrix}
1/4 & 1/4 & 1/4 & 1/4 \\
1 & -1 & 0 & 0 \\
0 & -1 & 1 & 0 \\
0 & -1 & 0 & 1
\end{pmatrix}
$$

Helmert

Helmert contrasts. Compares categories of an independent variable with the mean of the subsequent categories. The general matrix form is

mean	(	$1/k$	$1/k$	...	$1/k$	$1/k$)
df(1)	(	1	$-1/(k-1)$	...	$-1/(k-1)$	$-1/(k-1)$)
df(2)	(	0	1	...	$-1/(k-2)$	$-1/(k-2)$)
.			.			
.			.			
df(k-2)	(	0	0	1	$-1/2$	$-1/2$)
df(k-1)	(	0	0	...	1	-1)

where k is the number of categories of the independent variable. For example, an independent variable with four categories has a Helmert contrast matrix of the following form:

$$
\begin{pmatrix}
1/4 & 1/4 & 1/4 & 1/4 \\
1 & -1/3 & -1/3 & -1/3 \\
0 & 1 & -1/2 & -1/2 \\
0 & 0 & 1 & -1
\end{pmatrix}
$$

Difference

Difference or reverse Helmert contrasts. Compares categories of an independent variable with the mean of the previous categories of the variable. The general matrix form is

$$
\begin{array}{llcccc}
\text{mean} & (& 1/k & 1/k & 1/k & \dots & 1/k\ ) \\
df(1) & (& -1 & 1 & 0 & \dots & 0\ ) \\
df(2) & (& -1/2 & -1/2 & 1 & \dots & 0\ ) \\
& \cdot & & & \cdot & & \\
& \cdot & & & \cdot & & \\
df(k{-}1) & (& -1/(k{-}1) & -1/(k{-}1) & -1/(k{-}1) & \dots & 1\ )
\end{array}
$$

where k is the number of categories for the independent variable. For example, the difference contrasts for an independent variable with four categories are as follows:

$$
\begin{array}{cccc}
(\ 1/4 & 1/4 & 1/4 & 1/4\ ) \\
(\ -1 & 1 & 0 & 0\ ) \\
(-1/2 & -1/2 & 1 & 0\ ) \\
(-1/3 & -1/3 & -1/3 & 1\ )
\end{array}
$$

Polynomial

Orthogonal polynomial contrasts. The first degree of freedom contains the linear effect across all categories; the second degree of freedom, the quadratic effect; the third degree of freedom, the cubic; and so on for the higher-order effects.

You can specify the spacing between levels of the treatment measured by the given categorical variable. Equal spacing, which is the default if you omit the metric, can be specified as consecutive integers from 1 to k, where k is the number of categories. If the variable *drug* has three categories, the subcommand

```
/CONTRAST(DRUG)=POLYNOMIAL
```

is the same as

```
/CONTRAST(DRUG)=POLYNOMIAL(1,2,3)
```

Equal spacing is not always necessary, however. For example, suppose that *drug* represents different dosages of a drug given to three groups. If the dosage administered to the second group is twice that to the first group and the dosage administered to the third group is three times that to the first group, the treatment categories are equally spaced, and an appropriate metric for this situation consists of consecutive integers:

```
/CONTRAST(DRUG)=POLYNOMIAL(1,2,3)
```

If, however, the dosage administered to the second group is four times that given the first group, and the dosage given the third group is seven times that to the first, an appropriate metric is

```
/CONTRAST(DRUG)=POLYNOMIAL(1,4,7)
```

In either case, the result of the contrast specification is that the first degree of freedom for *drug* contains the linear effect of the dosage levels and the second degree of freedom contains the quadratic effect.

Polynomial contrasts are especially useful in tests of trends and for investigating the nature of response surfaces. You can also use polynomial contrasts to perform nonlinear curve fitting, such as curvilinear regression.

Repeated

Compares adjacent levels of an independent variable. The general matrix form is

```
mean      (1/k   1/k   1/k   ...   1/k   1/k )
df(1)     (  1    -1     0   ...     0     0 )
df(2)     (  0     1    -1   ...     0     0 )
 .                  .
 .                  .
 .                  .
df(k-1)   (  0     0     0   ...     1    -1 )
```

where k is the number of categories for the independent variable. For example, the repeated contrasts for an independent variable with four categories are as follows:

```
(1/4   1/4   1/4   1/4 )
(  1    -1     0     0 )
(  0     1    -1     0 )
(  0     0     1    -1 )
```

These contrasts are useful in profile analysis and wherever difference scores are needed.

Special

A user-defined contrast. Allows entry of special contrasts in the form of square matrices with as many rows and columns as there are categories of the given independent variable. For MANOVA and LOGLINEAR, the first row entered is always the mean, or constant, effect and represents the set of weights indicating how to average other independent variables, if any, over the given variable. Generally, this contrast is a vector of ones.

The remaining rows of the matrix contain the special contrasts indicating the desired comparisons between categories of the variable. Usually, orthogonal contrasts are the most useful. Orthogonal contrasts are statistically independent and are nonredundant. Contrasts are orthogonal if:

- For each row, contrast coefficients sum to 0.

- The products of corresponding coefficients for all pairs of disjoint rows also sum to 0.

For example, suppose that *treatment* has four levels and that you want to compare the various levels of treatment with each other. An appropriate special contrast is

(	1	1	1	1)	weights for mean calculation
(	3	−1	−1	−1)	compare 1st with 2nd through 4th
(	0	2	−1	−1)	compare 2nd with 3rd and 4th
(	0	0	1	−1)	compare 3rd with 4th

which you specify by means of the following CONTRAST subcommand for MANOVA, LOGISTIC REGRESSION, and COXREG:

```
/CONTRAST(TREATMNT)=SPECIAL( 1  1  1  1
                             3 -1 -1 -1
                             0  2 -1 -1
                             0  0  1 -1 )
```

For LOGLINEAR, you need to specify:

```
/CONTRAST(TREATMNT)=BASIS SPECIAL( 1  1  1  1
                                   3 -1 -1 -1
                                   0  2 -1 -1
                                   0  0  1 -1 )
```

Each row except the means row sums to 0. Products of each pair of disjoint rows sum to 0 as well:

Rows 2 and 3: $(3)(0) + (-1)(2) + (-1)(-1) + (-1)(-1) = 0$

Rows 2 and 4: $(3)(0) + (-1)(0) + (-1)(1) + (-1)(-1) = 0$

Rows 3 and 4: $(0)(0) + (2)(0) + (-1)(1) + (-1)(-1) = 0$

The special contrasts need not be orthogonal. However, they must not be linear combinations of each other. If they are, the procedure reports the linear dependency and ceases processing. Helmert, difference, and polynomial contrasts are all orthogonal contrasts.

Indicator

Indicator variable coding. Also known as dummy coding, this is not available in LOGLINEAR or MANOVA. The number of new variables coded is $k - 1$. Cases in the reference category are coded 0 for all $k - 1$ variables. A case in the ith category is coded 0 for all indicator variables except the ith, which is coded 1.

Bibliography

Agresti, A. 1990. *Categorical data analysis*. New York: John Wiley and Sons.

Ashford, J. R., and R. D. Sowden. 1970. Multivariate probit analysis. *Biometrics*, 26: 535–546.

Berenson, M. L., and D. M. Levine. 1992. *Basic business statistics, concepts and applications*. Englewood Cliffs, N.J.: Prentice Hall.

Bishop, Y. M. M., and S. E. Fienberg. 1969. Incomplete two-dimensional contingency tables. *Biometrics*, 25: 119–128.

Bishop, Y. M. M., S. E. Fienberg, and P. W. Holland. 1975. *Discrete multivariate analysis: Theory and practice*. Cambridge, Mass.: MIT Press.

Bowker, A. H., and G. J. Lieberman. 1972. *Engineering statistics*. 2nd ed. Englewood Cliffs, N.J.: Prentice Hall.

Box, G. E. P., and N. R. Draper. 1969. *Evolutionary operation: A statistical method for process improvement*. New York: John Wiley and Sons.

Carter, W. H., Jr., G. L. Wampler, and D. M. Stablein. 1982. *Regression analysis of survival data in cancer chemotherapy*. New York: Marcel Dekker.

Corbeil, R. R., and S. R. Searle. 1976. Restricted maximum likelihood (REML) estimation of variance components in the mixed model. *Technometrics*, 18: 31–38.

Cox, D. R., and D. O. Oakes. 1984. *Analysis of survival data*. London: Chapman and Hall.

Crowley, J., and M. Hu. 1977. Covariance analysis of heart transplant survival data. *Journal of the American Statistical Association,* 72: 27–36.

Delany, M. F., and C. T. Moore. 1987. American alligator food habits in Florida. Unpublished manuscript.

Embury, S. H., L. Elias, P. H. Heller, C. E. Hood, P. L. Greenberg, and S.L. Schrier. 1977. Remission maintenance therapy in acute myelogenous leukemia. *Western Journal of Medicine*, 126: 267–272.

Friereich, E. J., et al. 1963. The effect of 6-mercaptopurine on the duration of steroid-induced remission in acute leukemia. *Blood*, 21: 699–716.

Giesbrecht, F. G. 1983. An efficient procedure for computing MINQUE of variance components and generalized least squares estimates of fixed effects. *Communications in Statistics, Part A— Theory and Methods*, 12: 2169–2177.

Goodnight, J. H. 1979. A tutorial on the SWEEP operator. *The American Statistician*, 33: 149–158.

Haberman, S. J. 1973. The analysis of residuals in cross-classified tables. *Biometrics*, 29: 205–220.

_____. 1979. *Analysis of qualitative data*. Vol. 2. New York: Academic Press.

_____. 1982. Analysis of dispersion of multinomial responses. *Journal of the American Statistical Association*, 77: 568–580.

Heimann, R. Unpublished breast cancer data. Department of Radiation Oncology, University of Chicago.

Hemmerle, W. J., and H. O. Hartley. 1973. Computing maximum likelihood estimates for the mixed A.O.V. model using the W transformation. *Technometrics*, 15: 819–831.

Hess, K. R. 1995. Graphical methods for assessing violations of the proportional hazards assumption in Cox regression. *Statistics in Medicine*, 14: 1707–1723.

Hicks, C. R. 1982. *Fundamental concepts in the design of experiments*. 3rd ed. New York: Holt, Rinehart and Winston.

Hocking, R. R. 1985. *The analysis of linear models*. Monterey, Calif.: Brooks/Cole.

Huynh, H., and G. K. Mandeville. 1979. Validity conditions in repeated measures design. *Psychological Bulletin*, 86: 964–973.

Jennrich, R. I., and P. F. Sampson. 1976. Newton-Raphson and related algorithms for maximum likelihood variance component estimation. *Technometrics*, 18: 11–17.

Jennrich, R. I., and M. D. Schluchter. 1986. Unbalanced repeated measures models with structured covariance matrices. *Biometrics*, 42: 805–820.

Johnson, N. L., S. Kotz, and A. W. Kemp. 1992. *Univariate discrete distributions*. New York: John Wiley and Sons.

Johnson, R. A., and D. W. Wichern. 1988. *Applied multivariate statistical analysis*. London: Prentice Hall International, Inc.

Kalbfleisch, J. D., and R. L. Prentice. 1980. *The statistical analysis of failure time data*. New York: John Wiley and Sons.

Kleinbaum, D. G. 1996. *Survival analysis: A self-learning text*. New York: Springer-Verlag.

Koch, G., S. Atkinson, and M. Stokes. 1986. Poisson regression. In: *Encyclopedia of Statistical Sciences*, Vol. 7, S. Kotz and N. Johnson, eds. New York: John Wiley and Sons.

LaMotte, L. R. 1973. On non-negative quadratic unbiased estimation of variance components. *Journal of the American Statistical Association*, 68: 728–730.

Lee, E. T. 1992. Statistical methods for survival data analysis. New York: John Wiley and Sons.

Mauchly, J. W. 1940. Significance test for sphericity of a normal *n*-variate distribution. *Annuals of Mathematical Statistics*, 11: 204–209.

McCullagh, P., and J. A. Nelder. 1989. *Generalized linear models*. 2nd ed. London: Chapman and Hall.

Miller, R. G., G. Gong, and A. Munòz. 1981. *Survival analysis*. New York: John Wiley and Sons.

Milliken, G. A., and D. E. Johnson. 1992. *Analysis of messy data*. Vol. 1, *Designed experiments*. New York: Chapman and Hall.

Olsen, C. L. 1976. On choosing a test statistic in multivariate analysis of variance. *Psychological Bulletin*, 83: 579–193.

Patterson, H. D., and R. Thompson. 1971. Recovery of inter-block information when block sizes are unequal. *Biometrika*, 58: 545–554.

Potthoff, R. F., and S. N. Roy. 1964. A generalized multivariate analysis of variance model useful especially for growth curve problems. *Biometrika*, 51: 313–326.

Rao, C. R. 1973. *Linear statistical inference and its applications*. 2nd ed. New York: John Wiley and Sons.

Rao, C. R., and J. Kleffe. 1988. *Estimation of variance components and applications*. Amsterdam: North-Holland.

Searle, S. R. 1987. *Linear models for unbalanced data*. New York: John Wiley and Sons.

Searle, S. R., G. Casella, and C. E. McCulloch. 1992. *Variance components*. New York: John Wiley and Sons.

Searle, S. R., F. M. Speed, and G. A. Milliken. 1980. Population marginal means in the linear model: An alternative to least squares means. *The American Statistician*, 34:4, 216–221.

Snedecor, G. W., and W. G. Cochran, 1980. *Statistical methods*. 7th ed. Ames: Iowa State University Press.

Speed, F. M. (1979). Choice of sums of squares for estimation of components of variance. *Proceedings of Statistical Computing Section*, 55–58. Alexandria, Va.: American Statistical Association.

Stablein D. M., W. C. Carter, Jr., and G. L. Wampler. 1980. Survival analysis of drug combinations using a hazards model with time-dependent covariates. *Biometrics*, 36: 537–546.

Winer, B. J., D. R. Brown, and K. M. Michels. 1991. *Statistical principles in experimental design*. New York: McGraw-Hill.

Subject Index

Syntax Index